THE STATES OF PERFECTION

This translation of *Les États de Perfection* is published by
arrangement with Editions Fleurus, Paris, publishers of the
work in French.

ABBÉ GASTON COURTOIS

THE
STATES OF PERFECTION

ACCORDING TO THE TEACHING OF THE CHURCH

PAPAL DOCUMENTS

FROM LEO XIII TO PIUS XII

PREFACE BY

HIS EMINENCE VALERIO CARDINAL VALERI

Prefect of the Sacred Congregation of Religious

Translated by Rev. John A. O'Flynn, L.S.S., St Patrick's
College, Maynooth

DUBLIN

M. H. GILL AND SON LTD

1961

FIRST PUBLISHED, 1961

M. H. GILL AND SON LTD.,
50 UPPER O'CONNELL STREET, DUBLIN

THE NEWMAN PRESS,
WESTMINSTER, MD., U.S.A.

PRINTED AND BOUND
IN THE REPUBLIC OF IRELAND
AT THE PRESS OF THE PUBLISHERS

TABLE OF CONTENTS.

PREFACE

SACRED CONGREGATION
OF RELIGIOUS

Rome, 13 June 1958

Very Reverend Father,

It was a happy thought of yours to bring together in a single volume the pontifical documents that have appeared up to 1 January 1958 dealing with the states of perfection, namely Orders, religious Congregations, Societies of the common life and Secular Institutes. Nothing that is relevant to this subject has been overlooked by you in this rich collection, and the occasional notes which supplement the text are evidence of the care with which you have made the collection.

Those souls who have committed themselves to the path of the evangelical counsels, whatever be the particular state of perfection to which they belong, will be grateful to you for this work. You are placing in their hands a veritable anthology of the life of perfection. God grant that they will appreciate and make good use of the riches, both doctrinal and practical, which it contains.

It is unnecessary to add that your work will commend itself also to all priests who, in one capacity or another, exercise their ministry among religious, whether men or women. Directors, confessors, chaplains, preachers of retreats, etc., will find here a sound theology of the religious life, both contemplative and apostolic; they will find in it a spirituality drawn from the very sources of the Gospel and the magisterium, and principles and authoritative guidance relating to the contemporary problem of adapting the states of perfection to the needs of the Church and of souls at the present day. The essential and unchangeable principles of the life of perfection are there clearly distinguished from the subsidiary and contingent elements which must be modified.

Ignorance or forgetfulness of that distinction has, as you know,

ix

been the cause of very unfortunate errors in recent times. To keep religious, both men and women, in step with the times: that is something which obviously can be done only by following the wise directives many times repeated by their supreme Superior, the Pope, Vicar of Jesus Christ. It is he in fact who rules over the life and activities of those who make the profession of achieving to the best of their powers the essential aim of the Church, namely sanctity.

Here it is surely appropriate to recall the supremely tactful and appropriate words addressed by Pius XII to the Brothers of the Christian Schools of Rome: " To keep up to date, that is a popular expression nowadays; by all means, but only on condition that one does not destroy the precious book as one might tear the leaves from a calendar." Your book, Very Reverend Father, will be the trustworthy guide in bringing about the adaptation which remains true to essentials.

This work will be no less useful to the faithful, to the relatives of those who belong to the states of perfection, to all those who are interested in the spiritual atmosphere in which their children, their brothers and sisters, or their friends live. And how many generous souls, who are seeking for the right path, will be able to find here the decisive call summoning them to follow Christ more closely, to share his life of poverty, humility and submission, in order to labour more efficaciously for his work of salvation and redemption.

All this means that this collection will make an appeal to a very wide public, and that it will be of interest to everyone who takes the trouble to read it. It is a timely production, and, as you desire, it will make a worthy complement to the work on *The Catholic Priesthood* published by Monsignor Veuillot.

Very Reverend Father, your numerous spiritual writings, the retreats which you have preached, your ministry among the Parochial Teaching Sisters of France, have already won for you the acquaintance and esteem of consecrated souls; with the publication of this collection, it may be said that you have rendered service to the states of perfection in all lands. The Cardinal Prefect of the Sacred Congregation of Religious is happy to offer you felicitations and to thank you very sincerely.

Wishing the work the widest possible circulation, I give my blessing to you, the author, and I beg you kindly to accept this expression of my devoted sentiments in Jesus Christ.

VALERIO CARDINAL VALERI,
Prefect

VERY REV. FR. GASTON COURTOIS
8 Via del Monte Pramaggiore
ROME

INTRODUCTION

Some years ago in this same collection the volume on *The Catholic Priesthood* prepared by Monsignor Veuillot was published; it provides a rich harvest of pontifical documents, from Leo XIII to Pius XII, to serve as material for our meditations on that vital theme.

It was felt that it would be useful, and indeed timely, to present in the same way the actual teaching of the Church on the religious state. The religious state is that form of consecrated life to which the Lord has called more than a million women, and more than 200,000 men, of whom about 130,000 are priests, out of a total of some 400,000 priests now in the various parts of the world.

In a work such as this, where the principal teachings of the Popes of the present century on the religious life are brought together, we are given the opportunity of better appraising the true excellence, that is so often misunderstood, of the religious life, and also the importance of the rôle which it fills in the life of the Church today as in the past. One can form a better estimate of its ever-present requirements, and at the same time, see the gradual evolution, the extension, and the new forms of consecration to God in the pursuit of perfection.

On the one hand we see that the supreme Pontiffs, without mitigating in the least the severity and even the austerity of rules, are calling for an adaptation prudently tempered to the conditions of life and above all of the apostolate at the present day; on the other hand, we hear them give their blessing and encouragement to new forms of the dedicated life; and to these they give the title of " states of perfection," just as to the ancient Orders and old-established Congregations.

The Church is a mother who is ever young. As a mother she is a wonderful teacher of the souls who seek God; she warns against dangers, places signs at danger points, encourages progress, puts on guard against the hardening effects of routine; she recalls to all the ideal by distinguishing carefully that which is accessory from what is essential. Ever young she gives guidance by her magisterium in every generation to religious souls in their search for perfection. When brought face to face with new problems, she lays down the new conditions of the apostolate and even of life; she gives, with astonishing insight, directions that are sure, and authorizes, indeed encourages, bold advances along new routes which she has herself surveyed.

This combination of prudence and daring, which bears the stamp of the Spirit whose wisdom tells us that he acts *suaviter et fortiter*, is not the least of the surprises produced by this collection of texts.

It is for this reason that this book, which at the outset was to have the title of *The Religious State*, has taken the wider title of *States of Perfection*.

The " state of perfection " is so called because, through the medium of the three evangelical counsels, it removes the principal obstacles to the effort to achieve personal sanctity and facilitates the progress of souls towards charity in the unreserved and complete giving of themselves to God and to others. While the term " religious state " seems reserved to the Orders and Congregations, " state of perfection " embraces likewise societies of the common life without public vows, and above all the Secular Institutes whose development is one of the characteristic features of recent times.

The literal translation of *status perfectionis* as " state of perfection " is liable to lead to various misunderstandings: it might, for example, give the impression that those who live in these states have personally reached perfection, or that these states represent a sort of monopoly, outside which one could not attain perfection. It might perhaps be better to speak of *the juridical or canonical state of striving towards perfection*. But, with Horace, we must reconcile ourselves to current usage, while taking the precautions in speech which are necessary in order to avoid regrettable misunderstandings.

The concept of " Secular Institute," moreover, has its origin not so much in a personal idea of holiness of life, as in the necessity to adapt the apostolic ministry to the needs of a society which, since it no longer comes to the cloisters in search of shelter, silence and the advice it needs, must have in its midst living witnesses to those values of which society stands in need. The masses no longer come to the church, and still less to the cloister, to find that leaven which they need. That leaven must be injected into society in order to make it rise. This does not mean that monasteries, cloisters, Orders, Congregations, are now outmoded; because in the first place, God be thanked, a large part of the Christian people is still directly and beneficially influenced by them; and also because the members of Secular Institutes, who are the salt and the leaven of that dull mass of materialistic and dehumanized humanity, are themselves in need of the support of religious strictly so-called, if they are to retain their beneficent power to transform.

There is no question, therefore, of a competition between the forces of sanctity, and still less of any devaluation of the religious life; rather, by the extension of these states of perfection, there is an enrichment, in the service of all mankind, of the Church *circumdata varietate.*

God grant that this work will not only present the evidence that this is the case, but that it will encourage many generous souls to respond joyfully and whole-heartedly to the call of the supreme Pontiffs, so that each one in its own place, in the providential setting which best fits its capacities, will bring to fulfilment what the loving Father desires for it.

G.C.

FOREWORD

SOURCES

The reference to the official source of published documents is always given in a footnote at the beginning of each papal document.

SUB-TITLES

Save where the contrary is stated, the various sub-titles are not taken from the official papal text; they are proper to this edition.

INDEXES

Chronological, canonical, scriptural and analytical indexes will be found at the end of the volume.

MARGINAL NUMBERS

The marginal numbers refer to the divisions of the pontifical documents, and are proper to this edition. In the indexes at the end of the volume, the reference is *always* to the marginal numbers.

SOURCES AND ABBREVIATIONS

A A S   *Acta Apostolicae Sedis*. Commentarium officiale, Rome, 1909 (first volume) ff.

A S S   *Acta Sanctae Sedis*. Rome, 1865-1908. From T. XXXVII (1904) this collection has the sub-title: Ephemerides Romanae a SSmo. D. N. Pio PP. X authenticae et officiales Apostolicae Sedis actis publice evulgandis declaratae.

B P   *Actes* de Léon XIII, Pie X, Benoit XV, Pie XI et Pie XII. Text latin et traduction française. Maison de la Bonne Presse, Paris (1878 ff.).

C I C   *Codex Juris Canonici*.

D C   *La Documentation Catholique*. La Bonne Presse, Paris, 1919 (first volume) ff.

2

E S P   *Enchiridion de Statibus Perfectionis.* Documenta Ecclesiae
          Sodalibus instituendis. Rome, 1949. Officium Libri Catholici.

F P A   Funk, *Patres Apostolici.*

O R   *L'Osservatore Romano.*

P G   Migne, *Patrologiae Cursus Completus*, Series graeca, Paris, 1857
          (first volume) ff.

P L   Migne, *Patrologiae Cursus Completus*, Series prima latina,
          Paris, 1844 (first volume) ff.

S V S   Cattin P. et Conus H.Th., *Aux Sources de la vie spirituelle.*
          Documents. Éditions Saint-Paul, Fribourg-Paris, 1951.

          Discorsi e Radiomessagi di Sua Santità Pio XII. Milano, Società
          editrice " Vita e Pensiero," 1941 (first volume) ff.

          The Catholic Priesthood. Mgr. P. Veuillot. M. H. Gill & Son,
          Dublin, 1957.

          Revue des Communautés Religieuses. Eegenhoven-Louvain, 1925
          (first volume) ff.

LEO XIII 1878-1903

LETTER "TESTEM BENEVOLENTIAE" ON THE DANGERS OF ACTIVISM

22 January 1899

EXTRACTS

At the end of the last century, a certain tendency had arisen to make a distinction between active virtues and passive virtues. On the plea of their practical value, the importance of zeal, dedication and the spirit of organization was emphasized, and virtues like obedience, mortification and humility were depreciated as outmoded and unsuited to the conditions of modern life. It was only a short step from that to depreciation of the religious life. In a letter to Cardinal Gibbons, Archbishop of Baltimore, Leo XIII reacted vigorously against this tendency. This key-document gives decisive evidence of the esteem in which the religious life is held by the Church.[1]

Misleading distinction between active and passive virtues. What is one to think of this division 1 of the virtues? The answer is clear, for there is not and cannot be a truly *passive* virtue. In the words of St. Thomas: *Virtus* denotes a certain perfection of the potency; now the goal of potency is act, and the act of virtue is nothing other than the good use of free will;[2] this, of course, will be aided by the grace of God, if there is question of an act of supernatural virtue.

To maintain that some Christian virtues are more suited to one period than to another is to forget the words of the Apostle: *Those whom he foreknew, he also predestined to be conformed to the image of his Son.*[3]

---

[1] *ASS* XXXI (1898-99), pp. 476 ff. This same theme was taken up subsequently by 1a Pius XII in the Letter *Cum proxime*, 16 June 1944, which he addressed to the Vicar General of the Society of Jesus. In it he warned religious against that "naturalism" in the apostolate which leads to the heresy of action (*AAS* XXXVI (1944), p. 239).

[2] St. Thomas, *Summa Theologica*, I-II, q. 55, art. 1.

[3] Romans 8: 29.

2   Christ is the teacher and the model of all sanctity; all who
desire to take their place in the abode of the blessed must adapt
their conduct to the standard which he has laid down. Now
Christ does not change with the passing of the centuries: *He is
the same yesterday and today and forever.*[4] The words: *Learn of me,
because I am meek and humble of heart,*[5] apply therefore to men of
every age; at all times Christ reveals himself *obedient unto death*; [6]
true for every age are the words of the Apostle: *They that are
Christ's have crucified the flesh, with the vices and concupiscences.*[7]

Would that at the present day there were many more who
cultivated these virtues, as did the saints of former times, who
by their humility, their obedience, their abstinence, were
mighty in work and word, to the great benefit not only of religion,
but also of public and civil life.

3   **The distinction leads**   From such an attitude almost of
       to contempt of the   contempt for the evangelical virtues,
       religious life.   which are wrongly described as *passive*
                              virtues, it was an almost inevitable
consequence that disrespect for the religious life itself should
gradually take hold of men's minds. And this is a feature which
is common to all the advocates of these novel views, as we
gather from some of their statements concerning the vows taken
by religious Orders. For they declare that these vows are wholly
out of harmony with the mentality of our age, inasmuch as they
restrict the bounds of human liberty; that they are more suited
to weak personalities than to the strong, and that, instead of
notably assisting Christian perfection and promoting the good
of human society, they are rather an obstacle and a hindrance
to both one and the other.

---

[4] Hebrews 13: 8.
[5] Matthew 11: 29.
[6] Philippians 2: 8.
[7] Galatians 5: 24.

The Church has always held religious life in high esteem.
The complete falsehood of these assertions is quite clear from the practice and teaching of the Church, which has always given the highest approval to the way of life of religious. Nor is that approval undeserved; for those are people who, having being called by God, of their own accord embrace the religious life, and not content with the duties which the commandments lay upon all, follow the path of the evangelical counsels, and thus show themselves to be energetic and well-trained soldiers for the army of Christ. Are we to believe that this is characteristic of pusillanimous souls, or that this is a useless procedure or even injurious to perfection of life? Those who thus bind themselves by the obligation of vows, far from suffering the loss of liberty, in fact enjoy a much fuller and more noble freedom, the *liberty with which Christ has set us free.* 4

Value of religious life for the Church.
It is also asserted that the way of life of religious is entirely useless or of very little assistance to the Church; this sentiment, apart from being offensive to religious Orders, is one which nobody who is acquainted with the history of the Church will for a moment accept . . . At the present time, in our own day, with what readiness and great benefit to the Catholic cause do not religious societies give their services, wherever they are established . . . From among their ranks, no less than from the rest of the clergy, the Christian people have preachers of the word of God and directors of conscience, youth has teachers, and the whole Church countless models of sanctity. The same tribute of praise goes to those who follow the active way of life, and to those who, being attracted by solitude, dedicate themselves to prayer and to bodily mortification. How well these latter also have deserved of human society in the past, and also at the present time, is well known to those who understand the power of the *assiduous prayer of the just man*[9] 5

---

[8] Galatians 4:31.
[9] James 5: 16.

to placate and conciliate almighty God, especially when that prayer is joined to bodily mortification.

6   If, however, there are some who prefer to form a group, without being bound by vows, they may follow their preference; such an institution is not new in the Church nor deserving of disapproval. But they are to avoid ranking it above the religious Orders.

APOSTOLIC CONSTITUTION "CONDITAE A CHRISTO"

8 December 1900

EXTRACTS

This Apostolic Constitution remains one of the key documents relating to Congregations of simple vows. Gradually simple vows have come to be sufficient to constitute the religious state. By this Constitution, the relations are defined between bishops and Congregations of diocesan law on the one hand, and Congregations of pontifical law on the other.[1]

Congregations of simple vows may be either of diocesan law or of pontifical law.

The Church founded by Christ has, **7** by divine institution, such strength and fecundity that in former times it has brought forth many, and in the present age is giving birth to an even greater number of religious societies both of men and of women; these, having undertaken the sacred obligation of *simple vows*, make it their object to devote themselves in righteousness to various works of religion and mercy. The majority of these societies, being urged on by the charity of Christ, have reached out beyond the narrow limits of an individual city or diocese; and having acquired something of the character of a perfect society, in virtue of one and the same rule and a common government, they are constantly expanding further.

These Congregations are of two kinds: some, having received **8** only episcopal approbation, are therefore called *diocesan*; there are others concerning whom there has been also a decision of the Roman Pontiff, either by his examination of their laws and statutes, or because in addition he has given them his commendation and approbation.

Now there are some who hold that uncertainty still prevails concerning the rights of bishops in relation to these two classes of religious families, and likewise concerning their obligations towards the bishops. In fact, as far as *diocesan* Congregations are concerned, the question is not difficult to solve; because they

---

[1] *ASS* XXXIII (1900-1901,) pp. 341-347.

have been introduced and flourish solely by the authority of the sacred prelates.

9   But a more serious problem arises in connection with the others, which have been honoured by the approbation of the Holy See. Because these in fact extend into several dioceses, and everywhere they follow the same law and are subject to the same régime; in consequence, the episcopal authority over them must admit a certain restriction and accept certain limits.

How far these limitations extend may be gathered from the form of decision customarily employed by the Apostolic See in giving approval to such associations, namely that a certain Congregation is approved as a pious society of simple vows, *under the direction of a moderator general, without prejudice to the jurisdiction of Ordinaries, in conformity with the sacred canons and apostolic constitutions.*

By this it is made clear that such Congregations are not classed as *diocesan*, and that they cannot be subject to the bishops, save within the limits of each diocese, without prejudice however to the administration and rule of their supreme moderator. As it is unlawful for the supreme superiors of these societies to intrude upon the rights and power of the bishops, similarly bishops are forbidden to arrogate to themselves any of the authority of these same superiors. If the contrary were to be allowed, these Congregations would have as many superiors as there are bishops in whose dioceses their members reside, and there would be an end to unity of administration and rule.

10   The authority of the superiors of the Congregations and the authority of the bishops should be in complete accord; and that makes it necessary that each should thoroughly understand the rights of the other and keep them intact.

In order to secure this fully in the future, without any controversy, and in order that the authority of bishops, which we, as is right, wish to see everywhere inviolate, may not anywhere be prejudiced, it has been decided, on the advice of the Sacred Council for Bishops and Religious Orders,[2] to enact

10a   [2] It was only in 1908 (29 June) that, in the course of a complete reorganization of the pontifical administration, the Sacred Congregation of Religious was instituted (Apost. Const. *Sapienti consilio, AAS* I (1909), pp. 9-10).

two chapters of prescriptions: one for associations which have not yet secured the commendation or approbation of the Apostolic See, the other for associations whose laws have been recognised by the Apostolic See, or whose institute has received the commendation or approval of the Apostolic See.

CONGREGATIONS OF DIOCESAN LAW

The first chapter includes the following prescriptions:

I. It is for the bishop not to receive into his diocese any 11 recently founded Congregation, until he has first become acquainted with its rules and constitutions and approved them: having verified, namely, that they are not contrary to faith or upright morals, nor opposed to the sacred canons and decrees of the Pontiffs, and whether they are suitable for the aim proposed for the Congregation.[3]

II. No house of a new Congregation can be legitimately 12 founded, except with the assent and approval of the bishop. The bishop shall not grant permission for the foundation, until a diligent enquiry has been made concerning the qualities of those who request it: whether they are persons of correct and upright sentiments, gifted with prudence, and chiefly guided by zeal for the glory of God and desire for the salvation of themselves and others.

III. Bishops, as far as possible, instead of founding or 13 approving a new society of a particular kind, shall more profitably secure the services of one of those already approved which professes a similar kind of activity. Except perhaps in mission territories, approval is not to be granted to any Congregations which, without having a definite and special aim, undertake all manner of works of piety and charity, even though these are quite distinct in character from one another.

[3] Some years later, Pius X, by the Motu Proprio *Dei Providentis*, 16 July 1906, gave further precise directives: " No bishop may authorize in his diocese the foundation of a new Congregation without having received by letter the authorization of the Apostolic See "; cf. infra, n. 57.

Bishops shall not permit the foundation of any society which lacks the revenues necessary for the subsistence of its members. Only with the greatest precautions, and indeed with difficulty, shall they approve of Congregations who live on alms, or Congregations of women who assist the sick in their own homes by day and night. If any new Congregation of women has as its purpose to open in its houses hospitals for the reception of both men and women; or, if it is proposed to open similar establishments for the reception of infirm priests, who in their illness are to be cared for by the sisters, such projects shall not receive episcopal approval, without mature and strict examination. Moreover, bishops shall not on any account give permission for houses of female religious, where for payment men and women coming from outside are given board and lodging.

14   IV. No diocesan Congregation may pass into other dioceses, except with the consent of the two bishops, the bishop of the place which they are leaving and the bishop of the place to which they wish to transfer.

15   V. If it should happen that a diocesan Congregation expands into other dioceses, nothing of its nature or laws may be changed, except with the consent of each of the bishops in whose diocese it has a house.

16   VI. Once they have been approved, Congregations are not to be extinguished, except for grave causes and with the consent of the bishops in whose jurisdiction they have been. Bishops may, however, suppress individual houses, each in his own diocese.[4]

17   VII. The bishop shall be informed about each young girl individually who seeks the religious habit, and also about those who are about to take vows, at the completion of probation; it will be for him to make the customary enquiries and, if there be no obstacle, to admit them.

18 VIII. The bishop has the power of dismissing professed women religious of diocesan Congregations, releasing them

16a   [4] Subsequently, in accordance with canon 493 (cf. *infra*, n. 79), the Holy See reserved to itself the right to suppress a Congregation, even one of diocesan status.

from their vows, perpetual as well as temporary, with the sole exception (at least on his own authority alone) of the vow of perpetual chastity. Care must be taken, however, lest by such remission of vows, the right of others be violated; such violation will take place, if remission be granted without the knowledge of the superiors and they are legitimately opposed to it.

IX. Superioresses, in accordance with the constitutions, shall be elected by the sisters. The bishop, however, shall preside at the voting either in person or through a delegate; he has full power to confirm or annul the election in accordance with his conscience. 19

X. The bishop has the right of inspection of the houses of any diocesan Congregation, and also the right to be informed of the zeal for virtue, the discipline and the economic administration. 20

XI. It is the duty of bishops to designate priests for the performance of sacred functions, for Confessions and for preaching, both for diocesan Congregations and for others, and also to make regulations for the dispensation of the sacraments: this point is defined in detail in the following chapter (n. VIII). 21

CONGREGATIONS OF PONTIFICAL LAW

This second chapter, dealing with Congregations whose rules have been examined, or whose institute has been commended or approved by the Apostolic See, contains the following prescriptions: 22

I. The acceptance of candidates, and their admission to the holy habit or profession of vows, belongs to the superiors of the Congregations; the bishop, however, retains intact the power granted by the Council of Trent, that, when there is question of females, in virtue of his office he examines them before they take the habit and also before they make their profession. It likewise belongs to the superiors to organize the individual families, to dismiss novices and professed, with due observance, however, of all that the rules of the institute and pontifical decrees prescribe. The right to appoint to offices and functions, both those which concern the entire Congregation and those exercised in individual houses, belongs to the assemblies or *chapters* and to the particular councils. In the chapters of female Congregations held for the purpose of assigning offices, the bishop in whose diocese they are held, shall preside in person or through another, as the delegate of the Apostolic See.

23   II. The dispensation of vows, whether they be temporary or perpetual, belongs exclusively to the Roman Pontiff. No bishop is given the right to modify the constitutions, inasmuch as they are approved by the Apostolic See. Similarly, bishops may not change or restrict the authority enjoyed by superiors either of the entire Congregation or of individual communities in accordance with the constitutions.

24   III. Bishops have the right, each in his own diocese, to permit or forbid the foundation of new houses of the Congregations, or the erection by them of new churches, also the opening of oratories whether public or semi-public, the celebration of Mass in private oratories, the public exposition of the blessed Sacrament for the veneration of the faithful. It is also for the bishops to regulate solemnities and supplications which are public.

25   IV. If houses of Congregations of this class have *episcopal enclosure*, the bishops retain intact the rights which are granted in this matter by pontifical laws. If any house, however, has *partial enclosure*, it will be for the bishop to see that it is duly observed and to repress any abuse that may creep into it. [5]

26   V. The members of these Congregations, both men and women, are subject to the power of the bishop in respect

25a   [5] In the Apostolic Constitution *Sponsa Christi*, 21 November 1950 (*AAS* XLIII (1951), pp. 5-24), Pope Pius XII reviewed and modified these regulations on the subject of the enclosure of nuns, which had become incompatible with " the works of education and of charity" undertaken by Orders and Congregations of women. Cf. *infra*, nn. 338-340, 348.

of the *internal forum*. In the *external forum*, however, they are subject to him in respect of censures, the reservation of cases, dispensation of vows which are not reserved to the supreme Pontiff alone, the declaration of public prayers, dispensations and other concessions, which bishops are empowered to impart to the faithful who are subject to them.

VI. If any members of these Congregations request promotion 27 to sacred Orders, the bishop shall be careful not to promote them, even though they are living in his diocese, except on the following conditions: that they be proposed by their own superiors; that the requirements of canon law concerning *dimissorial* or *testimonial* letters be duly fulfilled; that they have a *titulus ordinationis*, or certainly have been lawfully exempted from it; that they have studied theology, in accordance with the decree *Auctis admodum*, dated 4 November 1892.[6]

VII. Over Congregations which live by questing, bishops 28 shall retain the rights mentioned by the decree *Singulari quidem* promulgated by the Congregation of Bishops and Religious Orders on 27 March 1896.[7]

VIII. In matters of the spiritual order, Congregations are 29 subject to the bishops of the dioceses in which they are established. It will be for the bishops, therefore, to designate for them priests for sacred functions and to approve preachers. If the Congregations are female, the bishop shall also designate both ordinary and extraordinary confessors, in accordance with the constitution *Pastoralis curae*, published by our predecessor Benedict XIV, and the decree *Quemadmodum*, issued by the Congregation of Bishops and Religious Orders on 18 December 1890; the same decree applies also to Congregations of men who are not promoted to sacred Orders.[8]

[6] *ASS* XXV (1892), pp. 312-315.
[7] *ASS* XXVIII (1896), pp. 555-558.
[8] *ASS* XXIII (1890), pp. 505-508.

30   IX. The administration of property, which the individual
                Congregations possess, shall pertain to the superior
                general or superioress general and their respective
                councils; the revenues of individual families are to be
                administered by their own superiors, in accordance with
                the laws of each institute. The bishop cannot demand
                any account of them. But when funds have been assigned
                or bequeathed to a certain house for divine worship or
                for the performance of works of beneficence in that
                place, the superior of the house shall have the adminis-
                tration of these funds; he shall, however, make a report
                to the bishop, and shall show himself completely
                obedient to him; so that neither the superior general
                nor the superioress of the entire Congregation may con-
                ceal any of this property from the bishop, or withdraw
                from it or convert it to other uses. The bishop, therefore,
                shall examine, as often as it seems good to him, the
                accounts of receipts and expenditure of such goods; he
                shall also take care that the capital is not diminished and
                that the revenues are not wrongly expended.

31   X. Wherever houses belonging to Congregations have
                attached to them establishments such as women's
                homes, orphanages, hospitals, schools, refuges for the
                instruction of children, all these shall be subject to
                episcopal vigilance in what concerns the teaching of
                religion, upright conduct, exercises of piety, the
                administration of the sacred rites, without prejudice
                however to the privileges which may have been granted
                by the Apostolic See to such colleges, schools and
                institutions.

32   XI. In the houses of any Congregations which profess simple
                vows, the bishops, each in his own diocese, have the
                right to inspect churches, sacristies, public oratories
                and confessionals, and to issue appropriate regulations
                and orders concerning them. In Congregations of priests,
                only the superiors shall have cognisance of matters of
                conscience and discipline, and likewise of economic
                matters. In Congregations of women, however, as well

as in Congregations of men who are not priests, it will be for the bishop to inquire whether discipline is flourishing in accordance with the rules, whether sound doctrine or upright morals have suffered any detriment, whether the enclosure has been violated, and whether the sacraments are received with due regularity and frequency in accordance with the statutes. If the bishop should perhaps find something deserving of reproof, he shall not take an immediate decision; he shall admonish the superiors to look after the matter; and if they prove negligent, he shall personally take steps. If, however, matters of importance, which brook no delay, are in question, he shall take an immediate decision; that decision, however, he shall communicate to the Congregation of Bishops and Religious Orders.

Especially on the occasion of visitation, the bishop shall make use of his rights which we mentioned above in respect of schools, refuges and other institutions there enumerated. As for the economic affairs of Congregations of women and also of men who are not priests, the bishop shall take cognisance only of the administration of funds or bequests which have been assigned for sacred worship, or for the assistance of the inhabitants of the place or the diocese.

LETTER TO CARDINAL RICHARD ON THE *RAISON D'ÊTRE* OF RELIGIOUS ORDERS

23 December 1900

EXTRACTS

The year 1900 was marked by the multiplication of attacks on the religious Orders. These attacks and calumnies reached the ears of the general public in the Press. The Holy Father, in this Letter to Cardinal Richard, speaks strongly in defence of the Orders.[1]

33 **Origins and purpose of the religious life.** The religious Orders, as everyone knows, have their origin and *raison d'être* in those sublime evangelical counsels, which our divine Redeemer spoke, for the course of all time, to those who desire to attain Christian perfection—those are strong and generous souls who, by prayer and contemplation, by saintly austerities and by the observance of certain rules, strive to climb to the very summits of the spiritual life. The religious Orders have come into existence through the action of the Church, which gives the sanction of her authority to their government and discipline, and they form an élite part of the flock of Christ. They are, in the words of St. Cyprian, " the honour and adornment of spiritual grace," [2] and at the same time they bear witness to the holy fecundity of the Church.

The promises which religious make, freely and spontaneously, after mature reflection on them in the novitiates, have been regarded and respected by all ages as sacred things and as the sources of the rarest virtues.

34 The object of the vows undertaken is twofold: first, to raise the persons who pledge themselves to these vows to a higher degree of perfection; secondly, to prepare them, by purifying

[1] *Acta Leonis XIII*, XX, pp. 340-341.
[2] *De disciplina et habitu virginum*, c. III (*PL* IV, 455).

and strengthening their souls, for an exterior ministry to be exercised for the eternal salvation of the neighbour and for the relief of the countless woes of humanity.

Religious Orders in the service of the mission of the Church. Thus, labouring under the supreme direction of the Apostolic See to achieve the ideal of perfection proposed by our Lord, and living under rules which have absolutely nothing contrary to any form of civil government, religious institutes co-operate magnificently in the mission of the Church; that mission which consists essentially in the sanctification of souls and in doing good for mankind.

That is the reason why, wherever the Church is in possession of her liberty, wherever the natural right of every citizen is respected to choose the way of life which he considers most in accord with his tastes and moral betterment, there too religious Orders have arisen as a spontaneous growth from the Catholic soil, and the bishops have with good reason regarded them as most valuable auxiliaries of the sacred ministry and of Christian charity.

Religious Orders in the service of civil society. It is not to the Church alone that the religious Orders have rendered immense services since their first beginnings: civil society itself has also benefited. Theirs is the merit of having preached virtue to the masses by the apostolate of example no less than by the word; they have formed and ennobled men's minds by the imparting of learning, both sacred and profane; they have even added to the inheritance of the fine arts by works both brilliant and of abiding worth. Their learned men shed lustre on universities by the profundity and extent of their learning, while their houses became the refuges of knowledge of things divine and human and, during the collapse of civilization, saved from certain ruin the masterpieces of ancient wisdom; frequently other religious penetrated into inhospitable territories, into swamps or impenetrable forests; there, by drainage and reclamation, braving all manner

35

36

3

of fatigue and danger, they cultivated the soil by the sweat of
their brow, while they also exercised the care of souls; around
their monasteries and in the shadow of the Cross, they founded
centres of population that became villages or thriving towns,
which were ruled with gentleness, and where agriculture and
industry first began their tremendous progress.

37   When the shortage of priests or the needs of the times
demanded it, one could see legions of apostles coming forth
from the cloisters, men eminent for sanctity and learning; these
gave valiant assistance to the bishops, and they exercised a most
beneficial influence on society, by appeasing discords, by
extinguishing hatred, by bringing people to a sense of duty,
and by restoring to a place of honour the principles of religion
and of Christian civilization.

38   Such, in brief, are the meritorious services
Their abiding rendered by religious Orders in the past.
worth.   Impartial history has recorded them, and it
would be superfluous to dwell on them at greater length.
Neither their activity, nor their zeal, nor their love for the
neighbour, has become less in our own day. The good which
they are doing is clear to the eyes of everyone, and their virtues
shine with a distinction which no accusation and no attack
can tarnish.

LETTER TO THE SUPERIORS GENERAL OF ORDERS AND RELIGIOUS INSTITUTES

29 June 1901

EXTRACTS

In the atmosphere of persecution which then prevailed in France, the first victims were the Orders and religious institutes. The Holy Father made it a point to manifest his sympathy to the superiors general, and gave them some motives of comfort and encouragement.[1]

Sorrowful protest against persecution of religious Orders. At all times, but especially in the time of severe trials, as at the present moment, religious families have received from this Apostolic See special testimonies of affectionate and far-seeing solicitude. 39

The grave attacks which, in some countries, have recently been launched against the Orders and institutes subject to your authority are a source of profound grief to us. The holy Church grieves for these attacks, because she feels both wounded to the quick in her rights and seriously hampered in her action; that action, if it is to be exercised in freedom, needs the assistance of the two branches of the clergy, the secular and the regular; indeed, whoever touches either her priests or her religious, touches the Church in the very apple of her eye. 40

For our own part, as you know, we have tried by every means to avert from you a persecution that is so shameful, and at the same time to save these countries from misfortunes as great as they are undeserved. That is the reason why, on many occasions, we have pleaded your cause with all our power, in the name of religion, of justice and of civilization. It was in vain that we hoped that our remonstrances would not go unheeded. 41

For now, in these very days, we see in fact, in a nation exceptionally rich in religious vocations, that the public authority

[1] *ASS* XXXIII (1901), pp. 716 ff.

has approved and promulgated special measures, concerning which we raised our voice some months ago in the hope of warding them off.

42   Being mindful of our sacred duties, and following the example of our illustrious predecessors, we absolutely reprobate these laws; they are contrary to the right, which is based on natural law and the law of the Gospel and confirmed by constant tradition, to form an association in order to lead a manner of life that is not only above reproach in itself, but even particularly holy. These laws are likewise contrary to the absolute right of the Church to found religious institutes, subject exclusively to her authority, in order to assist her in the fulfilling of her divine mission, while at the same time they yield benefits of the highest value both in the religious and civil spheres, to the great advantage of this noble nation itself.

43   **Motives of consolation: they are persecuted because of loyalty to Jesus Christ.** Among the many motives of encouragement to which faith gives birth, call to mind, beloved sons, this solemn declaration of Jesus Christ: *Blessed are you when they revile you and persecute you and speak every manner of evil against you, speaking falsely, for my sake.*[2] Reproaches, calumnies, tribulations, all these will fall upon you *for my sake; then you are blessed.* In fact, charges against you have been multiplied without restraint in order to humiliate you; but the sad truth is nevertheless obvious to all who have eyes to see. The true reason for persecuting you is the deadly hatred of the world for the *City of God*, which is the Catholic Church. The real intention is to banish from society, if possible, the saving action of Christ, that action which is universally beneficent and salutary. Everyone is aware that religious, both men and women, form an élite in the City of God: it is they who represent in a special way the mind and the mortification of Jesus Christ; it is they who, by observance of the evangelical counsels, strive to bring Christian virtues to the summit of perfection; it is they who in many different

[2] Matthew 5: 11.

ways powerfully support the action of the Church. It is not surprising, therefore, that nowadays, as in other ages and with other forms of injustice, the *City of the World*, and especially those men who by impious pacts are more closely bound in servile subjection to the *Prince of this world* himself, should rise up against religious.

It is clear that they regard the dissolution and extinction of the religious Orders as a skilful maneouvre towards the realization of their pre-conceived plan to force Catholic nations into the road of apostasy and of abandonment of Jesus Christ. But if that be the case, one can say of you in all truth: *Blessed are you*, for you are hated and persecuted solely by reason of the way of life which you have freely chosen because of your attachment to Christ.

If you were to follow the maxims and desires of the world, the world would not disquiet you; indeed it would even load you with its favours. *If you had been of the world, the world would love its own*, but because you follow a path which is contrary to the world's ways, you are exposed to affronts and war. *Therefore the world hates you*.[3] Christ himself has foretold it to you. And so he now looks upon you with all the greater complaisance and predilection, because he sees you as even more in conformity with himself when you suffer for justice' sake. Let you inasmuch as *you share in the sufferings of Christ, rejoice*.[4] Set your hearts on courage like that of those heroes who *went from the presence of the Sanhedrin rejoicing that they were counted worthy to suffer reproach for the name (of Jesus)*.[5]

44

Sympathy and appreciation of men of good will. The just pride, which comes from the witness of your conscience,[6] is supported, without your seeking for it, by the blessings of all upright men. All those who are genuinely concerned for the peace and prosperity of the nation consider that no citizens are more devoted and more useful to their country than members of the religious Con-

45

---

[3] John 15: 19.   [4] I Peter 4: 13.
[5] Acts 5: 41.   [6] II Corinthians 1: 12.

gregations; and they tremble at the thought of losing, together with you, so many benefits which stand or fall with your existence. There is a whole multitude of the needy, the abandoned, the wretched, for whose relief you have founded and maintain institutions of all kinds with an understanding and spirit of charity which are worthy of all admiration. There are the fathers of families who have entrusted their children to you, and who hitherto have relied upon you to give them religious and moral training, that healthy, vigorous education, fruitful in manly virtues, which was never more needed than in our own epoch. There are the priests who found in you excellent assistants for their own important and laborious ministry. There are the men of every class who, in this time of perversion, find useful directions and an incentive to upright conduct in your counsels, which have added authority from the integrity of your life. There are especially the sacred pastors, who honour you with their confidence; they regard you as the experienced instructors of the young clergy, and recognise in you the *true lovers of the brethren and of the people*,[7] who offer unceasing prayers and expiations for them to the divine mercy.

46   But no one can more correctly appreciate the outstanding merits of the religious Orders than we ourselves who, from this supreme See, have the duty of watching over the needs of the universal Church.

Already, in other official pronouncements, we have made special mention of this. For the moment let it suffice to praise the great zeal with which they follow not only the directives, but even the least desires of the Vicar of Jesus Christ; they undertake all manner of works beneficial to the Christian religion and to society, which he proposes to them, going forth into the most inhospitable lands, braving perils of every kind and facing even death itself.

47   If we count it among the most cherished memories of our long pontificate, that we have raised a great number of servants of God to the honours of the altar, that memory is all the more pleasing because the majority of these saints belonged to

[7] II Maccabees 15: 14.

institutes of regulars, either as their founders or as simple religious.

For your consolation we also wish to recall that, among men **48** of the world who are distinguished by their position and their grasp of social needs, there are not wanting persons of upright and impartial mind, who stand up to praise your labours and to defend your inviolable right as citizens, and your even more sacrosanct liberty as Catholics.

Indeed, one needs only not to be blinded by passion, to see how shortsighted and how ignoble it is to strike at men who, without hoping or asking for anything for themselves, give their lives completely to the service of society. Consider simply the zeal with which they apply themselves to developing in the children of the people those germs of natural goodness, which otherwise would be suffocated to the detriment of the children, and also to the detriment of others. These are the precious seeds which, with the aid of grace, the religious cultivate patiently and assiduously, protecting them from every deadly attack and guiding them to maturity. Thus it is that under their influence those splendid fruits, enlightened love of the truth, uprightness, the sense of duty, firmness of character and ready generosity in making sacrifices, reach full development. And what could be better calculated than these qualities to ensure the order and prosperity of States?

However, beloved sons, since the **49** **The appropriate** malice of the world persecutes you to **attitude for religious** the point even of pretending that it is **in face of persecution.** beneficial and praiseworthy to trample underfoot, in your persons, the most sacred rights, and since the world imagines that it is thus *giving glory to God*,[8] you shall bow in adoration of the designs of God with confident humility. If sometimes he allows right to be overcome by violence, he permits this only in the higher perspective of a greater good; besides, it is his way to give efficacious help, and that in ways unforeseen, to those who suffer for him and trust in him.

[8] John 16: 2.

If he places obstacles and opposition in the path of those who by their state profess Christian perfection, it is in order to test and strengthen their virtue; more particularly, it is in order to invigorate and temper anew souls that have been in danger of growing feeble in a long period of peace.

50   Strive then to conform to these fatherly designs of God. Devote yourselves with redoubled ardour to a life of faith, of prayer and saintly works. See to it that among you regular discipline flourishes, with fraternal union of hearts, humble and eager obedience, austere detachment and fervour for the praise of God. May your thoughts be noble, your resolutions generous and your zeal indefatigable, for the glory of God and the extension of his kingdom!

Inasmuch as the evil of the times has already inflicted or now threatens you with dispersion, you will realize that the circumstances impose on you the duty of defending the integrity of your spirit as religious against the distractions of contact with the world.

51   . . . And now, religious of every age, whether young or old, lift up your eyes to your illustrious founders! Their maxims speak to you, their statutes are your guide, their example shows you the way! May it be at once your fondest and most saintly preoccupation, to listen to their words, to follow their rules, to imitate their example! It was thus that many of your elders acted in times of the greatest trials. Thereby they handed on to you a rich heritage of invincible courage and sublime virtues. Show yourselves worthy of these your fathers and brothers, so that all of you can say, with justifiable pride: *We are the children and the brothers of the saints.*

It is thus that you will secure the greatest benefits for yourselves, for the Church and for society. By making the effort to attain that degree of sanctity to which God has called you, you will carry out the designs of his providence in your regard; and you will merit the superabundant recompenses which he has promised you. The Church, that tender mother, who has lavished her favours on your institutes, will receive from you, by way of return, ever more loyal and efficacious co-operation in her mission of peace and salvation.

Peace, salvation: these are the two urgent requirements in 52
contemporary society, which is undermined by so many causes
of corruption and enfeeblement. In order to rouse it from leth-
argy, to raise it up, to lead it back repentant to the feet of our
most merciful Redeemer, there is need for men of high virtue,
of inspiring words, of apostolic heart, who have at the same time
the power of mediators to bring down heavenly graces. You
will be such men, we are quite sure, and you will thus become
the most timely and outstanding benefactors of society.

Beloved sons, the love of Christ prompts us to say one final 53
word to confirm in your hearts the sentiments which animate
you towards those who attack your institutes and hamper your
activity.

Even as your conscience binds you to maintain an attitude that
is both firm and dignified, so also the way of life you profess
obliges you to show yourselves always gentle and kind; because
it is religious particularly in whom should be found the
resplendent perfection of that true charity, which is moved
indeed by compassion, but does not know anger.

It is saddening, no doubt, that ingratitude should be your
reward and that you are thus spurned, but let the faith strengthen
you! Faith brings to your mind the solemn exhortation: *Overcome
evil by good*.[9] It brings before your eyes the incomparable
magnanimity of the Apostle: *We are cursed and we bless; we are
persecuted and we endure; we are calumniated and we bless*.[10] Above
all, faith invites you to repeat the supplication of the supreme
benefactor of the human race, Jesus Christ, as he hung on the
Cross: *Father, forgive them*.[11]

Therefore, beloved sons, *be strengthened in the Lord*.[12] You
have with you the Vicar of Jesus Christ, you have with you
the whole Catholic world, which gazes upon you with affection,
respect and gratitude.

From heaven above, your glorious fathers, your glorious
brethren, give encouragement. Your sovereign Head, Jesus

[9] Romans 12: 21.
[10] 1 Corinthians 4: 12-13.
[11] Luke 23: 34.
[12] Ephesians 6: 10.

Christ, girds you with his strength and shields you with his valour.

Beloved sons, turn to his divine Heart with filial confidence and with fervent prayers. In that Heart you will find all the strength required to triumph over the most furious passions of the world. There is a word which echoes down through the centuries, a word which is ever living and always full of consolation: *Have confidence, I have overcome the world.*[13]

53a   [13] John 16: 33. Some months later the Holy Father returned to this subject and protested even more energetically against the odious measures affecting religious: " As for the religious Orders and Congregations, the practice of the evangelical counsels made them the glory of society no less than of religion; in the eyes of the enemies of the Church, this made them only the more culpable, and they have been mercilessly made the target for contempt and animosity from all sides. It is for us an immense grief to be obliged to recall those heinous measures, quite unjustified and condemned by every upright mind, of which again quite recently religious have been made the victims . . . And it is thus that men and women, themselves sprung from the people, and who have renounced the joys of the family in order to consecrate to the service of all men, in peaceful associations, their youth, their talents, their strength, even their very lives, have been treated as malefactors . . . have been excluded from the common rights of all " (Encyclical Letter, *Pervenuto*, 19 March 1902, *ASS* XXXIV (1901-2), pp. 513-532).

SAINT PIUS X 1903-1914

LETTER TO THE SUPERIOR GENERAL OF THE BROTHERS OF THE CHRISTIAN SCHOOLS

23 April 1905

EXTRACTS

The Brothers of the Christian Schools had undergone a severe trial; many of their schools were closed. In order to continue their work of teaching, a certain number had gone abroad, while others had taken to wearing lay dress. In addition to the sufferings caused by their dispersion, there were treacherous attacks that were liable to dishearten the goodwill of some and to create troubles of conscience. On the occasion of the Chapter General the Holy Father recalls the primacy of the religious life.[1]

We have heard that you are shortly to hold the solemn 54 chapter of your Order, and we gladly take this occasion of conveying to you and to your subjects our paternal good wishes, though we deem that you already fully realize our friendly interest.

For in these calamitous times through which France is passing, when a cruel war is being waged against the Church, we consider it necessary that the voice of the commander-in-chief should frequently resound in the ears of those who are engaged in the struggle for justice and truth, so as to stimulate their efforts by words of praise or warning. For you, who in a particular way have deserved well of your countrymen, and yet have for long been bearing the brunt of fierce attacks by the enemy forces, our command is that you stand firm and courageous, and that, as far as the difficulties of the times permit, you shall retain the character of your Institute.

We hear that a view is gaining ground that you should give 55 first place to the instruction of children, and that the religious

[1] *ASS* XL (1905), pp. 658 f.

profession should take second place to this; it is said that this is demanded by the outlook and requirements of the present age. We refuse absolutely to allow that view to have any weight with you and other similar institutes, whose function as religious is to instruct the youth. A remedy must indeed be found, as far as possible, for the grave evils which press on society, and consequently concessions must be made in many things; but one must beware of yielding to such an extent that the dignity of saintly institutions should suffer, and even the very patrimony of sacred doctrine be adversely affected.

56   Let the principle be firmly established therefore, as far as you are concerned, that the religious way of life is far superior to ordinary life; and, if you have the grave duty of teaching as an obligation to your neighbours, the obligations which bind you to God are graver still. It is evident, moreover, that if hitherto you have been outstanding teachers and educators of youth, a fact which has won for you even publicly the highest tributes of praise, the explanation of this excellence lies in the discipline whereby your Order has provided for your formation. Continue to observe and to love that discipline, as you are doing, with the greatest loyalty and devotion to your superiors, and with supreme unity among yourselves; for the rest, obey the dictates of conscience and trust in God.[2]

---

[2] The fidelity of the Brothers to their religious life has been, as Saint Pius X promised, richly blessed by divine providence. Fifty years later, his Holiness Pius XII, when receiving in audience the chapter general of the Brothers, paid them this splendid tribute: " We hold your religious family in high esteem, not only because of the incomparable results achieved throughout the whole world in the domain of instruction and education, and in the preparation of future workers, but also because of the fruits of sanctity which it has borne for three centuries, fruits which it will continue to bear in the future, provided you remain faithful to the spirit of your holy founder. The complete giving of yourselves in loving self-denial, in profound fidelity to the rule, in conscientious and intelligent application to the duties of your state, that should remain the essential feature of your life as religious. For it is upon your interior life that the spiritual fruit of your labours depends. Do not imagine that you are failing in charity when you reserve for God and for your soul all the time which the rule consecrates to prayer in common and in private. Such a mark of humility and confidence will secure from the Master of your souls, for yourselves and for your pupils, the graces of light and strength, which nowadays are more than ever necessary for anyone who wishes to perform the work of Christian education " (OR, 27 May 1956).

THE STATES OF PERFECTION

MOTU PROPRIO " DEI PROVIDENTIS "

16 July 1906

EXTRACTS

The Apostolic Constitution Conditae a Christo [1] *had laid down the regulations concerning the foundation of Congregations of simple vows and their relations with the bishops. But in order to avoid wrong steps at the outset, which would require grave modifications when a diocesan Congregation sought approbation of the Holy See, the Holy Father issued the following supplementary regulations.* [2]

1. No bishop or Ordinary of any place, unless he has received 57 by letter the permission of the Apostolic See, shall found a new Congregation of either sex or permit it to be founded in his diocese.

2. The Ordinary, in order to secure this permission, shall 58 approach the Sacred Council of Bishops and Regulars by means of a written petition, in which he shall set out the following: the identity and character of the founder of the new Congregation, and the motive which has led him to propose to found it; the form of words in which the name or title of the Congregation to be founded is expressed; the form, colour, material and the parts of the habit to be worn by novices and professed members; the nature of the activities which the Congregation proposes to undertake, and their number; what resources are available to assure the permanence of the Congregation; whether there are similar institutes in the diocese, and the works on which they are engaged.

3. Once the permission of the Sacred Council has been 59 received, there shall be no further obstacle to prevent the Ordinary establishing the new Congregation or permitting it to be established, but it must be with the title, habit, the purpose and other qualifications which have been examined, approved

[1] Cf. *supra*, nn. 7-32.
[2] *ASS* XXXIX (1906), pp. 344-346.

or designated by the same Sacred Council; these may not subsequently be changed at any time, except with the consent of the Sacred Council.

60   4. The Ordinary shall examine the constitutions of the Congregation being founded; but he shall not give them approval until he has seen to it that they are in conformity with the norms which the Sacred Council has decreed in this matter.

61   5. The Congregation having been founded, even though in the course of time it has extended into several dioceses, it shall remain subject to the jurisdiction of the Ordinaries, so long as it has not received the testimony of pontifical approbation or praise, as is decreed in the Constitution *Conditae* of our predecessor.

BENEDICT XV
1914–1922

INSTRUCTION "ILLUD SAEPIUS" OF THE SACRED CONGREGATION OF RELIGIOUS: QUALITIES REQUIRED FOR ADMISSION TO RELIGION

18 August 1915

As requests for dispensation from vows increased, probably being occasioned by the war, the Sacred Congregation of Religious, on the command of the Holy Father, sent a reminder to superiors of their grave responsibilities in relation to the admission, the spiritual training and supervision of members of their religious institutes. This instruction was not published in the Acta Apostolicae Sedis.[1]

Regrettable defections. It happens all too frequently that religious, even though bound by solemn vows, petition this Sacred Congregation for dispensation of these vows, in order to live a secular life outside the cloister. It is unnecessary to say how deeply the heart of the Holy Father is afflicted by these requests. For frequently, as a result of these unfortunate departures from the bosom of religious communities, grave dishonour is brought on the Orders themselves, there is serious disturbance of the regular discipline, great harm is done to the Church of God and a dangerous occasion of scandal is given to the faithful. His Holiness, whose most earnest desire is that these unfortunate cases should cease altogether or at least become less frequent in future, through the intermediary of this Sacred Congregation, has submitted for examination by all heads of religious societies the following two points, in which will be found the root cause and origin of these deplorable lapses: the absence of the divine call or vocation and the loss of vocation.

It is not to be overlooked at this point that the Sacred Council of Trent and the Roman Pontiffs, with supreme wisdom and

62

---

[1] *Enchiridion de Statibus Perfectionis*, I, pp. 340-344.

sanctity, enacted norms and precepts to ensure that the discipline of religious should never fall short of that dignity and perfection which was the aim of their founders, but should rather constantly make further progress. If these precepts and provisions, as well as the norms and rules of the religious societies, were duly observed, the lapses which we have deplored would rarely if ever take place. For then there would be no admission of postulants who lack a divine vocation; candidates quite unworthy of the religious state would not take vows; nor would those who had taken their vows be compelled to abandon monastic life in order to look to their eternal salvation.[2]

63   **Responsibilities of Superiors.** Whenever a man religious leaves his Order, the superior of the Order, if he has weighed everything diligently before the Lord, will readily perceive that all too often he himself is not free from fault and has failed in his responsibility. This neglect of duty usually takes place in the admission of candidates, or in their formation for the religious life, or in the supervision of them after they have taken their vows.

—Admission made too easy because of shortage of vocations.

64   Nowadays because of the scarcity of those who, moved by God's inspiration, seek to enter a religious society, it not infrequently happens that young men are admitted to the novitiate who are indeed endowed with intellectual qualities and other qualifications which are esteemed by men, but do not meet the approval of the Judge who sees in secret.

—Inadequate formation of novices.

65   In the training of novices for the monastic life, which should be carried out properly and steadfastly, this is what sometimes happens, when superiors of religious allow themselves to be influenced by particular considerations: for instance, they are captivated by the nobility and distinction of a family, or

---

[2] Since the obligations of religious life are too severe for these religious who lack a genuine vocation, they incur the risk of endangering the eternal welfare of their souls.

attracted by the utility and advantages of their resources, or influenced by their numerous relationships and powerful connexions, while they completely neglect to close the doors of the monastery against worldly inclinations and to prevent them from establishing within it a dangerous domination.

—Lack of authority.

Finally, in the supervision of religious who are already bound 66 by vows, it sometimes happens that superiors of Orders, through weakness of character, or fear or indifference, are gravely at fault: for example, when in order not to hurt a subject who is violent and quarrelsome, or to avoid offending a distinguished speaker or an outstanding professor, they entrust functions that call for both prudence and judgment, and which moreover are not free from all danger, to religious whose learning and experience may seem to fit them for these duties, but who lack the qualities which are the most essential of all.

Similarly superiors of religious families are at fault and fail in their responsibility, when they do not hesitate to grant privileges which are gravely prejudicial to poverty, chastity, obedience and other virtues, and thereby the way is opened to a manner of life and discipline which is very far removed from the perfection laid down for religious Orders.

Who will deny that the blame for all this should be laid on those appointed to guide and rule religious societies? And what answer will these superiors make to the eternal Judge, on that dread day, when he will ask what they have done to lead their brethren to the heavenly pastures?

—Conclusions.

The following, therefore, are absolutely essential for religious Orders; to admit to their membership only those who, under 67 the influence of God's inspiration, purpose to enter worthily into religion; to give those who have been admitted steady and solid training for the monastic life; to secure the perseverance in their vocation of those who are professed, through obedience to the rules of the society and especially by never departing from the pontifical directives.

68   **The directives**   It is opportune to mention here the Apostolic
      of Pius IX.   Letter *Ubi primum* sent on 17 June 1847 by the
      supreme Pontiff, Pius IX of happy memory,
to all superiors of religious families. In this Letter, that great
head and teacher of the Catholic faith gave wholesome precepts
and laid down norms of the greatest utility which, unfortunately,
with the lapse of time and also through negligence have been
completely forgotten.

—Admission of postulants.

69   This is what he said about the admission of postulants to the
novitiate: " The well-being and dignity of every religious family
depends entirely on the care taken in the admission of novices
and on the excellence of their training; we earnestly exhort
you, therefore, to make careful investigations beforehand into
the character, disposition and conduct of those who are about
to enter your religious family; and you shall also diligently look
into the purpose, outlook and motive by which they are led to
enter the regular life."

—Formation of novices.

70   Concerning the training of novices for the religious life, he
wrote: " When you have ascertained that, in embracing the
religious life, their only aim is the glory of God, the good of the
Church, their own salvation and that of others, make it your
particular care to have them educated to piety and holiness by
the very best teachers, during the period of novitiate prescribed
by the rules of the Order, and to give them the very best training
in all the virtues and for that form of the regular life which they
have begun."

—Supervision of professed religious.

71   Finally, concerning the continued supervision and progressive
development of those who are professed, the Letter says: " In
view of the position which you hold, and the responsibility
which you bear, you shall spare no efforts to ensure that the
religious who are subject to you shall meditate seriously on the

vocation to which they have been called, and show themselves
worthy of it in their conduct, and at all times strive scrupulously
to fulfil the vows which they once made to God. With most
watchful care you shall see to it that they follow in the footsteps
of their distinguished forbears, observing the holy discipline
and setting their face completely against the worldly allurements
and spectacles and occupations which they have renounced;
never slackening in prayer, they shall devote themselves to
meditation on heavenly things, to learning, to reading, and apply
their energies to the salvation of souls in accordance with the
statute of their Order; mortified in the flesh, but raised to
life in the spirit, they shall present to the people of God models
of modesty, humility, sobriety, benignity, patience and justice;
above reproach for integrity and chastity, fervent in charity,
deserving of honour for wisdom, they shall give offence to no
one, but afford an example of good works to all so that the
adversary may be put to shame, since he has nothing evil to say
about them."

The Holy Father, Benedict XV, makes these supremely   72
practical and timely norms and precepts his own; moreover, he
not merely desires and advises that they be carefully, constantly
and exactly observed by all superiors of Orders, but in virtue
of his Apostolic authority, imposes them under a grave obligation
of conscience.

Obedience of religious and charity of Superiors. All those who rule over religious   73
communities shall bear in mind, how-
ever, that no one can discharge his
responsibility unless the charity of Christ
urges him. It is the duty of those who are subject to the rule
and authority of superiors to obey those who are placed in
authority over them, and in a certain way to recognise and
respect in them the person of Jesus Christ himself; but it is
extremely difficult nevertheless, because of the weakness of
human nature, to give this obedience, if the person of the
superior, especially in relation to charity, fails to reflect the
person of Jesus Christ, who himself is charity. For it is one and
the same law which lays down obedience for subjects and charity

for superiors; and consequently, where obedience is wanting, one will easily discern, when all things are carefully examined, that as a rule charity also is lacking. Hence, when a religious loses his vocation and leaves the convent, the superior, who remains in the monastery, appears to stand more in need of the mercy of God than the one who leaves the cloister.

74 The first requirement, therefore, to secure observance of regular discipline, which is the chief means to ensure that the divine call will persist, is that the superiors of religious institutes should be "possessed of charity and gentleness, be sympathetic, lovers of the brotherhood, merciful, men to whose rule others will willingly submit."

Conclusion.

75 In view of all these considerations, this Sacred Congregation, on the mandate of the supreme Pontiff, earnestly commends to all religious, and especially to their superiors, that they give careful consideration to all that is set out in this document and keep it constantly in mind; the Congregation also commands them to observe all the norms and precepts, religious by observing obedience, the superiors by always exercising charity. When this is carried out in practice, it is beyond question that religious communities will be able easily to achieve the sanctity which corresponds to their condition and to the intention of their founders, and as a result to constantly flourish and prosper more and more.

What the Holy Father particularly desires, and he confidently hopes that it will be realized, is that never in the future will those who lack a vocation enter within the doors of the cloister; and that those who, moved by an impulse from God, have entered religion, will lead a true form of monastic life to the very end. Thus both superiors and their brethren, who all alike have left all things and followed Jesus Christ, will enter the heavenly Jerusalem bearing the merits of sanctity, penance and all the virtues, and will there receive a hundredfold reward and possess life eternal.

CODE OF CANON LAW

27 May 1917

EXTRACTS

The Code of Canon Law, which had been drawn up by the command of Pius X,[1] was promulgated by Benedict XV in the Apostolic Constitution Providentissima Mater *(27 May 1917), and came into force a year later (19 May 1918). Very many canons of the Code deal with the religious life. It is not possible to give them all here, but the present selection includes the greater part of the canons which are calculated to bring out the spirit of the religious life and to define the obligations which it entails.[2]*

THE RELIGIOUS STATE

Canon 487.—The religious state, or stable common life, by which the faithful undertake, in addition to the common precepts, to observe the evangelical counsels by vows of obedience, chastity and poverty, is to be held in honour by all.[3]   76

Canon 488.—In the canons which follow, the meaning of terms is as follows: 77

1° By the name *Religion* is meant a society, approved by legitimate ecclesiastical authority, in which, in accordance with the particular laws of the society, the members take public vows, either perpetual vows, or temporary vows which have to be renewed at the expiration of the appointed time, and thus strive for evangelical perfection.

2° By *Order* is meant a religious society in which solemn vows are taken; by *Monastic Congregation* is meant the union

---

[1] Motu Proprio *Arduum sane*, 17 March 1904 (*ASS* XXXVI, p. 549).   76a
[2] See the Index of canons of the Code at the end of this volume.
[3] The three vows are, therefore, essential constituents of the religious state properly   76b
so called. The vows must be public in the canonical sense (can. 1308, § 1) that is, received by a competent superior (or superioress) in the name of the Church, for the Church must know who are the faithful who are religious.

of several autonomous monasteries under the same superior; by *Exempt Religion* is meant a religious society, with either solemn or simple vows, which is withdrawn from the jurisdiction of the local Ordinary; by *Religious Congregation* or by *Congregation*, without further qualification, is meant a society in which only simple vows, whether these be perpetual or temporary, are taken;

3° By *Religion of pontifical law* is meant a society which has received approbation or at least a decree of praise from the Apostolic See; by *Religion of diocesan law* is meant a society which has been established by Ordinaries, but has not yet received this decree of praise;

4° By *Clerical religion* is meant a society in which the majority of members receive the priesthood; otherwise it is a *Lay religion*;

5° By *Religious House* is meant a house of any kind of religious society; by *Regular House* is meant a house of an Order; by *Domus Formata* is meant a religious house in which at least six professed religious live, of whom at least four shall be priests if there is question of a clerical religious society;

6° By *Province* is meant the union of several religious houses under the same superior, forming part of one and the same religious society;

7° By *Religious* are meant those who have taken vows in some religious society; by *religious of simple vows*, those who have taken their vows in a religious Congregation; by *regulars*, those who have taken vows in an Order; by *sisters*, women religious who have simple vows; by *nuns*, women religious whose vows are solemn, or, unless the contrary be clear from the nature of the case or the context, women religious whose vows are solemn by the institute, but for some places are simple by reason of a prescription of the Apostolic See;

8° By *Major Superiors* are meant the Abbot Primate, the Abbot Superior of a Monastic Congregation, the Abbot of an autonomous monastery, though it belong to a monastic Congregation, the Supreme Moderator of a religious society, the Provincial Superior, their vicars and others who have power like provincials.

ERECTION AND SUPPRESSION OF RELIGIOUS SOCIETIES

Canon 492, § 1.—Bishops, not however the vicar capitular 78 or vicar general, have the power to found religious Congregations; but they shall not found them or permit them to be founded, without consulting the Apostolic See; if there is question of tertiaries living in common, it is further required that they be aggregated to his religious society by the supreme moderator of the first Order.

§ 2.—A Congregation of diocesan law, even though in the course of time it has extended into several dioceses, so long as it has not received the testimony of pontifical approval or praise, remains diocesan, being fully subject to the jurisdiction of the Ordinaries in accordance with the law.

§ 3.—Neither the name nor the habit of a religious society already established can be assumed by those who do not legitimately belong to that society; neither can they be assumed by a new religious society.

Canon 493.—No religious society, even though it be only of 79 diocesan law, once it has been legitimately established, and even though it consists of only a single house, can be suppressed except by the Holy See; it is also reserved to the Holy See to make decisions about the property in the particular case, always without prejudice to the wishes of the donors.

Canon 494, § 1.—It is for the Apostolic See alone to divide 80 a religious society of pontifical law into provinces, to unite provinces already established or otherwise modify their limits, to found new provinces or suppress existing ones, to separate autonomous monasteries from a monastic Congregation and unite them to another.

§ 2.—When a province has been extinguished, it is for the general chapter, or, outside the time of the chapter, for the general moderator with his council, unless the constitutions provide otherwise, to make decisions about the property of the province, without prejudice to the laws of justice and the will of the founders.

Canon 495, § 1—A religious Congregation of diocesan law 81 cannot establish houses in another diocese, except with the consent of both Ordinaries, namely the Ordinary of the place where the principal house is situated and the Ordinary of the place to which the Congregation wishes to transfer; the Ordinary of the place from which the Congregation is going shall not however refuse consent without a grave reason.

§ 2.—If a Congregation of diocesan law should expand into other dioceses, no change may be introduced into its rules, except with the consent of each of the Ordinaries in whose dioceses the Congregation has houses, without prejudice to matters which, in accordance with canon 492, § 1, had been subjected to the Apostolic See.

82   **Canon 496.**—No religious house shall be erected, unless it can be prudently judged that fitting provision for the residence and the support of the members will be available from its own resources, or from the customary alms or in some other way.

83   **Canon 497 § 1.**—To erect an exempt religious house, whether it be a *domus formata* or *domus non formata*, or a monastery of nuns, or any religious house whatsoever in places subject to the Sacred Congregation de Propaganda Fide, the *beneplacitum* of the Apostolic See is required and also the consent of the local Ordinary given in writing; in other circumstances the permission of the Ordinary is sufficient.

§ 2.—Permission to establish a new house implies the faculty, for clerical religious societies, of having a church or public oratory attached to the house, without prejudice to the prescription of canon 1162, § 4,[4] and authorisation to perform sacred services, in conformity with the requirements of law; for all religious societies, the permission implies the faculty of performing the pious works which are proper to the religious society, without prejudice to conditions attached in the permission itself.

§ 3.—For the building and opening of a school, hospice or other similar building that is separated from a religious house, even one that is exempt, the special written permission of the Ordinary is necessary and sufficient.

83a   [4] Even members of a religious society, though they have received consent from the local Ordinary for the erection of a new house in the diocese or city, must nevertheless obtain the permission of the local Ordinary before they build a church or public oratory in a certain and determinate place.

§ **4.**—For the conversion to other uses of an established house, the same formalities are required as are visualized in § 1, unless the conversion in question be of a kind which, without prejudice to the laws of the foundation, concerns merely the internal régime and religious discipline.

Canon 498.—A religious house, whether a *domus formata* or *non formata*, if it belongs to an exempt religious society, cannot be suppressed without the *beneplacitum* of the Apostolic See; if it belongs to a non-exempt Congregation of pontifical law, it can be suppressed by the supreme moderator, with the consent of the Ordinary of the place; if it belongs to a Congregation of diocesan law, it can be suppressed by the sole authority of the Ordinary of the place, after he has heard the moderator of the Congregation, without prejudice to the prescription of canon 493, if there is question of a single house, and without prejudice to the right of recourse to the Apostolic See, the recourse to have suspensive effect. 84

Canon 499, § 1.—All religious are subject to the Roman Pontiff, as their supreme superior, and they are bound to obey him also by reason of their vow of obedience. 85

§ **2.**—The Cardinal Protector of any religious society, unless the contrary be expressly provided for in special cases, does not possess jurisdiction over the society or the individual members; he cannot interfere in the internal discipline or in the administration of the society's property; his only function is to promote the good of the society by his counsel and patronage.

Canon 500, § 3.—No religious society of men can, without a special apostolic indult, have subject to it religious Congregations of women, or keep the care and direction of these women religious as specially entrusted to itself. 86

Canon 509, § 2.—1° Local superiors shall take care that at least once a year, on appointed days, the particular constitutions of the society are read publicly, and also decrees which the Holy See commands to be read publicly. 87

THE CONFESSIONS OF RELIGIOUS

Canon 518, § 2.—Religious superiors, who have the power of hearing confessions, can, with due observance of the require- 88 ments of law, hear the confessions of their own subjects, who spontaneously and of their own initiative request to be heard by them; but they shall not do this habitually without grave cause.

§ 3.—Superiors shall beware of inducing any of their subjects, either personally or through another, by force, fear, importunate persuasion or in any other way, to confess their sins to them.

89   **Canon 520, § 1.**—To each house of women religious there shall be appointed a single ordinary confessor, who shall hear the sacramental confessions of the entire community, unless there be need for a second or several confessors, because of the great number of religious or for other just cause.

§ 2.—If any woman religious, for the peace of her soul, and for greater progress in the way of God, asks for some special confessor or spiritual director, the Ordinary shall readily grant this request; he shall, however, be vigilant lest abuses creep in from this concession; if any abuses have arisen, he shall eliminate them with caution and prudence, without prejudice to liberty of conscience.

90   **Canon 521, § 1.**—For each community of women religious there shall be appointed an extraordinary confessor who is to come to the religious house at least four times a year, and to whom all the religious shall present themselves, at least to receive his blessing.

§ 2.—Local Ordinaries, in whose territories communities of women religious exist, shall designate for each house some priests, to whom these religious can easily have recourse for the sacrament of Penance in particular cases, without the necessity of approaching the Ordinary in every case.

§ 3.—If any woman religious asks for one of these confessors, no superioress is allowed, either personally or through others, directly or indirectly, to seek the reason for the petition, to oppose it either by words or acts, or to show in any way that she is annoyed by it.

91   **Canon 522.**—If, notwithstanding the provisions of canons 520 and 521, a woman religious, for the peace of her conscience, goes to a confessor who has been approved by the local Ordinary

for women, the confession, made in any church or oratory, even a semi-public oratory, is valid and lawful, every contrary privilege being revoked; nor can the superioress forbid it or make enquiries about it, even indirectly; and the religious are not obliged to make any report to the superioress.

Canon 523.—All women religious, when they are gravely ill, 92 even though not in danger of death, can send for any priest approved for the hearing of women's confessions, even though he is not appointed for religious, and make their confession to him as frequently as they wish, while the grave illness lasts; and the superioress cannot prohibit them from doing so, either directly or indirectly.

Canon 524, § 3.—The confessors of women religious, both 93 ordinary confessors and extraordinary, shall not in any way involve themselves in the internal or external régime of the community.

Canon 526.—The ordinary confessor of women religious shall 94 not perform his office for more than three years; the Ordinary however can confirm him for a second, or even a third period of three years, if he is unable to provide otherwise because of the shortage of priests suited for this office, or if the majority of the women religious, including those who have not the right of voting in other matters, have by a secret vote agreed upon the confirmation of the same confessor; alternative provision must be made for those who dissent, if they so desire.

Canon 530, §. 1—All religious superiors are strictly forbidden 95 to induce in any way the persons subject to them to make a manifestation of their conscience to them.

§ **2.**—Subjects, however, are not prohibited from opening their souls fully and spontaneously to their superiors; indeed it is to their advantage to approach their superiors with filial confidence, and to set out to them, if they are priests, their doubts also and the anxieties of their conscience.

ADMISSION INTO RELIGION

Canon 538.—Any catholic can be admitted into a religious 96 society, provided that he is not barred by an impediment recognised by law and is motivated by a right intention, and is fitted to carry out the obligations of the religious life. [5]

97   **Canon 539, § 1**—In religious societies of perpetual vows, all women and, if there be question of a religious society of men, lay brothers (*conversi*), before admission to the novitiate, shall perform postulancy for at least six complete months; but in religious societies of temporary vows, the necessity and length of postulancy are to be decided in accordance with the constitutions.

§ 2.—The major superior can prolong the prescribed time of the postulancy, but not beyond another period of six months.

98   **Canon 540, § 1.**—The postulancy shall be performed either in the novitiate house or in another house of the religious society in which discipline according to the constitutions is exactly observed under the special care of an approved religious.

§ 2.—Postulants shall wear a modest dress, one that is different from the dress of the novices.

§ 3.—In monasteries of nuns, aspirants are bound by the law of enclosure while they are performing their postulancy.

99   **Canon 541.**—Postulants, before they begin their novitiate, shall make a retreat for at least eight complete days; and in accordance with the prudent judgment of the confessor, they shall also make a general confession of their past life.

100   **Canon 542.**—Without prejudice to the prescriptions of canons 539-541, and also the other requirements of the constitutions of each religious society,

1° The admission of the following to the novitiate is invalid:

Those who have belonged to a non-Catholic sect;

Those who have not reached the age required for the novitiate; [6]

Those who have been induced by force, grave fear or fraud to enter religion, or whom a superior has been in the same way induced to receive;

A married person, so long as the marriage lasts;

96a   [5] By impediments we are to understand those which arise from the natural law, for example from an urgent obligation of justice, or those which arise from the general law. (Cf. can. 542).

100a   [6] According to canon 555, the required age is fifteen complete years.

Those who are or who have been bound by the ties of religious profession;

Those who are liable to a penalty because of a grave crime committed for which they have been or can be accused;

A bishop, either residential or titular, even though he has only been designated by the Roman Pontiff.

Clerics who by the institution of the Holy See are bound by oath to labour for the good of their diocese or of the missions, for the length of time that the obligation of the oath remains.

2° The admission of the following is valid, but unlawful:

Clerics in sacred Orders, if the local Ordinary has not been consulted, or if he is opposed because their departure would involve grave loss to souls, which cannot otherwise be avoided;

Those who are in debt and incapable of paying;

Those who are under an obligation to render accounts or who are involved in other secular business from which the religious society might fear litigation and difficulties;

Children who are bound to assist their parents, namely father or mother, grandfather or grandmother who are in grave need, and parents whose assistance is necessary to bring up or educate their children;

Those who are destined for the priesthood in the religious society, but who would be precluded from it by an irregularity or other canonical impediment;

Orientals into Latin religious societies, without the permission in writing of the Sacred Congregation for the Oriental Church.

Canon 543.—The right of admitting to the novitiate and to subsequent religious profession, whether temporary or perpetual, belongs to the major superiors with the vote of the council or chapter, according to the particular constitutions of each religious society. 101

Canon 544, § 1.—In every religious society, all aspirants, before admission, are bound to furnish testimony of the reception of Baptism and Confirmation. 102

§ **2.**—Men aspirants are bound also to furnish testimonial letters of the Ordinary of their place of birth and of every place in which, after the completion of their fourteenth year, they have spent more than a year, the period of a year being continuous morally: all contrary privileges are extinguished.

§ **3.**—If there is question of admitting those who were in a seminary, a college or in the postulancy or novitiate of another religious society, there are also required testimonial letters which, according to the different cases, are given by the rector of the seminary or college, after having heard the Ordinary of the place, or by the major superior of the religious society.

§ **4.**—For the admission of clerics, in addition to the testimony of ordination, it suffices to have the testimonial letters of the Ordinaries in whose dioceses they have resided after ordination for longer than a period of a year that was morally continuous, without prejudice to the prescription of § 3.

§ **5.**—For a professed religious, who by apostolic indult is transferring to another religious society, the testimony of the major superior of his former religious society suffices.

§ **6.**—In addition to these testimonies required by the law, superiors, who have the right of accepting aspirants into the religious society, can demand other testimonials which appear to them to be necessary or useful for this purpose.

§ **7.**—Finally, women shall not be received without previous careful investigations concerning their character and conduct, without prejudice to the prescription of § 3.

103   **Canon 545, § 1.**—Those who, by the prescription of law, are bound to give testimonial letters, shall give them, not to the aspirants themselves, but to the religious superiors, free of charge, within three months of the time they were requested, sealed and closed; and if they have to do with persons who were in a seminary, a college, or in the postulancy or novitiate of another religious society, they shall be signed by the superior under oath.

§ **2.**—If for grave reasons they reach the judgment that they cannot reply, they shall submit the reasons to the Apostolic See within the same period.

§ **3.**—If they reply that the aspirant is not sufficiently known to them, the religious superior shall supply this deficiency by means of another accurate investigation and trustworthy report; if they send no reply, the superior who seeks the testimonial shall inform the Holy See that no reply was received.

§ 4.—In their testimonial letters, after instituting a diligent investigation even by means of secret information, they are bound to make their report, under a grave obligation of conscience concerning the truth of what is reported, on the birth, conduct, character, life, reputation, condition and learning of the aspirant: stating whether he has been the subject of an inquiry, whether he is impeded by a censure or irregularity or other canonical impediment, whether his own family needs his assistance; and finally, if there is question of persons who were in a seminary or college, or in the postulancy or novitiate of another religious society, what was the reason for their dismissal or spontaneous departure.

Canon 546.—All who shall have received these informations are strictly obliged to observe secrecy concerning both the information received and the persons who gave it. 104

Canon 552, § 1.—The superioress, even of exempt women religious, is bound to inform the local Ordinary, at least two months beforehand, about the forthcoming admission to the novitiate and also about admission to profession, whether temporary or perpetual, solemn or simple. 105

§ 2.—The local Ordinary or, if he is absent or impeded, a priest deputed by him, at least thirty days before the novitiate or before the profession, as set out above, shall diligently and gratuitously, without however entering the enclosure, investigate the will of the aspirant, to see whether she has been subjected to force, or has been deceived, and whether she understands what she is doing; and if the pious purpose and freedom of the will of the aspirant is clearly established, then the aspirant can be admitted to the novitiate or the novice to profession.

THE NOVITIATE

Canon 553.—The novitiate begins with the reception of the habit, or in any other way prescribed in the constitutions. 106

107   **Canon 555, § 1.**—In addition to the other requirements for the validity of novitiate enumerated in canon 542, in order to be valid, the novitiate must be performed:

1° After the novice has completed at least fifteen years of age;

2° For a full and continuous year; [7]

3° In the house of the novitiate.

§ 2.—If a longer time is prescribed in the constitutions for the novitiate, this longer period is not required for the validity of profession, unless the contrary be expressly stated in the same constitutions.

108   **Canon 556, § 1.**—The novitiate is interrupted, so that it must be begun and completed anew, if the novice, having been dismissed by the superior, has left the house; or if the novice has, without permission of the superior, left the house with the intention of not returning; or if, even with the intention of returning, the novice has remained outside the house for more than thirty days, with or without a break, for any cause, even with the permission of superiors.

§ 2.—If the novice, with the permission of superiors or compelled by force, has remained outside the limits of the house, but under the obedience of the superior, for more than fifteen days, but not for more than thirty days, even when these are not continuous, it is required and is sufficient for the validity of the novitiate that the days thus passed be supplied; if the absence was not for more than fifteen days, superiors can prescribe that this period be supplied, but this is not necessary for validity.

§ 3.—Superiors shall not grant permission to remain outside the bounds of the novitiate, except for a just and grave cause.

§ 4.—If the novice is transferred by superiors to another novitiate house of the same religious society, the novitiate is not interrupted.

107a   [7] Cf. canon 34, § 3, 3°: A complete year of novitiate means a calendar year, not counting the first day, and the completion of the year coincides with the end of the last day of the same date.

Canon 558.—In religious societies which have two classes of members, the novitiate performed for one class is not valid for the other class. 109

Canon 559, § 1.—For the instruction of novices a master of novices is to be placed in charge, who shall be at least thirty-five years of age, professed for at least ten years since first profession, and distinguished for prudence, charity, piety and religious observance; and, if there is question of a clerical religious society, he shall be a priest. 110

§ **2.**—If the number of novices or other just cause makes it advisable, a *socius* to the master of novices shall be appointed, and he shall be immediately subject to him in all that concerns the régime of the novitiate; he shall be a man of at least thirty years of age, a professed religious for at least five years since first profession, and shall also possess the other qualities which are necessary and useful.

§ **3.**—Both the master of novices and the *socius* shall be free from all duties and burdens, which could hinder the care and direction of the novices.

Canon 561, § 1.—Only the master of novices has the right and duty of making provision for the instruction of the novices, and he alone is responsible for the régime of the novitiate; so that no one else is entitled to interfere in these matters, on any pretext, except the superiors to whom this is permitted by the constitutions and the visitors; in respect of the discipline of the whole house, the novice master, like the novices, is subject to the superior. 111

Canon 562.—The master of novices is bound by a grave obligation to apply all diligence to secure that his pupils are sedulously exercised, in conformity with the constitutions, in the discipline of religious life in accordance with canon 565.[8] 112

Canon 571, § 1.—A novice can freely leave the religious society; and a novice can be dismissed by the superiors or by 113

[8] Canon 565 specifies the means to be employed in this training: study of the Rule and Constitutions; assiduous meditation and prayer; learning of all that concerns the vows and the virtues; practical ascetic exercises. 112a

the chapter, in accordance with the constitutions, for any just cause, without any obligation on the superior or chapter to reveal the reason to the person dismissed.

§ 2.—After the completion of the novitiate, if he is judged to be suitable, the novice shall be admitted to profession, otherwise he shall be dismissed; if a doubt remains about his fitness, the probationary period can be prolonged by the superiors, but not beyond six months.

§ 3.—Before the taking of vows, the novice shall perform spiritual exercises for at least eight entire days.

RELIGIOUS PROFESSION

114   **Canon 572, § 1.**—For the validity of any religious profession, it is required:

1° That the person about to make religious profession shall have reached the prescribed age in accordance with canon 573; [9]

2° That the legitimate superior shall admit the person to profession in accordance with the constitutions;

3° That the profession shall have been preceded by a valid novitiate in accordance with canon 555;

4° That the profession shall be made without force, grave fear or fraud;

5° That the profession shall be express;

6° That the profession shall be received in accordance with the constitutions by the legitimate superior, acting personally or through another.

§ 2.—For the validity of perpetual profession, whether solemn or simple, it is further required that it shall have been preceded by temporary simple profession in accordance with canon 574.

115   **Canon 574, § 1.**—In every Order, whether of men or of women, and in every Congregation which has perpetual vows, the novice, after completion of the novitiate, shall, without

---

[9] Sixteen years complete for temporary profession; twenty-one years complete for perpetual profession.

prejudice to the prescription of canon 634,[10] before making perpetual vows, whether solemn or simple, make in the novitiate house itself a profession of simple vows to last for three years, or for a longer period, should more than three years be required to reach the age for perpetual profession, unless the constitutions demand yearly professions.

§ 2.—The legitimate superior can prolong this time, temporary profession having been made anew by the religious, but not beyond another period of three years.

Canon 575, § 1.—When the period of temporary profession has been completed, the religious, in accordance with canon 637, shall either make perpetual profession, solemn or simple according to the constitutions, or shall return to the world; but, even during the time of temporary profession, the religious, if considered unworthy of taking perpetual vows, can be dismissed by the lawful superior in accordance with canon 647. 116

Canon 576, § 2.—A written statement that religious profession has been made, signed by the professed religious and at least by that person also before whom the profession was made, shall be kept in the archives of the religious society; moreover, if the profession is solemn, the superior who receives the profession is bound to inform the parish priest of the place where the professed person was baptized, in accordance with canon 470, § 2. 117

THE OBLIGATIONS OF RELIGIOUS

Canon 593.—Each and every religious, superiors as well as subjects, has the duty, not only to observe faithfully and completely the vows which they have undertaken, but also to conform their lives to the rules and constitutions of their own religious society and thus to strive for the perfection of their state. 118

[10] Canon 634: If a solemnly professed religious or one who has made profession of perpetual simple vows, should have transferred to another religious society with solemn or simple perpetual vows, after the novitiate, and having omitted the temporary profession mentioned in canon 574, the religious shall be admitted either to solemn or simple perpetual profession, or return to the original religious society; the superior has however the right to submit the religious to a longer probation, but not for more than a year from the completion of the novitiate. 115a

119   **Canon 594, § 1.**—In every religious society the common life shall be observed exactly by all, even in matters of food, dress and furniture.

§ **2.**—Everything acquired by religious, even by superiors, in accordance with canons 580, § 2 and 582, 1°, shall be entered into the goods of the house, province or religious society, and any money and all securities shall be deposited in the common funds.

§ **3.**—The furniture of religious shall be in conformity with the poverty which they profess.

120   **Canon 595, § 1.**—Superiors shall take care that all religious:

1° Make a retreat each year.[11]

2° Assist at Mass daily, if they are not legitimately impeded, give time to mental prayer, and devote themselves sedulously to the other duties of piety which are prescribed by the rules and constitutions.

3° Have recourse to the sacrament of Penance at least once a week.

121   **Canon 608, § 1.**—Superiors shall take care that religious subject to them, and who have been designated by them, especially in the diocese in which they live, shall gladly give their services, when requested by the local Ordinaries or parish priests in order to provide for the needs of the people, both within and without their own churches or public oratories, without prejudice to religious discipline.

§ **2.**—On the other hand, local Ordinaries and parish priests shall gladly avail themselves of the assistance of religious, especially those who reside in the diocese, in the sacred ministry and above all in the administration of the sacrament of Penance.

122   **Canon 611.**—All religious, whether men or women, can freely send letters, which are not liable to any inspection, to the Holy See and to the legate of the Holy See in the country, to the Cardinal Protector, to their own major superiors, to the superior of the house if he should be absent, to the local Ordinary

120a   [11] In his Encyclical *Mens nostra* on spiritual exercises, 20 December 1929, Pope Pius XI commented on this article of the Code: "The annual retreat is, in fact, the mystic *tree of life* (Gen. 2: 9), whose fruit, for individuals and communities, will be that renown for sanctity which should be enjoyed by every religious family . . . (*AAS* XXI (1929), p. 700).

to whom they are subject, and if there be question of nuns who are subject to the jurisdiction of regulars, even to the major superiors of the Order; and from all of these, the same religious, both men and women, can receive letters which are exempt from inspection by anyone.

QUESTING FOR ALMS

Canon 621, § 1.—Regulars, who by their institute are given 123 the name of mendicants and are such, can seek alms in the diocese in which their religious house is situated, with the sole permission of their superiors; but outside the diocese they need also the permission in writing of the Ordinary of the place in which they wish to collect alms.

§ 2.—Local Ordinaries, especially of the neighbouring dioceses, shall not refuse or revoke this permission, except for grave and urgent causes, if the religious house cannot possibly live by questing for alms solely in the diocese in which it is constituted.

Canon 622, § 1.—All other religious belonging to Congrega- 124 tions of pontifical law, without the special privilege of the Holy See, are forbidden to quest for alms; if this privilege shall have been secured by them, they shall also require the permission of the local Ordinary given in writing, unless a contrary provision be made in the privilege itself.

§ 2.—Religious belonging to Congregations of diocesan law cannot engage in questing for alms without the permission given in writing both of the Ordinary of the place in which their house is situated, and also of the Ordinary of the place in which they desire to seek alms.

§ 3.—Local Ordinaries shall not give permission to quest to the religious mentioned in §§ 1-2 of this canon, especially where there are convents of regulars who are mendicants in name and in fact, except where it is clear to them that there is a real need of the house or pious work, which cannot otherwise be met; if the need can be provided for by questing within the place or district or diocese in which they are resident, the Ordinaries shall not give wider permission.

§ **4.**—Without an authentic and recent rescript of the Sacred Congregation for the Oriental Church, Ordinaries of the Latin Church shall not permit any oriental of whatsoever order or dignity to collect money within their territory, and neither shall they send a subject of their own into dioceses of the Oriental Church for the same purpose.

125   **Canon 623.**—It is not permitted to superiors to entrust the task of collecting alms save only to professed religious of mature age and outlook, especially when women religious are in question; the task shall never be entrusted to those who are still engaged in their studies.

INSTRUCTION OF THE SACRED CONGREGATION OF RELIGIOUS ON THE SECOND YEAR OF THE NOVITIATE

3 November 1921

EXTRACTS

Canon 565, § 3 insists on the spiritual formation of novices, to the exclusion of other matters, during the year of novitiate. The present Instruction, coming some years after the Code, gives details as to the extent to which institutes that have a second year of noviceship may employ novices of the second year.[1]

There are several religious societies whose constitutions 126 prescribe a second year of noviceship and the power is given to the superiors to employ the novices, during that year, in performing the works of the institute . . .

I. This shall be permitted, provided the fundamental laws of noviceship are respected. Consequently it is to be borne in mind that the purpose of the novitiate is the formation of the souls of the novices in everything that concerns the extirpation of evil ways, the control of the movements of the mind, the acquisition of virtues and also the knowledge of the regular life by study of the constitutions; it is thus the novices will learn how to strive for Christian perfection by the profession of the evangelical counsels and of vows, which is precisely the aim of every religious. And it is with good reason that a novitiate of more than a year is prescribed in some institutes, in those especially whose religious are employed on exterior works, inasmuch as being distracted by many cares, and more exposed to the dangers of the world, these require a more solid and stable spiritual foundation. Therefore this Sacred Congregation lays down that, even during the second year of the novitiate, the discipline of the spiritual life shall be tended to before any other functions.

[1] Instruction *Plures exstant*, *AAS* XIII (1921), pp. 539-540.

127   II. It shall be lawful, however, in the second year of the novitiate, for male or female novices to engage in the works of the Institute, provided the constitutions allow it; this however shall be done with prudence and moderation, and only for the instruction of the novices; the novices shall never be engaged in these works to such an extent that they perform duties by themselves alone (e.g., by taking the place in schools of absent teachers or their assistants, or by ministering to the sick in hospitals); they shall rather perform these works under the direction and vigilance of a responsible religious, man or woman, who will instruct them by word and guide them by example.

128   III. If it is ever permitted by the constitutions that a novice, whether male or female, in the second year of the novitiate, be sent outside the house of the novitiate to perform the works of the institute, this shall be only as an exception, and provided there is a grave cause which makes it advisable; this grave cause must be envisaged from the standpoint of the novice, male or female; as, for example, that they cannot be sufficiently instructed in the novitiate house, or would not otherwise be able to remain there. But never, under any pretext, can the need or utility of the religious society be considered a sufficient cause, as for example if, because of the shortage of religious, novices were to be substituted for them in the works of the Institute.

129   IV. Whether the novices have been in the novitiate house, or outside it, they shall abstain from all exterior works for two months before profession; if they have been outside the novitiate, they shall be recalled to it, so that for an entire period of two months they shall prepare themselves for making their profession, strengthening themselves in the spirit of their vocation.

PIUS XI

1922—1939

APOSTOLIC LETTER "UNIGENITUS DEI FILIUS" ON THE STUDIES OF RELIGIOUS

19 March 1924

This Apostolic Letter, sent to the superiors general of Orders and religious Congregations, treats in some detail of the responsibilities of superiors in relation not merely to the spiritual formation, but also the intellectual training of their subjects.[1]

Origin of the religious life.

When the only-begotten Son of God came   130
into the world to redeem the human race,
he gave the precepts of spiritual life by which
all men were to be directed to their appointed end; in addition,
he taught that all those who wished to follow more closely in
his footsteps should embrace and follow the evangelical counsels.

Everyone who commits himself, by a solemn undertaking
made to God, to observe these counsels, is freed from the
hindrances which impede mortal men on the way to sanctity,
for instance the possession of wealth, the cares and anxieties
of marriage, the excessive enjoyment of all things; besides, he
progresses towards perfection of life on a way that is so straight
and free from obstacles, that he might be said to have already
cast anchor in the haven of salvation.

The constant concern of the Church for religious.

Thus it is that, from the earliest   131
centuries of the Christian religion,
souls have never been wanting who,
at the call of God, have nobly and
generously denied themselves everything, and set out on that
way of perfection and followed it to the end; history shows
clearly that men and women, in an unbroken line, have con-

[1] *AAS* XVI (1924), p. 133-148.

secrated and dedicated themselves to God in the various Orders
which the Church has approved and confirmed in the course of
centuries. And indeed, though the religious life by its nature
is one and indivisible, it takes many different forms; for each
in accordance with its own distinctive institute, and for the
glory of God and the benefit of their neighbour, religious
societies give themselves to serve God in different ways and
undertake different works of charity and beneficence. And thus
from this great variety of religious Orders, like to so many
different fruit-bearing trees sown in the field of the Lord, there
comes a great and varied harvest of fruits for the salvation of
mankind. Surely there is nothing more beautiful to behold than
the homogeneity and universality of these societies; though all
have one and the same aim, each has its own field of activity
and toil, which is in some degree distinct from the others.
This is indeed the usual way of divine providence, that whenever
new needs are to be met, new religious institutes arise and
flourish.

132   Consequently, the Apostolic See, under whose banner and
immediate command the religious Orders take their place in
the army of the Church, mindful of the benefits which in the
course of time they have conferred upon the Church and the
State, has always made them the object of its special care and
goodwill: for not only has the Apostolic See reserved it to itself
to revise and approve their rules and statutes, and defended
them most earnestly in difficult times and circumstances, but it
has also never failed to recall them to the original high dignity
and sanctity of their institute, whenever that was necessary.[2]

133   That care and concern of the Church for observance of the
rules and promotion of holiness of conduct among religious, is
shown in the very commands and exhortations of the Council
of Trent: " All regulars, both men and women, shall regulate
and order their lives in accordance with the prescription of the
rule of which they have made profession; and above all, they

132a   [2] Cf. especially: Leo XIII, Letter to Cardinal Richard, 23 December 1900, supra,
nn. 33-38; Letter to Superiors General, 29 June 1901, supra, nn. 39-53; Pius X, Letter
to Superior General of the Brothers of the Christian Schools, 22 April 1905, supra,
nn. 54-56.

shall observe faithfully what pertains to the perfection of what they profess: the vows of obedience, poverty and chastity, and any other special vows or precepts which are characteristic of any rule and Order, as part of their essential structure, and as a means of preserving common life, food and dress." [3]

And in the Code of Canon Law, before coming to the legis- 134 lation in this field, the religious state is defined and briefly described as a " stable common life by which the faithful undertake, in addition to the common precepts, to observe the evangelical counsels by vows of obedience, chastity and poverty " . . . and strive for evangelical perfection; this statement is followed by the splendid declaration that the religious state " is to be held in honour by all." [4]

We ourselves clearly showed our reliance on the virtue and 135 active assistance of religious, when for the first time we lovingly addressed all the bishops of the Catholic world in our Encyclical Letter *Ubi Arcano*; in putting forward remedies for the countless evils which afflict human society, we had more than one reason for saying that we placed solid hope in the regular clergy for the effective application of these remedies. [5]

Before that, when we sent to the Cardinal Prefect of the 136 Congregation of Studies the Apostolic Letter *Officiorum Omnium*, we of course included, in the care and consideration for the proper training of clerics destined for the sacred ministry which filled our mind, the pupils of religious Orders; because our comments and decisions on this matter are in great part relevant also to those religious who are destined for the priesthood. [6]

However, that ardent charity and vigilant concern for your interests which occupies our mind, beloved sons, strongly urges us to address you in a special Letter, in order to admonish you on certain matters; if your pupils reproduce these admoni-

[3] Council of Trent, *Sess.* XXV, chapter 1, *de Regul.*
[4] *CIC*, canons 487-8. Cf. *supra*, nn. 76, 77.
[5] Cf. Pius X, Encyclical Letter *Ubi arcano*, 23 December 1922, *AAS* XIV (1922), p. 673-700. Speaking of " the importance of the rôle " of religious, the Pope said in particular: " They rouse the faithful, who constantly see such examples, to raise their aspirations to higher things, and they obtain this result by devoting themselves to the good works by which Christian benevolence relieves all sufferings of body and soul." 135a
[6] Cf. Pius XI, Apostolic Letter *Officiorum Omnium*, 1 August 1922, *AAS* XIV (1922), pp. 449-58.

tions in their conduct and daily practice, then their life and activity will be everything that their unique and exalted vocation demands of them.

137   **Fidelity to the spirit of their Founders.**   Our first word is one of exhortation to all religious to look to their founder and the author of their rule as a model, if they want to share abundantly and with certainty in the graces which flow from their vocation. For when these noble figures established their institutes, can it be said that they did anything other than obey the inspiration of God? All of their followers, who manifest in themselves the characteristic quality which the founders wished to be the stamp of their own society, are certainly not untrue to their origins. Therefore their disciples, like good children, shall give their hearts and minds to defending the glory of their founding father and legislator, by obedience to his prescriptions and counsels, and by drinking deeply of his spirit; for never will they fall short of the duties of their state, so long as they travel in the footsteps of their founder: *And their children for their sakes remain forever.* [7]

God grant that they will obey the rules of their institute with such unassuming demeanour, and hold fast to the way of life which they have fashioned since entry into it, that they will daily show themselves more worthy of their religious state: for by their fidelity, they cannot fail to obtain the aid of heavenly grace in the sacred ministry which it falls to them to perform throughout their lives.

In all their activity, however, they shall have only one object: *The kingdom of God and his justice.* [8] Now this is a matter which we wish to be kept in mind, beloved sons, particularly in sacred missions and in the instruction of youth, to which your activity is mainly directed.

[7] Ecclesiasticus 44: 13.
[8] Matthew 6: 33.

The advice of Benedict XV to missionaries. Therefore care shall be taken in regard 138 to the apostolate, as our immediate predecessor so wisely admonished,[9] lest the propagation of the Gospel among foreign nations be turned by them into propaganda for their own land or nation or be made an instrument for aggrandizement; their only aim shall be the salvation of unbelievers, and missionaries shall occupy themselves with the promotion of earthly advantages and benefits only in so far as they are seen to conduce to eternal life.

The religious training of pupils: grave duty of teachers. As for religious whose function it is 139 to teach and educate the young, they shall studiously avoid the danger of being so carried away by an excessive desire to impart to their pupils the knowledge of subjects, excellent in themselves, that they neglect to give their minds and hearts a thorough religious training; the outcome of such neglect would be that the pupils would leave school with a vast knowledge of literary subjects, but quite devoid of that sacred learning whose absence deprives men of the most beautiful and precious adornment and leaves them in the direst need: *Vain are all men, in whom there is not the knowledge of God.*[10] The seraphic Doctor aptly comments: " This is the final fruit of all forms of knowledge: that in everything faith be built up, that God be honoured, that conduct be duly ordered; that the consolations be drawn, which come from the union of bridegroom and bride, which is itself the outcome of charity." [11]

CHIEF PURPOSE OF THIS LETTER: EXHORTATION TO EARNEST STUDY

Now since it is essential that the ministers of the Church 140 should highly esteem and thoroughly master this knowledge of sacred things, the principal object of this Letter is to exhort religious, whether they are already ordained or preparing for

---

[9] Cf. Benedict XV, Apostolic Letter *Maximum Illud*, 30 November 1919, *AAS* XI 138a (1919), pp. 440-5.
[10] Wisdom 13: 1.
[11] St. Bonaventure, *De reductione artium ad Theol.*, n. 26.

admission to the priesthood, to assiduous study of the sacred sciences; unless they are thoroughly acquainted with these subjects, they will not be capable of fulfilling properly the duties of their vocation.

The primary, if not the sole purpose of those who have consecrated themselves to God, is to pray to him and to contemplate or meditate upon divine things; now how can they discharge that important duty unless they have a profound and thorough knowledge of the teachings of our faith?

141 **Sound theological training required for contemplatives . . .** We would wish to bring this matter particularly to the attention of those who lead the contemplative life of the cloister. It is a mistake for them to think that, if theological studies were neglected before ordination or subsequently abandoned, they can easily dwell in the heights and be raised up to interior union with God, even though they lack that abundant knowledge of God and of the mysteries of the faith which is derived from the sacred sciences.

142 **. . . and even more necessary for active religious.** As for other religious, who may be engaged in teaching, in preaching, in cleansing souls from sin in the sacrament of Penance, or attached to the missions or in daily contact with the people, will not the performance of these various functions of the sacred ministry gain in power and efficacy in proportion to the brilliance and extent of their erudition? The Holy Spirit has declared through the prophet that knowledge of divine things, knowledge that is both profound and abundant, is of obligation for a priest: *The lips of the priest shall keep knowledge.*[12] How should the priest, the representative of the *God of knowledge*,[13] the minister and teacher of the *New Covenant, the salt of the earth* and *the light of the world*,[14] from whose lips the Christian people expect words of salvation, how should he be devoid of solid learning?

[12] Malachy 2: 7.
[13] I Samuel 2: 3.
[14] Matthew 5: 13, 14.

Anyone who undertakes the sacred ministry without training or competence should tremble for his own fate, for the Lord will not suffer his ignorance to go unpunished; it is the Lord who has issued the dire warning: *Because thou hast rejected knowledge, I will reject thee, that thou shalt not do the office of priesthood to me.*[15]

If ever there was an obligation on priests to be men of learning, it is even more pressing at the present time; indeed scientific knowledge is nowadays of such importance and so closely linked with everyday affairs that everyone professes to act in the name of science—as generally happens, those who do not understand what scientific knowledge is are most emphatic in this declaration. We should spare no effort, therefore, to secure the support of every branch of human learning which can be of assistance to the Catholic faith; in the light of these sciences the beauty of revealed truth will shine out before the eyes of all, and the specious and fanciful objections and theories, which a science falsely so-called is wont to urge against the dogmas of the faith, will receive timely refutation. 143

Our faith, as Tertullian so splendidly expressed it, " sometimes desires only one thing, that it be not condemned unheard."[16] Nor should we forget the words of St. Jerome: " The holiness of the unlearned is of no benefit to anyone else; while it builds up the Church of Christ by a meritorious life, it does equal damage if it fails to refute opponents . . . It is the duty of the priest, therefore, to give information when he is asked about the law."[17] The priest, therefore, whether secular or regular, has the duty to diffuse Catholic teaching ever more widely, and also to show clearly the meaning of that doctrine and to undertake its defence; Catholic doctrine not only contains the answer to whatever objections adversaries may bring forward, but also the power to attract minds that are free from prejudice, if only it is set out clearly. The teachers of the Middle Ages were well aware of this, and following the lead of Thomas Aquinas and Bonaventure, they strove with all their powers to acquire the 144

---

[15] Osee 4: 6.
[16] Tertullian, *Apol.*, I (PL I, 260).
[17] St. Jerome, *Epistola 53 ad Paulinum*, CV 54, 557 (PL, XXII).

widest measure of theological learning and then to impart it
to others.

145   There is the further consideration, beloved sons, that by the
earnest application of their intellectual and physical resources
to their studies, the members of your institutes cannot fail to
draw more copiously upon the sources of the spiritual life, and
thus carry with distinction the dignity of the vocation which
they have accepted. Anyone who makes the sacred sciences the
subject of his studies is undertaking a task which involves toil,
effort and sacrifice; there is no room here for slackness or that
laziness which is the *mother and teacher of a multitude of evils*.[18]
The intellectual concentration which is required in study
accustoms us to avoid hasty decisions and rash actions; it makes
it easier to control passions which, if they are not held in check,
quickly lead to deterioration and to the abyss of vice. In this
connection St. Jerome said: " Love the study of the Scripture and
you will not be attracted by the vices of the flesh "; [19] " knowledge of the Scriptures brings forth virgins." [20]

146   **Interior life of**   There is another reason why a religious
        religious to be   should pursue these studies, namely that
        nourished by study.   in virtue of his vocation he is obliged
in conscience to seek after perfection.

No one can efficaciously strive for that perfection or attain
it with certainty except through the practice of the interior life;
now where can one find more abundant means for the development and nourishment of this interior life than in the sacred
sciences? Constant daily meditation upon the wonderful gifts of
nature and grace, which almighty God has bestowed so abundantly upon the world and upon individuals, consecrates the
thoughts and the affections and raises them to heavenly things;
it fills men's minds with the spirit of faith and brings them into
the closest union with God. There is no one who more closely
resembles Jesus Christ than the man who has so assimilated the

[18] Ecclesiasticus 33: 29.
[19] St. Jerome, *Epistola 125 (al. IV) ad Rusticum (PL XXII, 1078).*
[20] St. Jerome, *Comment. in Zach.,* l. II, c. X (*PL XXV, 1409*).

divinely revealed doctrine on faith and morals, that it is, as it were, the sap and life-blood of his existence.

It was supreme wisdom therefore on the part of the founders 147 of religious Orders when, following in the footsteps of the Fathers and Doctors of the Church, they emphatically recommended the study of the sacred sciences to their disciples. Indeed it is a fact established by experience, beloved sons, that those religious who have most given their heart to the study of theology, have also generally attained to a high level of sanctity. On the other hand, those who abandoned this sacred duty have often begun by losing their fervour and, not infrequently, have fallen so low as even to violate their vows. Hence all religious shall bear in mind the words of Richard of St. Victor: " Would that everyone of us would persevere in these studies until the sun goes down, and gradually the love of vanity would lose its ardour, and the flame of concupiscence having been withdrawn, the fires of carnal thoughts would die down." [21] We also exhort religious to take to themselves the prayer of St. Augustine: " May your Scriptures be my chaste delight: in them I shall not be led astray, nor from them shall I lead others astray." [22]

Since such outstanding advantages accrue to religious from 148 constant and devoted study of sacred doctrine, it is manifest, beloved sons, that you must exercise the greatest vigilance, lest your subjects should lack the means of deepening their knowledge of theology and of pursuing theological study at every stage of their lives.

Advice for recruiting and formation of aspirants. In this connection, it will be of 149 immense benefit to the young aspirants to the life of the cloister, to have correct instruction and training for their minds and souls imparted from the very outset. A first point is this: in family life, because of the misfortunes of the times, the provision made for the Christian education of the children is inadequate; adolescents, though exposed to widespread cor-

[21] Richard of Saint Victor, *De diff. sacrif. Abr. et Mariae*, 1 (*PL* CXCVI, 1049).
[22] Saint Augustine, *Confessions*, l. XI, c. II, n. 3 (*PL* XXXII, 810).

rupting influences, are lacking in the solid religious instruction which alone can bring man's mind into conformity with the commands of God and even with the standard of what is good and right; it follows from this that there is no more useful undertaking possible for you in this department than the founding of minor seminaries or colleges for the reception of adolescents in whom some signs of vocation are discernible; we are glad to see that this is being done in some places.

150   However, in this matter you must avoid the danger against which our predecessor of holy memory, Pius X, warned the superiors of the Order of St. Dominic; [23] that is, you shall avoid the hasty admission, or acceptance in groups, of young people, when it is uncertain whether their choice of this saintly way of life is of God's inspiration. The choice of young candidates for the religious life shall be made with mature consideration and with prudence; and you shall earnestly see to it that, in addition to formation in piety suited to their age, they also receive instruction in the subjects which are usually taught in secondary schools; in this way, they are not to come to their novitiate before the completion of the course of humanities, unless a serious cause makes it advisable to decide otherwise. [24]

151   It is a duty of justice, as well as of charity, that you should apply all the resources of your industry and diligence in this instruction of the young. If, because of the smallness of the institute, or for other reasons, a province has not the means of making provision properly for this instruction, in accordance with the prescriptions of canon law, these young people are to be sent to another province or study centre, where they can be properly taught, in accordance with the prescription of canon 587.

152   In the lower schools the prescription of canon 1364, 1° shall be strictly observed: " Religious instruction shall hold the first place, and it shall be taught with the greatest diligence and in a manner suited to the capacity and age of each one." Only books which Ordinaries shall have approved, are to be used

150a   [23] Cf. Pius X, Letter *Cum Primum* to the Master General of the Dominicans, 4 August 1913, *AAS* V (1913), p. 387.
    [24] Cf. *CIC*, canon 589.

in this subject. Moreover, to mention the matter in passing, even the students of scholastic philosophy shall not cease from the study of religion; they will find it very advantageous to make use of that golden book, the *Roman Catechism*, in which one finds it difficult to say whether the richness of sound doctrine or the elegance of the Latin tongue is the more to be admired. If your clerics become accustomed, from the prime of life, to draw upon that source of sacred doctrine, then in addition to being better prepared for the study of theology, they will gain from the use of this splendid work the competence to give wise instruction to the people and to refute the usual false views brought against revealed doctrine.

The study of Latin. The directives on the study of Latin, to which, in the Apostolic Letter *Officiorum Omnium*,[25] we admonished the Catholic bishops to give their diligent attention, we now advise and command you, beloved sons, to observe in the classes for languages: for your pupils too are subject to the law of the Code, which prescribes for students of the sanctuary: " In regard to languages, they shall learn accurately Latin and their native tongue especially." [26] The importance for young religious of a good grasp of Latin is evident, not only from the fact that the Church employs Latin as an instrument and bond of unity, but also from the fact that it is in Latin that we read the Bible, in Latin we sing the Psalms, in Latin we celebrate Mass and in Latin we perform nearly all the sacred rites. There is the further fact that the Roman Pontiff addresses and teaches the whole world in Latin, and the Roman Curia makes use of this language alone when expediting business and making decrees which affect the whole community of the faithful. For those who are not at home with Latin, access is more difficult to the many great volumes of the Fathers and Doctors of the Church, very many of whom made use only of Latin in the exposition and defence of Christian wisdom. Take a deep interest, therefore, in the acquisition of

153

[25] Pius XI, Apostolic Letter *Officiorum omnium*, 1 August 1922, *AAS* XIV (1912), pp. 452-4.
[26] *CIC*, canon 1364, 2°.

an accurate and practical use of Latin by your clerics, who will one day be in the service of the Church.

154   **Advice for noviceship.** At the end of the secondary course all the pupils and candidates, whose clear intention it is to consecrate themselves to God, and who have won the approval of their superiors by their good character, intelligence, spirit of piety and integrity of conduct, shall be admitted to the novitiate; there, as in a training ground, they shall devote themselves specially to learning the principles of the religious life and its virtues.

155   The great importance of diligent training of the minds of novices at this time is clear not only from the testimony of masters of the spiritual life, but even more from experience; no one achieves and retains the perfection of the religious state, unless the foundations of all the virtues are already laid down at this time. Hence, putting aside all other studies and their attractions, the novices shall set their minds on this alone: under the wise guidance of their master, to devote themselves to the practices of the interior life and to the acquisition of the virtues, especially those virtues which are closely linked with the vows of religious life, namely poverty, obedience and chastity.[27]

At this time the writings of Saint Bernard, of the seraphic Doctor Bonaventure, of Alphonsus Rodriguez, and of those authors who, in each Order, flourished as masters of spirituality, will be most useful for reading and meditation; the worth and efficacy of these works, far from diminishing with age and the passage of time, seems rather at the present day to be augmented. The novices shall never forget this truth: as they are in the novitiate, so will they be for the remainder of their lives, and generally it is but a vain hope that they will make up later on, by renewal of the spirit of noviceship, for a novitiate which has been performed with little or no fruit.

---

[27] Cf. *CIC*, canons 553 to 571, some of which are given above, nn. 107-113.

ADVICE FOR TIME OF SCHOLASTICATE

—Studies should be complete.

Your next concern, beloved sons, shall be that the pupils, 156
who have completed their novitiate, are assigned to houses where
the observance of the holy rule flourishes and other things are
so arranged that they can most exactly and with the greatest
benefit complete the prescribed and regular courses of philosophy
and theology. We say the *prescribed* and *regular* courses: that is,
no one shall be advanced to a higher grade without having made
sufficient progress in a lower grade; and moreover, no part of
the course of studies shall be passed over, nor shall there be
any shortening of the time which is to be devoted to these subjects in accordance with the prescription of the Code. It would,
therefore, be imprudent—to say the least—for superiors who,
perhaps in order to meet the needs of a brief space of time,
want their subjects to reach sacred Orders by a short cut, in
order to be able to make use of their services sooner.

Is it not well established by experience that those whose
studies have been rushed and disordered, can scarcely ever
repair this defect in their training; and that whatever advantage
may sometimes have been gained by this premature reception
of Orders, it vanishes in the long run and comes to nothing,
because these religious are necessarily less well fitted for the
sacred ministry?

—Spiritual formation to be continued in the scholasticate.

See to it also that the young religious, who are engaged in 157
the study of philosophy and theology, do not relax in their
striving for virtue; indeed they should continue to avail themselves of outstanding masters of spirituality, so that one day,
as befits religious, they may be examples of solid doctrine
combined with holiness of life.

Strictness in choice of professors.

There is a point to which we direct your attention in a 158
particular way, namely the choice of thoroughly suitable teachers
of the higher disciplines; they should be men whose own way

of life is a model, and also be of the highest scholarly competence in the subjects in which they are obliged to instruct their students. No one, therefore, shall be appointed as professor, or lecturer, unless he has praiseworthily completed the courses of philosophy, theology and the allied subjects, and has sufficient skill and capacity to teach. Besides, you shall not overlook the directive of the Code of Canon Law: " It shall be seen to that there are separate professors for each subject, at least for sacred Scripture, dogmatic theology, moral theology and ecclesiastical history." [28] These shall not spare any pains in striving to turn their pupils into saintly and hardworking apostles of Christ, men well equipped with all the adornments of learning and prudence, which will give them the capacity to instruct the simple and unlearned, to confute those puffed up by a science falsely so-called, and to protect all against the contagion of errors; these errors commonly creep in almost unnoticed, and for that reason represent all the greater danger to the welfare of souls. If happily your pupils prove eager to make progress in the broad expanses and along the roads of Christian wisdom, and indeed are found to excel, then the joy of this abundant harvest will compensate, in a measure beyond belief, for the toil which you have devoted to so salutary an occupation.

—*Fidelity to Saint Thomas.*

159   You shall, however, regard as sacred and inviolable the regulation which, in conformity with canon law, we formulated in the Apostolic Letter about seminaries and clerical studies: [29] namely that in teaching philosophy and theology professors shall follow faithfully the scholastic method, according to the principles and teaching of Aquinas.

For the scholastic method and the angelic doctrine of Thomas, which our predecessors have at all times praised in the highest terms, are particularly suitable, as is known to all, for the clarification of revealed truths and for the brilliant refutation of the errors of every age. The angelic Doctor, in the words of our

[28] *CIC*, canon 1366, 3°.
[29] Cf. Pius XI, *Officiorum omnium*, 1 August 1922, *AAS* XIV (1922), p. 454-55.

predecessor of immortal memory, Leo XIII, " with his overflowing endowment of divine and human knowledge, appropriately
compared to the sun . . . secured for himself this triumph, that
alone he overcame all the errors of former generations, and
supplied the weapons to ensure victory over the constant
succession of errors which future ages would bring." [30] The same
pontiff rightly said: " Those who wish to be true philosophers,
and religious above all should wish it, shall place the principles
and foundations of doctrine on Saint Thomas." [31]

The importance for your pupils of not departing in any way 160
from the scholastic method, is clear too from this further
consideration: an intimate relationship exists between philosophy
and revelation, and the scholastics so combined and brought
them together in a wondrous harmony that they shed light one
on the other, and are a most valuable mutual aid. It is impossible
that they should be in conflict, as some foolishly contend, for
both come from God, the supreme and eternal truth, and while
philosophy sets down and expounds the claims of reason,
revelation presents the proofs of faith; in fact they so harmoniously agree, that one complements the other.

From this it follows that an ignorant and incompetent
philosopher can never become a learned theologian, and anyone
who is completely devoid of theological learning cannot be an
outstanding philosopher.

On this point Saint Thomas rightly observed: " From the 161
principles of faith a conclusion is proved for believers, in the
same way as from the natural first principles a conclusion is
proved for all; and so theology also is a science." [32]

To put the matter in another way: from reason, which is a
participation of the divine light, philosophy deduces the first
principles of natural knowledge, enunciates these principles and
explains them; in the same way, from the light of supernatural
revelation, which enlightens and strengthens the intellect by
its shining light, theology derives the truths of faith, develops
and explains them; so that philosophy and theology are two

[30] Leo XIII, Encyclical Letter *Aeterni Patris*, 4 August 1879, *ASS* XII (1879-80), p. 108.
[31] Leo XIII, Letter *Nostra erga*, 25 November 1898, *ASS* XXXI (1898-9), p. 264.
[32] Saint Thomas, *Summa Theologica*, II-II, q. 1, art. 5, ad 2.

rays from the same sun, two streams from the one source, two buildings raised on one foundation. Human learning is indeed a marvellous thing, provided it holds fast in docility to the doctrines of faith; but if it disregards them, it is inevitable that the same learning will fall away into many errors and foolishness of different kinds.

162   But if, beloved sons, your pupils put into the service of sacred learning the sum of human learning which they shall have acquired; if, in addition, they are on fire with eager love for the revealed truth, they will be, and will be recognized as men of God, and both by word and example they will bring immense blessings to the Christian people. For indeed, *All Scripture inspired by God*—or to take the interpretation of Saint Thomas —the sacred doctrine which has been received with the added light of divine revelation, *is useful for teaching, for reproving, for correcting, for instructing in justice, that the man of God may be perfect, equipped for every good work.*[33]

—Development of the spirit of faith.

163   But lest young religious should labour in vain in the vast fields of sacred and profane learning, the spirit of faith above all must be nourished in them; if that spirit grows weak, they will become like men whose vision is dimmed, and will be incapable of penetrating supernatural truths. It is no less important that they should pursue their studies with a right intention. Saint Bernard said: " There are some who seek to learn merely for the sake of knowing, and that is shameful curiosity . . . and there are some who seek to learn in order to sell their knowledge for money or for honours, and that is filthy desire for gain; but there are others who seek to learn in order that they may edify, and that is charity; and there are those also who seek to learn in order that they may be edified, and that is prudence." [34] Let your young students, therefore, make it the sole object of their studies to please God and to gain from them the greatest possible spiritual advantage for themselves and their neighbours.

[33] II Timothy 3: 16-17.
[34] Saint Bernard, *In Canticum, Sermo* XXXVI, 3 (*PL* CLXXXIII, 968).
[35] Saint Augustine, *Sermo* CCCLIV *ad Cont.*, c. VI (*PL* XXXIX, 1566).

—Need for humility.

Learning without virtue is a source of offence and danger   164
rather than of real benefit. It is generally true that those who
show overweening pride, because of the learning they have
acquired, lose the faith and blindly rush headlong to spiritual
death. Students, therefore, must take every means to ensure
that the virtue of humility, which is necessary indeed for everyone
but particularly to be practised by them, is part of their innermost being; let them remember that God alone is supremely
wise by his own nature; the learning that a man may acquire,
however extensive it may be, is as nothing compared with the
things of which he remains ignorant. Saint Augustine has well
remarked: " Saint Paul said: knowledge puffs up. Well then,
must you turn your back on knowledge, and make a choice of
ignorance, in order to avoid being puffed up? If that be the case,
why am I addressing you, if ignorance is better than knowledge?
. . . Love knowledge, but give preference to charity. Knowledge
puffs up, if it stands alone. But charity edifies, and it does not
allow knowledge to become puffed up. And so knowledge puffs
up, where charity is not present to edify; but where charity
edifies, knowledge is placed on a solid foundation."

If, therefore, your students bring to their labours the spirit   165
of charity and of piety, which are the source and foundation of
the other virtues, and make these permeate their studies as a
preservative to ward off corruption, there can be no doubt
that the adornment of their learning will make them more
pleasing to God and more useful to the Church.

Advice for religious formation of lay members. To conclude, let us turn our thoughts   166
to those religious who, though not called
to the priestly dignity, have however
pronounced the same religious vows as
priests, and are no less linked to God and bound by the duty
of seeking after perfection. Even though perhaps unlettered and
unacquainted with higher studies, they too can climb to the
highest level of sanctity; the proof lies in the fact that many
of them, because of a life of piety wholly above reproach, are the

constant object of the highest admiration of Catholics or, having had their names inscribed by the authority of the Roman Pontiff in the catalogue of the saints, are regarded and invoked as intercessors and patrons before God.

These *conversi* or lay members of religious societies, because of their status, are not exposed to the dangers which sometimes threaten priests who are religious, as a consequence of the very dignity of their office; but they enjoy similar privileges and spiritual helps, which every religious society is wont to accord to all its children alike with maternal providence; it is right, therefore, that they should highly esteem their religious vocation and thank God for it with grateful heart, frequently renewing the purpose, which they undertook on the day of their profession, of living in accordance with their vocation until their last breath.

167　At this point, beloved sons, we cannot refrain from urging you to pay attention to your grave obligation of seeing that the lay brethren, both during their period of probation, and through the rest of their life, never lack the spiritual helps which they need in order to make progress and persevere; it may be that they will need all the greater help, the more humble their condition and the more lowly the services they perform. Consequently, superiors should take account of the capacity of individuals and of the difficulties likely to be encountered, when reaching a decision about the house where each one will reside and the tasks they will perform. If at any time they fall short of their religious duties, superiors shall leave nothing undone with fatherly zeal to bring them back firmly but gently to holiness of life. Especially, superiors shall not cease to instruct lay members either personally or by entrusting them to suitable priests for instruction in the great and eternal truths of the faith; anyone who knows these truths and reflects on them, whether living in the world or within a religious house, will receive many inspirations to virtue from them.

168　We wish what we have just said to apply to all members of lay Congregations also; indeed these need to be equipped with a fuller knowledge of religion, and with education well above the average, because they generally are obliged by their very office to devote themselves to the instruction of the young and adolescents.

These are the matters, beloved sons, which in the spirit of fatherly love we have thought well to communicate to you, concerning the organization of your studies and other matters of no less importance; we do not doubt that, as befits your respect for our own person, and in accordance with your burning zeal to promote the development of your respective institutes, you will gladly and obediently accept them; so also we wish them to be imprinted on the minds of your novices and scholastics, and, in the future, through the good prayers of your founding fathers and legislators, may they bring many benefits and advantages to your institutes.

APOSTOLIC CONSTITUTION "UMBRATILEM"

8 July 1924

EXTRACTS

In this Constitution the Holy Father stresses the apostolic value of the contemplative life, of which the Carthusians give an outstanding example.[1]

The power of the contemplative life. There are souls who by their choice of state follow the contemplative life, set apart from the turmoil and follies of the world, and so live in that state that they give their mind fully to the contemplation of the divine mysteries and the eternal truths and, by earnest and unceasing supplications to God, pray for the welfare of his kingdom and its constant extension; in addition, by the mortification of mind and body prescribed by rule or voluntarily undertaken, they expiate and atone not so much for their own faults as those of others—all such must surely be said to have chosen the best part, like Mary of Bethany.[2] For no more perfect condition and rule of life can be offered to men than that which, in answer of course to the call of the Lord, they choose and embrace; and by the intimate union with God and the interior holiness of those who lead a solitary life in the silence of the cloister, that spectacle of radiant sanctity is greatly enriched, which the Church, the immaculate Spouse of Jesus Christ, affords for all to behold and to imitate. Nor is it surprising that ecclesiastical writers of former times, in order to extol the power and efficacy of the prayers of these religious, even went so far in their explanations as to compare them with the prayers of Moses.

They recalled the famous episode, when Josue gave battle to the Amalecites in the plain, and Moses, on the neighbouring mountain top, prayed and implored God for the victory of his people: so long as he kept his hands raised to heaven, Israel was triumphant;

---

[1] *AAS* XVI (1924), pp. 385-389.
[2] Cf. Luke 10: 42.

but, when through weariness he had lowered his hands, then the Amalecites were gaining the victory over the Israelites; and so Aaron and Hur held up his arms on either side, until Josue emerged victorious from the battle.[3] In this we have a very apt symbol of the prayers of the religious we have referred to: the power of their prayers comes from the august sacrifice of the altar, and from the practice of penance, the one recalling Aaron, the other Hur. For, as we have already said, it is a solemn and primary purpose of these religious, acting in a certain way on behalf of all, to offer and dedicate themselves to God as victims and sacrifices of expiation, for their own salvation and that of others.

The antiquity of anchoretic life. It is for this reason that even in remote antiquity this perfect way of life, which has proved beneficial to all Christianity to a degree that is almost beyond belief, took firm root in the Church and became widely diffused. For, to say nothing of the ascetics, who, from the very beginnings of the Christian religion, were accustomed to live such an austere life, even without leaving their own homes, that they were called by Cyprian " the choicest portion of the flock of Christ," it is an established fact that, when many of the faithful of Egypt fled into the Egyptian desert, because of the persecution of Christians under the emperor Decius, and when they realized the great value of this solitary life for the attainment of perfection, they persevered in their undertaking, even when peace was restored to the Church. It is known too that of these anchorites, who were so numerous that as many of them were said to live in the deserts as there were citizens in the cities, some continued to live apart from all human contacts, while others, following the lead of St. Anthony, begin to join together in the *lauras*. From this gradually arose the institute of the common life, with definite rules to govern and regulate it. This institution spread quickly in all the regions of the Orient, and then throughout Italy, the provinces of Gaul and proconsular Africa, with monasteries being established everywhere.

[3]Cf. Exodus 17: 8-13.

172   The institute, since it had for its whole purpose that monks, each in the retirement of his cell and entirely free and detached from any exterior ministry, should turn their minds solely to heavenly things, has brought wonderful benefits to Christian society; for the clergy and people of that period could not fail to derive great benefit from the example set before them of men who were carried by the love of Christ to the heights of perfection and of austerity, who imitated the interior and hidden life which he had lived in the home at Nazareth, and who, as victims consecrated to God, made up what was wanting of his sufferings.

173   **Departures from the primitive ideal.** But, with the passage of time, the institute of the contemplative life, as it is called, in its most rigorous form, lost something of its original fervour and declined. Though monks refrained from the care of souls and other exterior ministries, it came about, gradually and almost imperceptibly, that they combined works of the active life with the study and contemplation of divine things. For they deemed that they should, as the bishops insistently requested, give their services in support of the labour of priests overwhelmed by the requirements of their task; or they decided that it would be opportune to undertake the responsibility of public instruction, which Charlemagne was promoting. Moreover, in the generally disturbed conditions of those times, monasteries had not perhaps escaped without some damage and relaxation of discipline. It was, therefore, a matter of supreme concern for the Church that this saintly form of life, which for so many centuries had existed intact in the monasteries, should be restored to its original condition; thus the Church would never want for intercessors, persons free from every other responsibility, who would constantly implore the divine mercy and bring down from heaven upon men, all too careless of their own salvation, blessings of every kind.

Mission of Saint Bruno. Now the goodness of God, who provides for the needs and the well-being of his Church at all times, made choice of Bruno, a man of eminent sanctity, to restore the contemplative life to its primitive integrity and distinction. For this purpose Bruno founded the Carthusian Order, which he thoroughly imbued with his own spirit; he also furnished it with rules which would effectively influence the members of the Order to traverse speedily the path of interior sanctity and austere penance, in complete detachment from the exercise of any exterior ministry or office; these rules would also stimulate them to persevere, with unremitting fervour, in that same strictness and austerity of life.

And it is a well-known fact that the Carthusians have been, for almost nine centuries, so faithful to the spirit of their founder and lawgiver that this Order, contrary to the experience of other religious societies, has never in the course of that long period stood in need of correction or reform, as it is called.

Who could fail to admire those religious who, in complete seclusion and cut off from the society of men for the whole span of life, in order to promote the eternal salvation of mankind by a hidden and silent apostolate, dwell each of them in the solitude of his cell, and never depart from it for any cause, for any necessity, at any time of year? At fixed hours of day and night, they gather in the sacred edifice, not to recite the Psalms, as other Orders do, but to chant together—*viva et rotunda voce*—the entire divine Office, without the support of musical instruments and in accordance with the very ancient Gregorian melodies of their own codices. How should God in his mercy fail to grant the prayers of these saintly religious, who thus raise their suppliant voices for the Church and the reform of mankind?

Papal esteem for the Carthusians. Bruno himself enjoyed the esteem and good will of our predecessor Urban II, who had experience of Bruno's learning and sanctity as his pupil in the schools of Rheims, and subsequently as Pope summoned him to his side and made use of his services as a counsellor; in the same way the Carthusian Order, whose simplicity and unsophisticated way of life were a further recommendation, has constantly enjoyed the special favour of the Apostolic See. We ourselves bear no less affection to the Carthusians, and are equally desirous to see this salutary institute extend and develop ever more widely.

176   **The abiding value of the Carthusian Order.** For if ever in the past the Church had need of such anchorites, it is supremely necessary at the present day that this institution should exist and flourish; because we see so many Christians, neglectful of meditation on heavenly things, or even without any consideration or thought for eternal salvation, who engage in a mad pursuit of earthly riches and bodily pleasures, and who adopt pagan ways, totally opposed to the Gospel, which they flaunt in both private and public life.

177   There may be some who still consider that those virtues, which are wrongly described as passive, have long since gone out of date, and that the ancient discipline of the cloisters should give way to a wider and more liberal exercise of the active virtues; that opinion, which our predecessor of immortal memory, Leo XIII, refuted and condemned,[4] is quite evidently gravely offensive and fatal to the doctrine and practice of Christian perfection. Indeed, it is not hard to understand that a much greater contribution to the growth of the Church and the salvation of mankind is made by those who are constantly occupied with the duty of prayer and mortification, than by the workers who till the field of the Lord; for if they did not bring down from heaven an abundant rain of divine graces, the evangelical labourers would gather but a meagre harvest from their toil.

It is scarcely necessary to speak of the great hope and expectation which the Carthusians arouse in us: by reason of their obedience to the rule of the Order, not merely with exact observance but with a certain generosity of spirit, their souls will be readily formed to a higher degree of sanctity; and consequently it is impossible that these religious should fail to be powerful intercessors with the merciful God for the Christian people.

177e   [4] Cf. Leo XIII, Letter *Testem benevolentiae,* 22 January 1899, *ASS* XXXI (1899), p. 471-6); cf. *supra,* nn. 1-6.

LETTER OF CARDINAL PACELLI TO
RELIGIOUS ORDERS

15 March 1936

*In this letter Cardinal Pacelli, Secretary of State of Pope Pius XI, speaks
to religious superiors about Catholic Action, urging that Catholic Action
groups be formed in all colleges.[1]*

Readiness of religious to support Catholic Action. You are well aware of the great hopes 178
for the Christian renewal of society
which the Holy Father places in Catholic
Action; you know the comfort brought
to him by the reports, coming even from mission territories,
about the continuous development of this work and the precious
fruits which the Lord is producing through it.

It was a particular source of consolation to him, to see the
whole-hearted readiness with which certain Orders and Congregations of men and of women have made available for Catholic
Action subjects of theirs who, by the pen, by the word, by their
co-operation, have helped to develop Catholic Action and are
ensuring that it will bear fruit. The august Pontiff has several
times taken occasion to express his approval and satisfaction.
Once again recently, in his letter of last October to the bishops
of Brazil,[2] he expressed the desire that the assistance given by
religious societies " should surpass all others in effectiveness and
extent."

Course for training religious to carry out this mission. It is to be expected, therefore, in 179
accordance with the recommendations of
that important document, that special
courses will be organized to prepare
religious for the discharge of these new obligations, so that
through preaching and the various activities inspired by their
zeal, the faithful will be stimulated and trained for the apostolate
of Catholic Action.

---

[1] *OR*, 4 June 1936.
[2] Letter *Quamvis nostra* to the bishops of Brazil, 27 October 1935, *AAS* XXVIII (1936),
p. 161.

180   Since one of the chief meritorious services of religious is their preaching to the clergy, especially at retreats, they will, as a result of this better preparation, be able to inculcate with greater competence and authority, together with other obligations of priests, their duty in relation to Catholic Action; this latter the Holy Father, in his first encyclical,[3] declared to be " one of the principal duties of the pastor of souls." And without any doubt, the co-operation of religious will be no less effective in the education of youth, who are very largely under their direction, in conditions of time and place which are as much as one could desire.

181   **Catholic Action in educational establishments.** The august Pontiff, in various circumstances, has declared emphatically that the training in the spirit of the apostolate, which is characteristic of Catholic Action, is an essential element of education in modern times, a firm bulwark of the Christian life, and that it is a special grace to be called to an apostolate which is so intimately linked with the apostolate of the priesthood. A wise teacher cannot forget this; by overlooking it, he would narrow down the horizons for good which should be opened wide to the generous souls of the young; he would deprive the Church of valuable assistants and would hardly attain all the objectives of a true Christian education.

On the other hand, this formation contributes to the well-being of schools. No one can question the inestimable benefits which are gained by mutual good example, by action which wins over companions who are less good, by the endeavour to transform the life of a college into a more real preparation for work; these activities will subsequently, either during holidays or after the completion of studies, expand in the organizations of Catholic Action. The young will thus be better equipped to overcome the many grave dangers of modern social environment, which, as is only too well known, brings about the downfall of many, even of those who have been educated in Catholic schools.

[3] Encyclical *Ubi arcano*, 23 December 1922, AAS XIV (1922), p. 673-700.

For all these grave reasons the Holy Father had already 182
recommended the establishment of *Internal Associations,* which
are happily flourishing in many institutions. He also asked that
the *Pious Associations* under the care of religious should be
encouraged " to give their providential assistance to Catholic
Action, . . . by influencing and guiding their members into it:
that applies particularly to Institutes and Congregations which
bring the young together in order to preserve the fruits of
Christian education."

If, in addition, religious are not content merely to direct 183
their own prayers to this purpose, but strive to persuade those
subject to their spiritual direction to pray for Catholic Action
and to join the organization, their co-operation will be truly
complete, and from it will come a fruitful harvest for Catholic
Action and, consequently, for the entire Church. By obedience
to these directives, religious will continue their glorious
traditions of whole-hearted promptness in meeting the needs
of souls and answering the wishes of the Vicar of Christ, at this
time when so many difficulties are encountered in protecting
the young who are menaced by so many enemies and especially
by communist propaganda. It will be an act of true charity to
co-operate in full accord with the secular clergy for the diffusion
of the kingdom of Christ, which is the constant desire of the
sovereign Pontiff.

INSTRUCTION "POSTQUAM PIUS" OF THE SACRED CONGREGATION OF THE SACRAMENTS TO PREVENT ABUSES OF FREQUENT COMMUNION

8 December 1938

The almost universal practice of daily Communion in seminaries, colleges and religious communities could, in certain circumstances, constitute a form of social pressure that might interfere with the liberty of individual souls. The Holy Father gives precise directives to prevent possible abuses.[1]

184 **The decrees of Pius X.** Since Pius X of holy memory encouraged the faithful to frequent and daily Communion by the decree *Sacra Tridentina Synodus*,[2] issued on 20 December 1905 by the Sacred Congregation of the Council, and also invited children to the same practice by the decree *Quam singulari*[3] of this Sacred Congregation, issued on 8 August 1910, which decrees the Code of Canon Law[4] has made its own, it is well known to everybody that the practice of frequent and daily Communion has happily become widespread.

185 This practice, the source of countless blessings, is not only to be praised, but should be spread even more widely, not merely among the faithful in general, but also among young people and children, in conformity with the precept imposed by the above mentioned decrees and with due observance of the relevant norms there laid down.

" Frequent and daily Communion . . . is to be promoted as much as possible in clerical seminaries . . . and in other Christian educational establishments of every kind." [5] And " those who have the care of children must make every effort that, after their first Communion, the children shall frequently approach the Holy Table, even daily if possible, as is desired by Christ and our mother, the Church, and that they shall do so with all the devotion of which they are capable at their age." [6]

---

[1] *Enchiridion de Statibus Perfectionis*, I, pp. 523-530.
[2] *ASS* XXXVIII (1905), pp. 400-409.
[3] *AAS* II (1910), pp. 577-583.
[4] *CIC*, canon 863.
[5] *Sacra Tridentina Synodus*, n. 251, 7.
[6] Decree *Quam singulari*, n. 6.

I. But, just as frequent and daily Communion is to be praised, 186
so also there must be insistence on observance of the conditions
which are necessary, namely the *state of grace* and a *right intention*.
At the same time, suitable precautions must be taken so that no
one will eat this Bread unworthily. For the Apostle says:
Whosoever shall eat this bread, or drink the chalice of the Lord un-
worthily, shall be guilty of the Body and of the Blood of the Lord.[7]

Danger of abuses. The danger of unworthy reception of Com- 187
munion can be seen to be inherent in the very
practice of frequent and daily Communion, which
is so widespread, for it is the nature of men to have but little
esteem for things to which they are accustomed; that danger
is increased when the faithful, especially the young, approach
the Holy Table not individually, but generally and in a body,
as happens daily in seminaries and religious communities; it
also happens frequently in colleges and institutions for the
Christian education of the young, and sometimes also in the
gatherings which are held at Easter time, or some other solemn
occasion, for the purpose of receiving the Holy Eucharist.

For it can happen that someone, though conscious of grave
sin, may nevertheless approach the Holy Table because he is
influenced by the example of his companions and by the empty
fear that he would arouse wonder in others, especially superiors,
and thus fall under suspicion of having committed a grave fault.

II. Therefore, in order as far as possible to prevent every 188
abuse, this Sacred Congregation has considered it necessary to
seek appropriate remedies and to communicate them to the
pastors of souls. These remedies are as follows:

REMEDIES

—*Fuller instruction of consciences.*

1° Preachers and directors of conscience, when exhorting 189
the faithful, especially younger people, either publicly or in
private, to frequent and daily Communion, shall not be content
merely to exhort, but shall at the same time clearly teach:

[7] I Corinthians, 11: 27.

(a) that daily Communion is not of obligation; *(b) that it cannot be practised unless the necessary conditions are fulfilled.*

190   (a) Frequent and daily Communion is undoubtedly commended highly, but there is no law which makes it obligatory; it is, therefore, left to the piety and devotion of each individual. This is so true that even the obligation of paschal Communion is qualified by the clause, " unless perhaps on the advice of his own priest, for some reasonable cause, the person considers that he should for a time abstain from receiving it." [8] For this reason there is no ground for wonder or suspicion if, in a place where the practice of daily Communion is in use, someone abstains from time to time. And, if this truth is clearly set out, that vain fear, which can be the occasion of unworthy reception of Communion, will be completely uprooted.

191   (b) Holy Communion, which is *life to the good*, is also *death to the wicked*. The first requirement, therefore, is the *state of grace*. A horror of sacrilege should be thoroughly inculcated, and attention be directed to the law which lays down: " No one, who is conscious of the guilt of mortal sin, however convinced he may be that he is contrite for it, shall go to holy Communion without first making sacramental Confession [9] . . . "

192   A *right* or *pious intention* is also required; " it consists in this, that a person approach the Holy Table not as a matter of routine, or through vanity, or for human considerations, but with the desire to please God, to be united more closely with him in charity and to avail himself of this divine remedy for his weaknesses and defects." [10]

Moreover, " in order that frequent and daily Communion be received with greater prudence and be crowned with greater merit, the advice of the confessor should be taken." [11]

—*Frequent Confession encouraged.*

193   2° Together with frequent Communion, frequent Confession also should be encouraged: not that confession must be made before each Communion, unless one is conscious of mortal sin,

[8] *CIC*, canon 859, § 1.
[9] *CIC*, can. 856.
[10] *Sacra Tridentina Synodus*, n. 251, 2.
[11] *Ibid.*, n. 251, 5.

but that the faithful living in communities should go to confession not merely on the appointed days but should also have the opportunity, without any comment of their superiors, of freely going to the confessor of their choice; and it is a matter of special importance that they should be able to make their confession even a short time before Communion.

(a) Hence pastors of souls shall make every effort to provide for each community, according to the number of the members, one or two confessors to whom each one can freely go. They shall keep in mind the norm which prescribes that, where the practice of frequent and daily Communion is in honour, an opportunity for frequent and daily sacramental confession must also be provided, as far as possible. It is also desirable that all communities should fairly frequently have available to them other confessors from among those who are approved. 194

(b) As for seminaries, there are the prescriptions of canons 1358, 1361 and 1367 of the Code of Canon Law; these prescribe that there must be at least two ordinary confessors and a spiritual director in every seminary, and in addition to the ordinary confessors, other confessors are to be designated to whom the students can freely go; if these confessors live outside the seminary, and a student requests that one of them be summoned, the rector shall bring him, without seeking in any way the reason for the request or showing that he takes it ill. If the confessors live in the seminary, the student can go to them freely, without prejudice to the discipline of the seminary. Let superiors weigh the grave judgment of St. Alphonsus, namely that students of a seminary are in grave danger of committing sacrileges if they always confess their sins to confessors known to them.[12] Bishops shall see to it that students go to the sacrament of Penance at least once a week. 195

—*Regulations of canon law concerning freedom of choice of confessors.* 196
(c) In relation to all religious communities of men and of women, the provisions of law are taken from canon 518 and the subsequent canons, and they are to be scrupulously observed,

[12] Cf. St. Alphonsus, *Regolamento per i Seminari,* § 1, n. 3.

taking account of their letter and spirit. " In each house of a cleri-cal religious society, several lawfully approved confessors, in proportion to the numbers of the members, shall be appointed, and they shall have the faculty, in an exempt religious society, of absolving even from cases reserved in the religious society." [13] " Superiors shall beware of inducing any of their subjects, either personally or through another, by force, fear, importunate per-suasion or in any other way, to confess their sins to them." [14] " If a religious, even exempt, for peace of conscience goes to a confessor who is approved by the local Ordinary, even though not in the list of those designated, the confession is valid and lawful, any contrary privilege being revoked; and the confessor can absolve the religious even from sins and censures reserved in the religious society." [15] "For each community of women religious there shall be appointed an extraordinary confessor who is to come to the religious house at least four times a year, and to whom all the religious shall present themselves, at least to receive his blessing." [16] " Local Ordinaries, in whose territories communities of women religious exist, shall designate for each house some priests, to whom these religious can easily have recourse for the sacrament of Penance in particular cases, without the necessity of approaching the Ordinary in every case." [17] " If any woman religious, for the peace of her soul and for greater progress in the way of God, asks for some special confessor or spiritual director, the Ordinary shall readily grant this . . ." [18] Likewise " if any woman religious asks for one of these confessors (designated by local Ordinaries for each house of women religious), no superioress is allowed, either personally or through others, directly or indirectly, to seek the reason for the petition, to oppose it either by words or acts, or to show in any way that she is annoyed by it." [19]

197   Furthermore, if, notwithstanding these provisions, " a woman

---

[13] *CIC*, canon 518, § 1.
[14] *Ibid.*, canon 518, § 3; cf. *supra* n° 88.
[15] *Ibid.*, canon 519.
[16] *Ibid.*, canon 521, § 1; cf. *supra*, n° 90.
[17] *Ibid.*, canon 521, § 2; cf. *supra*, n° 90.
[18] *Ibid.*, canon 520, § 2; cf. *supra*, n° 89.
[19] *Ibid.*, canon 521, § 3; cf. *supra*, n° 90.

religious, for the peace of her conscience, goes to a confessor who has been approved by the local Ordinary for women, the confession, made in any church or oratory, even a semi-public oratory (or any other place lawfully destined for the confessions of women), is valid and lawful, every contrary privilege being revoked; nor can the superioress forbid it or make enquiries about it, even indirectly; and the religious are not bound to make any report about it to the superioress."[20] Similarly: "all women religious, when they are gravely ill, even though not in danger of death, can send for any priest approved for the hearing of women's confessions, even though he is not appointed for religious, and make their confession to him as frequently as they wish, while the grave illness lasts; and the superioress cannot prohibit them from doing so, either directly or indirectly."[21]

Nuns who are bound by the law of enclosure, and who are not allowed to go out or to go to their own church or to a semi-public oratory, enjoy the same faculty: these may send for a confessor approved for the confessions of women whom they prefer, to come to the ordinary confessional of the monastery to hear their confession; and, if they are gravely ill, even to their own room, with the necessary precautions, nor may the superioress forbid it directly or indirectly. 198

—Need for tact and discretion on part of superioresses.

Therefore the ecclesiastics who are responsible for communities of women religious shall earnestly endeavour to prevent superioresses from enquiring even indirectly why the women religious who are subject to them send for another confessor or go to him; and they shall admonish the superioresses that they have no power to prevent this in any way. The ecclesiastics in question shall realize that it can easily happen that women religious are excessively afraid to ask the superioress to whom they are subject for an extraordinary confessor, and consequently that they are unable freely to make provision for the welfare of their conscience. They shall therefore attentively watch lest in a matter 199

[20] CIC, canon 522; cf. supra, n° 91.
[21] CIC, canon 523; cf. supra, n° 92.

of such importance the liberty wisely established by the sacred canons for women religious should be diminished.

200 The exercise of this liberty of conscience should, of course, be suitably harmonized with regular observance of the discipline of each community; the local Ordinaries shall see to it that this discipline is kept intact, and it is also their duty to take measures lest abuses creep in, in consequence of the liberty allowed, or, insofar as abuses have crept in, to have them removed cautiously and prudently, always without prejudice to liberty of conscience.[22]

201 In lay religious societies of men also, an ordinary and an extraordinary confessor are to be appointed; and if a religious requests a special confessor, the superior shall grant this, without in any way seeking the reason for it or showing that he is annoyed by it.

202 (d) Finally, in all communities of young people of either sex, as far as possible it must be seen to carefully that, at the time when Communion is being distributed, a confessor is at hand to whom there is ready access.

203 **Particular measures against undue pressure.** III. In addition to these general remedies, the superiors of individual communities shall have recourse to other means suitable for securing the same end.

—A clear statement by superiors.

204 (a) The superior shall say to his subjects in unmistakeable terms that, while in general he is pleased with their frequent going to the Holy Table, he does not note it as a matter for rebuke if individuals abstain, but rather sees in this the sign of liberty and of an upright and delicate conscience. The superior shall not contradict his words by his way of acting, and he shall not give any indication from which it would seem that he takes note of those who frequently go to Communion and praises them, while disapproving others.

205 In seminaries and similar institutions, where at stated times

[22] CIC, canon 520, § 2; cf. supra, n° 89.

a judgment on each student is given by superiors in relation to piety, study and discipline, the said superiors shall take no account of greater or less assiduity in receiving the holy Eucharist, when giving their judgment on the progress of the young person in piety.

—Avoidance of the term "general Communion."

(*b*) In communities of boys and of girls there shall never be proclaimed a " general Communion " to be carried out with special solemnity; and even outside communities, the very expression " general Communion " should either not be used, or the meaning of this expression should be properly explained: namely that all are invited to the Holy Table, but that no one is compelled to come, and that individuals have full power and liberty to abstain from it. As regards religious communities, note should also be taken of what is laid down in the decree *Sacra Tridentina Synodus*, n° 8 : " If there are any institutes, either of solemn or of simple vows, in whose rules or constitutions, or even in their calendars, there are found to be certain days for which Communions are fixed and commanded, such regulations are to be regarded as merely directive and not as having the power of precepts." 206

—No hindrance of liberty.

(*c*) At the time when communicants approach the Holy Table, everything must be avoided that would create greater difficulty for a young person who wishes to abstain from Communion, and to do so in a manner which will be less noticed; hence there shall be no express invitation to the Sacred Table, no strict and almost military order in coming up, no insignia to be carried by the communicants, etc. 207

—Communion of the sick.

(*d*) The superior of the community shall see to it that Holy Communion is not brought to the sick who do not expressly ask for it. 208

—Precautions at gatherings of Catholics.

209   (e) Promoters and directors of gatherings of youth, which are announced, e.g., in public schools for the purpose of receiving Communion, shall take note of the fact that there are dangers in these gatherings akin to those which arise in communities; they must take every precaution to remove these dangers, not merely by announcing that everyone is free to go to Communion or to abstain, and by providing a sufficient supply of confessors, but also by endeavouring to avoid everything which could expose those who do not go to Communion to the wonder of others, as has been already said.

PIUS XII
1939—1958

DISCOURSE TO THE GENERAL CONGREGATION OF THE SOCIETY OF JESUS

17 September 1946

EXTRACTS

The Holy Father availed himself of the occasion afforded by the general congregation of the Society of Jesus to give certain precise directives to the Order, whose members make a special vow of obedience to him. This was their first general congregation after the war, and the Pope emphasized the importance of fidelity on several points of asceticism and doctrine.[1]

. . . . But certain conditions must be complied with by you, if this our confident hope is to be happily fulfilled, and if you yourselves are to fulfil our expectation.

Fidelity to the Constitutions. First of all, you must be steadfastly faithful 210 to your constitutions and to all their prescriptions. The institutes of your Order, if it be thought appropriate, can be altered here and there to accommodate them to the new circumstances of the age; but what is primary in them should not in any way be touched and should always firmly abide.

—Especially the third year of probation, meditation and silence.

For example: the third year of probation, which other 211 religious societies have adopted in imitation of you, and to which is due that stream of interior life that flows ever more richly in you; the customs of meditation and silence, and especially

---

[1] *AAS* XXXVIII (1946), p. 383-5. At the XXXth General Congregation, the Holy 210a
Father was to recall with redoubled emphasis the religious requirements in an Order
such as the Society of Jesus. Cf. *infra*, nn. 634-46.

91

the regulations handed down from your predecessors about the instruction of your pupils shall also be preserved intact. Now your traditional formation is prolonged, but for that reason it is telling and efficacious. A long span of time is required in order that the mighty oak be solidly established, and similarly the formation of the man of God always calls for prolonged patience. A check therefore should be placed on that generous impetuosity of the young, which carries them prematurely into the field of action; too hasty activity destroys rather than builds, and it is injurious to the person who acts thus and even to the apostolic activities themselves.

—*The spirit of Saint Ignatius.*

212   If you wish to be genuine and fearless apostles, then strive assiduously, having been wholly formed in and imbued with the spirit of the *Exercises* of your holy father Ignatius, to acquire the solid supernatural virtues and to devote all your powers with ardent faith to the service of Christ the Lord; strive to increase in this way the riches of heavenly grace within you, inasmuch as you are living members of the mystical Body of Christ.

—*Renunciation.*

213   Moved by the inspiration of the charity of the divine Redeemer, subdue the sentiments of evil self-love; deny yourselves, especially by holding in check and controlling the movements of your minds, and by the discipline of this renunciation you will be made fit and ready to discharge all duties and to endure the most arduous trials.

—*Obedience.*

214   Another result of this will be that the virtue of obedience will never rest upon unstable foundations. Obedience is your badge, your boast, your source of strength; its chief object is that you should be completely in compliance with the behest of your superiors, without complaints, without murmurings, without that reprehensible critical spirit, the disease of our time,

which dissipates strength and makes apostolic undertakings sluggish and sterile. With the inspiration of charity the onerous tasks, which are imposed by an austere obedience, will become light burdens for you; when that charity is present, God is present, because *God is love.* May you have in you that *charity which is from a pure heart and a good conscience and sincere faith.* [2]

Fidelity to doctrine. It is your duty to be both in name and in fact not merely true religious, but also men of great learning. You perform, by word and writing, the office of teaching theology, Scripture and the other ecclesiastical sciences, and also philosophy; this is an outstanding honour for you, a noble task, but a heavy responsibility also rests on you for this ministry you have undertaken. For one and all of those who have been entrusted with this charge, the words of the Apostle cry aloud: *O Timothy, guard the deposit, avoiding profane novelties of speech and contradictions of so-called knowledge.* [3] 215

—Fidelity to St. Thomas.

Members of the Society of Jesus, therefore, in order faithfully to fulfil this great hope, shall observe with all diligence their own laws, which command them to follow the doctrine of Saint Thomas " as the more solid, more sure, more approved and more in agreement with the constitutions." 216

—Fidelity to the magisterium.

They shall also, with the inflexible constancy which is traditional in your ranks, hold fast to the magisterium of the Church; to use the very words of the holy founder of your Society; they shall have " a mind ready and prompt to obey in everything the true Spouse of Christ our Lord, which is our holy Mother the hierarchical Church "; and " believing that between Christ our Lord, the Bridegroom, and the Church, his Bride, there is the same spirit, who rules and guides us for the salvation of our souls." [4] 217

[2] I Timothy 1: 5.
[3] I Timothy 6: 20.
[4] *Spiritual Exercises, Regulae ad sentiendum cum Ecclesia,* 1a et 3a.

218 **The spirit which** While it is a primary duty to cultivate
     should guide research. the faith, members of the Society are
                             also bound to acquire an accurate and
thorough scientific learning; moreover, following the illustrious
traditions of their Order, they should strive to promote, as far
as possible and in whatever way possible, the progress of
knowledge.

Let them be convinced that by following this path, however
difficult it may be, they can make a very great contribution to
the greater glory of God and the building up of the Church.
Moreover, both in speaking and in writing, they should so
express themselves for the men of their time that they will be
understood and gladly listened to. It follows from this that in
the setting out and clarification of questions, in the conduct
of discussions, and also in the choice of the mode of presentation,
they should prudently adapt their speech to the particular genius
and propensity of the times. But no one must disturb or upset
what ought not to be changed. There has been too much talk,
with too little investigation, of a " new theology " which, with
everything constantly evolving, must also evolve and be always
progressing and never reach finality. If such an opinion were to
be accepted, what would become of the unchanging dogmas of
the Catholic Church, and of the unity and stability of the faith?

219   While therefore you regard it as a sacred and solemn duty to
revere the eternal truth, labour also to investigate studiously
and to solve the problems which the passage of time brings to
the fore, especially if these are problems that can create obstacles
and difficulties for learned Christians; in fact, by shedding light
on these problems, turn the obstacle into a help, and use it to
strengthen their faith. Nevertheless, when new or free questions
are discussed, let the principles of Catholic teaching shine always
before your minds. Whatever sounds completely new in Catholic
theology ought to be examined with vigilance and caution;
what is certain and sure must be distinguished from what is
put forward as conjecture, from what a passing and not always
praiseworthy fashion can introduce even into theology and
philosophy; the hand of friendship should be extended to the
erring, but no concession should be made to erroneous opinions.

APOSTOLIC CONSTITUTION
"PROVIDA MATER ECCLESIA"

2 February 1947

This historic document has as its purpose to ratify the existence of Secular Institutes and to define the rules which govern them. That represents a new complement added to the Code of Canon Law, in conformity with the needs of the present time.[1]

Constant Care of the Church for States of Perfection

1. Mother Church, with provident care, has always striven, with most earnest and motherly affection, to render constantly worthy of their heavenly purpose and angelic calling,[2] those her specially beloved children, who dedicate their whole life to Christ the Lord and follow him freely in the arduous path of the counsels, and also to regulate wisely their way of life; there are countless documents and records of Pontiffs, Councils and Fathers which bear witness to this fact, and the entire course of ecclesiastical history as well as the whole system of canonical discipline down to our own times is evident proof of it.

2. Indeed, from the very infancy of Christianity, the Church in her magisterium set out to clarify the call to perfection contained in the doctrine and example of Christ[3] and the Apostles,[4] giving sure teaching on the manner in which a life dedicated to perfection should be conducted and suitably

220

221

---

[1] *AAS* XXXIX (1947), pp. 114-124. The full title of the Constitution is: "Apostolic Constitution *Provida Mater Ecclesia* on the Canonical States and Secular Institutes for acquiring Christian perfection."

[2] Cf. Tertullian, *Ad uxorem, lib.* 1, c. iv (*PL* 1, 1281); Ambrose, *De virginibus,* 1, 3, 11 (*PL* XVI, 202); Eucherius Lugd., *Exhortatio ad monachos,* 1 (*PL* L, 865); Bernard, *Epistola* CDXLIX (*PL* CLXXXII, 641); *ibid., Apologia ad Guillelmum,* c. x (*PL* CLXXXII, 912).

[3] Cf. Matthew 16: 24; 19: 10-12, 16-21; Mark 10: 17-21, 23-30; Luke 18: 18-22, 24-29; 20: 34-36.

[4] Cf. 1 Corinthians 7: 25-35, 37-38, 40; Matthew 19: 27; Mark 10: 28; Luke 18: 28; Acts 21: 8-9; Apocalypse 14: 4-5.

8

organized. As a result of her warm encouragement and propagation of complete dedication and consecration to Christ, it came
about that from the earliest times Christian communities
spontaneously afforded for the evangelical counsels a good soil,
prepared for the seed and assuring an excellent harvest; [5] and
soon afterwards, as can easily be established from the apostolic
Fathers and ancient ecclesiastical writers, [6] the profession of the
life of perfection had already reached such a flourishing condition
in different churches, that those who followed this way of life
began to constitute within the Church a clearly recognised rank
and social class, who were known variously as ascetes, *con-
tinentes*, virgins, and by other titles, and they were the recipients
of many marks of praise and honour. [7]

222   3. In the course of the centuries the Church, faithful to
Christ her Spouse and ever true to herself, under the guidance
of the Holy Spirit, moving forward continually and securely,
has gradually evolved the discipline of the state of perfection
down to the promulgation of the present-day Code of Canon
Law. With motherly affection for those who willingly were
making public and external profession of perfection of life in
different forms, she has given constant support in two respects
to their whole-hearted dedication to so holy a purpose. To begin
with, the Church not only accepted and recognized the individual
profession of perfection—a profession however always made in
the sight of the Church and in a public manner, as for instance
the ancient and liturgical ceremony of the blessing and consecra-

---

[5] Cf. Luke 8: 15; Acts 4: 32, 34-35; 1 Corinthians 7: 25-35; 37-38; 40; Eusebius,
Historia Ecclesiastica, 111, 39 (*PG* XX, 297).

[6] Ignatius, *Ad Polycarpum*, V (*PG* V, 724); Polycarp, *Ad Philippenses*, V, 3 (*PG* V,
1009); Justin, *Apologia I pro christianis* (*PG* VI, 349); Clement of Alexandria, *Stromata*
(*PG* VIII, 224); Hippolytus, *In Proverb.* (*PG* X, 628); id., *De Virgine Corinthiaca* (*PG* X,
871-4); Origen, *in Num.*, hom. II, 1 (*PG* XII, 590); Methodius, *Convivium decem virginum*
(*PG* XVIII, 27-220); Tertullian, *Ad uxorem*, lib. I, c. vii-viii (*PL* I, 1286-7); id., *De
resurrectione carnis*, c. viii (*PL* II, 806); Cyprian, *Epistola* XXXVI (*PL* IV, 327); id.,
Epistola LXII, II (*PL* IV, 311); id., *Testimonia adv. judaeos*, lib. III, c. lxxiv (*PL* V, 771);
Ambrose, *De viduis*, II, 9 ff. (*PL* XVI, 250-1); Cassian, *De tribus generibus monachorum*,
V (*PL* XLIX, 1094); Athenagoras, *Legatio pro christianis* (*PG* VI, 965).

[7] Acts 21: 8-10; cf. Ignatius of Antioch, *Ad Smyrn.*, XIII (*PG* V, 717); id., *Ad Polyc.*,
V (*PG* V, 723): Tertullian, *De virginibus velandis* (*PL* II, 935 f.); id., *De exhortatione casti-
tatis*, c. vii (*PL* II, 922); Cyprian, *De habitu virginum*, II (*PL* IV, 443); Jerome, *Epistola*
LVIII, 4-6 (*PL* XXII, 582-3); Augustine, *Sermo* CCXIV (*PL* XXXVIII, 1070); id., *Contra
Faustum Manichaeum*, lib. V, c. ix (*PL* XLII, 226).

tion of virgins [8]—she also enacted prudent legislation for and strenuously defended this profession and also attributed many canonical effects to it.

The Church's Preference for a Wisely Ordered Community Religious Life

However, from the time of the peace of Constantine, the 223 particular favour and very special care of the Church were rightly and deservedly exercised in favour of that full and more strictly public profession of perfection, which was undertaken within the societies and communities which had been established with her permission or approval or by her command.

4. It is well known to everyone how intimately and essentially 224 the history of the holiness of the Church and of the Catholic apostolate is bound up with the story and annals of the canonical religious life, as that life, through the constantly vivifying grace of the Holy Spirit, ever expands in its wondrous variety and is strengthened by a new unity that is ever more profound and stable. It is not surprising if the Church, holding faithfully even in the sphere of law to the procedure which the providential wisdom of God clearly indicated, of set purpose has tended to and organized the canonical state of perfection in such fashion as quite rightly to have made it one of the corner-stones on which to erect the edifice of ecclesiastical discipline. A first consequence of this is that the public state of perfection is counted among the three principal states recognized by the Church, and from it alone the Church derives the second class and rank of canonical persons. [9] A matter that is indeed worthy of attentive consideration: while the other two classes of canonical persons, namely clerics and laics, by divine law, which is supplemented by ecclesiastical regulations, [10] derive from the Church inasmuch as it is a society hierarchically constituted and organized, the class of religious, on the other hand, being placed between clerics and laics, can be common to both clerics and laics, [11] and it derives

---

[8] Cf. Optatus, *De schismate donatistarum,* lib. VI (*PL* XI, 1071 ff.); *Roman Pontifical,* II; De benedictione et consecratione virginum.

[9] *CIC,* can. 107.

[10] *CIC,* can. 107, 108 § 3.

[11] *Ibid.,* can. 107.

wholly from the close and special relationship to the end of the Church, namely sanctification, and the efficacious and adequate means to achieve it.

225   5. The Church did not leave matters there. Lest the public and solemn profession of sanctity should prove fruitless and vain, the Church, with ever increasing rigour, refused to give her recognition to this canonical state of perfection except in societies erected and regulated by herself, namely in religious societies,[12] whose general form and system had won the approval of her teaching authority, after mature and unhurried examination, and in every single case after she had submitted the institute and statutes to repeated scrutiny, not merely in relation to doctrine and in the abstract, but also by applying the test of practical experience. These matters are so strictly and precisely defined in the law of the Code, that in no case, not even by way of exception, will the canonical state of perfection be recognized, unless the profession of perfection is made in a religious society approved by the Church. Finally, the canonical discipline of the state of perfection, as a public state, was wisely so regulated by the Church that for clerical religious societies, in those matters generally which concern the clerical life of the religious, the religious society takes the place of the diocese, and enrolment in a religious society takes the place of clerical incardination into a diocese.[13]

Need to Supplement the Legislation of the Code on the Religious State

226   6. The Code, the work of Pius X and Benedict XV, in the second part of Book II which is devoted to religious, by means of a diligently collected, revised and carefully prepared body of legislation for religious, gave manifold confirmation, even in its public aspect, to the canonical state of perfection; with great wisdom it rounded off the work begun by Leo XIII of happy memory in his immortal Constitution *Conditae a Christo*,[14]

---

[12] *Ibid.*, can. 488, 1; cf. *supra*, n. 77.
[13] *Ibid.*, can. 111 § 1; 115; 585.
[14] Apostolic Constitution *Conditae a Christo Ecclesiae*, 8 December 1900; cf. *supra*, nn. 7-32.

and admitted Congregations of simple vows among religious societies strictly so-called; and thus it seemed that nothing further remained to be added to the discipline of the canonical state of perfection. The Church, however, with her characteristic broadness of mind and heart, in a truly maternal gesture, saw fit to add a brief section to the legislation for religious, as a very timely complement.

In it [15] the Church decided to give a rank corresponding fairly 227 completely with the canonical state of perfection, to other societies well deserving of the Church herself and frequently also of civil society; these societies, though they lacked certain of the juridical formalities required for the complete canonical state of perfection, for example public vows,[16] nevertheless are linked by a close resemblance and kinship with true religious societies, in other matters which are regarded as belonging to the substance of the life of perfection.

7. By means of all these wise and prudent arrangements, 228 inspired as they are by great love, the fullest provision was made for the great multitude of souls who, having renounced the world, desired to embrace a new canonical state strictly so-called, one solely and completely consecrated to the acquiring of perfection. But the God of all kindness who, without acceptance of persons,[17] repeatedly invited all the faithful to the pursuit and practice of perfection [18] everywhere, by the wonderful design of his divine providence, so arranged that even in a world so depraved by vices, especially in our times, many groups of chosen souls have flourished and still continue to flourish; these not only burn with zeal for individual perfection, but by a special vocation of God remain in the world, and they can find excellent new forms of associations that are excellently adapted to contemporary requirements, in which they are enabled to lead a life particularly suited to the acquiring of Christian perfection.

8. While we earnestly commend to the prudence and zeal 229

---

[15] Tit. XVII, Bk. II.
[16] CIC, can. 488, 1° and 7°; 487; cf. supra nn. 76-77.
[17] Cf. II Chronicles, 19: 7; Romans 2: 11; Ephesians 6: 9; Colossians 3: 25.
[18] Cf. Matthew 5: 48; 19: 12; Colossians 4: 12; James 1: 4.

of spiritual directors the noble strivings of individuals for perfection, in the forum of conscience, our concern now is with the associations which, in the eyes of the Church, in the external forum as it is called, seek earnestly to guide their own members to a life of solid perfection. We are not here concerned with all associations, which sincerely seek after Christian perfection in the world; there is question here only of those associations which, in their internal constitution, in their hierarchical form of government, in the full and unqualified dedication which they demand from their members properly so-called, in their profession of the evangelical counsels, in their manner of performing ministries and exercising the apostolate, come very close in substance to the canonical states of perfection and especially to societies without public vows,[19] though they do not practice the religious common life but follow other exterior forms of life.

Secular Institutes: Need to Legislate for Them

230   9. These associations, which henceforth shall be called " Secular Institutes," began to be founded, not without a special inspiration of divine providence, in the first half of the last century; they were founded with the object of faithfully following " the evangelical counsels in the world and to perform with greater freedom the duties of charity, which the evil conditions of the times had made difficult or impossible for religious communities." [20] The older of these Institutes gave a good account of themselves; they gave adequate concrete proof, and indeed ever-growing proof, that by the strict and prudent choice of members, by careful and sufficiently prolonged training, by adequate, firm and yet adaptable regulation of life, with the special call of God and with the aid of divine grace, there could be secured with certainty, even in the world, a consecration of oneself to God which was sufficiently strict as well as efficacious, not merely interior but exterior, and

[19] Tit. XVII.
[20] Decree *Ecclesia Catholica* of the Sacred Congregation of Bishops and Regulars, 11 August 1889 (*ASS* XXIII, p. 634).

almost equivalent to the consecration of religious; [21] it was
evident too that here was a particularly timely means of gaining
access and exercising the apostolate; for all these reasons, " these
societies of the faithful, just like true religious societies, received
the praise of the Holy See " [22] more than once.

10. The happy growth of these Institutes showed ever more
clearly how they could, in many different respects, become an
efficacious aid of the Church and of souls. To truly lead the life
of perfection at all times and places; to embrace it in many cases
where the canonical religious life was impossible or inconvenient;
to bring about the thorough Christian renewal of families,
professions and civil society, by intimate daily contact with a
life perfectly and entirely consecrated to sanctification; to
exercise a varied apostolate and to perform works of the ministry
in places, times and circumstances, to which access by priests
and religious was forbidden or impracticable—such are the
objects for which these Institutes can easily be called into
service. On the other hand, experience has shown that difficulties
and dangers sometimes were not absent, and indeed could arise
quite easily from this freely conducted life of perfection, in the
absence of the external aid of a religious habit, without the help
of a common life, and without the vigilance of the Ordinaries
(by whom indeed this way of life could easily be overlooked)
and of the superiors, who were frequently far away.

Discussions also began about the juridical nature of these
Institutes, and about the mind of the Holy See in giving approval
to them. Here we consider it opportune to make mention of
the decree *Ecclesia Catholica* which was issued by the Sacred

[21] In his Apostolic Letter to Madame Marie Stiltz, superioress general of the Society
of the Daughters of St. Francis de Sales, Pius X wrote as follows, on 13 April 1910:
" It is not given to all to become religious. Some are called to that state. All, however,
are bound to strive to reach the perfection to which God calls them. For us, who hold
here on earth the place of the eternal Pastor, it is an obligation to encourage with all
our power the Institutes which, though they are not religious Institutes, mark out for
the faithful a more dependable road for the acquiring of perfection. And consequently,
in addition to the religious life properly so-called, there have been founded Associations,
Confraternities and Third Orders. The Church shows favour to these associations, she
approves and honours them, for they are extremely useful for progress of the spiritual
life. Thanks to them and to the zeal of the faithful, souls are guided in the sure paths
that lead to salvation " (*AAS* II (1910), p. 320).

[22] Decree *Ecclesia Catholica* of the Sacred Congregation of Bishops and Regulars.

Congregation of Bishops and Regulars, and was confirmed on
11 August 1889 by our predecessor of immortal memory,
Leo XIII.[23] In that decree it was not forbidden to give a decree
of praise and approval to these Institutes; but it was specified that
the Sacred Congregation, when giving praise or approval to
these Institutes, wished to praise or approve them, not as religious
societies of solemn vows, nor as genuine religious Congregations
with simple vows, but simply as pious associations in which,
in addition to the lack of other requirements of the present-day
discipline of the Church, there is no making of religious
profession properly so-called; whatever vows be taken, if
any, are regarded as private, not public vows which are received
by a legitimate superior in the name of the Church. Moreover,
these associations, as the Sacred Congregation added, are given
praise or approval on the essential condition that they are fully
and perfectly made known to their respective Ordinaries, and
are entirely subject to their jurisdiction. These prescriptions
and declarations of the Sacred Congregation of Bishops and
Regulars made a timely contribution to the shaping of the
character of these Institutes, and guided their development and
progress without proving a hindrance.

233   11. In the present century Secular Institutes have multiplied
silently, and they have taken many quite different forms, either
autonomous or linked in various ways with religious Orders or
societies. The Apostolic Constitution *Conditae a Christo* [24]
made no provision in regard to them, as it was concerned only
with religious Congregations. The Code of Canon Law also
deliberately refrained from speaking of them, and left it to
subsequent legislation to make the required provision for them,
because the time did not yet appear to be ripe.

234   12. Having given repeated consideration to all these matters,
as our sense of duty demands, and also by reason of our paternal
love for those souls who so generously strive after sanctity in
the world; and at the same time purposing to make a wise and
strict discernment of societies, so that only those will be
recognised as genuine Institutes which make authentic profession

23 *ASS* XXIII, p. 634.
24 Cf. *supra*, nn. 7-32.

of the full life of perfection; with a view to avoiding the dangers of erecting more and more new Institutes, which not infrequently are founded imprudently and without due consideration; in order, moreover, that those Institutes, which are deserving of approval, may obtain the special juridical organization which suitably and fully meets their character, aims and circumstances, we have planned and decreed to do for Secular Institutes what our predecessor Leo XIII of immortal memory so prudently and wisely achieved for Congregations of simple vows by the Apostolic Constitution *Conditae a Christo*. And so by this Letter we approve the general statute of Secular Institutes, which had been diligently examined by the Supreme Sacred Congregation of the Holy Office insofar as it pertains to its competence, and which has been carefully drawn up and revised by the Sacred Congregation of Religious, by our order and under our direction; and by our Apostolic authority, we declare, decree and determine all that follows.

13. The foregoing having been thus constituted, we depute the Sacred Congregation of Religious to see to the carrying out of all these things in practice, and grant to it all the faculties that are necessary and opportune.

THE SPECIAL STATUTE OF SECULAR INSTITUTES

ARTICLE I

Christian societies, clerical or lay, whose members, in order to acquire Christian perfection and to exercise the apostolate fully, profess in the world the evangelical counsels, are known by the proper title of Institutes or Secular Institutes, in order to be distinguished suitably from other common associations of the faithful.[25] These Institutes are subject to the norms of this Apostolic Constitution.

235

---

[25] *CIC*, Bk. II.

ARTICLE II

236   § 1. Secular Institutes, since they do not admit the three public vows of religion,[26] and do not impose on their members the common life or residence beneath the same roof, in accordance with the canons:[27]

  1° In law, and by rule, they are not and cannot properly be called religious societies[28] or societies of the common life;[29]

  2° They are not bound by the proper and special legislation of religious societies and societies of the common life, nor can they avail themselves of this legislation, except insofar as some prescription of this legislation, especially that which applies to societies without public vows, by way of exception, shall have been legitimately adapted and applied to them.

237   § 2. Without prejudice to the general norms of canon law which concern them, Institutes are governed by the following prescriptions, representing as it were their own proper legislation, and corresponding more closely to their special character and condition:

  1° The general norms of this Apostolic Constitution, which constitute what may be called the proper statute of all Secular Institutes;

  2° The norms which the Sacred Congregation of Religious, as necessity demands and experience advises, shall have decided to issue by way of interpretation of this Apostolic Constitution, or by way of completing and applying it, for all or for some of these Institutes;

  3° The particular constitutions, approved in accordance with the articles which follow, which prudently adapt the general and particular norms of law mentioned above (1° and 2°) to the objects, requirements, and conditions—which can be very different—of the individual Institutes.

---

[26] *Ibid.*, can. 1308 § 1 and 488, 1°; cf. *supra*, n. 85.
[27] *Ibid.*, can. 487 f. (cf. *supra*, n. 76 f.) and 673 f.
[28] *Ibid.*, can. 487 and 488, 1°; cf. *supra*, nn. 76-7.
[29] *Ibid.*, can. 673 § 1.

ARTICLE III

§ 1. In order that a pious association of the faithful, in 238 accordance with the articles which follow, be capable of being erected as a Secular Institute, it must fulfil the following requirements (§§ 2-4) in addition to the other general conditions:

§ 2. In relation to consecration of life and the profession of 239 Christian perfection:

Associates, who desire to be enrolled in the Institute as members in the stricter sense, in addition to performing those exercises of piety and self-denial to which all who aspire to the perfection of the Christian life must devote themselves, are bound to strive efficaciously for this perfection by those special means also which are set out below:

1° By the profession made before God of celibacy and perfect chastity, a profession which is to be confirmed by a vow, oath or consecration binding in conscience, in accordance with the constitutions;

2° By a vow or promise of obedience, so that being bound by a stable link they may dedicate themselves wholly to God and to works of charity or of the apostolate, and be in all things under the authority and morally continuous guidance of their superiors, in accordance with the constitutions;

3° By a vow or promise of poverty, by virtue of which they have not the free use of temporal goods, but only a defined and limited use, in accordance with the constitutions.

§ 3. In relation to the incorporation of members in their 240 own institute, and the tie which arises from this incorporation: The bond between a Secular Institute and those who are strictly members should be:

1° Stable, in accordance with the constitutions, whether perpetual, or temporary and to be renewed at the end of the period; [30]

---

[30] CIC, can. 488, 1°; cf. supra, n. 77.

2° Mutual and full, so that, in accordance with the constitutions, the member gives himself completely to the Institute, and the Institute takes care of the member and is responsible for him.

241 § 4. In relation to the common residences and houses of Secular Institutes:

Secular Institutes, though they do not, in accordance with law, impose on their members a common life or residence beneath the same roof, nevertheless should, as a matter of necessity or utility, have one or more community houses, in which:

1° The superiors, especially those who hold supreme or regional authority, can reside;

2° Members can reside or come to stay, in order to receive or complete their training, or to perform spiritual exercises and for other such purposes;

3° Members can be received when, through ill-health or for other reasons, they are not able to provide for themselves, or if it is not expedient that they should reside in private either in their own home or with others.

ARTICLE IV

242 § 1. Secular Institutes shall depend on the Sacred Congregation of Religious, without prejudice to the rights of the Sacred Congregation de Propaganda Fide, in accordance with canon 252, § 3, concerning societies and seminaries destined for the service of the missions.

243 § 2. Associations which do not fulfil the definition or do not fully profess the purpose stated in Article I, and those also which lack any of the elements enumerated in Articles I and III of this Apostolic Constitution, are regulated by the law governing associations of the faithful, which are dealt with in canons 684 ff, and they depend on the Sacred Congregation of the Council, without prejudice to canon 252, § 3, in respect of mission territories.

ARTICLE V

§ **1.** Bishops, but not vicars general or vicars capitular, 244
have power to found Secular Institutes and to erect them as
moral persons, in accordance with Canon 100 §§ 1-2.

§ **2.** Bishops, however, shall not found such Institutes nor 245
allow them to be founded, without consulting the Sacred
Congregation of Religious, in accordance with canon 492, § 1
and the Article which follows.

ARTICLE VI

§ **1.** With a view to the granting by the Sacred Congregation 246
of Religious of permission to erect Institutes, to bishops who
consult it beforehand about the erection of Institutes in accordance with Article V § 2, the Congregation must be given
information on all those matters which are specified in the
Normae (nn. 3-5) given by the same Congregation for the erection
of a Congregation or society of the common life of diocesan
law, with the appropriate adaptations in accordance with the
judgment of the Congregation; it must also be informed of
other matters which have been introduced by the style and
practice of the same Sacred Congregation, or shall hereafter
be introduced.

§ **2.** When permission has been received by bishops from
the Sacred Congregation of Religious, there shall be nothing
to prevent them freely exercising their own right and proceeding
to erect the Institute. Bishops shall not omit to officially inform
the Sacred Congregation that the Institute has been erected.

ARTICLE VII

§ **1.** Secular Institutes, which have received approbation 247
or the decree of praise from the Holy See, become institutes of
pontifical law.[31]

[31] *CIC*, can. 488 § 3; 673 § 2; cf. *supra*, n. 77.

248   § **2.** In order that Institutes of diocesan law may secure the *decretum laudis* or decree of approbation, in general those requirements must be met, with the adaptations that are appropriate in the judgment of the Sacred Congregation of Religious, which are prescribed and defined in the *Normae* (nn. 6 ff) and by the style and practice of the same Sacred Congregation in regard to Congregations and societies of the common life, or may be defined in the future.

249   § **3.** The procedure for the first approval of the Institutes and their constitutions, for the further approval, if the case arises, and for the definitive approval, shall be as follows:

1° The first discussion of the case, which shall have been prepared in the usual manner and clarified by the *votum* and report of at least one consultor, shall take place in the Consultors' Commission, under the direction of the Secretary of the Sacred Congregation or of someone taking his place;

2° Next, the whole matter shall be submitted to the examination and decision of a plenary session of the Sacred Congregation, under the presidency of his Eminence the Cardinal Prefect, and, if it be considered necessary or useful, with expert or specially expert consultors invited to examine the case more thoroughly;

3° The decision of the plenary session shall be reported by the Cardinal Prefect or Secretary in an audience of the Holy Father and submitted to his supreme judgment.

Article VIII

250   Secular Institutes, in addition to their own present and future laws, are also subject to the local Ordinaries, in accordance with the existing law for non-exempt Congregations and societies of the common life.

ARTICLE IX

The internal régime of Secular Institutes, in accordance with   251
the character, aims and circumstances of the individual Institutes,
can be hierarchically arranged like the régime of religious
societies and societies of the common life, with the appropriate
adaptations in accordance with the judgment of the same
Sacred Congregation.

ARTICLE X

No change is made by this Apostolic Constitution in relation   252
to the rights and obligations of Institutes, which are already
founded and have been approved by bishops, after consultation
with the Holy See, or have been approved by the Holy See itself.

These provisions we publish, declare and sanction, and we
also decree that this Apostolic Constitution is and shall be firm,
valid and effective, and that it has and obtains its full and entire
effects, any contrary provisions notwithstanding, even those
worthy of most special mention. No one may, therefore,
violate this Constitution promulgated by us, or rashly oppose it.

Given in Rome, at Saint Peter's, 2 February, feast of the
Purification of Our Lady, 1947, the eighth year of our pontificate.

ENCYCLICAL LETTER "FULGENS RADIATUR" FOR THE FOURTEENTH CENTENARY OF THE DEATH OF ST. BENEDICT

21 March 1947

EXTRACTS

On the occasion of the fourteenth centenary of the death of St. Benedict, Pope Pius XII recalled the characteristics of the rule of the patriarch of the West and the achievement of the Order founded by him; the world still stands in need of these services. [1]

253 **Wisdom of the Benedictine rule.** Thus those special and particular norms and precepts of the eremetical life, which previously, for the most part, were not strictly defined and codified, but frequently depended on the will of the coenobiarch, gave way to the Benedictine monastic rule; this rule is an outstanding achievement of Roman and Christian wisdom, in which the rights, duties and functions of monks are regulated by evangelical kindness and charity; it has been and still is a highly efficacious means of arousing many to the pursuit of virtue and progress in holiness.

254 For in this Benedictine rule, supreme prudence is allied with simplicity, and Christian humility goes with generous courage; gentleness tempers severity, and healthy freedom ennobles the obedience which is demanded. In it correction is characterized by firmness, but forbearance and kindness impart the gentleness that attracts; precepts are strictly binding, but obedience gives quiet to minds and peace to souls; the solemnity of silence is pleasing, but conversation is graced by a sweet charm; while the force of authority is not lacking, weakness is not left without support. [2]

[1] *AAS* XXXIX (1947), pp. 137-155.
[2] Cf. Bossuet, *Panégyrique de saint Benoît*, Oeuvres Complètes, Vol. XII, Paris, 1863, p. 165.

We cannot be surprised, therefore, that " the monastic rule, of remarkable discretion and clarity of expression, which Benedict, the man of God, wrote," [3] nowadays receives the highest praise from all men of wisdom; and it gives us pleasure here to outline briefly and place in clear light the essential features of that rule, for we are confident that this will give satisfaction and prove useful, not only to the very numerous family of the saintly patriarch, but also to others of the clergy and Christian people.

The monastic community is so constituted and organized that   255 it is comparable with a Christian household; the abbot, or coenobiarch, presides over it, as the father of a family, and all are bound to be subject entirely to his paternal authority. Benedict said: " We consider it expedient, in order to safeguard peace and charity, that the regulation of the monastery should depend on the will of the abbot." [4] Consequently each and everyone is bound to obey him scrupulously as a duty of conscience, [5] and to see and respect in him the authority of God himself. Anyone however who, in virtue of the function entrusted to him, has undertaken to rule the souls of monks and to stimulate them to evangelical perfection of life, shall diligently reflect and consider that one day he will be obliged to render an account for them to the Supreme Judge; [6] and hence in this extremely grave charge he shall so conduct himself that he will be awarded the just reward, when " in the fearsome judgment of God, the accounting will take place." [7] Moreover, whenever very important matters are to be dealt with in the monastery, he shall summon all the members, and he shall listen to and carefully weigh their advice, freely given, before reaching the decision which to him appears best. [8]

. . . It is easy to discern and to appreciate in these principal   256 norms and doctrines, which serve as a sample of the Benedictine rule, not only the prudence and opportuneness of that monastic

---

[3] St. Gregory, *Lib. Dial.*, II, 36 (*PL*, LXVI, 200).
[4] *Rule of St. Benedict*, c. 65.
[5] *Ibid.*, c. 3.
[6] *Ibid.*, c. 2.
[7] *Ibid.*, c. 2.
[8] *Ibid.*, c. 3.

9

rule, and its wonderful correspondence and harmony with man's nature, but also its importance and supreme dignity. For in that dark and turbulent era, when agriculture, the arts and crafts, literary pursuits and studies, sacred and profane, were held of no account and were unhappily neglected by nearly all, within the Benedictine monasteries, on the other hand, an almost countless number of farmers, artisans and learned men constantly grew up; these men not only did all in their power to preserve intact the memorials of ancient learning, but also established peace and concord between the nations, old and new, which frequently were engaged in war with one another, and recalled them to industrious pursuits; they rescued them from renascent barbarism, from devastation and disasters, and happily brought them back to the gentleness of Christian and civilized conduct, to patient toil, to the light of truth, to the restoration of civilized relations, in conformity with the demands of wisdom and charity.

257   And that was not all: for a vital element in the Benedictine way of life is that all, whether they are engaged in manual or intellectual labour, should each make it the principal aim and the object of their striving, constantly to turn themselves to Christ and to be on fire with the most perfect love of him. For indeed earthly things, even the whole of the world's goods, are incapable of satisfying the human soul which God has created to reach himself; rather is it true that these earthly things have from their creator the function of moving and turning us to reach God, as it were by successive steps, until we possess him. Consequently, it is vital above all that "the love of Christ be given the first place"; [9] "that nothing be deemed dearer to one than Christ"; "that nothing whatsoever be preferred to Christ, who leads us to eternal life." [10]

258   This burning love for the divine Redeemer must be accompanied by charity for our neighbours, all of whom we should embrace as brethren and assist them by every means. Therefore, while hatred and rivalries provoke and drive men to conflict; and while robbery, murder and countless miseries and afflictions flow

[9] *Ibid.*, c. 4.
[10] *Ibid.*, c. 72.

from the disorder and agitation of peoples and conditions, Benedict lays down for his followers these saintly precepts: " The most solicitous care is to be devoted to hospitality for the poor and pilgrims especially, for it is rather Christ who is received in their persons "; [11] " all guests who come are to be received as Christ himself, because he will say one day: *I was a stranger and you took me in* "; [12] " above and before all, care must be taken of the sick, in order to serve them as Christ himself, because he said: *I was sick and you visited me.*" [13]

The beneficent influence of the Benedictine Order. . . . The immense influence for good 259 which the power and efficacy of the Benedictine institute exercised upon that first period, and the countless great benefits which it conferred even upon subsequent centuries, must be recognized by all who study and rightly evaluate the course of human events without prejudice, on the basis of historical truth and with sound judgment. For in addition to the fact, already mentioned, that the Benedictines, throughout that dark age, in the midst of ignorance and general ruin, were practically alone in preserving learned manuscripts and literary works, which they carefully transcribed and explained, they were also among the first to cultivate the arts, sciences and teaching, which they promoted with all their power.

. . . Indeed, just as in a former age the Roman legions 260 marched forth upon the consular roads, striving to bring all nations under the rule of the Eternal City, so also at this period countless battalions of monks, whose weapons are *not carnal, but powerful unto God*,[14] were despatched by the supreme Pontiff, in order to spread effectively to the very ends of the earth the peaceful kingdom of Jesus Christ, not by the sword, or violence or slaughter, but by the Cross and the plough, by truth and charity.

Wherever these unarmed battalions, consisting of heralds of the Christian religion, of artisans, farmers and teachers of the sciences, human and divine, set their feet, there the un-

[11] *Ibid.*, c. 53.   [12] *Ibid.*, c. 53.   [13] *Ibid.*, c. 36.
[14] II Corinthians 10: 4.

cultivated forest lands were brought under the plough; centres of crafts and arts arose; men were raised up from their savage and rude way of life and trained to civilized social intercourse, while the living example of the teaching and virtue of the Gospel shone before their eyes.

261   Countless apostles, burning with heavenly charity, travelled through the unknown and turbulent regions of Europe; they watered these lands with their sweat and the generous sacrifice of their blood, and when the inhabitants had been pacified, they brought to them the light of Catholic truth and sanctity . . .

Indeed, not only Britain, Gaul, The Netherlands, Friesland, Denmark, Germany, Pannonia and Scandinavia, but many also of the Slav countries, take pride in the fact that they were evangelized by these monks; they look to them as their proud boast and the illustrious founders of their civilization.

262   From the Benedictine Order how many bishops have come, men who ruled existing dioceses with wisdom, or who founded not a few new dioceses, and by their labours in them produced a fruitful harvest! How many masters and distinguished scholars, who established celebrated seats of studies and of the liberal arts, and not only brought enlightenment to countless minds clouded by errors, but in general contributed to the progress of learning, both sacred and profane.

And finally, how many who were outstanding for shining sanctity, who, when adopted into the Benedictine family, strove for evangelical perfection with all their powers, and by the example of their virtue, by their preaching and the wonderful signs they performed by God's gracious favour, spread the kingdom of Jesus Christ by every means! Very many of these, as you well know, venerable brethren, were either clothed in the episcopal dignity or even shone with the majesty of the supreme pontificate. It would be too long to recount individually each of these apostles, saints and supreme pontiffs, whose names are written in letters of gold in the annals of the Church; and in fact, such is the splendour of these names, so great is their importance in the course of history, that they easily come to the minds of all.

. . . It is not only past ages which are 263
Abiding actuality of the Benedictine Order. indebted for innumerable benefits to this patriarch and the institute which he founded; our own age too can learn many important lessons from him. First of all, as indeed we believe to be the case, the members of the great Benedictine family shall learn to follow with ever greater zeal his splendid example, and to give effect, each in his own life, to the principles and the models of his virtue and sanctity. For thus surely it will come to pass that they will whole-heartedly give the response of fruitful conduct, which is appropriate to that heavenly call which they followed, led by a divine inspiration, when they entered the monastic life; not only that, but they will secure for themselves serene peace of conscience and make excellent provision for their eternal salvation; and they will also be able to make a fruitful contribution to the general welfare of the Christian people and to the promotion of the glory of God.

Moreover, citizens of every rank of society, if they meditate 264 attentively on the life of St. Benedict, and upon his precepts and splendid achievements, cannot fail to be moved by his gentle inspiration and powerful influence; they will see for themselves that even our age, with all its grave material and moral calamities, with the dangers and losses that have brought disorder and anxiety, can look to him for the necessary remedies. Above all, let them bear in mind and give deep consideration to the truth that the sacred principles of religion, and the laws of conduct which it lays down, are the most dependable and solid foundations of human society; if they be overthrown or weakened, it is inevitable that there will be a gradual collapse of everything that pertains to right order, to peace and to the prosperity of citizens and nations.

A distinguished mind of the ancient pagan world had already discerned this truth which, as we have seen, the history of the Benedictine Order places in such clear light: " You, the pontiffs, . . . more effectively protect the city by religion, than by the very walls that surround it." [15] The same author said: " . . .

---

[15] Cicero, *De natura deorum*, II, c. 40.

when they (sanctity and religion) are set aside, the consequences are disorder of life and great confusion; and I wonder whether, if piety towards the gods disappears, loyalty also and the fellowship of human society, and justice, the most excellent of virtues, will not also vanish." [16]

265   The first and principal duty, therefore, is this: to reverence the supreme God, and to submit to his most sacred laws both in private and in public; if they be disregarded, no human power can exercise control sufficient to keep in check and moderate the passions and desires aroused in the hearts of man. For religion alone constitutes the foundation of what is just and good.

266   There is still another lesson taught by the saintly patriarch, and it gives advice which this our age sadly needs: God is not only to be honoured and worshipped, but is to be loved as a father, with ardent charity. Nowadays this charity has unfortunately grown cold and listless, with the result that there are many who strive for earthly things rather than heavenly; and this striving is so immoderate that frequently it leads to disorders, and stirs up rivalries and bitter hatred. But, inasmuch as the eternal God is the author of our life, and since countless benefits are bestowed on us by him, it is the duty of all to love him with supreme love, and to turn and direct to him in the first place ourselves and all that is ours.

267   And from this love of God should spring that fraternal charity for men, all of whom, of whatever race, nation or social class, we must hold as our brothers in Christ; thus from all nations and from all classes of society will be formed a single Christian family, which will not be divided by the excessive seeking of their own advantage by individuals, but will rather be united by the amicable exchange of practical aid.

268   These are the precepts, which of old inspired Benedict so that he enlightened, restored, heartened, and raised the moral standards of the decadent and troubled society of his time; if nowadays they were generally adopted and in force, undoubtedly our age too would more easily be able to escape from such a fearful catastrophe, to repair the material and moral damage and bring effective and timely remedies to bear on its immense evils.

[16] *Ibid.*, I, c. 2.

The lawgiver and founder of the Benedictine Order teaches   269
us another truth, venerable brethren—a truth which nowadays
men like to proclaim aloud, but all too frequently it is not put
into practice as it should—namely that man's labour is not
something devoid of dignity, something hateful and troublesome,
but rather something to be loved, something honourable and
joyful.

The life of labour, whether it be exercised by the tilling of the
fields, by gainful occupation or by intellectual pursuits, does
not debase but ennoble men; it does not reduce them to
slavery, but rather makes men the masters and controllers of
their environment and of the things on which they toil. Jesus
himself, as a youth, while still living in obscurity within the
walls of the home, did not disdain the carpenter's trade in the
workshop of his foster-father; he willed to consecrate human
toil by the sweat of his divine person.

Let everyone reflect, therefore, not merely those who study
literature and the sciences, but those too who toil in manual
occupations in order to secure their daily bread, that they are
engaged in a noble occupation, whereby they can provide not
merely for their own needs but also serve the good of all society.
But, as the patriarch Benedict admonishes, they shall act with
mind and heart raised to heaven; they shall labour not by
compulsion but by love; and finally, even when defending their
lawful rights, they shall not act with envy of the lot of others,
they shall not proceed with disorders and tumult, but calmly
and with right order. They shall always remember the divine
words: *In the sweat of thy brow thou shalt eat bread*; [17] that is a
precept to be observed by all men as a matter of obedience and
expiation.

This above all they shall constantly remember: each day we   270
must make even greater efforts to rise above earthly and passing
things—whether they be matters of keen intellectual study and
research, or things handled in laborious toil—and strive for the
heavenly things which abide for ever; it is only when we have
attained these that we shall be able to enjoy true peace, serene
rest and eternal happiness.

[17] Genesis 3: 19.

MOTU PROPRIO "PRIMO FELICITER"

12 March 1948

A year after the promulgation of the Apostolic Constitution Provida Mater,[1] *the supreme Pontiff felt obliged to give precise indications about the " secular " character of the Institutes which bear this title.*[2]

271   Now that the first year since the promulgation of our Apostolic Constitution *Provida Mater Ecclesia* has happily run its course, having before our mind the great multitude of souls hidden *with Christ in God*,[3] who in the world aspire to sanctity and gladly consecrate their whole life to God *with great heart and willing mind*[4] in the new Secular Institutes, we cannot refrain from giving thanks to the divine goodness, for this new phalanx, which has reinforced the army of those who profess the evangelical counsels in the world; we give thanks too for this powerful aid which has providentially strengthened the Catholic apostolate in these disturbed and calamitous times.

272   The Holy Spirit, who unceasingly re-creates and renews the face of the earth,[5] which is daily ravaged and defiled by so many great evils, has called to himself, by a great and special grace, a great number of beloved men and women, to whom we lovingly impart our blessing in the Lord; for the world to which they do not belong[6] and in which nevertheless by God's disposition they are to remain, these, brought together and organized in Secular Institutes, are called to be the unfailing salt which, with its power renewed by their vocation, does not lose its savour;[7] they are to be the light which, even amidst the world's darkness, gives light and is not extinguished;[8] they are to be that small but efficacious leaven which, working at all times and places and mingling in every class of society, from the

[1] Cf. *supra*, nn. 220-252.
[2] *AAS* XL (1948), pp. 283-286.
[3] Colossians 3: 3.
[4] II Maccabees 1: 3.
[5] Cf. Psalm 103: 30.
[6] Cf. John 15: 19.
[7] Cf. Matthew 5: 13; Mark 9: 49; Luke 14: 34.
[8] Cf. John 1: 5; 8: 12; 9: 5; Ephesians 5: 8.

lowest to the highest, endeavours by word, example and every means, to reach and permeate each and every one, until it so transforms the entire mass of men that it will be wholly leavened in Christ.[9]

To ensure that the numerous Institutes, which have arisen everywhere as a result of this consoling pouring forth of the Spirit of Jesus Christ, will be effectively directed in accordance with the norms of the Apostolic Constitution *Provida Mater Ecclesia*, and that they will yield the abundant harvest of holiness which is hoped for; and likewise, in order to secure that, like an army solidly and skilfully drawn up in battle array,[10] they will be able to fight valiantly the battles of the Lord in the special and general activities of the apostolate, we have great joy in confirming the afore-mentioned Apostolic Constitution, and after mature deliberation, motu proprio, with certain knowledge and in virtue of the fullness of Apostolic authority, we declare, decree and order the following: 273

I. Societies, either of clerics or of lay persons, which profess Christian perfection in the world, if they are found to possess certainly and fully the elements and requisites prescribed in the Apostolic Constitution *Provida Mater Ecclesia*, should not and cannot be arbitrarily left among the ordinary associations of the faithful,[11] on any pretext whatsoever; they must necessarily be brought into line with and raised to the nature and form proper to Secular Institutes, which is eminently in accord with their character and needs.   274

II. In this elevation of societies of the faithful to the higher form of Secular Institutes [12] and in carrying through the organization, whether general or particular, of all Institutes, it is always to be borne in mind that the proper and special character of these Institutes, namely their *secular* character, in which lies their entire *raison d'être*, must be made clear in every respect. There shall be no curtailment of the full profession of Christian perfection, solidly based on the evangelical counsels and truly   275

---

[9] Matthew 13: 33; I Corinthians 5: 6; Galatians 5: 9.
[10] Cf. Canticle 6: 3.
[11] *CIC*, canon 684-725.
[12] Cf. N. 1.

religious in substance, but the practice and profession of
perfection is to be *in the world*; it is a perfection, therefore,
which must be adapted to life in the world in everything which
is lawful and which is compatible with the duties and activities
of this perfection.

The entire life of members of Secular Institutes, since it has
been consecrated to God by the profession of perfection, should
be made an apostolate; this apostolate should be performed
steadfastly and piously, with such purity of intention, intimate
union with God, generous selflessness and courageous self-denial,
and love of souls, as not only to reveal the interior spirit which
animates it, but also to nourish and renew that spirit ceaselessly.
This apostolate, which embraces the entire life, is constantly
so deeply and sincerely felt in these Institutes, that, by the aid
and counsel of divine providence, an ardent thirst for souls
appears happily not only to have been the occasion of this consecration of life, but to a great extent also has determined their
specific character and form; and it is indeed remarkable how
their specific aim, as it is called, seems to have demanded and
created the generic aim also. This apostolate of Secular Institutes
must be faithfully carried on, not merely *in the world*, but also,
so to speak, *from the world*, and, consequently, through the
professions, activities, forms, places and conditions corresponding
to this secular condition.

276   III. The prescriptions concerning the canonical discipline of
the religious state are not applicable to Secular Institutes, and
in general the legislation for religious should not and cannot
be applied to them, as the Apostolic Constitution *Provida Mater
Ecclesia* [13] prescribes. On the other hand, whatever features in
the Institutes are found to be harmoniously combined with their
secular character, provided they do not in any way present an
obstacle to the full consecration of the entire life and are in
harmony with the Constitution *Provida Mater Ecclesia*, may be
retained.

277   IV. A hierarchical, interdiocesan and universal constitution,
modelled on the organic body, can be applied to Secular

---

[13] Art. II, § 1.

Institutes,[14] and this application should undoubtedly give them internal strength, together with a wider and more effective exterior influence and stability. However, in this work of organization, which must be adapted to each individual Institute, account must be taken of the nature of the end which the Institute aims at, of its intention to expand on a larger or smaller scale, of the degree of development and maturity which the Institute has reached, of the circumstances in which it finds itself, and of other matters of this kind. Nor are those forms of Institute to be rejected or despised, which are established in a confederation and wish to retain and moderately encourage their local character in individual nations, regions and dioceses, provided that this local character is lawful and permeated by the sense of the catholicity of the Church.

V. Secular Institutes, even though their members live in the 278 world, by reason nevertheless of that full consecration to God and to souls which, with the approval of the Church, they profess, and also by reason of the hierarchical, interdiocesan and universal organization which they can have in various degrees, are rightly and deservedly classed among the states of perfection juridically organized and recognized by the Church herself, in virtue of the Apostolic Constitution *Provida Mater Ecclesia*. It was designedly, therefore, that the Institutes were assigned and entrusted to the competence and care of that Sacred Congregation which is responsible for the régime and care of the *public states of perfection*.

Consequently, while always safeguarding, in accordance with the tenor of the canons and the express prescription of the Apostolic Constitution *Provida Mater Ecclesia*,[15] the rights of the Sacred Congregation of the Council over ordinary pious sodalities and pious unions of the faithful [16] and the rights of the Congregation de Propaganda Fide over societies of ecclesiastics and seminaries for foreign missions,[17] we have decreed that all societies everywhere, even those which have ordinary or even

---

[14] *Provida Mater Ecclesia*, Art. IX.
[15] *Ibid.*, Art. IV, §§ 1-2.
[16] *CIC*, canon 250, § 2.
[17] *Ibid.*, canon 252, § 3.

pontifical approval, when they are recognized to have the elements and requisites which are proper to Secular Institutes, must necessarily and immediately be brought into line with this new form, in accordance with the norms already enunciated;[18] and also, in order to safeguard unity of direction, that they should rightly be assigned and entrusted exclusively to the Sacred Congregation of Religious, within which a special office for Secular Institutes has been set up.

279   VI. We paternally commend to directors and assistants of Catholic Action and of other associations of the faithful, within which training for a life that is integrally Christian and, at the same time, an initiation into the exercise of the apostolate, is given to so many élite youth who have received a heavenly calling to higher things, either in religious Orders and societies of the common life or even in Secular Institutes, to give generous encouragement to these saintly vocations; we ask too that they should give a helping hand, not only to religious Orders and societies, but also to these genuinely providential Secular Institutes, and gladly to make use of their assistance, without prejudice to their internal discipline.

By our authority we commit the faithful execution of all these things, which we have laid down motu proprio, to the Sacred Congregation of Religious and to the other above-mentioned Sacred Congregations, to local Ordinaries and directors of societies whom it concerns, each in so far as the decrees affect him.

The prescriptions which we enact by this Letter, issued motu proprio, we command that they are to be perpetually valid and firm, notwithstanding anything whatsoever to the contrary.

Given in Rome, at St. Peter's, 12 March 1948, at the beginning of the tenth year of our pontificate.

---

[18] Cf. N. 1.

INSTRUCTION " CUM SANCTISSIMUS " OF THE SACRED CONGREGATION OF RELIGIOUS ON SECULAR INSTITUTES

19 March 1948

The Sacred Congregation of Religious was empowered by the Apostolic Constitution Provida Mater Ecclesia *to regulate Secular Institutes; here it gives new precise directives, which were intended to prevent from the outset any kind of misunderstanding or erroneous interpretation.*[1]

When the Holy Father promulgated the Apostolic Constitution *Provida Mater Ecclesia*,[2] he graciously deputed the Sacred Congregation of Religious, to whose competence Secular Institutes are entrusted, to ensure the more effective execution of all the wise provisions of the Constitution, granting to it all the faculties necessary and useful for this purpose. 280

Among the functions and duties which, in consequence of this pontifical delegation, are incumbent on the Sacred Congregation, as the Constitution expressly states, it is to be noted that, " as necessity demands and experience advises . . . either by way of interpretation of the Apostolic Constitution or by way of completing and applying it,"[3] the Congregation is empowered to issue norms which are deemed necessary or useful, either for Secular Institutes generally, or for some of them in particular.

Now, though it is preferable to postpone complete and definitive norms relating to Secular Institutes to a more opportune time, lest the present-day development of these Institutes should be dangerously restricted, it is advisable nevertheless that certain matters, which were not clearly grasped and rightly interpreted by all in the Apostolic Constitution *Provida Mater Ecclesia*, should immediately be clarified and ensured against error, in 281

---

[1] *AAS* XL (1948), pp. 293-297.
[2] Cf. *supra*, nn. 220-252.
[3] Cf. *supra*, n. 237.

the strictest compliance with the prescriptions laid down by the Holy Father in the Letter *Primo Feliciter*, issued motu proprio on the 12th day of this month.[4]

282   Consequently, the Sacred Congregation has decided to issue, in the form of an Instruction, a clearly ordered collection of the principal norms which are rightly to be regarded as fundamental, if Secular Institutes are to be solidly established and organized from the beginning.

283   1°—In order that an association, even one intensely dedicated to the profession of Christian perfection and to the exercise of the apostolate in the world, qualify for the right to assume the name and title of *Secular Institute*, it must have not only each and every one of the elements which, in accordance with the Apostolic Constitution *Provida Mater Ecclesia*, are listed and defined as necessary and integral parts of Secular Institutes; [5] it is also absolutely essential that it should be approved and erected by a bishop, this Sacred Congregation having first been consulted. [6]

284   2°—All associations of the faithful, which have the character and qualities described in the Apostolic Constitution, are everywhere, by law, in accordance with that Constitution, dependent on this Sacred Congregation of Religious, whether in territories of common law or in mission territories; [7] they are subject to the special statute of the Constitution, and they may not, for any reason or on any title, according to the Letter *Primo Feliciter*, remain among the ordinary associations of the faithful, without prejudice to the prescription n. 5 of this Instruction.

285   3°—To secure permission for the erection of a new Secular Institute, the bishop of the place, and no one else, should approach this Sacred Congregation, giving a clear exposition of all the matters laid down in the norms issued by the Sacred Congregation of Religious [8] for the erection and approbation

---

[4] Cf. *supra*, nn. 271-279.
[5] Art. I and III; cf. *supra*, nn. 235 and 238-41.
[6] Art. V, § 2, art. VI; cf. *supra*, nn. 245-6.
[7] Art. IV, §§ 1 and 2; cf. *supra* 242-3.
[8] 6 March 1921, 3-8 (*AAS* XIII (1921), pp. 312-319).

of Congregations, with however the adaptations appropriate to the circumstances.[9]

Drafts of the constitutions (at least six copies) are also to be sent, drawn up in Latin or another language accepted in the Curia, and in addition directories and other documents which can help to an understanding of the character and spirit of the association. The constitutions should contain all those matters which have reference to the nature of the Institute, the categories of members, the régime, the form of consecration,[10] the bond which arises from incorporation of members into the Institute,[11] the community houses,[12] the method of training members and the exercises of piety.

4°—Associations which, before the Constitution *Provida Mater Ecclesia*, had been lawfully erected or approved by bishops, in accordance with the earlier legislation, or which had obtained some form of pontifical approbation as lay associations, in order to qualify for recognition by this Sacred Congregation as Secular Institutes, either of diocesan law or pontifical law, must forward to the Sacred Congregation documentary evidence of their erection or approval, the constitutions by which they have hitherto been ruled, a brief account of their history, discipline and apostolate, and also, especially if they are of diocesan law only, testimonies of the Ordinaries in whose dioceses they have houses. When all these have been considered and attentively examined, in accordance with Articles VI and VII of the Constitution *Provida Mater Ecclesia*, the permission for erection or decree of praise may be granted, as the circumstances of the case indicate. | 286

5°—As for associations which were recently founded, or are insufficiently developed, and those also which are constantly making their appearance, even though they give good ground for hope that, all going well, they will grow into solid and genuine Secular Institutes, it will be more advisable that they should not immediately be submitted to the Sacred Congregation with a view to securing from it permission to erect | 287

---

[9] Art. VII; cf. *supra*, nn. 247-9. [10] Art. III, § 2; cf. *supra*, n. 239.
[11] Art. III, § 3; cf. *supra*, n. 240. [12] Art. III, § 4; cf. *supra*, n. 241.

them. As a general rule, which shall not admit of exception save for grave causes that are strictly established, these new associations, until such time as they have sufficiently proved themselves, shall be kept and exercised under the paternal rule and protection of the diocesan authority, at first as mere associations, which have an existence in fact rather than in law; then, according to the circumstances, they are to be developed under some one of the forms of associations of the faithful, such as a pious union, sodality or confraternity, not all at once but step by step and by degrees.

288   6°—During these preliminary developments (n. 5), which must furnish clear proof that the associations in question have as their purpose complete consecration to the life of perfection and to the apostolate, and moreover that they possess all the characteristics required in a true Secular Institute, it must be carefully seen to that nothing is allowed to these associations, interiorly or exteriorly, that goes beyond their actual present status, and that would appear to correspond to the specific character and nature of Secular Institutes. Those things especially are to be avoided which, if permission for erection into a Secular Institute is subsequently refused, could not easily be withdrawn or annulled, and which might seem to bring a certain pressure to bear on superiors to grant approval or to grant it too readily.

289   7°—To form a safe practical judgment on the question whether an association has the true nature of a Secular Institute, namely whether it efficaciously leads its members in their secular state and secular condition to that complete consecration and dedication which, even in the external forum, is an image of the complete state of perfection and, in substance, of the true religious state, the following points are to be carefully weighed:

290   (a) Do those associates, who are listed as members in the strict sense of the association, " in addition to performing those exercises of piety and self-denial " without which the life of perfection can only be described as a vain illusion, also profess practically and solidly the

three general evangelical counsels, in one of the different forms which the Apostolic Constitution admits? [13] Associates who aspire to evangelical perfection and strive to practise it in their own condition, even though they do not embrace each of the evangelical counsels at a higher level or are unable to do so, can be admitted as members in the wider sense of the term, and as incorporated into the association more or less effectively or by intention;

(b) Whether the bond, which mutually binds members strictly so-called and the association, is *stable, mutual* and *full*, in such a manner that, in accordance with the Constitution, the member gives himself wholly to the association and the association is already such, or gives serious grounds for the belief, that it will be capable and willing to take care of the member and take responsibility for him? [14]   291

(c) Whether and in what manner or by what title the association actually holds or is seeking to acquire the community houses, which are prescribed in the Apostolic Constitution,[15] in order to attain the aims for which these houses are organised?   292

(d) Are those things being avoided, which would be out of harmony with the nature and purpose of Secular Institutes, for example, the wearing of a habit which does not correspond with the secular condition, a common life exteriorly organized [16] after the manner of religious common life, or of something equivalent to religious life? [17]   293

8°—Secular Institutes, in accordance with Article II, § 1, 2° of the Apostolic Constitution *Provida Mater Ecclesia*, and without prejudice to Article X and Article II, § 1, 1° of the same Constitution, are not bound by the legislation that is   294

[13] Art. III, § 2.
[14] Art. III, § 3, 2°; cf. *supra*, n. 240.
[15] Art. III, § 4, cf. *supra*, n. 241.
[16] Art. II, § 1; art. III, § 4; cf. *supra*, nn. 236 and 241
[17] *CIC*, Bk. II, Tit. XVII, canons 673-681.

10

proper and special to religious societies or societies of the common life, and they cannot have recourse to that legislation. The Sacred Congregation, however, by way of exception, in accordance with the tenor of the Constitution,[18] can accommodate and apply to Secular Institutes certain individual prescriptions of the legislation for religious that are appropriate to them; it can also prudently draw upon that legislation for certain criteria of a more or less general character, that are proved by experience and that correspond to the intimate nature of things.

295   9°—In particular:

(a) Although the prescriptions of canon 500, § 3 [19] strictly do not refer to Secular Institutes, nor should they be applied to them as they stand, nevertheless one may rightly deduce from them a solid criterion and a clear directive for the approbation and organization of Secular Institutes.

296   (b) There is no obstacle, arising from canon law [20], to prevent Secular Institutes, as a special concession, from being aggregated to religious Orders and other religious societies also, and being entitled to derive assistance from them in various ways, and even, in a certain fashion, being directed by them morally; nevertheless, it is only with difficulty, after attentive consideration of the good of the Institutes, and careful weighing of the spirit, nature and purpose of the apostolate to which they are bound to devote themselves, and with appropriate precautions, that other forms of more strict dependence can be allowed, which might appear to interfere with the autonomy of the government of Secular Institutes and subject them to a more or less strict guardianship, even though these forms should be desired and sought by the Institutes themselves, especially by Institutes of women.

---

[18] Art. II, § 1, 2°; cf. *supra*, nn. 236-7.   [19] Cf. *supra*, n. 86.
[20] Cf. *CIC*, canon 492, § 1; cf. *supra*, n. 78.

10°—Secular Institutes, 297

(a) by reason of the state of complete perfection which they profess, and because of the total consecration to the apostolate which they impose, are obviously called to greater achievements, within this same kind of perfection and apostolate, than would be regarded as sufficient for the faithful, even the very best of them, who labour In merely lay associations or in Catholic Action or other pious works;

(b) they should however undertake the exercises of the apostolate and special ministries, which constitute the special ends of these Institutes, in such a way that their members—all confusion being carefully avoided—will be able, according to their powers, to give an outstanding example of disinterested, humble and constant collaboration with the hierarchy, to the other faithful who see and observe them, always without prejudice to their own interior discipline.[21]

11°— 298

(a) When the Ordinary, having obtained the permission of the Holy See, performs the erection of a Secular Institute, which had previously existed as an association *de facto* or as a pious union or sodality, he can decide whether it is expedient, for the purpose of determining the situation of persons and meeting the conditions required in the constitutions of the Institute, to take account of what has already been done, for example, probation, consecration, etc.

(b) In the first ten years of a Secular Institute, the years 299 to be counted from its erection, the bishop of the place can dispense from the requirements of age, time of probations, years of consecration and other similar matters, which are prescribed generally for all Institutes or for an individual Institute, with a view to offices, duties, grades and other juridical effects.

[21] Motu Proprio *Primo Feliciter*, VI; cf. n. 279.

300   (c) Houses or centres, which were founded before the
canonical erection of the Institute, provided they
were established with the permission of both bishops,
in accordance with canon 495, § 1,[22] become part of
the Institute by the very fact of its erection.

---

[22] Cf. *supra*, n. 81.

ALLOCUTION TO THE CLERICS REGULAR
OF THE MOTHER OF GOD
ON THE OBJECTS OF THE CATHOLIC SCHOOL

22 November 1948

EXTRACTS

The Holy Father took advantage of the occasion of the third centenary of the beatification of St. Joseph Calasanctius, patron of all popular Christian schools, to extol the mission of the teaching brother, and to recall the abiding importance of the Christian school.[1]

Tribute to the obscure teaching brother. . . . But we recall with particular appreciation and affection the "unknown" teaching brother, all those members of your Institute who by their unpretentious toil, all too often but little esteemed by the world, have formed thousands and thousands of children to knowledge and to every religious and civic virtue. 301

This is a very high ideal, for its supreme object is the supernatural formation, and consequently the eternal destiny, of the pupils entrusted to your care; it is moreover a far-reaching ideal, because its aim is to fashion here on this earth men who are above reproach for their intellectual, moral, scientific, social and artistic culture, in accordance with the condition, the capacities and the legitimate aspirations of each individual, in such a way that none of them will become a discard or misfit; and, on the other hand, that none will see closed to him the way which leads to the very heights.

That is a magnificent and saintly undertaking; in the teachers, it demands the gifts of judgment and tact which equip them 302

[1] This Allocution did not appear in the *AAS*. The original Italian text was published in *Discorsi e Radiomessagi di Sua Santita Pio XII*, vol. X (1948-9), pp. 285-289. On 12 July 1948, the Holy Father had sent, in connection with this centenary, an Apostolic Letter to Rev. Fr. Tomek, Superior General of the Clerics Regular of the Mother of God (*AAS* XL (1948), pp. 369-371). 301a

with the capacity to impart to each and every pupil, in the matter of knowledge that is both solid and deep, what is appropriate to him; it also calls for the art of moulding and adapting their instruction to the intelligence and capacity of the young pupils; above all it pre-supposes dedication, love and, within the measure of their powers, a holy enthusiasm, which arouses the spontaneous interest of the pupils and stimulates their eagerness for work.

303   Where then will you find this treasury of higher pedagogy, of which you have need? It is in your own interior spiritual life, in prayer, in study, to put it in a word, in the exact and faithful practice of those duties of your state, which your saintly founder has inculcated by his example, by the constitutions which he prescribed, and by his wonderful letters, which filial love, combined with careful and exact scholarship, has placed or will very soon place in your hands. From this incomparable teacher you will learn ever more perfectly what you have to know and to do and how to do it, what you have to suffer and how you are to imitate his magnanimity in sufferings; because education is above all a work of love and is the great school of love and of the Cross.

304   **Obligation of pupils to co-operate with teachers.** . . . You, therefore, who are growing up in the atmosphere of the schools of Joseph Calasanctius, you certainly cannot go every day to school, study diligently your lessons, perform conscientiously the tasks assigned, merely because you are obliged to do so, or even merely to enrich your minds with ever wider learning, and to refine your intelligence by exercise and culture, so as to assure yourselves of a becoming condition of life.

305   No; over and above these just and proper aims, education has the higher purpose of forming and perfecting in you the Christian who is worthy of his natural and supernatural character, one who is useful to society, whatever may be the office for which providence destines him. But, in order to fashion such men, have you ever given thought to the toil, the weary labour, the complete and continuous self-denial, to which your

teachers and professors must submit themselves? Do you realize
how much it costs them, they who love you as they do, to impose
on themselves the obligation of a work, which may indeed be
gladly undertaken, but is certainly austere, and the observance
of the discipline which although gentle is also strict? The
work of formation inevitably implies some restrictions. Now,
the restriction of discipline can be either submitted to with a
bad grace, or willingly accepted, or even generously and gladly
embraced by yourselves in filial collaboration with those who
are educating you. It is to such a collaboration that the pedagogy
of St. Joseph Calasanctius calls you, not only in your intellectual
studies, whether profane or religious, but also in your moral
and supernatural training; in this latter sphere there is question for
you not just of recording good results like simple machines that
are mechanically exact—there is question here of co-operation by
an activity that is at one and the same time docile and personal.

All this is true in general. But every age has its own distinctive
aspect, and Christian education must necessarily come face to
face with it. Consequently we deem that the Catholic school
has to keep in mind two special ends:

1°. In face of the restlessness, the inordinate multifariousness,   306
the tension of modern life, which is like a whirlwind in which
a man is caught up almost wholly and given no opportunity to
search his own heart; in face of the craze for success, which is
the standard by which everything is judged, without paying any
attention to whether it is true or false, good or bad, lawful or
unlawful, Catholic education is called upon to present in contrast
the man of clear, sure and profound convictions.

Is that not the lesson of everyday experience? Attend to this.
Anyone who has not solid principles is nowadays swept away
by the towering waves of ideological conflicts. This is the reason
why so many at present are turning their faces, full of hope,
towards the Church. She has behind her a wonderful record of
holiness and of great achievements, she is enriched by ancient
customs, by beauty and forms that are sublime. But that which
above all attracts souls to her, is that conviction, solid as a rock,
of the absolute truth, of the divine power of that faith, from
which everything else derives life and force.

307   2°. In face of that moral instability, to which youth is drawn in a thousand ways by books, pictures and films, it is the rôle of Catholic education to present the man who knows how to control himself, and to preserve and defend his dignity as a man and a Christian.

Catholic morality is broad-minded; it accepts and embraces all that finds its place within the reach of that dignity. But here there are clearly defined limits which it is not permitted to transgress. It is the glory and merit of strong souls to keep these limits inviolate always and in every circumstance; but grace is necessary and humble prayer in order to obtain it—the grace and prayer without which victory is impossible; it is essential that from his earliest years the young man should be trained to self-denial, to sacrifice and to self-control.

DECLARATION OF
THE SACRED CONGREGATION OF RELIGIOUS

19 May 1949

In reply to questions submitted concerning the nature of the obligations contracted by members of Secular Institutes, the Sacred Congregation of Religious gave the following declarations.[1]

1. The obligations contracted [2] by members properly so-called 308 of Secular Institutes cannot be light *ex genere suo et ex omni parte.*

2. On the contrary, it should rather be held that the juridical 309 bonds, on which the state of perfection of Secular Institutes rests, so oblige in conscience that the effects which they produce should be called grave *ex genere suo.*

3. For each individual case, there will be a grave obligation 310 only when the matter of this obligation, in accordance with the constitutions and the common teaching for similar bonds, must be considered certainly grave. In case of doubt, one must not declare that there is a grave obligation or one that is more grave, for example, on the ground that the obligation arises from or is formally reinforced by the virtue of religion.

4. What, in each Institute, is the nature of the juridical 311 bonds contracted by the members, and what is the ground on which the obligation rests, that is, in addition to justice and fidelity, is there question also of the virtue of religion, and in what way? This must be determined in accordance with the text of the constitutions, which should state the matter with precision, and also in accordance with the tenor of the formula of consecration or incorporation into the Institute in which these obligations are expressed.

---

[1] This was a private reply not published in the *AAS*; cf. Lemoine, *Le Droit des Religieux*, pp. 593-594.
[2] Art. II, § 2; cf. *supra*, n° 237.

312   5. Even when an obligation arises expressly from the virtue
of religion, the malice of sacrilege should not be attributed to
the non-observance of the juridical bonds, since there is question
of bonds or vows which, though they are not wholly private
vows, nevertheless cannot be, either by rule or in the strict
and specific sense, classed as public vows, and they do not
involve a public consecration of the person to God.

DISCOURSE TO THE MISSIONARY SISTERS OF THE KINGSHIP OF OUR LORD JESUS CHRIST

3 August 1949

On the occasion of the thirtieth anniversary of the foundation of this Institute,[1] Pius XII delivered this discourse in which he stressed the features which should characterize every Secular Institute.[2]

The balance sheet of the events of thirty years: that is what 313 you have come today to lay before us, beloved daughters; thirty years of vicissitudes, of toil and sanctification. Our heart and mind dwell with pleasure on that history, and on yourselves who represent it, because this is more than one of these charming family chronicles, all studded with memories and happenings that are recalled with pride and love. Despite its vicissitudes, or rather because of them also, this story teaches a lesson, an important lesson that has permanent and universal significance.

In addition to the example, in itself so consoling, of an intense spiritual and apostolic life, your history teaches also the lesson of thirty years of filial submission to the exhortations and the desires of the Church and its representatives, and of faithful perseverance in the path to the goal which you have set for yourselves; that submission and perseverance have been recompensed by a triumph more splendid than you could have hoped for, in the fulfilment day by day of the most saintly desires and most generous aspirations.

Truly you can chant with the Psalmist: *The Lord is my shepherd . . . he leads me by straight paths for the love of his name. Even though I walk through a dark valley, I shall not fear evil, because thou art with me.*[3]

---

[1] This society, which came into existence in 1919, was founded at Assisi by Rev. Fr. Gemelli, Rector of the Catholic University of Milan. In 1945 its Statutes were approved by the Sacred Congregation of the Council. In 1947 it counted about 2,000 members, especially in Switzerland and Italy, and it obtained a *decretum laudis* from the Sacred Congregation of Religious on 12 July 1948, thereby being established as a Secular Institute of pontifical law. Definitive approbation was granted to it in 1953.

[2] *Discorsi e Radiomessagi di Sua Santità Pio XII*, vol. XI (1949-50), pp. 167-169.

[3] Psalm xxii: 1, 3-4.

At each step that it took, your Institute saw itself favoured and encouraged, with however certain limitations or reservations which might have seemed to impede its progress. But notwithstanding these apparent obstacles, your work, the work of God in you and through you, proceeded at a steady and sure pace. Disappointments were inevitable, it is true; however, instead of becoming occasions of discouragement, as too often happens, they became an inspiration to you to new fervour and to sincere obedience, without murmuring and without hesitation.

What was the source of this wondrous and rare manner of feeling and acting, if not the sincerity and disinterestedness of your desires, free as they are from all attchment to the individual's own judgment and to personal and human designs?

314   And now your virtue and your generosity have been recognized by the Church, in a manner surpassing your expectation; for she has grafted you juridically into her own life, while allowing you to live in the world without belonging to the world. Is not that precisely the wish that Jesus expressed for his Apostles in his last prayer? You are women consecrated to God, recruited for the service of Christ; the pact is sealed. God knows that, the Church knows it, and you know it. The world does not know it; but it feels the beneficial effects which radiate from the Christian substance of your being and your apostolate. You are many in number and your vocation is to be the salt and sweet perfume of the earth, the leaven in the dough,[4] the light of the world.

315   You are firstly the leaven of the classes to which, by your birth, by your education, by your life since childhood, you belong and from which you have not separated; family relationships, bonds of friendship, professional links, these remain the same—and if you have some indefinable and almost imperceptible change to show in yourselves, it can only be a greater light in your eyes, a more frequent smile upon your lips, a greater grace in your manner, greater delicacy in your kindness, and more discretion in the sacrifice, the giving and the forgetfulness of your own selves. You will thus exercise a genuine and irresistible

4 Matthew xiii: 33.

attraction on those around you; and the man or woman who, though without being aware of it, comes under your salutary influence, will assume the tone and spirit which befit their position.

You are moreover the leaven in the groups of friends among 316 whom your activity and your devotion are exercised; these groups are excellent, rich in zeal, but it could easily happen, and sometimes does happen, that a less healthy leaven, a slight injection of self-love, of personal interest, of all too human exuberance, finds its way into them; and then the happy out-come, the tangible and unquestionable success, which is the fruit of natural genius and capacity, veils to some extent the power of the supernatural means; in these groups too, youthful and legitimate enthusiasm for the work might almost cause one to lose sight of him for whose service the work is intended.

Finally, you are the leaven of all that complex of persons and 317 things in the environment in which you discharge your daily task. And here, beloved daughters, a wide vista of works and of trials opens before your eyes. Already how unwearyingly you labour in the world of the school and of education, in the world of employees, among the liberal professions and in public ad-ministration, in the fields of health and of charity! Is it then such a small thing to be in that laboratory, in that administrative office, behind that cash-desk, in that teacher's chair, as one who inspires respect and trust, as one who has a healthy and elevating influence on those around, as one to whom the timid and faint-hearted come for the courage and daring to defend themselves and to struggle, as one who by her virtue and her love com-pensates for the affronts offered around her at every instant to the majesty and goodness of God?

But your influence extends even more widely and deeply in 318 the fruitful apostolic fields of Catholic Action. There undoubtedly lies your most grave responsibility, but it is a responsibility which, with full awareness of itself, keeps burning the fire of your first dedication to Christ and to the Church.

You have kindled this fire from the flame of the love of Christ, which burned in the incomparable saint of Assisi. Insistently therefore we beg and exhort you, beloved daughters, that what the disciples, both men and women, of the seraphic patriarch did in the thirteenth century, you too would accomplish now; the circumstances are of course completely different, but do you accomplish it with the same spirit.

319   Exert yourselves, each one of you in her own circle and her own way, to bring people to ponder on and truly deepen their understanding of their Catholic faith, as the supremely living reality, as something more living than the splendour and fascination of all earthly culture.

Bring into the world the spirit of Christian simplicity and self-denial in imitation of Francis, the knight captivated by the poverty of Christ, the hero who despoiled himself amidst those hungering for gold, the father of the friends of the people, Francis who was the messenger of conciliation and of peace.

LETTER TO CARDINAL MICARA ON ADAPTATION OF RELIGIOUS TO CONTEMPORARY CONDITIONS

12 November 1950

On the occasion of the first international congress of religious, held in Rome at the end of the Holy Year, the Holy Father reaffirms the confidence of the Church for the religious life.[1]

Approval and encouragement for the Congress. It is with very great joy that we have 320 learned that your Sacred Congregation has summoned at Rome, towards the end of this Holy Year, a congress of the chief members chosen from all religious Orders, from Congregations and societies and also from the present day Secular Institutes, which, having received the official approval of the Church, are earnestly devoting themselves at the present to the attainment of evangelical perfection.

Those who will take part in the congress will not be content, as befits their special way of life, merely to gain the indulgence of the Great Jubilee with zealous piety; they will also, in ready conformity to our desire, endeavour to restore and renew by suitable meditation the zeal for divine things and the ideals of apostolic activity; and throughout a week they will discuss in common and carefully investigate the manifold problems which in these troubled times are a source of concern to religious.

We are most desirous to give our warmest commendation and publicly to set the seal of our approval on this undertaking; for we are convinced that all who are bound to God by vows in the Catholic Church will follow the forthcoming meetings with all their heart and soul, and with earnest prayer to God, in order that they may be able to gather from them rich fruits for themselves and their Institutes.

[1] *AAS* XLIII (1951), pp. 24-26.

321 Need for wise and prudent adaptation. In the course of the studies to be held during the week, as we have already been informed, themes will be submitted for the consideration of those who profess the religious life, themes which undoubtedly appear to correspond to the most pressing contemporary demands of the religious life, especially in relation to the training of souls consecrated to God and the pursuit of works of the apostolate. What in fact is necessary is so to recreate and renew minds and wills, with the aid of the grace of the Holy Spirit, that as far as possible the new fashions of our time and the spiritual destitution of our age will be met.

322 Complete reform of oneself and of one's possessions is not by any means equivalent to the disowning or unreasoning contempt for what has been achieved by the laborious strivings of those who have gone before us, and which should be regarded as the glory and ornament of each one's religious society. Reform means rather not to lead a sluggish, idle life, but to reproduce in one's life the great deeds of those who have gone before, to nourish intensely the flame of piety; it means striving by every means that the holy laws of one's institute will not appear as a collection of exterior and useless regulations, *whose letter*, in the absence of the spirit, *kills*;[2] but that these laws will really be so many instruments of heavenly virtue, and that those who are bound to obey them will be enabled to form an ever keener desire for holiness and to spend all their powers, following the example of St. Paul, in securing the salvation of their brethren.

323 The obligation for those consecrated to God to accommodate themselves to the changing ways of the age, does not by any means signify that they are to yield in the slightest to the demands of the world or to its foolish seductions and blandishments. Their duty rather is to ensure that they give a lead to all by integrity of life, and to turn every advance of science or the arts to the good of religion[3] . . .

[2] 2 Corinthians 3: 6.

324 [3] The supreme Pontiff found it necessary to insist once again on this problem of adaptation in the course of a solemn audience, granted on 6 May 1951, on the occasion of the centenary of the foundation of the Merode Institute at Rome, to the Brothers of the Christian Schools. The discourse was published in Italian in *L'Osservatore Romano*,

7 May 1951. " The glories of the past create for you obligations for the future . . . go forward on the path which has been smoothed by the toils of your predecessors. The secret of their success lies in the fact that they never remained static, while at the same time they never deviated from the clear path traced by your incomparable founder John Baptist de la Salle. ' Keep up with the times ': *that is a popular dictum nowadays; by all means, but on condition that one does not make this a pretext for tearing the precious book, by destroying the preceding pages, as one detaches the leaves from a calendar.*

The art of education is, in fact, under many aspects, the art of adaptation: adaptation to the age, temperament, character, capacity, requirements and just aspirations of the pupil; adaptation to all the circumstances of time and place, adaptation to the general rhythm of the progress of humanity. Now that which characterizes true Christian education, in this adaptation, is that its constant object is the total formation of the child and the adolescent, with the aim of making him a complete and balanced man, citizen and Catholic, rather than a would-be savant whose mind is encumbered with encyclopedic information that is undigested and confused. To develop by sound pedagogy the intellectual culture, to make use of the health, the bodily vigour and agility of the members secured by physical education, for the benefit of mental alertness and flexibility, to refine all the faculties, by the happy accord of senses and intelligence, in artistic formation, in order to give grace and attractiveness to their exercise, and thereby to give them greater efficacy and a wider range, and make them more acceptable: all that is splendid, but would have neither eternal value nor be sufficiently full, if religious culture were not added to it, to give all education its unity and true value, by its amplitude and magnificence.

There is a widespread error which limits religious instruction and education to a specified time, even though with programmes that are complete and wisely arranged. But true Christian education demands much more: it is a work which is continuous, permanent, progressive; it should permeate all teaching, even that which is profane, and should enter into the very depth of the soul. It consists, therefore, over and above methodical exposition of doctrine, in seeing and showing all things in the light of the great and divine truth; just as in gazing upon material creation, one does not see things in their true colours save in the light, sometimes obscured by clouds, of God's beautiful sun.

But education would still be incomplete were it to reach only part of its object; that is, were it to confine itself to securing the personal good, physical and moral, temporal and eternal, of the pupils. It must also form and prepare them to exercise upon their age and generation, and even upon future generations, a salutary influence, so that they will pass through the world leaving it after them a better and more beautiful place than they found it."

APOSTOLIC CONSTITUTION "SPONSA CHRISTI" CONCERNING THE STATUTE OF NUNS

21 November 1950

This Apostolic Constitution, in line with the general trend towards adaptation of the life of religious to the new requirements of our time, determines a number of points concerning the life, enclosure and activities of nuns. The text of this Apostolic Constitution was distributed to participants in the congress of Orders and Congregations of women, which was held at Rome from 26 November to 8 December 1950.[1]

HISTORICAL SKETCH
NUNS IN THE COURSE OF THE CENTURIES

325

Concern of the Church for consecrated virgins. The Church, the Spouse of Christ,[2] from the very beginning of her history, has manifested in repeated acts and significant gestures, which she has confirmed by the clearest documents, the esteem and maternal affection that gently inspired her dealings with virgins consecrated to God.[3]

Nor is this a matter for wonder; for Christian virgins, " the choicest portion of the flock of Christ," [4] actuated by charity, disdaining all the distracting cares of the world [5] and over-

---

[1] *AAS* XLIII (1951), pp. 5-24.

[2] Cf. Ephesians 5: 25-27; Apocalypse 21: 2-9; 22: 17; Hermas, *Vis.*, 4, c. 2 (*FPA* 1, 460); St. Methodius, *Convivium*, orat. 3 (*Thaliae*), c. 8 (*PG* XVIII, 72-5); orat. 7, 7 (*PG* XVIII, 133); St. Ambrose, *De virginitate*, I, 6, n. 31 (*PL* XVI, 208); *Exhortatio virginitatis*, c. 10, n. 67 (*PL* XVI, 372).

[3] St. Ignatius, *Epist. ad Polycarp.*, 5 (*FPA* I, p. 290): ad Smyrn., 12 (*FPA* I, p. 284); St. Justin, *Apologia* 1 *pro chirstianis*, 15 (*PG* VI, 349); St. Cyprian, *De habitu virginum*, 3 (*PL* IV, 455), 11 (*PL* IV, 462); St. Clement, *De virginitate*, II, III (*FPA* 2, 1-5); St. Athanasius, *De virginitate*, 24 (*PG* XXVIII, 280); St. Basil, *Liber de virginitate* (*PG* XXX, 670); St. Ambrose, *De virginibus* (*PL* XVI, 198 f.); *De virginitate* 5 (*PL* XVI, 286); *De instit. virg.*, 17, 104 (*PL* XVI, 345); St. Jerome, *Epist.* 22, 2 (*PL* XXII, 395); 22 (*PL* XXII, 409); St. Augustine, *Epist.* 188, 1 (*PL* XXXIII, 849); *De sancta virginitate* (*PL* XL, 397), especially 27 (*PL* XL, 410); St. John Chrysostom, *De virginitate*, 11 (*PG* XLVIII, 540), 34 (*PL* XLVIII, 556); St. Leander, *Regula*, Introd. (*PL* LXXII, 876 B); *Constitutiones Apostolicae*, 2, c. 57 (*PG* I, 731-34).

[4] St. Cyprian, *De habitu virginum*, 3 (*PL* IV, 455).

[5] Cf. I Corinthians 7: 32-33; St. Thomas, II-II, q. 186, a. 4.

coming that division of the heart which is so easy yet full of danger,[6] not only dedicated themselves wholly to Christ,[7] as the true Spouse of their souls,[8] but made a perpetual transfer [9] to Christ the Lord and to the Church of their entire life, adorned as it was with all the jewels of Christian virtues.[10]

This mystic transfer of virgins to Christ and their donation to the Church, in the early centuries of Christianity were enacted spontaneously, being accomplished in facts rather than by express formulae.

The Church gave an official character to vows of virginity. Subsequently, when virgins began to 326 constitute not only a particular class, but a state already well defined and a rank recognised by the Church,[11] the profession of virginity began to be made publicly, and consequently was confirmed by a bond that constantly grew more strict.[12] Then the Church, when accepting the holy vow or purpose of virginity, consecrated the virgin as a person inviolably

---

[6] Cf. I Corinthians 7: 32-33; St. Augustine, De sancta virginitate, 22 (PL XL, 407).

[7] II Corinthians 11: 2; Tertullian, De oratione, c. 22 (PL I, 1296); De virginibus velandis, c. 16 (PL II, 960); De resurrectione carnis, c. 61 (PL II, 932); De exhortatione castitatis, c. 13 (PL II, 978); St. Cyprian, De habitu virginum, 22 (PL IV, 474); St. Methodius, Convivium, orat. 7 (Procilae) cc. 2-4 (PG XVIII, 127, 128); St. Athanasius, Apologia ad Constantium imp., n. 33 (PG XXV, 640); De virginitate, c. 2 (PG XXVIII, 253); St. Basil, Epist. 199, c. 18 (PG XXXII, 717); St. Ambrose, De virginitate, 12 (PL XVI, 297); De virginibus, I, 7, n. 36 (PL XVI, 209), I, 11, n. 65, 66 (PL XVI, 218); St. Jerome, Epist., 22, nn. 2, 25 (PL XXII, 395, 411); St. Augustine, Epist., 188, 1 (PL XXXIII, 848); In Joannis Evangelium, tr. 9, n. 2 (PL XXV, 1459); St. Thomas, in I V Sent., d. 38, q. 1, a. 5.

[8] St. Cyprian, De habitu virginum, 4 (PL IV, 455); St. Methodius, Convivium, orat. 5 (Talusa), I, 4 (PG XVIII, 97, 101); St. Clement, De virginitate, 1 (FPA, 2, p. 1); St. Augustine, De sancta virginitate, 8 (PL XL, 400), 29 (PL XL, 412).

[9] St. Cyprian, De habitu virginum, 4 (PL IV, 455); St. Clement, De virginitate, cc. 2, 3 (FPA, 2, p. 1-5).

[10] Origen, in Rom., 9: 1 (PG XIV, 1205); St. Methodius, Convivium, orat. 2 (Aretes), c. 1 (PG XVIII, 204); orat. 8 (Theclae), c. 17 (PG XVIII, 173); St. Athanasius, De virginitate, 21 (PG XXVIII, 275); St. Ambrose, De virginibus, 1, 10 (PL XVI, 216); Exhortatio virginitatis, 12, n. 80 (PL XVI, 375); St. Jerome, Epist., 130, 14 (PL XXII, 1118); St. Augustine, Epist., 98, 6 (PL XXXIII, 362).

[11] St. Ignatius, Ad Smyrn. 13 (FPA, I, 287); Tertullian, De virginibus velandis, 14 (PL II, 957); Origen, in Num. homilia, II, I (PG XII, 591); St. Cyprian, De habitu virginum, 3 (PL IV, 455); St. Methodius, Convivium, orat. I (Marcel.) c. I (PG XVIII, 35); St. Clement, De virginitate, I (FPA, 2, p. 1); Constitutiones Apostolicae, 2, c. 57 (PG I, 731-4); St. Gregory Nyssa, De vita S. Macrinae (PG XLVI, 988); St. John Chrysostom, I Tim. 5: 9 (PG LI, 323).

[12] Tertullian, De oratione, c. 22 (PL I, 1294); De virginibus velandis, c. 11 (PL II, 954) c. 13 (PL II, 956); c. 14 (PL II, 957); c. 15 (PL II, 959); Clement of Alexandria, Stromatum, 3, 2 (PG VIII, 1104); 25 (PG VIII, 1197); Origen, in Levit. hom. 3, n. 4

dedicated to God and to the Church, in a solemn rite which is rightly regarded as one of the most beautiful monuments of the ancient liturgy; [13] and the Church clearly distinguished the virgin thus consecrated from others who bound themselves to God by merely private obligations.[14]

327   The profession of the life of virginity was protected by vigilant and rigorous asceticism; at the same time it was nourished and supported by all the practices of piety and the exercise of the virtues. The ancient teaching of the Fathers, of the Greeks and other Orientals as well as of the Latins, puts before us a true and very beautiful image of the Christian virgin. In their writings the Fathers most diligently and lovingly clarify and vividly depict everything, either interior or exterior, that could in any way concern virginal sanctity and perfection.[15]

The high degree to which the angelic way of life of these Christian virgins, in this first period of their history, corresponded to the exhortations and descriptions of the Fathers, manifesting the adornment of countless jewels of high heroic virtues, that is known to us in part by the direct and certain evidence of historical documents and monuments; and in part, with no less certainty, it may be inferred and deduced from other equally reliable sources.[16]

(PG XII, 428); in Num. hom. 23, n. 3 (PG XII, 748); In Epist. ad Rom. 9: 37 (PG XIV 1237); St. Cyprian, De habitu virginum, 4 (PL IV, 455); St. Ambrose, De institutione virg., c. 17 (PL XVI, 345); St. Nicetas, De lapsu virginis, c. 5 (PL XVI, 388); Conc. Illiberit. (a. 395), c. 13 (Mansi, 2, 8).

[13] Roman Pontifical: " De benedictione et consecratione virginum"; St. Ambrose, De institutione virg., c. 17 (PL XVI, 345); De virginibus, 3, c. 1 (PL XVI, 231); St. Nicetas, De lapsu virginis, 5 (PL XVI, 387); St. Jerome, Epist., 130, n. 2 (PL XXII, 1108); Sacramentarium Leonianum, 30 ad virgines sacras (PL LV, 129).

[14] Tertullian, De virginibus velandis, c. 14, 15 (PL II, 957); St. Basil, Epist., 199, c. 18 (PG XXXII, 717); Innocent I, Epist. 2 ad S. Victricium, c. 13 (PL XX, 478 f.); St. Gelasius I, Epist. 14, c. 20 (A. Thiel, Epist. RR. Pontificum, Brunsbergae, 1868, p. 373); Codex Theodosianus, 9, 25, 2; St. Ambrose, De virginitate, c. 5, n. 26 (PL XVI, 286); De institutione virginis, c. 17, 114 (PL XVI, 348).

[15] St. Polycarp, Epist., 5, 3 (FPA I, 303); Tertullian, De virginibus velandis (PL II, 935); St. Cyprian, De habitu virginum (PL IV, 451); St. Methodius, Convivium, orat. I (Marcel.), I (PG XVIII, 35); St. Athanasius, De virginitate, 3 f. (PG XXVIII, 253 f.); St. Basil, Epist., 173 (PG XXXII, 648); Constitutiones Apostolicae, 8, c. 24 (PG I, 1122); St. Ambrose, De virginibus, 2, 2 (PL XVI, 220); 3, 1-4 (PL XVI, 231); St. Augustine, De sancta virginitate, 31 f. (PL XL, 412 f.).

[16] St. Cyprian, De habitu virginum, 22 (PL IV, 474); St. Ambrose, De virginibus, I, c. 4, 5 (PL XVI, 203-5); c. 10 (PL XVI, 215); St. Augustine, De moribus Ecclesiae catholicae, I, c. 31, 68; c. 33, 70 (PL XXXII, 1339).

Especially after peace had been granted to the Christians, it gradually became more frequent for consecrated virgins, following the example of hermits and cenobites, to complement and set the seal on their vow of virginity by the express profession of the evangelical counsels of poverty and stricter obedience.[17]

Organization of female communities. Women who had made the profession 328 of virginity, and had already agreed to come together in a common life, as far as possible cut off from association with men, both for the love of solitude and as a defence against the grave dangers that threatened from every side in the corrupt Roman society, very soon, as conditions subsequently became more favourable, followed the example of the immense throngs of cenobites; they generally left to men the eremitical way of life, and practically all took up the practice of the cenobitical life.[18]

The Church generally commended to virgins the common life 329 understood in a wide sense; but for a long period, the Church did not wish to impose strictly the monastic life even on consecrated virgins, whom she left in the world, duly honoured, but nevertheless free. However, the number of liturgically consecrated virgins living in their own homes, or in a common life that was somewhat free, constantly diminished; finally they disappeared, in some places by reason of a juridical decision, everywhere in fact. Furthermore, in general they were not brought back again, and later were even prohibited.[19]

---

[17] St. Augustine, *Epist.* 211, c. 5, 6 (*PL* XXXIII, 960); 15 (*PL* XXXIII, 964); St. Caesarius, *Regula ad virgines*, c. 4, 19 (*PL* LXVII, 1107, 1110), c. 11, 16 (*PL* LXVII, 1109); St. Leander, *Regula*, 18 (*PL* LXXII, 890); Anonymus, *Regula ad virgines*, c. 17 (*PL* LXXXVIII, 1066).

[18] St. Basil, *Regulae fus.*, n. 35; *Regulae brev.*, 108-110 (*PG* XXXI, 1004, 1156), *Epist.* 55 (*PG* XXXII, 402); St. Ambrose, *De virginibus*, I, c. 10, n. 59 (*PL* XVI, 215), *in Luc.* 2, n. 8, 20, 21 (*PL* XV, 1636, 1640); St. Epiphanius, *Advers. Haereses*, 2, 67 (*PG* XLII, 174), *Expositio fid. cath.*, 21 (*PG* XLII, 822); St. Jerome, *Epist.*, 22, 17 (*PL* XXII, 404), 24, 3 (*ibid.*, 427), 66, 13 (*ibid.*, 646), 108, 19 (*ibid.*, 896), 130, 19 (*ibid.*, 1122); St. Augustine, *De moribus Eccl. cach.*, I, c. 31; 68, c. 33, 70 (*PL* XXXII, 1339 f.); *Aeteriae peregrinatio*, 23, 2, 3 (W. Heraeus, Heidelberg, 1908, p. 27).

[19] *Conc. Carth.* III (a. 397), c. 33 (*Mansi*, 3, 885); *Conc. Aurelian.* v. (a. 549), c. 19 (*Mansi*, 9, 133); Venantius Fortunatus, *Vita S. Radegundis*, c. 12 (*PL* LXXXVIII, 502); *Conc. Paris* V (a. 614), c. 12-13 (*Mansi*, 10, 542); c. 13, C. 27, q. i; *Conc. Aquisgr.* (a. 789), c. 39 (*Mansi*, 13, App. 3, 166); *Conc. Mogunt.* (a. 888), c. 26 (*Mansi*, 18 71); *Conc. Lat.* II (a. 1139), c. 26 (*Mansi*, 21, 532), c. 25, C. 28, q. 2.

330   In those circumstances, the Church turned her maternal solicitude especially to those virgins who, making choice of the best part,[20] completely abandoned the world, and adding strict poverty and full obedience to the profession of virginity, embraced complete Christian perfection in monasteries. By means of constantly stricter laws of enclosure,[21] the Church prudently provided exterior protection for the professed cenobitical life of these virgins. Interiorly, however, it so organized their way of life that gradually and imperceptibly the Church in her laws and religious asceticism clearly and precisely delineated the type of the nun or saintly woman completely dedicated to the contemplative life under rigid regular discipline.[22]

331   At the beginning of the middle ages, when the way of life of consecrated virgins still living in the world had completely ceased, nuns, having increased remarkably in numbers and fervour and variety, came to be regarded as the sole heirs *in solidum* and legitimate successors of the virgins of ancient times; [23] and not merely as heirs and successors, but as the faithful stewardesses and active administrators of the patrimony handed down to them who, having been enriched with five talents, had gained five more.[24] The liturgical monuments, canonical documents, and historical testimony of every kind, writings, sculpture, painting,

---

[20] Cf. Luke 10: 42.

[21] St. Caesarius, *Regula ad virgines*, 1 (*PL* LXVIII, 1107), 33, 34, 35 (*PL* LXVII, 1114); *Conc. Lat.* II (a. 1139), c. 26 (*Mansi*, 21 532), c. 25, C. 28, q. 2; Boniface VIII, *De statu regularium*, c. un. 3, 16 in 6°; *Conc. Trid. Sess.* 25, " De regularibus et monialibus " c. 5; Pius V, *Circa Pastoralis*, 29 May 1566, 1 (Gasparri, *Fontes* I. C., I, n. 112); *Decori*, 1 February 1570 (Gasparri, *Fontes* I C., I, n. 133); Benedict XIV, *Salutare*, 3 January, 1742 (*Bull. Rom.* XIV, I, p. 106).

[22] Cc. 11, 20-25, C. 18, q. 2; c. 8, *De statu monachorum et canonicorum regularium*, X, 3, 35, c. 2, *De statu monachorum et canonicorum regularium*, 3, 10 in Clem; *Conc. Trid. Sess.* 25, *De regularibus et monialibus*; Clement VIII, C. *Religiosae congregationes*, 19 June 1594 (*Bull. Rom.* ed. Taurin, 10, 146); *Nullus omnino*, 25 July 1599 (*Fontes I.C.*, 1, n. 187); C. *Cum ad regularem*, 19 March 1603 (*Fontes I.C.*, 1, 189); Gregory XV, *Inscrutabili*, 5 February 1622 (*Bull Rom.*, ed. Taurin., 12, 656); Innocent XI, *Litt. Encycl.* 9 October 1682 (Bizzari, *Collectanea*, 2, p. 374); C. *Cum ad aures* (Ferraris, *Prompta Biblioth*; v. *Eucharistia*); Benedict XIV, C. *Pastoralis Cura* (*Bull. Rom.* XIV, 2, 471).

[23] *Roman Pontifical*: De benedictione et consecratione virginum. Cf. note 13.

[24] Cf. Matthew 25: 20.

all these prove and establish this origin and dignity, and also the merits and sanctity of nuns.[25]

For several centuries, down to the end of the middle ages, as is clear from the Decretals and indeed from the whole corpus of canon law, nuns were the only women who, together with monks and canons regular, exemplified the state of perfection, which had already been so solemnly accepted and fully recognized, in order the more perfectly to manifest its public character.

Later, when many grave difficulties had been overcome, at first all friars, who were variously called Mendicants, Hospitallers, Ransomers, or by some other title, and, after about three centuries, the clerics called regulars, were classed as true religious and regulars, together with monks and canons regular; but all nuns, both those who were attached to the ancient monachism or canonical life and those being formed into the second Orders of the friars mendicant, as far as canon law is concerned, pursued the one, noble and ancient institute and embraced the same religious way of life. 332

Therefore, until the rise of the first Congregations of women, which appeared in the sixteenth or seventeenth century, the only women considered as nuns were those who in fact and in law made legitimate profession of religious life. Indeed, even after Congregations had received toleration and, in the course of time, had been received first in fact and then by a certain provisory legislation,[26] nuns alone, up to the promulgation of the Code of Canon Law, were admitted in strict law as true religious and regulars.[27]

[25] Honorius IV, C. *Ascendit fumus*, 24 September 1285 (*Bull. Rom.*, ed. Taurin., 4, p. 83); *Conc. Trid. Sess. 25, De regularibus et monialibus*, c. 1; Pius IV, Motu Proprio, *De Statu*, 5 April 1560 (*Bull. Rom.*, ed. Taurin., 7, 21); Pius V, C. *Decori*, 24 January 1570 (*Bull. Rom.* ed Taurin., 7, 808); Pius VI, *Litt. Quod aliquantulum*, 10 March 1791 (*Coll.* Brev. et Instructionum SS. DD. N. Pii P. VI, 1800, p. I, p. 47); *Conc. Vat. Schema Constit. Ecclesiae*, c. 15 (*Coll. Lacensis*, 7 appendix, 575); Leo XIII *Litt. Testem Benevolentiae*, 22 January 1899 (*Acta* Leonis XIII, 19, 5); *Litt. Au milieu*, 23 December 1900.

[26] C. un. *De Statu Regularium* 3, 16 in 6°; c. un. *De religiosis . . .*, 3, 11, in Clem; c. un. *De religiosis . . .*, 3, 9 in Extravag. Comm.

[27] S. C. Ep. et Reg. Bergom, 14 March 1841; ad 16 § 3 (Lucidi, *De visitatione sacrorum liminum*, II, n. 463); Gerunden., 9 May 1860, ad 2 (Bizzari, *Collectanea*, 2, p. 78, VI); Albien., 23 June 1860, ad 14 (Bizzari, p. 786, X); 16 September 1864 (Bizzari, p. 744 f.). *Rilievi circa gli Statuti della Congr. dei Fratelli della S. Fmaiglia*, art. I and 13 (Bizzai, p. 800, 803); *Normae secundum quas S. C. Ep. et Reg. procedere solet in approbandis novis institutis votorum simplicuum*, 28 June 1901, art. 32.

333   Should we at this point wish to consider the hidden interior of monastic life, how is one to recount or estimate the treasures of religious perfection hidden in these monasteries? Who shall tell what flowers and fruits of sanctity these closed gardens have brought forth to Christ and the Church; who shall recount the efficaciousness of prayer, the riches of devotion, and indeed the benefits of every kind, with which nuns have sought with all their powers to adorn, support and strengthen the Church, their Mother?

This strict and well-defined type of nun, that which is engraved in the pages of canon law and ascetical writings, was readily and faithfully accepted by countless Orders, monasteries and convents which have always existed in the Church, as far as its chief features are concerned, and was also tenaciously retained for many centuries. From this general fidelity and constancy, a compact unity has arisen in the sacred institute of nuns, which has always strongly resisted innovations of every kind, more vigorously indeed than any other institute of either sex. That, within certain just limits, is undoubtedly to be counted to its credit.

334   **Various forms of life practised by nuns.** This unity of nuns, which we have described, did not by any means prevent, either in regard to asceticism or interior discipline, the admission even from ancient times of different forms and variations; these variations are means whereby God, wonderful in his saints, has enriched and adorned his Spouse, the Church.

335   These different forms of the life of nuns appear to have arisen from variations of the same kind in the Orders and religious societies of men to which they were in some way attached. In fact, practically all monks, canons regular, and especially the mendicants, sought to establish second Orders; these, while always preserving in general the distinctive character of nuns, were seen to differ from one another in the same way as the first Orders. In the same way, in more recent times some Orders

of clerics regular and some Congregations of men have founded
orders of nuns corresponding to their own institute.[28]

These differences in the life of nuns are well deserving of the
closest attention, whether we have in mind the history of the
institute of nuns or the interior changes shared in common.
There is no doubt that, without destroying the general character
of the contemplative life and without prejudice to the chief
norms and principles of accepted discipline, these variations
have brought a new power for holiness to the ancient institute.[29]

In more recent times, especially towards the end of the
sixteenth century, new forms of Orders of nuns were introduced
and were gradually approved by the Church; for example, the
Institute of Saint Ursula, of Saint Angela, the Congregation of
Religious of Our Lady, the Order of the Visitation, the Society
of Our Lady, the nuns of Blessed Mary of Charity,[30] and many
others. These new foundations, being forced or morally compelled, from the very beginning of their foundation or
subsequently, to accept the general law for nuns then in force,
in order to be able to make profession of truly religious life—
the only form then recognized for women—were thus in various
ways preparing a reform of the law itself.

Such new forms of nuns, although they made profession of 337
the canonical contemplative life, and had finally accepted, with
difficulty but sincerely, in deference to the opinions then current,
strict pontifical enclosure duly adapted to their own way of life,
did not always nevertheless undertake the recitation of the divine
Office. But with laudable solicitude they undertook, as part
of their calling, many works of the apostolate and of charity

[28] S. C. Ep. et Reg., dec. Ecclesia Catholica, 11 August 1889 (ASS XXIII, 634).

[29] Leo XIII, Apostolic Constitution Conditae a Christo, 8 December 1900 (Acta Leonis XIII, 22, p. 317-327); Normae secundum quas S. C. Ep. et Reg. procedere solet in approbandis novis institutis votorum simplicium, 28 June, 1901.

[30] Paul V, C. Inter universas, 13 June 1612 (Règle et Constitutions de l'Union Romaine de l'Ordre de Sainte Ursula, 1936, p. 231-9); C. Debitum Pastoralis, 24 March 1614, loc. cit., p. 240-6); Salvatoris et Domini, 3 October 1616 (loc. cit., p. 246-50); Urban VII, Alias felicis, 6 November 1626 (loc. cit., p. 273); Paul V, Sacri Apostolatus, 23 April 1618 (Oeuvres de Saint-François de Sales, 1912, XVIII, p. 423); Paul V, Salvatoris et Domini, 7 Apr l 1607 (Inst tuto de la Compan a de Nuestra Senora, T.I., Constituciones Pontificias y Reglas aprobadas, Manresa, 1899, p. 7-14); Innocent X, Exponi nobis, 28 September 1645 (Bull. Rom., ad Taurin. 15, p. 403); Benedict XIV, In supremo, 26 September 1741 (Règle de Saint-Augustin et Constitutions pour les religieuses de la Congrégation de Notre-Dame de Charité du Bon Pasteur d'Angers, 1836, p. 39-41).

which were regarded as in harmony with their sex and their juridical status.

With the passage of the years, whether spurred by the example of new Orders or by the progress of Congregations and societies which strove to combine the fruitful exercise of charity, assistance and teaching with the life of perfection, or finally by reason of the general progress of ideas and things in every sphere, not a few monasteries of many Orders, who by their institute devoted themselves solely to the contemplative life, undertook in many places works of the apostolate,[31] with the approval and under the prudent guidance of the Holy See.

In consequence, gradually and imperceptibly it came about that the general institute of nuns not only embraced different Orders with their individual rules and constitutions, but that an even more profound division came to be recognized, namely between Orders and monasteries which followed the contemplative life solely, and Orders and monasteries in which, either by a special provision of the constitution or subsequent concessions of the Apostolic See, canonically approved works of the apostolate were suitably combined with the contemplative life.

Adaptations Required by Contemporary Conditions

338   In our own day the whole institute of nuns, both in those Orders and monasteries which hitherto had faithfully observed the contemplative life exclusively, and especially in those which by the direction of the Church happily combined the contemplative life with works of the apostolate, has been profoundly affected by the development of events and changes of circumstances. Indeed, when these Orders devote themselves to educational or other similar charitable activities, which nowadays, because of changed customs or by reason of the intervention of the State, are performed in a manner which is practically incompatible with some of the classic rules of pontifical enclosure, the rules of this enclosure have had to be wisely mitigated; thus, while the general nature of enclosure is retained, its rules can be harmonized with the above-mentioned activities.

---

[31] *Formulae S. C. de Religiosis*, n. 91.

The change was seen to be required for the welfare of holy Church and of souls, since if it had not been made, these works of the apostolate could not have been undertaken at all or at least not in that way. And it is not merely in relation to the apostolic Orders, but even in regard to merely contemplative Orders, that the circumstances of the times, and the great poverty from which they often suffer, have been judged to demand urgently mitigations or more liberal interpretations.

The law of enclosure especially needs modifications. Nowadays, for example, the social sense of men would scarcely tolerate the excessively strict interpretation of canon 601, even when there is question of contemplative nuns.[32] Consequently the Holy See with maternal care makes constantly more generous provision for several needs and advantages which, according to the formerly accepted estimation, were not judged sufficiently grave to justify any infringement of pontifical enclosure or exemption from it. Moreover, the security and inviolability of domiciles, which was one of the reasons for pontifical enclosure, and in various ways at different times together with other causes served to constitute and establish that enclosure, is nowadays more assured and guaranteed than formerly. 339

Distinguish between essentials and accessories. Having given this summary account of the origin and chief events of the sacred institute of nuns, we deem it opportune now to mark off accurately its proper and essential constituents, those which directly affect the canonical contemplative life of nuns as their primary and principal aim. Besides those original and primary features, whereby the canonical figure of nuns is clearly defined in the law, there are a number of accessory features of considerable importance; though not essential, they are nevertheless complementary to it, because they correspond well to the publicly avowed purpose of nuns and serve to ensure it. But we find some other things in the institute 340

---

[32] Canon 601 forbids a professed nun to leave the monastery without permission of the Holy See, except in the case of imminent danger of death or of other very grave evil.

of nuns which are neither necessary nor complementary; they are merely extrinsic and historical, since they certainly have their origin in the circumstances of former ages, and these conditions have greatly changed. When these elements are no longer beneficial, or if they can hinder a greater good, there does not appear to be any special reason for retaining them.

341   And so, while fully maintaining all the basic and principal elements of the venerable institute of nuns, we have decreed, in relation to other elements, which are to be regarded as extrinsic and accessory, to introduce cautiously and prudently those adaptations to present-day conditions, which will be able to bring not only greater dignity but also greater efficacy to this institute.

342   **Economic conditions of the times call for changes.**   We are moved, indeed constrained, to introduce these reasonable adaptations of the institute of nuns by the full information on the matter that we have received from all parts of the world, and by the certain knowledge derived from this information of the grave need in which nuns frequently, not to say always, exist. Indeed, there are not a few monasteries which, alas! are practically dying from hunger, distress, privation; many others, because of domestic difficulties, lead a hard life that is, generally, impossible to endure. In addition, there are monasteries which, though not living in dire need, not infrequently are languishing because they are completely segregated and cut off from any other monasteries. Besides, rules of enclosure which are sometimes too strict easily lead to grave difficulties. Finally, with the ever growing needs of the Church and of souls, and with the urgent need for the labour of all to come to their assistance in many ways, the time appears to have come in which monastic life in general, including even that of nuns dedicated to contemplation, should be harmonized with moderate participation in the apostolate.

    Our judgement on this matter has received frequent confirmation from the testimonies of local Ordinaries and religious superiors, which have reached us from some countries with absolute unanimity.

It will be useful to explain here some of the decrees that 343
are enacted in the *General Statutes* of nuns which are given
below; thus we can enunciate rules and principles by which
each of the individual prescriptions can easily and securely be
understood.

Changes must not   And in the first place, in relation to 344
hinder the   the contemplative life of nuns, that
contemplative life, which according to the mind of the
the principal aim Church has always been in force, must be
of monastic life. preserved intact and inviolable: namely
that all monasteries of nuns must always and everywhere make
the canonical profession of the contemplative life their primary
and principal aim.

For this reason the works and ministries to which nuns can
and should devote themselves, must be of such a kind and be
so regulated and arranged in regard to place, time, mode and
character, that the true and solid contemplative life, whether
of the entire community or of individual nuns, shall not only
be safeguarded but constantly nourished and strengthened.

Restoration of   Prescriptions and concessions were for- 345
solemn vows.   merly granted for certain regions, under the
pressure of circumstances, whereby solemn
vows were commuted to simple vows; [33] these concessions
must certainly be regarded as involving a dispensation that is
undesirable [34] (can. 19); and that all the more because such
exemption is opposed to a chief characteristic of nuns; for solemn
vows, which involve a closer and fuller consecration to God
than other public vows, are the canonically indispensable and
most essential quality of religious Orders.

---

[33] Vows are *solemn* when the Church recognizes them as solemn, otherwise they are
simple (can. 1308 § 2). In particular: (1) Solemn vows establish reciprocal and indissoluble
ties between the Order and the religious; (2) the religious are bound to private recitation
of the divine Office, if they have not taken part in the public recitation of it; (3) solemn
profession invalidates acts contrary to the vows which are capable of being nullified;
(4) a religious who has made profession of solemn vows is incapable of holding and
acquiring property.

[34] Latin, *dispensatio odiosa*, in the sense of " to be avoided."

346   Consequently, since prolonged experience in different places
has clearly shown that the solemn vows whether of men regulars
or of nuns, though ignored by civil law, can easily and without
trouble be observed, and likewise that suitable provision for
the security of other community goods can be otherwise
made, even if, as happens in some places, juridical personality
be denied to religious societies and monasteries; it is with good
reason that the legislation and the action of the Holy See for
many years have jointly made it their aim to restrict the undesirable exceptions to which we have referred,[35] and as far as
possible, to have them abolished. And indeed it is not right
that nuns should be deprived of the honour, the merit and the
joy of making the solemn vows which are proper to them.

Pontifical Enclosure

—*Major enclosure.*

347
In order to secure the better custody of the solemn vow of
chastity and of the contemplative life, so that the closed garden
of monasteries should be beyond the reach of worldly assaults,
safe from violation by cunning or ruses, immune from disturbance by worldly and profane contact, and become rather a
true enclosure of souls [36] in which nuns could more freely serve
God,[37] the Church with vigilant and wise solicitude established
a stricter form of enclosure, as an institution special to nuns;
this institution she organized carefully and gave it the perpetual
protection of grave pontifical sanctions.

This venerable enclosure of nuns, which is entitled pontifical
by reason of the supreme authority from which it emanates and
the sanctions which protect it interiorly and exteriorly, in this
Constitution is not only deliberately and solemnly confirmed
by us, account being taken of the different circumstances of
monasteries which hitherto have been subject to enclosure;

345a   [35] Pius VII, *Breve ad ep. Tornac.*, 24 June 1810 (Bizzari, *Collectanea*, II, p. 738); *Sacra
C. de Relig.*, 22 May 1912 (*AAS* XI (1919), p. 240); *S. C. de Relig.*, 23 June 1923 (*AAS*
XV (1923), p. 357); *S. C. de Relig.*, 6 February 1924 (*AAS* XVI (1924), pp. 96-101).
XV (1923), p. 357); *S. C. de Relig.*, 6 February 1924 (*AAS* XVI (1924), p. 96-101).
     [36] Hugo de Folieto, *De claustro animae* (PL CLXXVI, 1017).
     [37] Innocent IV, *ad Moniales S. Dominici de Im.*, 11 May 1252 (*Bull. Ord. Praed.*, I,
p. 206).

it is also prudently extended to those monasteries which hitherto, because of dispensations legitimately secured, were not bound by it.

Monasteries which profess the exclusively contemplative life, and which do not admit within the precincts of the religious house stable works of education, charity, recollection or others of the same kind, will retain or receive the form of pontifical enclosure which is dealt with in canons 600-602 of the Code of Canon Law; and this will be called *major* enclosure.[38]

—Minor enclosure.

But in those monasteries which, by their institute or by the lawful directives of the Holy See, within the monastic buildings harmoniously combine the practice of the contemplative life with certain ministries that harmonize with it, pontifical enclosure, while retaining what is necessary and essential to it,   348

[38] **Canon 600:** No one, irrespective of family, sex, condition or age, shall be admitted   347a
within the enclosure of nuns without the permission of the Holy See, save the following persons:

1. The local Ordinary or regular superior, when they are conducting a visitation of the monastery, or other visitors delegated by them, are permitted to enter within the enclosure, for purposes of inspection, and with the precaution that they are accompanied by at least one cleric or man religious of mature age;

2. The confessor or one who is taking his place can, with due precautions, enter within the enclosure to administer the Sacraments or assist the dying;

3. Heads of States who actually hold office and their wives, together with their retinue, and also Cardinals of the Holy Roman Church, can enter within enclosure;

4. It is for the superioress, having taken due precautions, to permit the entry of doctors, surgeons and others whose services are necessary; she must have secured beforehand at least the habitual permission of the Ordinary of the place; if, however, there is urgent necessity and time is not sufficient for requesting, this permission is lawfully presumed.

Canon 601, § 1.—No nun is permitted after profession to leave the monastery, even for a brief time, on any pretext, without the special indult of the Holy See, except   347b
for the case of imminent danger of death or of other very grave danger.

§ 2.—This danger, if time permits, is to be recognized in writing by the local Ordinary.

Canon 602.—The enclosure of a monastery of nuns should be so protected that,   347c
as far as possible, there will be no view into it by outsiders, nor view of outsiders from within it.

Canon 599, § 1.—If a house of men regulars has attached to it a hostel for intern   348a
students or other works proper to this religious society, if possible, at least a separate part of the house shall be reserved for the residence of the religious, and it shall be subject to the law of enclosure.

§ 2.—Even outside the enclosure, persons of the other sex shall not be admitted into those places reserved for extern or intern students or for the special works of this religious society, except for a just cause and with the permission of the Superior.

Canon 604, § 2.—The prescription of canon 599 shall be applied also to houses   348b
of religious Congregations, whether of men or of women.

is mitigated in some features which can be observed only with difficulty or not at all; in other matters, however, which are not regarded as so essential for the pontifical enclosure of the Code of Canon Law (can. 599, 604 § 2), pontifical enclosure is aptly complemented. This mitigated form of pontifical enclosure, thus adapted to present-day needs, shall be called *minor*, in order to distinguish it from the old more rigid enclosure; it can be granted to those monasteries also which, though they practise the contemplative life only, do not have solemn vows or lack some of the conditions which are rightly required for major enclosure by the jurisprudence and customary *stylus* of the Curia. A precise definition of all these elements of minor pontifical enclosure will be given below, in the *General Statutes* and in the *Instructions* to be issued by the Sacred Congregation of Religious by our authority and in our name.

349 **Federations of monasteries.** As for the autonomy of monasteries of nuns or independence from one another, we deem it opportune to repeat here and apply to nuns what we spoke designedly concerning monks in the homily we delivered in the patriarchal basilica of St. Paul-outside-the-Walls on 18 September 1947, at the end of the fourteenth centenary of the death of St. Benedict of Norcia.[39] With the changes of conditions there are many considerations which suggest and frequently demand a confederation of monasteries of nuns; by this an easier and more suitable distribution of duties can be made; the temporary transfer, which is useful and frequently necessary for various causes, of a nun from one monastery to another, economic assistance, the co-ordination of labours, the protection of common observance, and other such matters, will be made possible. That all these things can be done and secured, without any derogation of the essential autonomy or weakening of the strictness of enclosure or injury to recollection and the more severe discipline of monastic life, is established with certainty from the wide experience of monastic Congregations of men; the same is clear also from the numerous

[39] *AAS* XXXIX (1947), p. 454-455.

examples of unions and federations between nuns which have
been approved up till now. The formation of federations and
the approval of the statutes by which they shall be ruled remains,
however, reserved to the Holy See.[40]

Work by nuns. Not merely the natural law,[41] but the duty 350
of penance and satisfaction,[42] obliges all,
without exception even of men and women who are dedicated to
the life of contemplatives, to labour, either manual or intellectual. Labour, moreover, is the general instrument whereby the
mind is preserved from dangers and raised to higher things;
it is the means whereby we co-operate with divine providence
both in the order of nature and in the order which surpasses
nature; it is by labour that deeds of charity are performed.
Labour, finally, is the norm and chief law of the religious life,
and has been such even from its very beginnings, in accordance
with the dictum: "Pray and work." Indeed the discipline of
religious life has always in great part been based on the command
to work, and on the organization and performance of work.[43]

Work by nuns, considered from the aspect of eternity,
should be such that the nun who undertakes it will do so with
a holy purpose; that she will frequently think of God who is
present, carrying it out from obedience and joining with it
voluntary personal mortification. Labour carried out in this
spirit will be a potent and constant exercise of all the virtues,

---

[40] It is certain that the Holy See, while acting with great prudence and respect for 349a
acquired rights, views with satisfaction the movement towards Unions or Federations
on the part of religious communities which are animated with the same spirit and have
the same objective. Thus Pius XII, on 21 July 1939, congratulated the Canonesses
Regular of St. Augustine who, under the authority of Mother-Marie-Yvonne de Jésus,
of Malestroit, had brought about their Roman Union: "In a world that is avid for instruction, and finding yourselves face to face with female youth who are in many countries
menaced by the *éclat* of atheistic teaching, you have recognized the advantages of a
union between your various houses, in order the better to co-ordinate and then re-
apportion, with the aid of a superioress general, the intellectual resources at the disposal
of the entire body. And in order to make this Union more universal and indestructible,
you have made it immediately dependent on the Holy See. More than ever, therefore,
you will be daughters of the Church, because even in your very *name and title*, you
proclaim yourselves Roman" (*Discorsi e Radiomessagi di sua Santità Pio XII*, Milano,
Società editrice "Vita e Pensiero," t. I, p. 278-279.)

[41] Genesis 2: 15; Job 5: 7; II Thessalonians 3: 10.

[42] Genesis 3: 19.

[43] *Homily for XIVth centenary of the death of St. Benedict* (*AAS* XXXIX (1947), p. 453)

12

and a pledge of gentle and efficacious combination of the active with the contemplative life, following the example of the family of Nazareth.[44]

If however monastic labour be judged with reference to its nature or its disciplinary value, then by the rules, constitutions and traditional customs of each Order, it should be adapted to the strength of nuns; it should also be so ordered and carried out that, allowing for different times and circumstances, it will procure the necessary support for nuns and also contribute to the welfare of the poor, human society and the good of the Church.[45]

351   **Nuns should share in the apostolate of the Church.** The perfection of Christian life consists especially in charity,[46] and this charity, whereby we should love the Lord alone above everything and all men in him, is truly one and the same; Mother Church, therefore, demands of all nuns who canonically profess the contemplative life, together with perfect love of God, perfect charity towards the neighbour; in virtue of this charity and of their state all religious, men and women, should feel themselves wholly dedicated to the Church and to the needs of all the indigent.

All nuns, therefore, should realize thoroughly that their vocation is fully and wholly apostolic, that it is subject to no limits of place, time or events, that at all times and places it reaches out to everything that in any way concerns either the honour of their Spouse or the salvation of souls. But this universal apostolic vocation of nuns in no way hinders monasteries from having commended to their prayers the needs of the whole Church and of individuals or of groups of men.

352   The apostolate common to all nuns, whereby they are bound to be zealous for the honour of their divine Spouse [47] and to promote the welfare of the universal Church and of all the faithful, makes use chiefly of the three following means:

---

[44] Matthew 13: 55; Mark 6: 3.
[45] Ephesians 4: 28.
[46] I John 4: 16; Colossians 3: 16; St. Thomas, II-II, q. 184, a. 1.
[47] Off. S. Theresiae Virginis, 15 October; Pius XII, Mystici Corporis (AAS XXXV (1943), p. 241-5).

1° The example of Christian perfection; since their life, even without words, profoundly influences and constantly draws the faithful to Christ and to Christian perfection, and like a standard, arouses the good soldiers of Christ [48] to the lawful struggle and attracts them to the crown of victory;[49]

2° Prayer, which is offered both publicly in the name of the Church in the solemn seven-fold daily recitation of the canonical hours to God, and also in private prayer unceasingly offered to God in all its forms;

3° Zeal for self-dedication, so that, to the mortifications which arise from common life and the faithful observance of the rule, other exercises of personal self-denial are added; these may either be prescribed by the rules and constitutions or undertaken entirely voluntarily, in order generously to make up *those things which are wanting of the sufferings of Christ Jesus, for his body, which is the Church.* [50]

Having sketched the chief historical events of the institute of nuns and carefully described the limits within which it can be adjusted to the needs of life at the present day, we now propose to give the general norms according to which that adaptation should be brought about. The Sacred Congregation of Religious will give effect to the entire *Constitution* and *General Statutes* in relation to all federations of monasteries already existing or to be established in the future and in relation to each individual monastery; and by our authority, the Congregation will have power, by means of instructions, declarations, replies and other such documents, to perform everything which

353

[48] II Timothy 2: 3.

[49] II Timothy 4: 8.

[50] Colossians 1: 24. The Holy Father frequently came back to this theme of the special apostolate of consecrated souls, for example in the Encyclical *Sacra Virginitas*, 25 March 1954 (cf. nn. 482-552, especially 506-9 and 525). More recently the Encyclical Letter *Le pèlerinage de Lourdes*, 2 July 1957, on the centenary of the apparitions of Lourdes, gave him the opportunity of saluting " the multitude of consecrated souls, who in the Church dedicate themselves to innumerable good works. Their vows of religion dedicate them more than others to combat victoriously, und 'r the protection of Mary, against the unloosing upon the world of the unregulated passions of independence, riches and enjoyment; and so, at the call of the Immaculate Virgin, they will desire to stand against the assaults of evil with the weapons of prayer and penance and with the victories of charity " (*AAS* XLIX (1957), p. 617).

352a

has reference to the diligent and effective introduction of the constitution into force and the prompt and faithful observance of the *General Statutes.*

GENERAL STATUTES OF NUNS

ARTICLE I

354   §. 1—In this Constitution by the title nuns, in accordance with the law,[51] are understood, in addition to women religious with solemn vows, those also who have made profession of simple vows, either perpetual or temporary, in monasteries in which solemn vows are actually taken or should be taken in virtue of the institute; unless from the context or the nature of the case the contrary is quite certain.

355   § 2.—The following are in nowise contrary to the legitimate title of nuns and to the application of the legislation for nuns: (1) *Simple profession* lawfully made in monasteries (§ 1); (2) *Minor pontifical enclosure* which has been prescribed for or duly granted to monasteries; (3) *The exercise of works of the apostolate* in conjunction with the contemplative life, whether this be by virtue of constitutions which have been approved and confirmed by the Holy See for certain Orders, or by the legitimate prescription or concession of the Holy See to some monasteries.

356   § 3.—This Apostolic Constitution does not juridically concern: (1) The religious Congregations [52] and sisters who are members of them,[53] who by their institute pronounce only simple vows; (2) Societies of women who live in community like women religious, and their members.[54]

---

[51] Canon 488, 7; cf. *supra*, n. 77.
[52] Canon 488, 2; cf. *ibid.*
[53] Canon 488, 7; cf. *ibid.*
356a   [54] **Canon 673.**—1. A society, whether of men or of women, in which the members imitate the way of life of religious by living in common under the rule of superiors according to approved constitutio·s, but are not bound by the three customary public vows, is not properly a religious society, nor are the members properly designated by the name of religious.

2. Such societies are clerical or lay, of pontifical or diocesan standing, in accordance with canon 488, 3-4.

ARTICLE II

§ 1.—The special form of monastic religious life which nuns 357
are bound to lead under strict regular discipline, and for which
they are destined by the Church, is the canonical contemplative
life.

§ 2.—By the canonical contemplative life is understood, not 358
that interior and theological life to which all souls in religious
societies and even in the world are called, and which each
individual soul is everywhere capable of leading within itself;
it is rather the exterior profession of a religious discipline which,
by means of the enclosure, or by exercises of piety, prayer
and mortification, or finally by the works to which the nuns are
bound to dedicate themselves, is so orientated to interior
contemplation that the entire life and activity can easily and
should be effectively imbued with the desire for interior
contemplation.

§ 3.—If the canonical contemplative life under strict regular 359
discipline cannot be habitually observed, the monastic character
cannot be granted, nor can it be retained should it be already
possessed.

ARTICLE III

§ 1.—The solemn religious vows, which have been pro- 360
nounced by all the members of the monastery or by at least
one class of the members, constitute the principal mark by
which monasteries of women are juridically classed, not among
religious Congregations but among Orders of regulars.[55] All
religious who have made profession in these monasteries come
under the title of regulars in law, in accordance with canon
490,[56] and are properly called not sisters, but nuns.[57]

§ 2.—All monasteries, in which simple vows only are pro- 361
nounced, will be able to obtain the restoration of solemn
vows. Indeed, unless very grave reasons to the contrary stand
in the way, they shall take care to resume once again these vows.

---

[55] **Canon 488,** 2°; cf. *supra*, n. 77.
[56] **Canon 490:**—What is laid down for religious, even though expressed in the 360a
masculine, holds equally for women religious, unless from the context or the nature of
the subject the contrary is clear.
[57] **Canon 488,** § 78 ; cf. *supra*, n. 77.

362 § **3.**—The solemn ancient formulae of the consecration of virgins, which are found in the *Roman Pontifical*, are reserved to nuns.

ARTICLE IV

363 § **1.**—The stricter enclosure of nuns, which is called pontifical, while retaining always and for all monasteries the characteristics which are, as it were, natural to it, shall henceforth be distinguished into two kinds: *major* and *minor*.

364 § **2.**—1° *Major* pontifical enclosure, that which is described in the Code (can. 600-602),[58] is fully confirmed by this our Apostolic Constitution. The Sacred Congregation of Religious, by our authority, will declare the causes for which a dispensation may be granted from major enclosure, so that, while its essential nature is left intact, it may be better adapted to the conditions of our times.

2° In all monasteries which profess only the contemplative life, major pontifical enclosure should be the rule in force, without prejudice to § 3, 3°.

365 § **3.**—1° *Minor* pontifical enclosure shall retain those elements from the ancient enclosure of nuns, and will be protected by those sanctions, which are expressly defined in the Instructions of the Holy See as necessary for the preservation and defense of its natural character.

2° To this minor pontifical enclosure are subject monasteries of nuns of solemn vows who, either by their institute or by legitimate concession, so undertake ministries that bring them into contact with outsiders, that several of the religious and a notable part of the house are habitually devoted to these ministries.

3° Likewise, each and every monastery, even though exclusively contemplative, in which only simple vows are pronounced, must be subject to the prescriptions of this form of enclosure at least.

366 § **4.**—1° Major or minor pontifical enclosure is to be regarded as a necessary condition, not only in order that solemn

[58] Canon 600-602 ; cf. *supra*, n. 347a, b, c.

vows may be taken, but also in order that those monasteries in which simple vows are professed, should in future be regarded as true monasteries of nuns, in accordance with canon 488, 7°.[59]

2° If the rules of pontifical enclosure, at least of minor enclosure, cannot generally be observed, the solemn vows which may have been possessed are to be abolished.

§ 5.—1° Minor pontifical enclosure, especially in respect of those features whereby it is distinguished from the enclosure of Congregations or of Orders of men, shall be observed in those places where the nuns do not take solemn vows. 367

2° If however it clearly appears in some monastery that minor enclosure at least cannot be observed habitually, that monastery shall be transformed into the house of a Congregation or society.

ARTICLE V

§ 1.—It is nuns alone, of all those women consecrated to God, whom the Church deputes to offer the public prayer which is offered to God in her name, either in choir or privately;[60] and she places them by rule under a grave obligation, in accordance with their constitutions, to perform this prayer daily at the canonical hours. 368

§ 2.—All monasteries of nuns and the individual nuns who have made profession of solemn or of simple vows, are everywhere obliged to recite the divine Office in choir in accordance with canon 610, § 1 and their own constitutions. 369

§ 3.—In accordance with canon 610, § 3,[61] nuns who were absent from choir, if they have not made profession of solemn 370

---

[59] Cf. supra, n. 77.

[60] **Canon 610,** § 1.—In religious societies whether of men or women, in which the obligation of choir exists, in every house where there are at least four religious bound to choir who are not actually legitimately impeded, and even fewer than four, if the constitutions so enjoin, the divine Office shall be recited daily in common in accordance with the constitutions. 368a

§ 3.—In these same religious societies, whether of men or women, those who have made profession of solemn vows, except *conversi*, are bound to recite the canonical hours privately, if they were absent from choir.

[61] **Canon, 578,** 2°:—Those who have made profession of temporary vows (can. 574) are bound by the same obligation (as those who have made profession of solemn vows or simple perpetual vows) to observe the rules and constitutions, but, where the obligation of choir is in force, they are not bound by the law of reciting the divine Office privately, unless in sacred Orders or the constitutions expressly prescribe the contrary. 370a

vows, are not strictly obliged to private recitation of the canonical hours, unless their constitutions expressly make a different
provision; however, it is not only the mind of the Church, as
we said above (Art. IV), that solemn vows of nuns be everywhere
restored, but also that, if for a time they cannot be restored,
nuns who have made profession of perpetual simple vows should
faithfully perform the task of the divine Office.

371   § 4.—In all monasteries, the conventual Mass corresponding
to the Office of the day, in conformity with the rubrics, should
as far as possible be celebrated. [62]

ARTICLE VI

372   § 1.—1° Monasteries of nuns, unlike other religious houses
of women, by virtue of the Code and in accordance with its
norm, are *sui juris*. [63]

2° The superioresses of individual monasteries in law are
major superiors, and they are given all the faculties which belong
to major superiors, [64] unless from the context or the nature
of the case it is clear that certain faculties pertain to men only. [65]

373   § 2.—1° The ambit of this condition of being *sui juris* or
autonomous, as it is called, which belongs to monasteries of
nuns, is defined by common law and by particular legislation.

2° The juridical guardianship, which the law grants to local
Ordinaries or regular superiors in relation to individual
monasteries, does not suffer any derogation either from this
Constitution or from the federations of monasteries permitted
by the Constitution (Art. VII) and introduced by its authority.

3° The juridical relations of individual monasteries with local
Ordinaries or with regular superiors will continue to be ruled
by the common law and particular legislation.

374   § 3.—It is not defined in any way by this Constitution whether
individual monasteries are subject to the local Ordinary, or

371a   [62] **Canon 610**, § 2.—In religious societies of men, the Mass corresponding to the
Office of the day according to the rubrics should be celebrated daily and, as far as
possible, also in religious societies of women.
[63] Can. 488, 8°; cf. *supra*, n. 77.
[64] *Ibid.*
[65] **Canon 490.** cf. n. 360a.

are, within the limits of the law, exempt from his jurisdiction
and subject to a regular superior.

ARTICLE VII

§ 1.—Monasteries of nuns are not only *sui juris* or auton- 375
omous,[66] but also juridically distinct and independent of one
another, and are mutually linked and united by spiritual and
moral bonds only, even though they may be subject in law to
the same first Order or religious society.

§ 2.—1° The constitution of federations does not in any way 376
interfere with the mutual independence of monasteries, which
is rather admitted in fact than imposed by law; nor are these
federations to be regarded as prohibited by law or in any way
out of harmony with the nature and ends of the religious life
of nuns.

2° Though federations of monasteries are not prescribed by
general rule, nevertheless they are strongly commended by the
Holy See, not merely in order to prevent evils and inconveniences
which can arise from complete separation, but also to promote
regular observance and the contemplative life.

§ 3.—The constitution of any form of federation of monas- 377
teries of nuns and confederation of federations is reserved to
the Apostolic See.

§ 4.—Every federation or confederation must necessarily be 378
organized and ruled by its own laws which have been approved
by the Holy See.

§ 5.—1° Without prejudice to article VI, §§ 2, 3, and 379
safeguarding the principal characteristic of autonomy defined
above (§ 1), there is no obstacle, in establishing federations of
monasteries, after the example of certain monastic Congregations and Orders of canons or monks, to the introduction
of certain equitable modifications and remissions of this autonomy, which appear necessary or more useful.

2° Forms of federation, however, which appear to be
contrary to that autonomy of which we have spoken and to

[66] **Canon 488,** 8°; cf. n. 77.

approximate to the character of centralized government, are reserved in a special way to the Holy See, and cannot be instituted without an express concession from it.

380   § 6.—Federations of monasteries, by reason of the source from which they originate and the authority from which they directly depend and by which they are ruled, are of pontifical law in accordance with the norm of canon law.

381   § 7.—The Holy See, as the case demands, can exercise direct and immediate vigilance and authority over the federation through a religious assistant, whose function will be not merely to represent the Holy See but also to promote the preservation of the genuine spirit of the Order and to assist the superioresses in the right and prudent government of the federation by his activity and advice.

382   § 8.—1° The statutes of the federation must conform not merely to the prescribed norms to be elaborated by the Sacred Congregation of Religious by our authority, but also to the nature, laws, spirit and traditions, whether ascetical, disciplinary, juridical or apostolic, of each Order.

2° The principal object of the federation of monasteries is to give fraternal mutual help, not only by promoting the religious spirit and regular monastic discipline, but also by improving their economic situation.

3° Where circumstances call for it, in the approval of statutes, special norms will be given for the regulation of the faculty and the moral obligation of mutually asking for and giving nuns who are considered to be necessary for the government of monasteries, or for the training of novices in a common novitiate to be set up for all or for several monasteries, or finally to make provision for other moral or material requirements of the monasteries or nuns.

ARTICLE VIII

§ 1.—Monastic labour, in which nuns of the contemplative life also must engage, should as far as possible be in harmony with the rule, constitutions and traditions of each Order.

§ 2.—Work should be so organized that, together with the 384 other sources of income approved by the Church [67] and also the assistance supplied by divine providence, it will ensure for the nuns a secure and appropriate livelihood.

§ 3.—1° Local Ordinaries, regular superiors and superioresses 385 of monasteries and federations, are obliged to apply all diligence to see that nuns never want for the work which is necessary, suitable and remunerative.

2° Nuns for their part are bound by an obligation of conscience not only to gain honestly by the sweat of their brow the bread by which they live, as the Apostle admonishes, [68] but also, as the times demand, constantly to make themselves more competent for different kinds of work.

[67] **Canon 547, § 1.**—In monasteries of nuns, the postulant shall bring the dowry 384a laid down in the constitutions or determined by legitimate custom.

§ 2.—This dowry shall be handed over to the monastery before the reception of the habit, or at least the handing over shall be ensured in a form valid in civil law.

§ 3.—In religious societies of simple vows, in respect of the dowry of women religious, the constitutions shall be abided by.

§ 4.—The prescribed dowry cannot be condoned in whole or in part without the indult of the Holy See, if there be question of a religious society of pontifical standing. If there be question of a religious society of diocesan standing, it cannot be condoned without the permission of the local Ordinary.

Canon 548.—The dowry is irrevocably acquired by the monastery or religious 384b society through the death of the religious, even though she may have made only temporary vows.

Canon 549.—After the first profession of the religious, the dowry shall be invested 384c in safe, lawful and productive shares by the superioress with her council, with the consent of the local Ordinary, and of the regular superior if the house is dependent on him; but it is absolutely forbidden that the money be spent in any way before the death of the religious, even for the building of a house or the wiping out of a debt.

Canon 550, § 1. Dowries shall be administered with prudence and integrity in the 384d monastery or house where the superioress general or provincial superioress resides habitually.

2. Local Ordinaries shall carefully watch over the preservation of the dowries of women religious; and especially at the sacred visitation they shall demand an account of them.

Canon 582.—After solemn profession, without prejudice to particular indults of 384e the Apostolic See, all property which comes in any way to a regular:

1° In an Order which is capable of holding property, goes to the Order or province or house according to the constitution.

2° In an Order which is incapable of holding property, they are acquired by the Holy See.

[68] II Thessalonians 3: 10.

ARTICLE IX

386   All nuns, in order to be found faithful to their divine apostolic vocation, should not only apply the general means of the monastic apostolate, but shall also take care to observe the following:

§ 1.—Nuns who in their own constitutions or by legitimate prescriptions have well defined works of a special apostolate, are bound to dedicate and consecrate themselves faithfully to these, in accordance with their constitutions or statutes and prescriptions.

387   § 2.—Nuns who profess the exclusively contemplative life:

1° If in their own traditions they now have or in the past have accepted a special form of the exterior apostolate, they shall retain it faithfully, having adapted it to modern needs, and always safeguarding their own contemplative life; if they have lost it, they shall diligently take steps to restore it; if some doubt persists on the question of adaptation, they shall consult the Holy See;

2° On the other hand, if the purely contemplative life of the Order has never been combined in a permanent and stable manner with the exterior apostolate either by the approved constitutions of the Order or by tradition, then only in cases of necessity and for a limited time can the nuns be occupied, or be bound at least in charity to occupy themselves, with those particular or personal forms of the apostolate especially which are seen to be compatible with the contemplative life, as it is practised in the Order, in accordance with criteria to be fixed by the Holy See.[69]

387a   [69] Six years later, 25 March 1956, the Sacred Congregation of Religious was to publish a new Instruction *Inter Cetera* on the same important subject of enclosure. That Instruction gave precise details concerning the prescriptions of *Sponsa Christi* and gave effect to the principles laid down by that document. Specifically it stated: " Now, after some years of rich experience, having attentively given consideration to everything that has been submitted to the Holy See on this subject, and because with the introduction of minor pontifical enclosure by the Apostolic Constitution *Sponsa Christi* of 21 November 1950, the Instruction *Nuper Edito* of the Sacred Congregation of Religious, 6 February 1924 (*AAS* XVI (1924), pp. 96-112), no longer corresponds to the discipline in force, this Sacred Congregation has judged it possible and opportune to lay down other regulations and to completely regulate this matter. That is what it purposes by the present Instruction " (*AAS* (1956), pp. 512-26).

INSTRUCTION "INTER PRAECLARA" OF THE SACRED CONGREGATION OF RELIGIOUS ON MONASTIC LABOUR

23 November 1950

EXTRACTS

Two days after the publication of the Apostolic Constitution Sponsa Christi, *the Instruction* Inter Praeclara, *which gave a certain number of directives on the enclosure of nuns and federations of monasteries, made its appearance. Six years later, in the Instruction* Inter Cetera, *25 March 1956,[1] these matters were further defined. We give here only the extract concerning work in monasteries which is still in force.[2]*

XXVI—1° Since the temporal necessities of life, by the 388 ordination of divine providence, are sometimes so pressing that nuns are seen to be morally compelled to seek or accept other forms of work outside their customary labours, to modify their horariums, and indeed perhaps even to increase the time assigned to work, like the faithful in similar circumstances, as true religious they shall all promptly and humbly submit themselves to the dispositions of divine providence.

2° This, however, shall not be done with anxiety or frivol- 389 ously or arbitrarily, but with prudence as far as it is proved to be really necessary or suitable; they shall with simplicity of heart seek to strike a balance between fidelity to the letter and tradition and filial subjection to what is allowed and ordained by divine providence.

3° With these considerations in mind, the measures that 390 are deemed to be required shall be submitted to the religious or ecclesiastical authority, as the particular case calls for.

XXVII. Ecclesiastical and religious superiors are bound:

1° To seek and procure by all means fruitful work for nuns 391 who need it; they shall employ, if the case arises, in addition

---

[1] Cf. *supra*, n° 387a.
[2] *AAS* XLIII (1951), p. 44.

to other upright means, commissions of pious women or men, and even external societies instituted for this purpose, but with caution and prudence;

392   2° To watch prudently over the execution and order of the works performed, and the just price to be demanded for them;

393   3° To diligently make provision for the co-ordination of the activities and labour of different monasteries, so that they will mutually assist, replace and complement one another, and that even the appearance of competition between them will be completely absent.

ALLOCUTION "ANNUS SACER" TO THE
INTERNATIONAL CONGRESS OF RELIGIOUS

8 December 1950

At the closing of the first international congress of religious, which was held in Rome at the end of the Holy Year, the Holy Father delivered an Allocution fn which, in the light of certain contemporary problems, he emphasized the iundamental features of the religious life.[1]

The Holy Year, which without any merit of ours has by God's merciful favour proved fruitful of good in a measure that surpasses human calculations, has shown, in an astonishing series of manifestations, the potent faith and abundant vitality of our Mother, the Church of Christ. Among the events and undertakings of this year, which assume particular gravity and importance, a place is appropriately taken by your congress and the radiant fraternity of this gathering, which it is our great pleasure to salute at this moment, addressing it in terms of the warmest affection. · 394

Something that the annals of the Church have never before recorded—this is the first time that associations, whose members make it the aim of their lives to achieve evangelical perfection, have come together in such numbers as in these last few days, in order to deliberate on proposals concerning their common interests. · 395

The present times, in our opinion, absolutely demand the holding of such a congress. In fact, the transformation of conditions, which the Church must face; a certain number of opinions developed and spread, even within the Church, and touching on questions relating to the condition and state of moral perfection; the urgent demands of that apostolic labour of which you carry an abundant share; all this made it highly advisable that you should give your earnest attention to the proposed discussions and studies. · 396

Your work is now about to be brought to its conclusion. Your careful deliberations have given it life and animation; it has

[1] *AAS* XLIII (1951), p. 26-36.

given rise to manifold proposals and, we hope, it will be no less rich in practical virtuous achievements . . .

As a pledge of divine protection and light, to bring your congress to a happy conclusion, you implore the paternal blessing of the Vicar of Christ. Before according it to you, we deem it opportune to expound certain points which serve to clarify the essential features of the religious life; once these have been set in clear light, they will henceforth be a rule to guide your thoughts and actions.

397 **Clerics, religious, laity.** In the first place, it is well that we should state briefly what is the place of religious Orders and Congregations in the Church. You are well aware that our Redeemer gave a hierarchical constitution to the Church which he founded. He made a clear distinction between the Apostles and their successors together with those who assist them in their office, on the one hand, and on the other, the simple faithful; the structure of the kingdom of God on earth is formed by the union of these two. Consequently, it is ordained by divine law itself that clerics are distinct from the laity.[2] Between these two ranks there is the state of the religious life, which is of ecclesiastical origin; the reason for the existence of this state and the explanation of its value lie in the fact that it is intimately connected with the special purpose of the Church, namely to lead all men to the acquisition of holiness. Though every Christian is bound to attempt to reach that sacred pinnacle, following the guidance of the Church, the religious proceeds on a path which is entirely his own and relies upon helps of a higher nature.

398 **Secular clergy and religious clergy.** Moreover, the religious state is by no means reserved exclusively to either of the two groups which exist in the Church by divine ordinance; both clerics and laics can equally be religious, and the way to the clerical dignity is open equally to those who are religious and to those who are not. It is an error, therefore,

[2] *CIC*, can. 107.

in the appraisal of the foundations upon which Christ has founded his Church, to regard the particular form of the secular clergy, *qua* secular, as established and ratified by our divine Redeemer, while the particular form of the regular clergy, though good and legitimate, is regarded as secondary and subsidiary, on the ground that it derives from the secular clergy. Therefore, if one considers the order established by Christ, neither of the two particular forms of the twofold clergy enjoys a prerogative of divine law, because that law does not give preference to one rather than the other, nor does it exclude either of them. As for the difference between them, their mutual relations, the tasks to be entrusted to each of them in performing the work of human salvation, Christ left all this to be determined in accordance with the varying circumstances and needs of every age; or rather, to express our mind more definitely, he entrusted it to the decisions of the Church.

Secular and religious clergy exercise their ministry subject to the bishop. According to the precept of divine 399 law, there can be no doubt that the priest, whether secular or religious, is bound to fulfil his ministry in such a way that he assists the bishop and acts under his direction. This in fact is the customary practice in the Church, and it is clearly defined by the prescriptions of the Code of Canon Law which deal with religious who are parish priests and local Ordinaries.[3] Not infrequently in missionary territories, the whole of the clergy, including the bishop, belong to the ranks of the regular clergy. Let no one assert that this is a quite extraordinary and abnormal situation, to be regarded as temporary, and that, as soon as possible, the ecclesiastical administration should be handed over to the secular clergy.

Neither is the exemption of religious Orders in conflict with 400 the principles of the divinely given constitution of the Church; nor is it in any way incompatible with the law which obliges a priest to obey the bishop. For according to canon law, exempt religious are subject to the authority of the local bishop in so

---

[3] *CIC*, can. 626-31; 451 § 5.

13

far as the exercise of the episcopal ministry and the proper organization of the care of souls require it. And even apart from that, in the discussions about exemption which have taken place in the last ten years, perhaps sufficient attention has not been paid to the fact that exempt religious, even by the prescriptions of canon law, are at all times and places subject to the authority of the Roman Pontiff, as their supreme superior, and that they are bound to obey him by reason also of a vow of obedience.[4] Now the supreme Pontiff has ordinary and immediate jurisdiction not only over the universal Church, but over each diocese and the individual faithful.

It is clear, therefore, that the fundamental law enacted by God, which binds clerics and laics to submit to the rule of the bishop, is quite adequately complied with even in respect of exempt religious, and, finally, that both the secular and the religious clergy equally accord with the will and command of Christ.

401 **The clerical state and the religious state vis-à-vis the obligation of perfection.** There is another question which is closely connected with what we have said so far, and we propose now to explain and clarify it; it concerns the reason for which the cleric and the religious are bound to strive for absolute perfection of conduct.

402 It is contrary to the truth to assert that the clerical state, precisely as such and as it proceeds from divine law, demands by its nature, or at least in virtue of some postulate of its nature, that the evangelical counsels should be observed by those who belong to the clerical state, and, consequently, that it should or can be called the state of (acquiring) evangelical perfection. The cleric therefore is not bound by the divine law to practise the evangelical counsels of poverty, chastity and obedience; and especially he is not bound in the same way and for the same reason as one for whom this obligation arises from a public vow made when embracing the religious state. That, however, does not prevent the cleric from assuming these obligations privately and on his own initiative. Likewise, the fact that priests of the

---

[4] *CIC*, can. 499 § 1.

Latin rite are obliged to observe celibacy, does not in the least destroy or attenuate the distinction between the clerical and the religious state. But the reason why the regular cleric makes profession of the condition and state of perfection, is not because he is a cleric, but because he is a religious.

Place of Secular Institutes. It is true that by the Apostolic Constitution *Provida Mater Ecclesia* [5] we declared that the form of life, which is followed by Secular Institutes, is also to be accepted as a state of perfection publicly recognized, because the members are bound in some way to the observance of the evangelical counsels; that fact does not in any way contradict the doctrine just propounded. There is, of course, nothing to prevent clerics from merging in Secular Institutes in order to strive for the state of evangelical perfection by the choice of this form of life; but then they too are in the state of acquiring perfection, not as clerics, but because they are members of a Secular Institute. The evangelical counsels, which are proper to the religious state and are practised therein with the highest perfection, are adopted by the Secular Institute as a way of life which it is to follow; but it carries them out in such a manner that it is not dependent on the religious state, but has its own independent existence in an exterior form of life that does not necessarily belong to the above-mentioned perfection. 403

Reasons for entering religious life. We deem it opportune to dwell somewhat on the question: what reasons does the religious state offer for entering it? 404

There are those who assert that the religious state, by its own nature and purpose, which of course are not to be disapproved, is nothing more than a refuge afforded for the timid and anxious; these, being unable to face the perils of life with its storms, and not knowing how or being perhaps unwilling to support adversity, are led by indolence to bid farewell to the world and take refuge in the calm of the cloister; hence, such

[5] Cf. *supra*, n. 220-252.

people should rather be aroused to have confidence in the grace of God and in themselves, so that instead of seeking leisurely tranquillity, they will cast away this imaginary inclination of the soul and boldly confront the struggles of everyday life. Is this correct?

405 It is not our purpose now to weigh in the scales the question of the motives which prompt individuals to adopt the religious state. We wish to state the reason, the principal and true reason, for which the walls of the cloister are to be approached. It is a reason far removed from the opinion above-mentioned which, taken as a generalization, is false and unjust. For indeed, just as the purpose of entering the priesthood, so also the decision to enter the religious state and the firm constancy to remain faithful to that decision once taken, demand noble souls and an eager spirit of self-dedication. The history of the Church, which narrates the mighty achievements of the canonized saints and of religious institutes, and which tells of the outcome of missionary journeys and records ascetical teachings, and indeed even everyday experience, all make it clear as day that in the religious state no less than in the world men and women have shone with invincible and generous courage. Besides, those men and women religious who exhaust themselves in undertakings for the extension of the Gospel kingdom, who assist the sick, who educate the young, who work in the schools—do all these cut themselves off from the human community and turn their hearts away from it? Is it not the fact rather that the majority of them, like secular priests and lay helpers, are fighting in the front line for the cause of the Church?

406 **True religious obedience.** Here, however, we cannot refrain from drawing attention to a fact that is quite contrary to the opinion we have already cited. If it be the case that there is a decline in the numbers of those, especially young girls, who wish to enter the enclosed gardens of the religious life, all too frequently the reason is that it is thought to be too severe to be deprived of one's own free choice and to renounce one's freedom; that is what the vow of obedience by its nature involves. Indeed it is not the renunciation

of liberty for the love of Christ which is extolled by some as an exalted form of moral perfection, but the narrowing down of this self-denial. Therefore, they say, for the formation of the just and holy man, it is this norm which should be preferred: let liberty be limited, but only as far as is necessary, but let liberty be unchecked as far as possible.

We pass over the question whether the new foundation, upon 407 which they are endeavouring to raise up the edifice of holiness, will be as fruitful and firm in sustaining and increasing the apostolic work of the Church, as that furnished for 1,500 years by the ancient rule of obedience accepted for the love of Christ. For the moment, the point of chief importance is thoroughly to weigh this reasoning in order to bring to light its inner significance. For, if it be properly examined, it fails to recognize the nature of the evangelical counsel, and indeed it distorts it in a certain way to a contrary meaning. No one is in duty bound to impose on himself the evangelical counsel of perfect obedience, which is rooted in that rule of life whereby the free control of one's own will is renounced—no one, we repeat, whether there is question of individuals or of associations. They can, if they wish, regulate their life according to this new rule. But words should be understood and employed according to their meaning. Now, if this new norm be compared with the vow of obedience, it is not of the same supreme value, nor does it give expression to the sense of the passage of Scripture and the splendid example it proposes: *He humbled himself, becoming obedient even unto death.* [6]

It is misleading and an error, therefore, if, when advice is 408 sought about adopting the religious state, one offers only that norm or opinion for guidance, and wrongly neglects the inclination of the soul that has come for advice and the prompting of divine grace. Consequently, if there are unmistakable indications that it is the voice of God which has called someone to the summit of evangelical perfection, then without any hesitation, for the sake of accomplishing this exalted purpose, let that free immolation of liberty which the vow of obedience demands be proposed to him; it is a vow which, we declare,

[6] Philippians 2: 8.

the Church has studied carefully through the course of centuries; she has put it to the test of experience, defined and approved it. No one is to be pushed against his will into this pursuit of self-dedication; but if someone so wishes, then let no one dissuade, not to speak of hindering him.

409   So much for these matters. We now intend to say something about exterior works and the inner life. There are few questions which pertain to the regular life and in general to the religious life, and which in fact are of great importance, that have been more extensively treated than this. Nevertheless we wish to express our own mind also on this theme.

410   **Warning against existentialism.** It is not a mere chance that the origin and shaping of the philosophy popularly called "existentialism" should have taken place in our own time. The men of our day, living at a time when the course of events has brought difficult philosophical and religious questions to the fore for solution, are quite content to disregard the higher aspects and deem that it is quite sufficient for them to do what has to be done here and now. But he who professes our holy faith refuses, on the basis of such tenets, to concern himself merely with individual points of time and to allow himself to be carried along by the stream of life. He knows that the invisible things [7] are of supreme value and supremely true, and that they are so destined to last that they will never know failure.

But alas! despite warnings and exhortations, even ecclesiastics, not excepting religious, have been affected in no small degree by this contagion; and though they do not deny the supernatural which surpasses man's senses and all of nature, they do nevertheless depreciate it.

Can it be said that this grave and dangerous crisis has now been overcome? Thanks be to God that one may now hope so; some things that we see and that are revealed by events inspire us with this confidence.

---

[7] Cf. Hebrews 11: 1.

Union of active life with interior life. The most active forms of busy work 411 can be united with the rare riches of the interior life. Those two stars, St. Francis Xavier and St. Theresa of Jesus, who are shining examples of devotion to the regular life, prove this clearly.

Eager activity and care for the interior life not only demand that they should be closely linked, but that, at least in respect of appreciation and desire, they should go forward hand in hand. Where there is fervent activity, there should be found, with corresponding fervour, faith, prayers, the desire to dedicate oneself and all one possesses to God, the shining beauty of a conscience that is undefiled, obedience, patience in trials, active and vigilant charity towards God and the neighbour.

This applies not only to the members of religious societies 412 individually, if they are religious not merely in their outward religious habit but in their very souls; it also constitutes for the entire religious society the reason why religious life is solidly established before God and men, and is worthy of the fullest approbation. This is what the Church insistently demands of you: that your exterior activity be in harmony with your interior life and that the two constantly balance one another.

Do not all of you, clerics and laics alike, make the profession that you are embracing the state of evangelical perfection? If that be the case, then produce the fruits of that state, so that the mystical Body of Christ, which is the Church, may draw even more effective strength from your vigour and ardour. It is for this same reason that religious Orders dedicated to the contemplative life are in a certain way necessary to the Church, to which they bring an abiding bloom of beauty and a profusion of heavenly graces.

True charity comes from living faith. You are aware, of course, that it is 413 frequently said that charity towards the neighbour is gradually losing its religious nature and becoming worldly, laicized. But that beneficence which has no foundation in faith, but springs from another source, is not charity and cannot be called Catholic. Charity has a dignity, an inspiration and strength, which are lacking in mere philanthropy, even when it is endowed with riches and resources. Thus, Catholic religious sisters who attend the sick, when compared with those who practise the same function for humanitarian reasons or for a salary, have something which is different and more important. Sometimes they may take second place to others in regard to technical resources; and now also we exhort them to keep up with others in this department, and indeed even to surpass them. Nevertheless, when members of religious sisterhoods, in whom breathes the vital spirit of their institute, give their devoted care, being always prepared for the love of Christ to give their lives for those who are suffering from infirmity, then a certain atmosphere surrounds them, and in it virtue works wonders which neither technical invention nor medicine achieves.

Religious Orders and Congregations which profess the active life shall keep before their eyes and cherish everything that will reflect the sacred features of their work, and they shall nourish the fire of the Holy Spirit in the sanctuary of a clean conscience.

414   **Adaptation to con-**   Beloved children, we wish also to
temporary conditions   touch briefly on the desire and concern
of religious institutes to adapt them-
selves to changed times and to combine the old and the new in
a happy alliance.

—Need for adaptation;

415   When young people hear it said: " We must belong to our time." " Our endeavours must be equal to the demands of our time," they are inflamed with an unwonted ardour of spirit and, if they are serving in the ranks of religious life, it is towards this objective above all that they are eager to direct the strivings of their future religious activity. And indeed that is partly correct. For it has generally happened that the founding fathers of religious institutes conceived their new undertaking as a means of meeting needs or tasks of the Church that were then emerging and brooked no delay; consequently they adapted their under-takings to their own time. If you wish to follow in the footsteps

of your fathers, then act in the same manner as they did. Study the opinions, judgments and conduct of your contemporaries, among whom you live, and if you find there details that are good and just, make these precious elements your own; otherwise you will not be able to enlighten, help, support and guide your contemporaries.

—Limits of adaptation;

But the Church has a patrimony, one that is intact since her origin, that is invariable through the passing centuries, and that is perfectly suited to the needs and desires of the human race; the chief part of that patrimony is the Catholic faith, which recently again we have defended against new dangers by the Encyclical *Humani Generis*. [8] Guard carefully that faith in all its purity, being thoroughly convinced that it contains supremely potent powers, which enable it to transform any epoch. 416

Moreover, the aim of the state of perfection is part of that same patrimony, and you must strive to realize it with the greatest zeal; with the assistance and means which it offers, you are to become holy, and also to sanctify your neighbours directly or indirectly by your labours, so that they too, sharing ever more richly in divine grace, may live lives of piety and die in piety. To that same patrimony belongs that truth, so sublime, so primary, namely that the one way to perfection is deemed to be self-denial for the love of Christ. That is something which does not change with the changing times. 417

—Methods of adaptation;

There are circumstances, however, and indeed many of them, in which you can and ought to fall in with the character and needs of men and of the times. That adaptation is, to a great extent, already an accomplished fact; and now that you have compared your ideas and proposals, it is being thoroughly and completely carried out. That many laudable innovations have already been introduced by you is abundantly clear from all 418

---

[8] Encyclical *Humani Generis* on Catholic doctrine, 12 August 1950 (*AAS* XLII (1950), p. 561-78.

that you are doing, either individually or by your institutes, in schools, for the education of youth, for the relief of human miseries, for the cultivation and promotion of learning. Consequently it must be said, and no one can deny our assertion, that a vast mass of work is arising, if you are to meet the changed times with new and appropriate means.

419   But it is of supreme importance, in our judgment, that in this adaptation to the changing needs of the times which you are seeking, you should search out and sagaciously investigate what are the spiritual resources which lie beneath the surface in our contemporaries, the deep-seated desires which influence them, and the genuine aspect of their souls. We do not mean that aspect which reflects what is deserving of condemnation and reproach, or that which shows forth the tumults of the passions and the poison of vices. But in men, because they are men and, all the more, inasmuch as they are Christians, even though they are in error and emmeshed in faults, there is a notable amount of good, and also the aspiration to greater good. You must give your encouragement to inclinations such as these, you must meet these aspirations; taking prudent care, however, that you will not borrow from the world what is harmful and culpable, but rather that you will impart to it the good and holy qualities of your own which are in harmony with its healthy inclinations. The hesitant good in others, therefore, you shall tend, develop and make to increase; from it, as from particles of gold, fashion precious vessels, and as from streams, make rivers to flow.

—*Programme of adaptation.*

420   There are some who hold, and they are not perhaps in error, that there are three things which especially correspond to the character and inclinations of our age: latitude in thought and discussion, unity in planning and organization, speed in execution. Are not these three things also characteristic notes of the Gospel, are they not qualities of those who profess the Catholic faith in word and conduct? What greater expanse can be opened for our thoughts than that broad reach expressed in the words of the Apostle: *All things are yours: you indeed are of Christ and Christ*

is of God? [9] What closer unity of understanding and love than that simple and unified view expressed in the words of the divine Scriptures: *God all in all.*[10] *Thou shalt love the Lord thy God with thy whole heart and thy whole soul and thy whole mind and with all thy strength . . . Thou shalt love thy neighbour as thyself.*[11]

The admonition that we should be active and vigorous, and not detained by the harmful recollection of passing things, is contained in the words: *No one who puts his hand to the plough and looks back is fit for the kingdom of God.*[12] If you wish to raise your eyes to examples of virtue in which these three glorious qualities shone out, turn your thoughts to the Apostle Paul and to all who have accomplished in the Church of Christ outstanding deeds worthy of being remembered for ever.

CONCLUSION

Essentials of the religious life ; exhortation to fidelity, apostolic labour and unity. Now the aims which shine like beacons before you both in contemplation and in the active life, the same aims which the other children of the Church, priests and laity, must pursue, are Christian perfection and the salvation of the human race. But your special rôle is to make use of the most efficient means, namely the evangelical counsels by the taking of vows of religion; thus by assiduous warfare you will vanquish the concupiscence of the flesh, the concupiscence of the eyes and the pride of life;[13] and you will constantly grow in holiness and be energetic ministers of God in securing the salvation of mankind. Turn your thoughts and actions to the attainment of these sublime aims and *being rooted and founded in charity,*[14] solidly established by firm faith and rich in humility, neglect no opportunity of bringing men, your brothers, back to the Creator, the Redeemer, like lost sheep back to the shepherd.

As models of trustworthiness and fidelity, see to it that your conduct corresponds with your title, and that your whole way of life agrees with your profession. In the words of the Apostle

421

422

[9] I Corinthians 3: 23. [10] I Corinthians 15: 28.
[11] Mark 12: 30-31. [12] Luke 9: 62.
[13] Cf. I John 2: 16. [14] Ephesians 3: 17.

of the gentiles: *Being solicitous to keep the unity of the spirit in the bond of peace*;[15] may peace reign within you and between you, among the members of the same house or institute, and also with those who have been received into other institutes; may it reign between yourselves and all others who labour with you and with whom you labour to win souls for Christ. Away with controversies and discords which weaken and cripple even projects full of hope; the Church is like a field to be cultivated by apostolic labour, and it is immense in its area; the opportunity for toil and perspiration is not lacking for anyone.

423   If the pledges of the religious have the solid support of a life that is made a shining example at every stage by the inflexible observance of the rule, and if the priest considers that nothing is too burdensome or too hard, when there is question of the salvation of souls, then even at the present day the words will be verified in them which the Apostle uttered concerning the word of God, *which is living and effective and keener than any two-edged sword.*[16] To give an example: quite recently we have urged the faithful that in these calamitous times, in which the afflicted lot of so many and their pitiable destitution are so flagrantly opposed to excessive expenditure, they should lead a modest way of life and show themselves openhanded towards the neighbour bowed down with distress. Therefore, in such an urgent work of Christian perfection, of justice and of charity, do you surpass all others by your example, and lead them on to the imitation of Christ.

[15] Ephesians 4: 3.
[16] Hebrews 4: 12.

CIRCULAR LETTER OF THE SACRED CONGREGATION OF RELIGIOUS ON THE USE OF TOBACCO IN THE STATES OF PERFECTION

10 January 1951

Wars always bring a certain relaxation, and religious who, in the spirit of mortification, practised complete abstention from tobacco, have been led to relax their rule in the trenches or in prison camps. At the beginning of 1951, the Sacred Congregation of Religious thought it proper to address a circular to all superiors general in order to make clear the spirit in which there should be a tightening of discipline in this respect.[1]

During these last years, since the end of the war, a number 424 of consultations, complaints, and even denunciations and formal accusations concerning the use of tobacco by members of the states of perfection, have reached us from superiors, chapters general, and also from religious inspired by zeal for observance, and even from local Ordinaries.

In religious Orders and societies in which the use of tobacco is forbidden by the constitutions or by the legitimate received traditions or by the prescriptions of chapters and superiors, the intervention of the Sacred Congregation has been invoked in various ways, in order that this unlawful usage, which has been introduced here and there principally on the occasion of the war, should be effectively checked and extirpated.

As regards religious Orders and societies in which the use 425 of tobacco generally is not regarded as unlawful, it has been commented that it gives occasion to rather grave abuses. These abuses usually infringe on and undermine in many ways religious poverty, the spirit of mortification and even exterior modesty.

The question of the use and abuse of tobacco could have been treated on the occasion of the recent congress of states of perfection; but since, for various reasons, this was not done,

[1] This Circular was not published in the *AAS*.

the Sacred Congregation considers it its duty to discuss the
matter clearly and frankly with superiors general without delay,
in order to inform them of the standards to be observed concerning the use of tobacco, and to stimulate strongly their zeal in
checking abuses of tobacco, if any such are to be found in their
Orders and societies. For those who are members of the states
of perfection should be in this matter models to all of fidelity,
of Christian and religious poverty, of temperance and modesty.

426   The Sacred Congregation, therefore, includes in the following
general norms the criteria which are to be observed concerning
the use of tobacco:

I. In religious Orders, societies and institutes, in which,
either by the approved constitutions or by the lawful received
prescriptions of chapters and superiors, the use of tobacco is
either forbidden or very limited or strictly subject to conditions,
these lawful prescripts should be religiously observed and
insisted on. The Sacred Congregation considers these prescripts
as constituting part of the regular and religious mortification
and observance, and rightly and with good reason confirms and
maintains them.

427   II. In religious Orders, societies and institutes, in which the
moderate use of tobacco is accepted and lawfully exists, this
usage is to be so regulated that religious poverty is safeguarded
both in relation to expenses and to dependence on the superiors;
that the spirit of asceticism and of religious observance, which
constitutes one of the essential foundations of the states of
perfection, suffers no detriment; and finally that the use of
tobacco does not, by reason of the place, manner or time,
prove injurious to or in any way adversely affect good example
and the edification of the faithful or of outsiders.

428   III. To avoid these dangers (n. II) and to render more effective
the legitimate prescripts of the constitutions or chapters that
are actually in force (n. I), superiors together with their councils
can and should issue, if there is need, special norms regulating
the manner, quantity, time and place of the use of tobacco.

429   IV. Generally the Sacred Congregation is opposed to the
introduction of the use of tobacco, to the derogation of rules
in favour of its use, to the relaxation of discipline in this matter,

whether in religious Orders, societies or institutes. Indeed, we must frankly say, these relaxations, derogations and permissions, as experience proves, do not favour the religious spirit, and in 430 fact easily do it serious harm.

V. If, in a diocese, some norms for clerics have been given by the local Ordinaries concerning the use of tobacco, especially in public, superiors shall see to it by every means that these norms are religiously, faithfully and exactly observed by religious and by others who strive for evangelical perfection, as befits their public profession of holiness. If local Ordinaries inform superiors of violations of these rules or of abuses of tobacco by their religious subjects, the superiors shall take effective and diligent means to deal with them.

In communicating these matters to your paternity, I beg that you will convey to this Sacred Congregation whatever provisions had already been made in this matter in your religious society or which you will straightway decide to enact together with your Council.

Our holy Father Pius XII, Pope by divine providence, in an audience granted to the undersigned Cardinal Prefect on 8 January, has deigned to approve this circular Letter.

ENCYCLICAL "EVANGELII PRAECONES"
ON THE MISSIONS

2 June 1951

EXTRACTS

This Encyclical is directly concerned with missionary activity. It clearly defines its essential object, namely the establishment of the Church in mission territory. It also deals with numerous practical questions, such as the assistance of militant laity in Catholic Action, the formation of youth, charitable and social institutions. But in many passages it stresses the spirit of detachment which should inspire religious Congregations in the service of the missions. For this reason, these extracts have their place in a work devoted to the states of perfection.[1]

431 **The religious missionary's primary concern: the salvation of souls.** Our purpose is that the labour of the heralds of the Gospel should constantly grow more efficacious, and that not one drop of their sweat and their blood should be shed in vain; hence we wish here to explain briefly the principles and standards by which the activity and zeal of missionaries should be guided.

In the first place it is to be noted that a person who has received a heavenly vocation to teach the truths of the Gospel and Christian virtue to far-off pagan nations, has been given a very great and exalted function. For he consecrates his life to God, in order that God's kingdom may be spread to the very ends of the earth. He is not seeking his own interests, but those of Jesus Christ.[2] He considers as addressed to himself, in a special way, those splendid sayings of St. Paul: *For Christ, therefore, we are ambassadors;*[3] *for though we walk in the flesh, we do not war according to the flesh;*[4] *to the weak I became weak, that I might gain the weak.*[5]

[1] *AAS* XLIII (1951), p. 506, 510, 520.
[3] II Corinthians 5: 20.
[5] I Corinthians 9: 22.

[2] Philippians 2: 21.
[4] II Corinthians 10: 3.

He must, therefore, regard the country to which he is bringing the light of the Gospel as a second fatherland and love it with due charity; and so he will not seek material interests, nor the advantage of his own country or of his own religious institute, but rather what is for the salvation of souls. Certainly he should have an intense love for his own country and his own institute, but he should love the Church even more ardently. And he must remember that nothing will prove beneficial to his own institute, if it is detrimental to the welfare of the Church.

. . . On this matter, however, we **432** deem it opportune to direct attention **The religious should collaborate with local bishops.** to something that we consider should be carefully borne in mind, when missions, which previously had been entrusted to foreign clergy, are handed over to bishops and priests of the country to be tended and ruled. The religious institute, whose members have undertaken the first cultivation of this field of the Lord at the cost of heavy labour, need not entirely abandon this field when, by the mandate of the Sacred Congregation for the Propagation of the Faith, they entrust to other workers the vineyard which they have cultivated and which is now loaded with a rich harvest of fruits; it will be useful and appropriate if they continue to give assistance to the new bishop elected from the people of the place.

For even as in all other dioceses of the Catholic world religious generally give assistance to the local Ordinary, so also in mission territories, even though the missionaries belong to another race, they will not cease to engage in the holy combat as auxiliary forces; and thus happily will be fulfilled the words spoken by the divine Master at the well of Sichar: *And he that reapeth receiveth wages and gathereth fruit unto life everlasting: that both he that soweth and he that reapeth may rejoice together.* [6]

[6] John 4: 36.

14

433   **Not to regard the mission territory as their own property.**   . . . . In former times the vast field of the missionary apostolate was not defined by prescribed limits of ecclesiastical jurisdiction, nor was it entrusted for cultivation to religious Orders or Congregations together with the growing native clergy. That, however, is frequently the case nowadays, as is well known, and it even happens sometimes that certain regions have been assigned to religious of a particular province of the same religious institute.

We, of course, recognize the advantages of such an arrangement; since the organisation of Catholic missions is accelerated and facilitated by such methods and regulations. It can happen, however, that from this practice serious inconveniences and setbacks may arise, and it is opportune to remedy them as far as possible. Our predecessors have already treated of this subject in their Letters [7] which we have mentioned, and they laid down regulations of great wisdom which it pleases us here to repeat and confirm; and we paternally exhort you, " in accordance with your known and proved zeal for religion and the salvation of souls, to accept these norms with pious sentiments and minds ready to obey.

434   For since those territories, which the Apostolic See entrusted to your care in order that you should attach them to Christ the Lord, are generally of vast extent, it can sometimes happen that the number of missionaries from your respective institutes falls far below what the needs of the territory demand. Do not hesitate, therefore, to follow the practice in duly established dioceses; there it is customary for men religious, clerical or lay, from different institutes, and for sisters from different Congregations, to assist and help the bishop.

435   Similarly for the propagation of the Christian faith, for the instruction of the native youth of the country and for the securing of other such advantages, do not hesitate to summon and enlist as partners in your labours religious or missionaries who do not belong to your institute, whether they be priests or belong to so-called lay institutes. Religious Orders and Con-

433a   [7] Benedict XV, Apostolic Letter *Maximum Illud*, 30 November 1919 (*AAS* XI (1919), p. 440 f); Pius XI, Encyclical *Rerum Ecclesiae*, 28 February 1926 (*AAS* XVIII (1926), p. 65f).

gregations may take a saintly pride both in the mission to pagans
entrusted to them and in the conquests for Christ's kingdom
achieved by them to this day; but they shall remember that they
have not received a personal and perpetual right to the mission
territories; they hold them at the will of the Apostolic See,
which therefore has the right and duty to make provision for
their proper and full development. The Roman Pontiff does not,
therefore, satisfy the requirements of the apostolic office merely
by distributing territories of greater or less dimensions among
different institutes; what is of even greater importance, he
must at all times and with all solicitude make it his concern
that these institutes send to the territories entrusted to them
missionaries in such numbers, and above all of such quality,
that they will be abundantly sufficient to fill these broad expanses
with the light of Christian truth and to labour efficiently there."

DISCOURSE TO TEACHING SISTERS

13 September 1951

In September 1951, the first international congress of teaching sisters was held at Rome, with representatives from more than forty institutes. The Holy Father received them in special audience at Castel Gandolfo and took the opportunity of giving them a number of counsels and directives suited to their mission at the present day.[1]

436   We are particularly pleased to have the opportunity, afforded by your participation in the congress of teaching sisters, of speaking a word of sincere and paternal praise for the activity of sisters in the domain of the school and of education in Italy and throughout the whole Catholic world. How could the Church, in recent and very recent times, have carried out fully her mission, without the work which hundreds of thousands of sisters perform with such zeal in the spheres of education and charitable activity? And how could she accomplish it in our own day? Undoubtedly there are many other valuable female forces which, together with sisters or side by side with them, labour in the school and in education, or dedicate themselves to the apostolate of the laity.

We are thinking above all of the army of good Catholic women teachers in the State schools. But even they will not be astonished if today we say to you, beloved daughters, gathered around us as representatives of the Orders and religious Congregations dedicated to the apostolate of the school and education: God grant that the dedication, the love and the sacrifices which you make, generally in secret and without the light of publicity, for the love of Christ and the welfare of youth, will give a hundredfold return of good fruits in the future, as in the past. May the Lord recompense you for it, and may he pour forth on you the abundance of his divine favours.

[1] *AAS* XLIII (1951), p. 738-44.

The contemporary crisis : a conflict of generations. Our good wishes go forth all the more 437 fervently from our heart, because we feel with you the crisis through which your schools and your institutes of education are passing. It is a crisis which is expressed in the contrast: modern youth—sisters' schools. No doubt you have had ample opportunity to treat of this subject in your congress. Many points, which are no less important for you than for men religious, and which refer to the questions of your activity, have already been expounded by us in the Discourse of 8 December 1950.[2] Consequently we can confine ourselves here to one or more features of your problem, which seem to us more in need of consideration.

—Causes of this crisis.

If you have the painful experience that the teaching sister 438 and the young girl of today no longer understand one another, that is not a phenomenon peculiar to your crisis. For other teachers also, and often even for the parents themselves, the situation is not much better.

Indeed it is not just an empty expression to say that youth has changed, that it has become very different from what it was. Perhaps the radical reason for this difference in the youth of today is the one which has been made the subject of frequent observations and complaints: youth is wanting in reverence for many things which formerly, from childhood and quite naturally, were regarded with the most profound respect. However, the youth of today does not carry all the blame for this attitude. During the years of childhood it has lived through horrible things and has seen before its eyes the failure and miserable collapse of many ideals formerly highly prized. Thus it has become distrustful and recalcitrant.

It is right, moreover, to add that this complaint of lack of 439 understanding is not new; it is encountered in every generation, and it is reciprocal: between mature age and youth, between parents and children, between teachers and pupils. Half a

---

[2] To the international Congress of Religious; cf. *supra*, nn. 394-423.

century ago, and even earlier, it was frequently a question of
soft sentimentality: men and women liked it to be believed and
said that they were not " understood." Nowadays the complaint,
which is not free from a certain pride, turns rather on intellectual
attitudes. The result of this lack of understanding is, on the
one hand, a reaction that sometimes can go beyond just limits,
a tendency to reject everything that is new or has the appearance
of novelty, an exaggerated fear of rebellion against all tradition
—on the other hand, there is a lack of trust, which alienates
from all authority and which drives people to seek solutions
and advice, irrespective of competent judgment, with a sort
of infatuation that is ingenuous rather than reasoned.

—*Remedies*: (1) *Understanding*,

440
    To set out to reform youth and to win it over by keeping
it in subjection, to gain it by constraint, would be useless and
not always just. You will succeed much better in getting it to
give you its trust, if you apply yourselves, on your own part,
to understanding youth and to making yourselves understood by
youth, always safeguarding, of course, those truths and unchanging values which do not admit any change in the human
mind and heart.

    Understanding youth: that certainly does not mean giving
approval to everything and admitting everything in their ideas,
their tastes, their fantastic caprices and the spurious enthusiasms
of youth; but it consists above all in the discernment of whatever
of solid worth these contain and in the loyal recognition of it,
without laments or regrets; it consists also in seeking out the
origins of deviations and errors, which frequently are only the
unhappy outcome of attempts to resolve real and difficult
problems; and finally it consists in following with attention the
vicissitudes and the conditions of the present time.

441   —(2) *Making oneself understood*,

    Making oneself understood: this does not mean the adoption
of the misuses, the imprecisions, the confusions, the equivocal
neologisms of vocabulary and syntax; what it does mean is the

clear expression, in form that is varied and always exact, of one's own mind, while seeking to detect the thought of others and taking account of their difficulties and of their ignorance or inexperience.

—(3) Influence of profound faith.

On the other hand, it is equally true that even the youth   442 of today is fully accessible to true and genuine values. And it is precisely here that your share of responsibility begins. You must treat the young with naturalness and simplicity, each one of you acting according to individual character; but, at the same time, all of you are bound to give proof of that religious seriousness and that reserve, which even the world of today expects of you and behind which it should sense your union with God. It is not necessary that, when you find yourselves in the midst of young girls, you should be constantly speaking of God. But when you do speak of God, it should be in such a manner that they cannot fail to recognize—yes, this is a genuinely sincere sentiment which springs from profound conviction. And then you will gain the trust of your pupils, who will allow themselves to be persuaded and guided by you.

Is religious life an obstacle to education? And now let us come to what is   443 particularly and distinctively yours: the religious life, your habit, chastity, your rules and constitutions. Do all these perhaps make you less fitted or simply incompetent for the instruction and education of the youth of today?

—Principal answer: even non-practising Catholics have confidence in religious.

Let us take note of this first of all: Those who have the right   444 of educating, the parents, are not of that opinion. The sisters' schools are still sought after and preferred even by many who are only on the fringes of religion or even far from it. In how many countries do not the vocations of teaching sisters and the number of their schools still fall short of the demands! And that is not a mere chance! Consequently one might add, not only for Italy, but in general: From those who have a share in the forming of school legislation one has the right to expect a measure of justice, and we would say, of democratic spirit, which corresponds with the will of the parents; in that way the schools founded and directed by religious institutes would not be placed in worse conditions than schools founded by the State, and they would be accorded that liberty which is necessary for their development.

445   —*Necessity for certain adaptations.*

And now let us speak briefly about the religious life in itself.— The religious habit: select one of such a kind that it will be an expression of the inner character, of religious simplicity and modesty; then it will be a source of edification for all, even for modern youth.

446   Chastity, virginity (which implies also the inner renunciation of all sensual affection) does not make souls strangers to the world. It rather arouses and develops the powers of the soul for greater and more exalted tasks, which are beyond the resources of the individual family. Nowadays there are many teaching and nursing sisters who are, in the best sense of the word, nearer to life than ordinary people in the world.

The very regulations of the constitutions, taken according to the letter and the spirit, facilitate and secure for the sister all that she requires and must do, in our times, in order to be a good teacher or educator. That is obvious even on the purely technical side. For example, nowadays in many countries the sisters make appropriate use of the bicycle, whenever their work makes it necessary. At the outset it was something completely new, but not contrary to the rule.

447   It is possible that some points of the horarium, certain prescriptions which are nothing more than simple applications of the rule, certain customs which perhaps correspond with conditions in the past, but at present serve only to complicate the educational task, should be adapted to the new conditions. The major superiors and the general chapter shall take care to

proceed conscientiously in this matter, with clear foresight, prudence and courage and, wherever the case calls for it, they shall not fail to submit the proposed changes to the competent ecclesiastical authorities.

You wish to serve the cause of Jesus Christ and of his Church in accordance with the needs of the world of today. It would not then be reasonable to persist in usages or forms which impede that service or perhaps even make it impossible. Sisters engaged in teaching and education should be so well prepared and so equal to the exalted nature of their task; they should be so well acquainted with everything with which the young come into contact or by which they are influenced, that the pupils will immediately say: "We can go to the sister with our problems and difficulties; she understands us and helps us."

Requirements for teaching mission. This brings us on to speak of those school and educational requirements which we wish particularly to recommend to your care. 448

A great number of your schools have been represented to us and praised as very good. But not all of them. It is our keen desire that all should strive to become excellent.

—Competence.

That, however, presupposes that your teaching sisters have a perfect knowledge and command of their subject. Make provision, therefore, to give them a good preparation and formation, which will also meet the qualities and qualifications demanded by the State.[3] Give generously to them all that they need, especially in the matter of books, so that they will be able to follow up afterwards the progress of their subject, and thus give to their young pupils a rich and solid harvest of information. That is in conformity with the Catholic conception, which gleans 449

[3] The general conference of the bishops of Latin-America held at Rio de Janeiro, 25 July to 4 August 1955, echoed the concern of the Holy Father, when expressly asking major superiors, "in order to increase the efficiency of their sisters, to take steps to enable all to acquire solid spiritual, ascetic and doctrinal formation, and to have as many as possible gain, in the higher schools of religion, pedagogy, social services, nursing, diplomas which officially accredit them for their respective missions."

with gratitude everything that is naturally true, beautiful and good, because it is a reflection of the truth, goodness and beauty of God.

Furthermore: the majority of parents entrust their daughters to you for motives of Christian conscience. This, however, should not involve for them the disadvantage of an inferior standard of teaching in your schools. On the contrary, you should make it a point of honour to guarantee for these parents the very best instruction for their daughters, and that even from the elementary schools.

Do not forget either that competence and good teaching win for the sister the respect and consideration of the girls. And then she will be able to exercise a more profound influence on their character and their spiritual life.

—*Profoundly Christian pedagogy.*

450   In this connection we have no need to repeat to you what you well know, a matter which has no doubt been the subject of full discussion in your congress, namely that according to the Catholic sense the aim of the school and of education is to form the perfect Christian; or to apply this principle to your position, the purpose is to exercise such spiritual and moral influence and to establish such habits in the girl or young woman that, when subsequently left to herself, she will remain firm in the Catholic faith and put it into practice in its daily practical consequences; or at least that there will be solid grounds for the hope that the pupil will later live according to the principles and norms of her faith.

Your whole school and educational system would be futile, if this aim were not at the very heart of your work. That you should labour with all your powers for that end, that is what the Lord wants from you. He has called you to the mission of educating female youth to make them perfect Christians; he demands your full dedication to that mission, and one day he will call for an exact account of it.

451   The modern young girl! Better than many others you can estimate the problems as yet unsolved and the serious dangers,

which the recent changes in the female world, women's sudden introduction into all the departments of public life, have brought with them. Was there ever a time like the present, in which the young girl has needed to be won over and trained interiorly, in her profound convictions and in her will, for the cause of Christ and for virtuous conduct, in such fashion that she will remain faithful to him and to virtue, in spite of all temptations and obstacles, in everything from modesty of dress to the gravest and most anxious questions of life?

Never allow material advantages, the authority of an individual,   452 riches, political power or other similar considerations, to induce you to turn your back on your educational ideal and to become unfaithful to your mission! An examination of conscience during your congress might prove very salutary. This paternal exhortation is prompted only by our goodwill for you, because your cares are also ours and your happy success is ours also.

—Fraternal collaboration between religious communities.

To secure such a favourable outcome, harmony and generous   453 understanding between different religious communities can make a great contribution. Mutual acquaintance and encouragement, a saintly rivalry, cannot fail to prove advantageous to all. An excellent beginning has already been made; you have only, therefore, to continue to advance.

Conclusion: the help of the religious life itself. Your mission is not an easy one, just   454 as in general Christian education today is an aim not easily achieved. But in respect of the interior formation of the young girl, your religious vocation is for you a potent help. Lively faith, union with God, the love of Christ with which each one of you has had the opportunity of being permeated, in accordance with the spirit of your Congregation from the time of the novitiate; the vows, not only of chastity, but also and essentially, of obedience; common toil under a single guide and in the same direction—all this acts powerfully upon young minds—on the supposition, of course, that you yourselves are equal to your vocation.

May divine providence direct and guide all your plans and undertakings! May the grace of the Lord Jesus Christ fill your minds and hearts. May the Blessed Virgin and Mother Mary be for you a model, and may she protect you and intercede for you. With that wish we impart with all our heart to you here present, to your beloved sisters and to all the youth entrusted to your care, our Apostolic benediction.

ALLOCUTION TO THE DISCALCED CARMELITES

23 September 1951

On the occasion of the twenty-fifth anniversary of the foundation in Rome of the international college of the Discalced Carmelites, the Holy Father delivered the following Discourse. In it he emphasized the importance of the natural virtues and of complete sincerity in education to purity.[1]

. . . You are holding this congress from all your provinces 455 on the happy occasion of the twenty-fifth anniversary of the foundation in Rome of the international college of the Discalced Carmelites. And your chief concern and hope is that your religious institute, having thus gathered new strength and being adapted to the needs of a changed world, will by the merciful favour of God exercise its apostolic mission with the greatest possible efficiency.

We esteem highly this whole undertaking, and there are some matters which you have taken for treatment to which we give the highest praise. Nowadays the science and art of pedagogy makes a closer investigation of the whole basis and method by which the mind becomes constant, and perseveres in attachment to the good and virtuous, whatever the status of the individual may be.

Importance of the natural virtues. Your purpose is to study intensively 456 how this strength of character, which is to be prized above all else, grows and perseveres in man, and how the so-called natural virtues are formed and developed.

We consider that it was a salutary inspiration to undertake this study. For if it be true, and it certainly is true, that nature is perfected and not suppressed by supernatural grace, then the edifice of evangelical perfection must undoubtedly be raised on the foundation of these natural virtues. Before the young religious

[1] *AAS* XLIII (1951), pp. 734-738.

can become a shining example as a member of his society, he must strive to be a perfect man in the ordinary things of everyday life: he cannot scale the mountain-peaks, unless he is able to walk freely on the level ground.

457   He must therefore learn and manifest in his conduct the qualities which are the fitting adornments of man's nature and grace human relations: his bearing and appearance should be becoming, he should be reliable and sincere, faithful to his promises, he should control his acts and words, be respectful to all, avoid interference with the rights of others, and be patient, considerate and, above all, obedient to the laws of God.

458   As you well know, the whole structure of the so-called natural virtues is raised to the dignity of the supernatural life, especially when they are practised and cultivated with the object of becoming a good Christian or a worthy preacher and minister of Christ. And there is another consideration also. A religious house differs from the family home and roof; it is not the same and does not try to be, because within its walls zeal for dedication and self-denial for the love of Christ, and the austere penitential customs, involve some measure of discomfort and pain.

Nevertheless, as far as possible, the religious house shall endeavour to become a loved family home for each one of the religious community. And undoubtedly that will be achieved more easily, if all alike respect the foundation-structure of the natural virtues, which frequently indeed are the proof of abundant supernatural vigour and splendour.

459   **Religious obedience and respect for the human personality.** You will now be good enough to accept from our lips some points which have to do with the profession of religious vows and the due training of your novices. In the programme of subjects we find this theme set out for discussion: " Training to religious obedience; the exercise of authority and respect for the person of the subject." Certainly it is of the highest importance that supernatural obedience, nourished by the flames of love of God, should be cultivated and flourish in religious houses, strictly and assiduously and with

ready goodwill in accordance with the established rules. For is it not this that furnishes the solid support of religious life and discipline?

Is it not through the combined strength that comes from obedience, that the great undertakings of religious have gained in the past, as they will win in the future, such happy results? Recognize, therefore, and respect and gladly accept the salutary yoke of obedience as the burden of the strong! However, at the present time, when the machine is everywhere in control, and technical direction is infiltrating, permeating and fashioning everything to its own image, superiors shall be on their guard lest they treat their subjects as merchandise or machine-parts; they shall always respect in them the human personality.

Education in chastity : clear and appropriate instruction. What are we to say about chastity? 460 The questions which arise about chastity would require lengthy treatment, for they are questions of great gravity and importance. It is fitting that we should touch on some of them at least, even though superficially and briefly. The ancient Greeks and Romans, when speaking of matters relating to chastity, made use of a special term : αἰδοῖα— *verenda*; they used this term to signify that this was a subject that should be treated in a reverent manner. But this sense of reverence must not be taken to mean that there should be complete silence on the subject, and that in giving moral instructions there should be no mention of it, even with due care and circumspection. Young people must be given appropriate instruction in these matters; they must be allowed to indicate their problems, to ask questions without hesitation, and to receive an answer which is sure, clear and sufficiently explicit to give them light and confidence.[2]

Neither should anyone who has chosen to preserve virginity 461 belittle or despise marriage. Marriage is good, but virginity is better; the married state is honourable, but, according to the Gospel, higher still is the state of virginity which is embraced

[2] In the Encyclical *Sacra Virginitas* the Holy Father returned to this theme and insisted on the tact with which such initiation should be given. Cf. *infra*, n. 541.

for the love of Christ and made fruitful by charity. Perpetual virginity especially is a clean offering to God, a holy victim, the flower, the pride and joy of the Church, a mighty resource of strength, which the Church can neither repudiate nor neglect.

462   When, however, it is necessary to explain and give instruction about virginity, it should be thoroughly understood from the outset by everybody that chastity in general, including conjugal chastity, cannot be steadfastly preserved without the aid of God's grace; and this heavenly aid is all the more necessary when there is question of retaining chastity to one's dying breath; this is the reason why anyone who vows virginal chastity to God must struggle, as Jacob did with the angel, to secure a heavenly triumph by prayer and penitential zeal.

463   **Religious poverty and necessary resources.** And now something must be said about evangelical poverty. This poverty must be observed strictly at all times, in accordance with the established rules of your institute, whether in the life of the individual or the life of the community. But the manifold works of the apostolate, such as the care of souls, the embellishment of places of worship, the erection of suitable schools and their organisation, the foreign missions, the promotion of learning, and also the payment of just wages to servants, all these call for fairly extensive resources; and this must be accepted as normal and above criticism in the changed condition of the present time. But there should be proportion between activities and material resources, and the quest for resources should be kept within due bounds; if there should be a superfluity of means, it should be used in a spirit of brotherly emulation to relieve needs of every kind; it is not human foresight, which is always uncertain, but trust in the mercy and help of God, and the generous kindness which goes with it, that will ensure genuine success for religious and their undertakings and win for them the esteem of men.

Classical culture and knowledge of Latin. What a joy it is to us that you propose 464 to give your young novices a more liberal training in humane studies! These studies are excellent for the training of the developing mind, in order to ensure clarity and order in thought and speech and to avoid an empty flow of words, and also for the acquisition of other notable qualities of the well-trained intelligence. In these studies we have to deplore a regrettable development. For alas! there is a decline in the number and in the enthusiasm of those who study the Latin language, the glory of the priesthood. What praise is adequate for this imperial tongue, as the Greeks called it, which does not so much enunciate the truth as sculpture it, which appears in all its dignity in edicts and decisions, which is the liturgical language used in the Latin Church, and finally a bond of great value in the whole Catholic Church? Let there be no priest who cannot read and speak Latin with ease and facility! May God grant also that many of you may be distinguished by the capacity to write Latin concisely and elegantly!

For the Latin tongue, like Greek, is a treasury of incomparable 465 excellence, to which countless ecclesiastical writings have been committed from the early days of Christianity; the sacred minister who is ignorant of it must be regarded as deplorably lacking in mental refinement.

Fidelity to the Encyclical "Humani Generis." Finally, we praise highly your intention 466 to regulate your philosophical and theological studies in accordance with the directives given in our recently promulgated Encyclical *Humani Generis*.[3] It is with surprise and sorrow that we have learned that some have taken serious exception to that document, as though it were our purpose to halt the research which scientific progress demands and to forbid particular views which, up to now, could freely be discussed without danger to the faith in the schools of philosophy and theology. These people have been misled or are deceiving

---

[3] Encyclical *Humani Generis* on Catholic Doctrine, 12 August 1950 (*AAS* XLII (1950), p. 561-78).

themselves. It was not our purpose to restrict that freedom; what we undoubtedly intended, in virtue of our apostolic office, was to mark off Catholic truth from certain contemporary errors and exaggerations, and to guard and defend that unchanging truth, which is the common heritage of the Church and transcends all epochs and all forms of civilization and culture.

LETTER OF THE SACRED CONGREGATION OF EXTRAORDINARY ECCLESIASTICAL AFFAIRS: SECULAR AND REGULAR CLERGY

13 July 1952

The Allocution Annus Sacer [1] *of 8 December 1950 to the international congress of religious had led to a certain number of requests for clarification, especially on the part of Mgr. Charue, Bishop of Namur. In order to prevent all erroneous interpretation, the Sacred Congregation of Extraordinary Ecclesiastical Affairs gave the following clarifications in reply:* [2]

1. When it is said that a priest who wishes to strive for perfection must become a religious or at least become a member of a Secular Institute; and if a young man, who is undecided between the secular priesthood and entry into religion, is given the answer that it is a question of generosity; when it is asserted that one who decides for the secular clergy proves that he has not the generosity to give himself entirely to the service of God; if it is thought that a young man who is hesitating in this way cannot be advised to enter a seminary rather than a religious Order; if some go so far as to assert that the Church " tolerates " the secular clergy as a second-best, but that the ideal would be that all priests would be religious—all this is a false interpretation and an erroneous application of the Holy Father's Allocution of 8 December 1950. [3] The bishops are within their rights, if they oppose a form of propaganda for recruitment on

467

---

[1] Cf. *supra*, nn. 394-423.

[2] Note on the Discourse to Religious, published by the Bishop of Namur, Mgr. Charue (*Mandements*, 1952, T. 11, pp. 121-3). Mgr. Charue communicated this note to the clergy of his diocese, on 3 September 1952, in these terms: " Everything that touches on priestly vocation is a matter for the vigilance of the bishops. We therefore consider it our pastoral duty to request all the clergy of the diocese to read attentively the pontifical document which we are publishing here, and to conform their teaching strictly to it. By a letter of 13 July 1952, the Sacred Congregation of Extraordinary Ecclesiastical Affairs has transmitted to us, through the Apostolic Nunciature of Brussels, a detailed note of his Holiness, in reply to requests for clarification which had been submitted from various quarters to the Holy See."

[3] Allocution *Annus Sacer.*

the part of religious societies, which has theoretical foundations that are inexact and liable to lead into error, and which, in practice, is at least lacking in loyalty; bishops are also within their rights if they place proper and definite limits to such propaganda by an administrative decision.

468   2. The above-mentioned Allocution of the Holy Father had as its primary aim the clarification and definition of three points:

(a) What is the position of the regular clergy (*clerus religiosus*) in relation to the secular clergy (*clerus saecularis*) in the constitution given by Christ to his Church (pp. 27-29[4])? The answer was: . . . " if one considers the order established by Christ, neither of the two particular forms of the twofold clergy enjoys a prerogative of divine law, because that law does not give preference to one rather than the other, nor does it exclude either of them " (p. 28).

469   (b) What is the relation of the " cleric " and the " religious " in regard to the " state of perfection " considered as the state of the evangelical counsels (p. 29)? This was the answer: " The cleric is not bound by the divine law to practise the evangelical counsels of poverty, chastity and obedience; and especially he is not bound in the same way and for the same reason as one for whom this obligation arises from a public vow made when embracing the religious state. That, however, does not prevent the cleric from assuming these obligations privately and on his own initiative . . . The reason why the regular cleric makes profession of the condition and state of perfection is not because he is a cleric, but because he is a religious." Furthermore, it was expressly affirmed that even *Secular Institutes* realize the essence of the " state of perfection," " because the members are in some way bound to the observance of the evangelical counsels " (p. 29).

If " clerics " join together in such a *Secular Institute*, " then they too are in the state of acquiring perfection, not because they are clerics, but because they are members of a Secular Institute." (p. 30).

470   (c) What are the objective reasons for adopting the religious

---

[4] These page-references, which are given in the *Note* itself, refer back to the text of the Allocution *Annus Sacer* (*AAS* XLIII (1951), pp. 26-36).

state? What is said in the papal Allocution about the religious state, considered in itself, as a state of perfection, should not be identified, as has been done by certain religious societies in the manner of recruitment about which complaints have been made, with the vocation of the individual to personal perfection, whether within the " state of perfection " or outside it. The three points thus clarified are not immediately concerned with the individual person, but with the " state," its *de jure* status and its essential nature. They do not, therefore, touch upon the vocation of the individual to a particular state in the Church; nor do they touch on the vocation of the individual to personal perfection in the state which he has chosen; nor do they touch on the perfection actually attained by the individual in his state or his vocation.

The point under discussion, therefore, is not the personal 471 perfection of the individual. That perfection is measured by the degree of love, the degree of " theological charity," which is actually realized in the individual. The criterion of the intensity and purity of charity is, in the words of the Master, the fulfilment of the will of God. The individual is thus personally more perfect before God according as he carries out more perfectly the will of God. In this respect, the state in which he lives is of little importance, whether he be a layman or an ecclesiastic, or, if he is a priest, whether he be a secular or a regular.

It follows that it would not be correct to say that the secular 472 priest, in regard to his own personal sanctification, is any less called to perfection than the regular priest; or to say that the decision of a young man to follow the vocation of a secular priest is a determination to a lower personal perfection than if he had chosen the priesthood in the religious state. It is possible that it might be so; it is equally possible that one person's choice of a state other than the state of perfection may spring from a greater love of God and a greater spirit of sacrifice than another person's choice of the religious state.

Thus, as far as the priest is concerned, and this applies also 473 to the candidate for the priesthood, it is not difficult to perceive that by reason of the dignity and the duty of the priestly office, he too is called in a special way to personal perfection. That holds good even in the case where the individual who is clothed with the perfection of the priesthood is living lawfully in the " state of marriage," as is the case in the Oriental Rites.

474   By way of conclusion, therefore, it must be stated: the call of the individual to sanctity or personal perfection, and the adoption and permanent practice of personal perfection, cannot be identified with the question of the " state of perfection " in the juridical sense of the term. The state of perfection is so called and is such, inasmuch as, through the medium of the three evangelical counsels, it removes the principal obstacles which impede the effort to obtain personal sanctity; or, to speak more exactly, it is by its nature suited to the removal of these obstacles. But the mere fact of embracing the state of perfection does not mean that it necessarily realizes its potentialities in the life of the individual religious, that it actually leads to sanctity; that depends upon the effort of the individual, upon the measure in which, in co-operation with the grace of God, he applies the evangelical counsels in his life.

ALLOCUTION TO THE SUPERIORS GENERAL
OF FEMALE INSTITUTES AND CONGREGATIONS

15 September 1952

This Allocution was delivered by the Holy Father in the course of an audience granted to the superiors general of female institutes and Congregations of pontifical law who, for the first time in the history of the Church, were assembled in an international congress at Rome.[1]

We extend paternal greetings to you, beloved daughters, who 475 have come in such numbers to the international congress of superiors general of Orders and Congregations of women, and who now, at the end of your toils, when about to give effect to the results of your deliberations, come to seek from us the blessing of the Vicar of Christ.

When the Sacred Congregation of Religious proposed to us this congress, we felt obliged to weigh the matter: an international undertaking of this kind always involves considerable demands in time, money and personal effort. But the necessity for it, or at least the great advantages of such a congress, could not be denied. In fact, we felt obliged to admit the cogency of the reasons advanced for it; and the imposing assembly here before our eyes, your very countenances, your whole attitude, tell us of the immense goodwill that has been at work during these days.

Yes, beloved daughters, the reports from the congress, which has now concluded, have made clear the high sense of responsibility with which you envisage the service of God and how earnestly you wish to spend yourselves for your religious families and for the Church. For this purpose, you desire to hear from us a word of consolation and encouragement and some directives.

It is just a year since we treated in detail a series of questions which concerned the good estate of Orders and Congregations

[1] *AAS* XLIV (1952), pp. 823-826.

of female teaching religious and their adaptation in appropriate form to the contemporary situation.[2] A certain number, if not the greater part of the directives which we then gave, apply also to all other Congregations of women religious. The experiences of the year which has passed invite us to draw your attention to the directives which we formulated at that time. We ask of you courageously to conform with these directives, when your sisters and your own experience tell you that the time has come to take account intelligently of contemporary modes of life.

476   **Crisis of vocations.**
We have a very special motive for thus speaking to you. You are aware that Orders of women are passing through a rather serious crisis: we have in mind the decline in the number of vocations. That crisis has not yet of course reached every country. Even where the crisis is most severe, the intensity is not the same everywhere. But already at this moment it is a cause of disquiet, in a number of European countries. In a region where twenty years ago the female religious way of life was in full bloom, the number of vocations has fallen by half. And in that former time, nevertheless, there were grave difficulties to hamper the vocation of young girls, while nowadays exterior conditions seem to favour them, and one might regard it as a duty to be on guard against fictitious vocations.

—*Responsibility of those who do not praise Christian virginity.*

We do not wish to treat in detail of this crisis which causes us grave concern. Another occasion will provide an opportunity to do so.[3]

477   Today we wish only to say a word to all those, priests or laymen, preachers, orators or writers, who have never a word of approval or praise for virginity dedicated to Christ; for years, in spite of the Church's warnings and running counter to her mind, they have been giving priority, as a matter of principle,

---

[2] Discourse to the International Congress of Teaching Sisters, 13 September, 1951; cf. *supra*, nn. 436-54.

477a   [3] The Holy Father is thinking of the Encyclical *Sacra Virginitas*, which was promulgated on 25 March 1954; cf. *infra*, nn. 482-552.

to marriage over virginity; they even go so far as to present marriage as the sole means capable of ensuring the due development and natural perfection of the human personality. Let those who propound these views in words and in writing take account of their responsibility before God and before the Church. They must be counted among those principally responsible for a fact of which we can speak only with sorrow: while nowadays, within the Christian world and even everywhere outside it, more than ever calls are heard for Catholic sisters, it has regrettably been found necessary to refuse these requests time and again; indeed sometimes even longstanding activities, namely of hospitals and educational establishments, have had to be abandoned—all this because vocations do not meet requirements.[4]

---

[4] The meeting of the Cardinals and Archbishops of France was gravely concerned with the crisis of religious Congregations and, in March 1949, published this statement: " I. *Understanding and esteem of the religious life;* (a) To correct the opinion held by all too many of the faithful and Christian families on the subject of the religious vocation of young girls, it is essential that the priest be himself convinced of the excellence in itself of religious perfection. It appears that on this matter appropriate instruction could be given in the seminary; (b) The clergy shall be watchful to diminish the effects of exaggerated and clumsy propaganda for the lawful spirituality of Christian marriage; they shall not hesitate to teach the superiority of virginity consecrated to God to the state of marriage; (c) It is essential that the clergy should respect scrupulously a religious vocation which is certain, and not seek to hold a person back for the good of the parish or Catholic Action movements; (d) In the decision of a female vocation, the parish clergy, chaplains of Catholic Action movements and confessors, shall bear in mind the excellence of a life entirely consecrated to God by the practice of the evangelical counsels, as well as the advantages and the security offered by entry into a religious institute or a Secular Institute canonically approved by the Church.

" II. *Pastoral ministry among women religious;* the clergy, both secular and regular, shall show esteem, devotion and gratitude to the congregations and communities of women religious; they shall consider themselves in honour bound to correct the criticism directed against these religious, criticisms that are frequently unjust as well as being based on misunderstanding of the realities of religious life.

" The clergy cannot ignore the fact that it is from the priest that women religious expect an enlightened knowledge of the obligations and the privileges of their state of evangelical perfection.

" In particular, the clergy are bound to weigh their individual and collective responsibility in respect of women religious and the obligation which binds them to fulfil exactly the functions which canon law imposes: superiors, confessors, chaplains, preachers.

" The ministry to religious is to be esteemed as a select ministry, one that is particularly delicate, which may not be discharged without preparation or attention, under pain of inflicting grave damage to souls.

" Under this heading, it seems advisable to recommend: 1. The specialised training in each diocese of one or more priests, for the spiritual care of communities of women religious and for the instruction of the parochial clergy in their work as ordinary or extraordinary confessors, and for preaching to female religious; 2. An important place be given in pastoral publications for the use of the clergy to enlighten and assist them

477a

—Necessity for adaptation of customs and habits.

478 For yourselves, these are our recommendations: In this crisis of vocations, be watchful lest the customs, the way of life or the asceticism of your religious families should prove a barrier or be a cause of failures. We are speaking of certain usages which, if they had once a certain significance in a different cultural setting, do not possess it nowadays; they are such that a young girl, who is genuinely good and courageous, would find them simply hindrances to her vocation.[5] In our exposition on the subject last year, we gave various examples. To return to the subject and say a word on the question of dress: the religious habit should always express consecration to Christ; that is what everyone expects and desires. For the rest, let the habit be suitable and meet the requirements of hygiene. We could not fail to express our satisfaction when, in the course of the year, we saw that one or other Congregation had already taken practical steps in this regard. To sum up, in those matters which are not essential, adapt yourselves as reason and well-ordered charity advise.

in their ministry to women religious. 3. A more active participation by the regular clergy' who are familiar with the practice of the religious life and who are frequently united by bonds of spiritual kinship with female Congregations; 4. Finally, it is essential that the clergy should bring women religious into the stream of parish life, not leaving them without a part in those apostolic responsibilities which the clergy is more and more being led to entrust to the laity."

478a [5] It is quite obvious, without any desire to yield to a craving for change, that some developments are necessary in the anachronistic customs of certain communities. We can admire the psychological delicacy of the Holy Father, when writing on 4 November 1941 to the superioress of the Visitation of Annecy and to other superioresses of the Order of the Visitation, on the occasion of the tricentenary of the death of Saint Jeanne de Chantal, he prepared the way for the developments that were necessary: ". . . if, however, the Holy See, in special circumstances, in its wisdom deems it well to take a decision which seems novel to your Institute, you will undoubtedly accept it with entire submission, being wholly convinced that this decision will not prove disadvantageous to you, but will be for your good. That is a manner of acting, of course, which is commended to you by the obedience which you owe to ecclesiastical authority, and also by the eager and generous goodwill that urges you to accept all the decisions reached by that same authority, because it has judged that they are timely and salutary for you. *It is unnecessary therefore to bring forward reasons in support of our exhortations on this point,* because we see that there happily exists among you, between your different monasteries, as between the whole Order and the Holy See, a perfect communion of souls in profound charity " (*AAS* XXXIII (1941), p. 491).

Special Directives to superioresses.

Having said this, we put before you, beloved daughters, two insistent exhortations:

1°—Motherly affection in the direction of sisters.

It is no doubt true, as psychology affirms, that the woman invested with authority does not succeed as easily as a man in finding the exact formula for combining strictness with kindness and establishing the balance between them. That is an added reason for cultivating your motherly sentiments. You can, of course, say that the vows have exacted from your sisters, as from yourselves, a great sacrifice. They have renounced their family, the happiness of marriage and the intimacy of the home. It is a sacrifice of great value, of decisive importance for the apostolate of the Church, but it is still a sacrifice. Those of your sisters, who are most high-souled and refined, are the ones who feel this detachment most keenly. The word of Christ: *No one who puts his hand to the plough and looks back is fit for the kingdom of God,* [6] finds here its application to the full and, nowadays too, without reserve. But the religious Order must take the place of the family, as far as possible, and it is you, the superiors general, who are expected in the first instance to breathe the warmth of family affection into the community life of the sisters.

479

You must, therefore, yourselves be motherly in your exterior behaviour, in your words and your writings, even if sometimes this calls for exercise of self-restraint; but above all be motherly in your innermost thoughts, your judgments and, as far as possible, your sympathetic feeling. Pray every day to Mary, the Mother of Jesus and our mother, to teach you how to be motherly.

2°—Training of sisters for work and for their special task.

Here there shall be no pettiness; but rather be broad minded in your outlook. Whether it be a question of education, pedagogy, care of the sick, artistic or other activities, the sister

480

[6] Luke 9: 62.

should have this sentiment: mother superior is giving me the opportunity of a formation which will put me on an equal footing with my colleagues in the world. Give them also the possibility and the means of keeping their professional knowledge up to date.[7] That also is a point which we enlarged upon last year. We are repeating it in order to stress the importance of this requirement for the peace of soul and the active work of your sisters.[8]

480a   [7] Cardinal Valerio Valeri, in a letter to Mgr. Godfrey, Archbishop of Liverpool, on the occasion of the congress of men and women religious of Great Britain, held at Liverpool from 3 to 6 January 1956, echoes this thought of the Holy Father: "The responsibility of superiors is particularly grave on this point. It is their duty to ensure that balance which is indispensable for the health of the body and the soul. It is for them too, in accordance with the desire of the Holy Father, to equip their subjects with a professional and technical training which is not inferior to that of lay persons who perform the same function. Young men and women religious, who attend the universities, should be the object of particular solicitude on the part of superiors lest their spiritual life suffer injury of any kind."

480b   [8] A year before, on 31 July 1951, Rev. Fr. Larraona, Secretary of the Sacred Congregation of Religious, had sent a circular to all superiors general concerning the technical equipment of young women religious: "Our Sacred Congregation would feel that it was failing in its duty if it did not, moreover, draw your attention at this time to the grave obligation that falls on superiors general of female Congregations who dedicate themselves to education, to prepare their subjects in appropriate fashion, not merely from the point of view of religious formation, but also of technical preparation.

"The sublime mission of teacher, to which God our Lord calls the young sister, causes her to enter, with open heart and trusting soul, into the institute which she has freely chosen in the belief that she will find there the milieu in which her vocation will be able to flourish and fructify for the good of souls.

"It would be indeed rash to claim that, after the years of the postulancy and novitiate, which were devoted almost exclusively to the personal religious training of the young girl, she now can, straightway, without any special preparation, become a teacher; and still less can she be a responsible, capable and conscientious teacher, even for infants merely.

"Our Sacred Congregation knows well the difficulties in which reverend superiors general find themselves, in the face of the pressing requests of Ordinaries who, because of their concern for the immediate needs of the Christian people, ask for the opening of new houses and for the assistance of the Congregations for the education of the people.

"But, knowing well that the sister who is well prepared will be able, by herself, to accomplish real good among souls, even the youngest of them, the Congregation does not hesitate to recommend emphatically to those superiors to watch, with all possible care, not only the formation of the young sisters, in accordance with the spirit of the institute, but also their pedagogical and technical training; they can be assured that they are thus fulfilling a very strict duty of their delicate task, that they are labouring for the true welfare of their Institute, and are making an effective contribution to the apostolate of the Church " (Commentarium pro religiosis et missionariis, 1951, T. XXX, p. 262).

Conclusion

You have come, beloved daughters, from all parts of the world, 481
from far and near. Tell your sisters that we are grateful to them
for their prayer of which we ourselves stand so much in need;
for their good example which helps so powerfully to confirm
so many Catholics in their faith and to lead to the Church so
many who do not belong to the Church; for their labours in
the service of youth, the sick and the poor, on the missions and
in many other ways, which are all of the highest worth for the
growth and expansion of the reign of Jesus Christ over souls.
Tell your sisters that we extend to them all our affection; that
their cares are our cares, their joys our joys; that before all
we wish them the twofold strength of courage and of patience
in the task of achieving their own perfection and in the apostolate
which their divine Master and Spouse has assigned to them.

As a token of our paternal goodwill and as a pledge of the
triumphant grace and love of the divine Heart, we grant to you,
beloved daughters, to your sisters and their works, our Apostolic
benediction.

ENCYCLICAL "SACRA VIRGINITAS" ON CHRISTIAN VIRGINITY

25 March 1954

The supreme Pontiff, being concerned with certain errors on the subject of marriage, ecclesiastical celibacy and the state of perfect chastity of souls consecrated to God that had been gaining ground for some years, in this solemn document of the magisterium recalls the Catholic doctrine on the superiority of virginity to marriage.[1] Within this perspective the Encyclical treats of priestly chastity and also the chastity of religious, men and women.

482

Perpetual virginity essentially Christian. Holy virginity and perfect chastity dedicated to the service of God undoubtedly rank among the most precious treasures which the Founder of the Church bequeathed to the society which he established.

This is the reason why the holy Fathers declared that perpetual virginity is a heavenly gift introduced by the Christian religion. They rightly noted that the state of virginity imposed on the Vestals in pagan antiquity was only temporary,[2] and also that the Old Testament commanded the practice and preservation of virginity simply as a prerequisite for marriage;[3] furthermore, as St. Ambrose said: " We read that there were virgins in the temple at Jerusalem, but what does the Apostle say? *Now all these things happened to them in figure,*[4] as signs of things to come." [5]

483

Christian virginity from the origins of the Church to our own day. In fact this virtue has thriven and flourished in the garden of the Church ever since the apostolic age. In the *Acts of the Apostles,* the statement that the four daughters of Philip the deacon were virgins,[6] clearly refers to their state of life rather than to their youth. And not long after this, Ignatius of Antioch sends greetings to the virgins,

---

[1] *AAS* XLVI (1954), pp. 161-91.
[2] Cf. Ambrose, *De virginibus*, L.I., c. 4, 15; *De virginitate*, c. 3, 13 (*PL* XVI, 193, 269).
[3] Cf. Exodus 22: 16-17; Deuteronomy 22: 23-29; Ecclesiasticus 42: 9.
[4] I Corinthians 10: 11.
[5] Cf. St. Ambrose, *De virginibus*, L. I, c. 3, 12 (*PL* XVI, 192).
[6] Cf. Acts 21: 9.

who, together with the widows, already formed an important part of the Christian community of Smyrna.[7] In the second century, as St. Justin tells us, " many men and women now sixty and seventy years of age, who were instructed from childhood in the teaching of Christ, keep themselves unsullied."[8] Gradually the number of men and women who consecrated their chastity to God increased, and, at the same time, the rôle which they fulfilled in the Church grew in importance, as we have explained at greater length in our Apostolic Constitution *Sponsa Christi*.[9]

Moreover, the holy fathers, Cyprian, Athanasius, Ambrose, 484 John Chrysostom, Jerome, Augustine and many others, in their writings on virginity praised it in the highest terms. Their teaching, which has been further developed in the course of time by the Doctors of the Church and the masters of Christian asceticism, undoubtedly helps greatly to arouse in Christians of both sexes the resolve to dedicate themselves to God in perfect chastity and to confirm them in their purpose to persevere in perfect chastity until death.

The number of those who, from the origins of the Church 485 down to our own day, have offered their chastity to God, is beyond reckoning; some have kept their virginity intact, others have dedicated their widowhood to God after the death of their married partner, while others have made choice of a life of complete chastity in repentance for their sins. But all are outstanding for their common purpose to abstain from the pleasures of the flesh for the love of God. May the teaching of the holy Fathers on the glory and merit of virginity be for all of these an invitation, a support and a source of strength, which will enable them to persevere steadfastly in the sacrifice they have made, and never to take away or claim back even the tiniest part of the holocaust they have laid on the altar of God.

[7] Cf. St. Ignatius of Antioch, *Ep. ad Smyr.*, c. 13 (Ed. Funk-Diekamp, *Patres Apostolici*, vol. I, p. 286).
[8] St. Justin, *Apol. I pro christ.*, c. 15 (PG VI, 349).
[9] Apostolic Constitution *Sponsa Christi*, 21 November 1950 (*AAS* XLIII (1951), pp. 5-24); cf. *supra*, nn. 325-87.

486

Perfect chastity practised by simple faithful.

Perfect chastity is the subject of one of the three vows which constitute the religious state.[10] It is required also from clerics of the Latin Church in major Orders,[11] and from members of Secular Institutes.[12] It flourishes equally in many of the laity; for there are men and women who, without being established in the public state of perfection, nevertheless have resolved, or taken a private vow, to refrain entirely from marriage and from the pleasures of the flesh, in order to have greater freedom to serve their neighbours and to unite their soul with God more easily and more intimately.

To each and every one of these our beloved sons and daughters, who have in any way whatever consecrated soul and body to God, we turn with paternal affection and earnestly exhort them to confirm their holy resolve and to carry it out diligently.

487

Motive and purpose of this Encyclical.

Nowadays, however, there are some who have strayed from the straight path of truth in this matter; they so extol matrimony that in practise they put it above virginity, thereby disparaging chastity dedicated to God and ecclesiastical celibacy. Consequently, our sense of the duties of the Apostolic office demands that we should explain and defend, particularly at the present time, the doctrine of the high dignity of virginity, in order to guard Catholic truth against such errors.

---

[10] *CIC*, can. 487: The religious state, or stable common life, by which the faithful undertake, in addition to the common precepts, the observance of the evangelical counsels by vows of obedience, chastity and poverty, is to be held in honour by all.
[11] *CIC*, can. 132 § 1.
486a [12] Cf. Apostolic Constitution *Provida Mater*, 2 February 1947, art. III § 2 (*AAS* XXXIX (1947), p. 121); cf. *supra*, n. 239.

FIRST PART

THE EXCELLENCE OF CHRISTIAN VIRGINITY

The teaching of Christ on virginity. The first point to which we would 488 direct attention is that it is from the lips of the divine Spouse himself that the Church has received the essentials of her teaching on virginity.

The disciples considered that the bonds and burdens of matrimony, which the words of their Master had emphasized, were an unsupportable load, and they said to him: *If the case of a man with his wife be so, it is not expedient to marry*; [13] Jesus replied that not all understand this truth, but only those to whom it is given; for some are prevented from marriage by natural defect, others have been made incapable of marriage by the violence and malice of men, while others spontaneously and of their own free will abstain from marriage *for the sake of the kingdom of heaven*. And he concluded with the words: *He that can accept it, let him accept.* [14]

In these words the divine Master is not referring to physical 489 impediments to marriage, but to the free spiritual resolution to abstain perpetually from marriage and bodily pleasures. When he compares those who have resolved of their own free will to renounce these things, with those who, by nature or by human violence, are forced to make a like renunciation, is not the divine Redeemer teaching us the lesson that chastity, if it is to be really perfect, must be perpetual?

Christian virginity, primarily dedication to God. A further consideration, and this is 490 plainly taught by the holy Fathers and Doctors of the Church, is that virginity is not the Christian virtue unless it is embraced *for the sake of the kingdom of heaven*; [15] that is to say, unless we adopt this way of life in order the more easily to devote ourselves to divine things, the more surely to attain

[13] Matthew 19: 10.
[14] Matthew 19: 11-12.
[15] Matthew 19: 12.

16

eternal happiness, and the more readily to bring others also to the kingdom of heaven, by our earnest efforts.

491   Consequently, the distinction of Christian virginity cannot be claimed by men or women who abstain from marriage through selfishness or, as St. Augustine remarks,[16] in order to escape the responsibilities of marriage, or in order to have the proud, pharisaical boast of bodily integrity. The Council of Gangria [17] already of old censured the virgin or celibate, who refrained from marriage as though it were a state to be abhorred, and not for the sake of the beauty and holiness of virginity.

492   Moreover, the Apostle of the gentiles, speaking under the influence of divine inspiration, has this to say: *He that is without a wife is solicitous for the things that belong to the Lord, how he may please God. And the unmarried woman and the virgin thinketh on the things of the Lord, that she may be holy both in body and spirit.*[18] This, then, is the primary purpose and the principal reason of Christian virginity: to strive only for the things of God and to give one's whole mind and soul to them alone, to desire to please God in all things, to fix one's thoughts on him, to dedicate oneself body and soul entirely to him.

493   **Teaching of the Fathers on virginity . . .**   It is in this way that the holy Fathers always interpreted the words of Christ and the teaching of the Apostle of the gentiles: from the earliest ages of the Church they regarded virginity as a consecration of body and soul to God. Thus St. Cyprian demands of virgins that, " inasmuch as they have dedicated themselves to Christ, they must renounce carnal desires, and devote themselves body and soul to God . . . they should no longer seek to adorn themselves or to please anyone except their Lord."[19] The bishop of Hippo goes further: "Virginity is not honoured because it is virginity, but because it is consecrated to God . . . What we praise in virgins is not their virginity, but the fact that they are virgins consecrated to God by religious

---

[16] St. Augustine, *De sancta virginitate*, c. 22 (PL XL, 407).
[17] Cf. can. 9 (Mansi, *Coll. concil.*, II, 1096).
[18] I Corinthians 7: 32, 34.
[19] St. Cyprian, *De habitu virginum*, 4 (PL IV, 443).

continence." [20] Those princes among theologians, St. Thomas Aquinas [21] and St. Bonaventure, [22] relying on the authority of Augustine, teach us that virginity does not possess the constancy required for virtue, unless it is based on a vow to keep it intact perpetually. And undoubtedly those who bind themselves by a perpetual vow to preserve virginity are giving effect in the most complete and perfect way to the words of Christ about perpetual abstention from marriage, it cannot rightly be maintained that the decision of those who wish to keep open a way of withdrawing from their purpose is better and more perfect.

The holy Fathers regarded this bond of perfect chastity as a form of spiritual marriage, in which the soul is wedded to Christ; some in fact went so far as to compare a violation of this pledge to adultery. [23] St. Athanasius wrote that the Catholic Church was accustomed to describe as brides of Christ those who possessed the virtue of virginity. [24] And St. Ambrose, writing about a consecrated virgin, has this pithy comment: " A virgin is one who is wedded to God." [25] Indeed, as is clear from the writings of the same Doctor of Milan, [26] even as early as the fourth century the rite of consecration of virgins was very similar to that which the Church at the present day follows in the blessing of marriage. [27]

494

. . . and on the charity which should inspire the bride of Christ. For the same reason the holy Fathers exhort virgins to love their divine Spouse even more ardently than they would love their husbands, if they were married, and to obey his will in all their thoughts and actions. [28] St. Augustine writes as follows to virgins: " Love

495

[20] St. Augustine, De sancta virginitate, c. 8, 11 (PL XL, 400, 401).
[21] St. Thomas, Summa Theol., II-II, q. 152, a. 3 ad 4).
[22] St. Bonaventure, De perfectione evangelica, q. 3, a. 3, sol. 5).
[23] Cf. St. Cyprian, De habitu virginum, c. 20 (PL IV, 459).
[24] Cf. St. Athanasius, Apol. ad Constant., 33 (PG XXV, 640).
[25] Cf. St. Ambrose, De virginibus, L. I, c. 8, 52 (PL XVI, 202).
[26] Ibid., L. III, c. 1-3, n. 1-14; De institutione virginis, c. 17, 104-114 (PL XVI, 219-24, 333-6).
[27] Cf. Sacramentarium Leonianum, XXX (PL LV, 129); Pontificale Romanum: De benedictione et consecratione virginum.
[28] Cf. St. Cyprian, De habitu virginum, 4, 22 (PL IV, 443-4, 462); St. Ambrose, De virginibus, L. I, c. 7, 37 (PL XVI, 199).

with all your heart him who is the most beautiful of men;
you have the opportunity, for your heart is free from matrimonial ties . . . Seeing then that you would have owed great
love to your husbands, how much greater should not be your
love of him for whose sake you have resolved to have no
husband. May he be nailed to your heart, who for you was
nailed to the Cross." [29] Such indeed are the sentiments and
resolutions which the Church requires of virgins on the day of
their consecration to God, when she asks them to say: " For
the love of our Lord Jesus Christ, whom I have seen, whom I
have loved, in whom I have believed, whom I have preferred,
I have scorned the kingdom of the world and all earthly finery." [30]

496   It is love of the divine Redeemer, therefore, and it alone, that
gently compels a virgin completely to dedicate herself, body
and soul, to him, as St. Methodius, Bishop of Olympus, says in
the beautiful words which he places on the virgin's lips: " Thou
art everything, O Christ, to me. For thee I keep myself pure,
and with a shining lamp in my hand I hasten to meet thee, my
Spouse." [31] It is love of Christ that persuades a virgin to retire
for ever within the convent walls, in order to contemplate and
love her heavenly Spouse more easily and with greater freedom;
and it is the same love which inspires her to apply herself
unsparingly to the performance of works of mercy for the benefit
of others until the day of her death.

497   **Love and imitation of Christ, supreme motives of chastity.** With reference to men *who were not
defiled with women, for they are virgins,*[32]
John the Apostle declares: *These follow
the Lamb whithersoever he goeth.*[33] Let us
meditate on the advice given to all of these by St. Augustine:
" Follow the Lamb, because the flesh of the Lamb is virgin too
. . . you are right to follow him, by virginity of heart and
body, wherever he goes. For what does *following* mean if not
imitation? For Christ has suffered for us, leaving us an example,

---

[29] St. Augustine, *De sancta virginitate*, c. 54-5 (*PL* XL, 428).
[30] *Pontificale Romanum;* De benedictione et consecratione virginum.
[31] St. Methodius of Olympus, *Convivium decem virginum, orat.* XI, c. 2 (*PG* XVIII, 209).
[32] Apocalypse 14: 4.
[33] *Ibid.,* 14: 4.

as the Apostle Peter says, *that you should follow his steps.*"[34] Indeed, all these disciples and brides of Christ embraced the state of virginity, as St. Bonaventure said, " to become like Christ, the Spouse, because virginity makes virgins like to him.'[35] For their burning love for Christ could not be satisfied by merely spiritual bonds of union with him; it demanded to be put to the test by imitation of his virtues, and in particular, by conformity to his life, which was wholly spent for the welfare and salvation of mankind.

If priests, and men and women religious, and indeed all who 498 are in any way dedicated to the service of God, practise perfect chastity, the ultimate reason for this is that their divine Master remained a virgin during his life on earth. Thus St. Fulgentius exclaims: " This is the only-begotten Son of God, the only-begotten Son of the Virgin also, the one Spouse of all consecrated virgins, the offspring, the adornment and the recompense of holy virginity, the one whom holy virginity brought forth bodily, to whom holy virginity is spiritually espoused, by whom holy virginity is made to conceive and yet remain unsullied, by whom it is embellished so as to remain beautiful, by whom it is crowned so as to reign for ever in glory."[36]

Virginity frees the soul for service of God and the neighbour. Venerable brethren, we deem it 499 opportune at this point to undertake a further analysis and more careful elucidation of the reason why the love of Christ influences noble minds to abstain from marriage, and also to clarify the mysterious links between virginity and the perfection of Christian charity. Now in the teaching of Christ, to which we have already referred, it is implied that complete abstention from marriage relieves men of the grave responsibilities and duties which the married state entails. The Apostle of the gentiles, under the influence of divine inspiration, states the reason why abstention from marriage effects this liberation: *But I would have you to be without solicitude . . . But he that is with*

---

[34] I Peter 2: 21; St. Augustine, *De sancta virginitate*, c. 27 (PL XL, 411).
[35] St. Bonaventure, *De perfectione evangelica*, q. 3, a. 3.
[36] St. Fulgentius, *Epist.* 3, c. 4, 6 (PL LXV, 326).

a wife is solicitous for the things of the world, how he may please his wife, and he is divided.[37] In this context, however, it must be noted that the Apostle is not finding fault with husbands because they are concerned with their wives, nor censuring wives because they endeavour to please their husbands; he is declaring rather that they are torn between love of their partner and love of God, and that they are so pre-occupied by the pressing cares and duties of conjugal life that they cannot easily turn their minds to meditation on the things of God. For they are bound by the clear matrimonial obligation which states: *They shall be two in one flesh.*[38] Husband and wife are joined together, both in the sorrows and in the joys of life.[39]

500   It is easy to see, therefore, why those who seek to consecrate themselves to the service of God adopt the state of virginity as a kind of emancipation, so that they may serve God more completely and devote all their energies to the welfare of their neighbour. How, for example, could that wonderful herald of the Gospel, St. Francis Xavier, or that merciful father of the poor, St. Vincent de Paul, or that most zealous educator of youth, St. John Bosco, or that indefatigable "mother of emigrants," St. Frances Cabrini, how could they have sustained such immense burdens and accomplished such mighty deeds, if they had been under an obligation to provide for the spiritual and bodily needs of a family and married partner of their own?

501

Virginity promotes progress in spiritual life. There is a further reason why all those, who desire eagerly to devote themselves wholly to God and to the salvation of their neighbour, embrace the state of virginity. It is the reason which the holy Fathers emphasize, when they set out the advantages which can be secured by those who completely renounce the pleasures of the flesh in order to be better fitted for the enjoyment of the higher things of the spiritual life. Undoubtedly, as the Fathers themselves clearly state, such pleasure as lawfully belongs to marriage is

[37] I Corinthians 7: 32-33.
[38] Genesis 2: 24; cf. Matthew 19: 5.
[39] Cf. I Corinthians 7: 39.

by no means to be condemned; in fact, chaste wedlock is consecrated and elevated in dignity by a special sacrament. At the same time, it must be admitted that, since the unhappy fall of Adam, the lower faculties of human nature resist right reason and sometimes even lead a man to do wrong. In the words of the angelic Doctor, the use of marriage " holds back the soul from complete dedication to the service of God." [40]

Special motives for the priest to practise perfect chastity. In order that her sacred ministers 502 may acquire this spiritual liberty of soul and body, and avoid becoming involved in earthly business, the Latin Church demands that they should freely and willingly submit to the obligation of perfect chastity.[41] And, as was said by our predecessor of immortal memory, Pius XI, " though this law is not binding in all its rigour on the clergy of the Oriental Church, ecclesiastical celibacy is held in high honour by them, and in some cases, particularly for the higher grades of the hierarchy, it is a matter of obligation." [42]

Another point to consider is that sacred ministers do not 503 renounce marriage solely because of their apostolic ministry, but also because they serve the altar. For if the priests of the Old Testament abstained from the use of marriage while they were performing the services in the Temple, lest they should be declared legally unclean like other men,[43] it is surely much more appropriate that the ministers of Jesus Christ, who daily offer the sacrifice of the Eucharist, should possess perfect chastity. St. Peter Damian put his advice on this perfect priestly chastity in the form of a question: " If, therefore, our Redeemer so loved the bloom of perfect chastity that he was not only born of a virgin womb, but also fondly handled by a virgin foster-father, and this while he was still an infant crying in the cradle,

---

[40] St. Thomas, *Summa Theol.*, II-II, q. 186, a. 4.
[41] *CIC*, can. 132 § 1.
[42] Encyclical *Ad catholici sacerdotii* (*AAS* XXVIII (1936), p. 24-5).
[43] Cf. Leviticus 15: 16-17; 22: 4; I Samuel 21: 5-7; Pope St. Siricius, *Ep. ad Himer.*, 7 (*PL* LVI, 558-559).

by whom, I ask, does he wish his Body to be handled, now that he is reigning in all his immensity in heaven? " [44]

504 **Christian virginity superior to marriage.**   This is the principal reason why it must be held, as the Church clearly teaches, that holy virginity is more excellent than marriage: our divine Redeemer had already commended virginity to the disciples as a counsel of a more perfect way of life; [45] and St. Paul, having stated that the father who gives his daughter in marriage *doth well*, immediately adds: *He that giveth her not in marriage doth better.* [46] Several times in the course of his comparison of marriage with virginity, the Apostle reveals his own mind, especially in the words: *For I would that all men were even as myself . . . But I say to the unmarried and to the widows; it is good for them if they so continue, even as I.* [47]

505   If, therefore, as we have written, virginity is more excellent than marriage, this superiority undoubtedly is chiefly due to the fact that virginity aims at a higher purpose, [48] and also because it is a supremely effective means of consecrating oneself entirely to the service of God; on the other hand, the mind of one who is burdened by the cares and ties of matrimony is always to some extent *divided.* [49]

---

[44] St. Peter Damian, *De coelibatu sacerdotum*, c. 3 (PL CXLV, 384).
[45] Cf. Matthew 19: 10-11.
[46] I Corinthians 7: 38.
[47] I Corinthians 7: 7-8; cf. *ibid.*, 1 and 26.
[48] Cf. St. Thomas, *Summa Theol.*, II-II, q. 152, a. 3-4.

505a   [49] Cf. I Corinthians 7: 33. In a discourse to nursing sisters, 24 April 1957, the Holy Father came back to the same theme, referring to this passage of the Encyclical: " It is a truth of faith which we enunciated recently once more in the Encyclical *Sacra Virginitas* of 25 March 1954, that virginity is superior to the married state, because the virgin soul binds ties of absolute and indissoluble love directly with God, with the incarnate God, Jesus Christ. In fact, all that she has received as a gift from God to be a spouse and mother, she offers to him as a holocaust on the altar of complete and final renunciation. To reach to the heart of God, to love him and be loved by him, the virgin soul does not pass through other hearts; nor does it stop to dally with other creatures; there is nothing placed between the soul and Jesus, no obstacle, no curtain . . . It is only virgin souls who make the offering of that which for other loving creatures is an unattainable goal; for them the first step on their ascent is also the last; and the end of their ascent is at the same time a summit and a profound abyss." (*AAS* XXXXIX (1957), p. 291-296); cf. *infra*, n. 623.

The Spiritual Fruits of Virginity.

1° In the apostolic life.

The excellence of virginity stands out even more clearly when   506
we consider the rich fruit which it yields: *For by the fruit the
tree is known.*[50]

When we turn our thoughts to the countless companies of   507
virgins and apostles who, from the earliest ages of the Church
down to our own day, have abstained from marriage, in order
the more freely and more completely to devote themselves for
the love of Christ to the salvation of their fellow-men, we are
overcome by the most intense joy and satisfaction.[51] It is
certainly not our wish, nor would it be right, to disparage in
any way the meritorious work and the fruits of the apostolate
of the militants of Catholic Action; their salutary zeal can be
brought to bear even on people whom, in many cases, priests
and religious could never reach. Nevertheless, we know that it
is these latter who deserve the greatest credit for these charitable
works.

These noble souls assist and guide people of every age and
condition of life; and when they retire, exhausted or ailing,
they always bequeath this sacred mission to be carried on by
others. Thus it frequently happens that the new-born baby is
taken up by virginal hands, and is provided with everything
that the tender love of a mother could give it; when the child
grows and attains the use of reason, he is handed over to them
to be educated; they will instruct him in Christian doctrine,
develop his mind by suitable teaching and give him a proper
training and character formation. Anyone who is afflicted by

[50] Matthew 12: 33.
[51] Already in a Discourse of 21 October 1945 to the directors of female Italian   506a
Catholic Action, on " Women in social and political life " (*AAS* XXXVII (1945), p.
284-5), the Holy Father had stressed voluntary celibacy in accordance with the evangelical
counsel: " For nigh on twenty centuries, in all generations, thousands and thousands
of men and women, persons of the highest quality, freely renounce, in order to follow the
counsel of Christ, a family of their own, and the holy duties and sacred rights of matrimonial life. Does that perhaps imperil the common good of peoples and of the Church?
On the contrary: these noble souls recognize the association of the two sexes by union
in marriage, in view of the same common benefit, but if they withdraw from ordinary
life, from the beaten path, far from abandoning, they are consecrating themselves to
the service of humanity, in absolute disinterestedness in respect of themselves and their
own affairs, in an activity that is incomparably more ample, total and universal."

illness or disease will find them at hand, moved by the love of Christ to strive by careful attention and remedial treatment to restore him to health. The orphan, the one who is distressed by poverty or anxiety, the prisoner, none of them is left without consolation and help; for those sacred ministers, men religious and consecrated virgins, will look compassionately on him as an ailing member of the Mystical Body of Christ, remembering the words of the divine Redeemer: *For I was hungry, and you gave me to eat; I was thirsty and you gave me to drink; I was a stranger and you took me in; naked and you covered me; sick and you visited me; I was in prison, and you came to me. Amen I say to you, as long as you did it to one of these my least brethren, you did it to me.*[52] And how are we to sing adequately the praises of the heralds of the word of God? Far from their own land, at the cost of immense toil, they are converting the infidel multitudes to the Christian faith. What are we to say in praise of the sacred brides of Christ who give these missionaries such invaluable assistance?

508   To one and all we gladly pay the tribute contained in the words which we wrote in our Apostolic Exhortation *Menti Nostrae*: " Instead of completely losing the privilege of fatherhood, by reason of this law of celibacy, the priest actually enhances it to an immense degree; for he begets children not for this earthly and transient life, but for the heavenly and everlasting life." [53]

2° *In the contemplative life.*

509   But the fruitfulness of virginity is not limited to the external works and undertakings to which those who adopt virginity can devote themselves more freely and more completely; it is productive also of those perfect forms of love for the neighbour,

---

[52] Matthew 25: 35-36, 40.

508a   [53] *AAS* XLII (1950), p. 663. In a Discourse to the young girls of Italian Catholic Action, 24 April 1943, the Pope said: " It is within monasteries and religious Congregations that hearts open wide to take the whole world into their care; the young boys and young girls who consecrate themselves to God acquire a genuine spiritual fatherhood and motherhood . . . Virginity is of inestimable worth, both by the mystic value of their offering united to that of Christ, and by the total consecration of their powers to the great undertaking of spreading the faith in the world. *He that can take it let him take* (Matthew 19: 12): this saying of Christ, we would wish to proclaim in the ears of all young Christian boys and girls, giving it the character of a call and a pressing invitation " (*AAS* XXXV (1943), p. 134).

namely ardent supplication on his behalf, and the willing and
cheerful endurance of grave trials for the same motive. These
are the aims to which servants of God and brides of Christ,
especially those men and women who live within monastic
enclosure, have dedicated their whole lives.

Heroic sanctity, a fruit of virginity. Finally, the consecration of one's vir- 510
ginity to Christ is in itself such a
remarkable testimony of faith in the
kingdom of God, and so striking a proof of love for the divine
Redeemer, that it cannot be wondered at if it brings forth a
rich harvest of holiness. Indeed, those countless virgins and
apostolic workers, who are vowed to perfect chastity, shed
lustre on the Church by the sublime holiness of their lives. For
virginity imparts to souls a spiritual strength which, if need be,
is capable of carrying them even to martyrdom; that is the plain
teaching of history, which proposes for the admiration of the
world so many companies of virgins, from Agnes of Rome to
Maria Goretti.

Virginity, a witness to the ideal of Christian purity. It is not without reason that virginity 511
is called the angelic virtue, as St. Cyprian
rightly declares in writing to virgins:
" What we will be, you have already
begun to be. You already possess in this world the glory of the
resurrection, you are passing through the world without the
defilement of the world. While you persevere in chastity and
virginity, you are the equals of the angels of God." [54] To the
soul that is thirsting for the pure life and burning with desire
for the kingdom of God, virginity offers itself as *a pearl of great
price* for which a man *sold all that he had and bought it*. [55] Married
people, and even those who are sunk in the depths of vice, are
not infrequently moved to admiration by the shining purity of
virgins, and feel themselves inspired to rise above the pleasures
of the senses. The point made by Aquinas, when he wrote: " To

---

[54] St. Cyprian, *De habitu virginum*, 22 (*PL* IV, 462); cf. St. Ambrose, *De virginibus*,
L. I, c. 8, 52 (*PL* XVI, 202).
[55] Matthew 13: 46.

virginity . . . is ascribed the highest beauty," [56] no doubt explains why virgins attract everyone by their example. Moreover, do not all these men and women, by their perfect chastity, provide the clearest possible proof that this mastery of the soul over the bodily senses is an effect of divine aid and a mark of solid virtue?

512

Virginity, a reflection of the holiness of the union between Christ and the Church.

But the choicest fruit of virginity, one on which it is particularly pleasing to dwell, is this: consecrated virgins bring vividly before us the perfect virginity of their Mother, the Church, and show clearly the holiness of their own intimate union with Christ. It is primarily in order to give expression to this truth that those admirably chosen words were written, in which the bishop, when performing the rite of consecration of virgins, humbly entreats God: "That there might be noble souls who would disdain the carnal union of man and wife, but eagerly desire what it symbolizes, and while refusing to imitate what is done in marriage would yet prize what is signified by marriage." [57]

513   The supreme glory of virgins undoubtedly is to be the living images of that perfect integrity which unites the Church with her divine Spouse; that these virgins are a wonderful sign of the flourishing sanctity and spiritual fruitfulness which distinguish the society founded by Jesus Christ, this is a source of the deepest joy to the Church. St. Cyprian has well said on this matter: "Virginity is the bloom of the Church, the beauty that adorns spiritual grace, a source of joy, a perfect tribute of praise and homage, the image of God answering to the holiness of the Lord, the choicest portion of the flock of Christ. Through them the Church rejoices and her own glorious fruitfulness flourishes even more abundantly in them. The more the number of virgins increases, the greater is the joy of this mother." [58]

---

[56] St. Thomas, *Summa Theol.*, II-II, q. 152, a. 5.
[57] *Pontificale Romanum;* De benedictione et consecratione virginum.
[58] St. Cyprian, *De habitu virginum*, 3 (PL IV, 443).

SECOND PART

THE CHRISTIAN DOCTRINE OF VIRGINITY

Contemporary errors must be refuted. This doctrine of the excellence of virginity and celibacy, and of their superiority to marriage, was revealed by the divine Redeemer and by the Apostle of the gentiles, as we have already said; in the holy Council of Trent [59] it was solemnly defined as a dogma of divine faith, and it has always been unanimously held by the holy Fathers and Doctors of the Church. Moreover, we ourselves, like our predecessors, have availed ourselves of every opportunity to explain it and have given it strong commendation. However, in view of the fact that recently this traditional doctrine of the Church has been attacked in a way which involves grave danger and detriment to the faithful, our sense of duty has led us to the conclusion that it would be timely to deal with the subject once again in this Encyclical, and to unmask and condemn those errors which are so frequently put forward with a show of truth.

Life of the senses and balanced personality. In the first place, it is undoubtedly a departure from that common sense of upright men, which the Church has always respected, to regard the natural sex instinct as the dominant and most important of man's inclinations, and to conclude from this that man cannot restrain this appetite throughout his whole life without grave risk of disturbing his vital bodily functions, particularly his nervous system, and thus injuring the balance of his personality.

But as St. Thomas rightly remarks, the most deep-seated of man's inclinations is in fact the instinct of self-preservation; the sexual instinct takes a secondary place. And furthermore, it is a matter for man's rational power and control, which is a singular privilege of our nature, to regulate these fundamental instincts and to ennoble them by exercising proper mastery over them. [60]

514

515

516

---

[59] *Sess.* XXIV, can. 10.
[60] Cf. St. Thomas, *Summa Theol.*, I-II, q. 94, a. 2.

517   It is true, unfortunately, that as a result of the sin of Adam, our bodily faculties have been disturbed, so that the passions seek to control not merely the life of the senses but even our souls, by darkening our understanding and weakening our wills. But the grace of Jesus Christ is given to us, especially through the sacraments, in order that living by the Spirit we may reduce the body to subjection. [61] The virtue of chastity does not demand of us that we should be insensible to the stimulus of concupiscence, but that we should subordinate it to right reason and the law of grace, while we strive with all our might for what is noblest in human and Christian life.

518   Now in order to acquire this complete mastery of the soul over the bodily senses, it is not enough to refrain merely from acts which are directly contrary to chastity; it is absolutely essential to renounce willingly and generously everything that is opposed to this virtue whether proximately or remotely. For then the soul will be able to rule fully in the body and to lead its spiritual life in peace and liberty. How, then, can anyone who takes his stand on Catholic principles fail to see that perfect chastity and virginity, far from hindering the natural growth and development of men and women, in fact assist that growth and ennoble it to the highest degree.

519   **Conjugal life and union of souls with God.**   With sorrow we recently had to censure the opinion of those who go so far as to maintain that marriage is the only means of ensuring the natural development and due perfection of human personality. [62] It is, in fact, asserted by some that the divine grace given *ex opere operato* by the sacrament of Matrimony, so sanctifies the use of marriage that it becomes a more efficacious instrument than virginity for uniting individual souls to God, inasmuch as Christian marriage is a sacrament, whereas virginity is not. We denounce that doctrine as a dangerous error. It is true, of course, that this sacrament confers on the married couple the grace to fulfil holily the duties of the

---

[61] Cf. Galatians 5: 25; I Corinthians 9: 27.
[62] Allocution to superiors general of female Orders and religious Congregations, 15 September 1952 (*AAS* XLIV (1952), p. 824; cf. *supra*, n. 477).

married state; undoubtedly it strengthens the bonds of mutual affection which unite them; but it was not instituted for the purpose of making the use of marriage a more fitting instrument *per se* for uniting the souls of the married partners with God by the bond of charity.[63] Is it not the case rather, that when the Apostle Paul recognizes the right of the partners to abstain from the use of marriage for a time, in order to devote themselves to prayer,[64] he does so because such abstention gives greater freedom of soul to one who wishes to turn his thoughts to heavenly things and to give himself to God in earnest prayer.

Mutual assistance of husband and wife: " loneliness of heart " of consecrated souls. Finally, it cannot be held, as some maintain, that the " mutual assistance," [65] which the partners seek in Christian marriage, is a more perfect aid to the acquisition of personal sanctity than the so-called " loneliness of heart " of virgins and celibates. For even though it is true that all those who have embraced the state of perfect chastity have renounced this form of human love, it cannot be asserted in consequence that this privation involves a diminution and impoverishment of their human personality; because they receive from God, the giver of heavenly gifts, a spiritual aid which is vastly superior to the " mutual assistance " rendered by husband and wife to one another. By giving themselves completely to him who is the source of their existence and who shares his divine life with them, far from diminishing their personality, they enrich it immensely. For who has a better right than virgins to apply to themselves the wonderful words of the Apostle Paul: *I live, now, not I, but Christ lives in me.*[66] 520

This is the reason why the Church in her profound wisdom considers that the celibacy of priests must be maintained; she 521

[63] Cf. Decree of the Holy Office, *De matrimonii finibus*, 1 April 1944 (*AAS* XXXVI (1944), p. 103). 519a
[64] Cf. I Corinthians 7: 5.
[65] *CIC*, can. 1013 § 1: The primary end of marriage is the procreation and education of children; the secondary end is mutual assistance and remedy for concupiscence.
[66] Galatians 2: 20.

knows that celibacy is and will continue to be a source of spiritual graces, which will bring priests into ever closer union with God.

522   **Witness of the Christian**   At this point we deem it opportune
home and the apostolate also to refer briefly to another error:
of the priest.   there are some who, in order to deter
young boys from entering seminaries and young girls from joining religious institutes, try to convince them that the Church at the present day has greater need of the aid of men and women who practise Christian virtue in married life spent among their fellow-men, than of priests and consecrated virgins, who are withdrawn from human society by reason of the vow of chastity which they have taken. It is obvious, venerable brethren, that this theory is utterly false and pernicious.

523   It is by no means our intention to deny that Catholic husbands and wives, by the Christian example of their lives in all places and circumstances, can produce abundant salutary fruits by the witness of their virtue. But to argue from this that married life is to be preferred to complete dedication to God, is undoubtedly to sow confusion and pervert the proper order of things. Indeed it is our most earnest desire, venerable brethren, that those who are already married, or who wish to enter the married state, should receive timely instruction about their grave obligation not only to bring up properly and carefully the children whom they have or will have, but also to help others as far as lies in their power, by the witness of their faith and the example of their virtue. But we must entirely reprove, as the sense of

524   our duty demands, those who endeavour to dissuade young people from entering a seminary or joining a religious Order or taking sacred vows, on the plea that they can achieve greater spiritual good in the married state, as fathers and mothers of families, by the open and public profession of the Christian life. It would certainly be far more appropriate and correct to exhort with all earnestness the vast numbers of married people to lend their assistance as lay persons in promoting the works of the apostolate, than to seek to turn away from virginity the young people, unfortunately all too few nowadays, who desire to dedicate themselves to the service of God. The words of

St. Ambrose provide an apt comment on this point: " It has always belonged to the grace of the priesthood to sow the seeds of integrity, and to stimulate the desire for virginity." [67]

Practice of chastity does not isolate one from the community. We deem it necessary also to insist 525 that it is utterly false to assert that those who have dedicated themselves to perfect chastity are strangers to and out of touch with the human community. The consecrated virgins who dedicate their lives to the care of the poor and the sick, without distinction of race, social rank or religion, are not they as intimately in touch with the miseries and sufferings of these, and as tenderly moved with compassion for them, as if they were really their mothers? And similarly, is it not the example of his divine Master that moves the priest to perform the office of good shepherd, one who knows his flock and calls them by name? [68] It is precisely the perfect chastity which they practise, that causes priests, and men and women religious, to give themselves to the service of all, and to love all with the love of Christ.

Contemplatives too, because they offer not only their prayers and supplications, but also the immolation of themselves which they have made to God for the salvation of others, contribute greatly to the welfare of the Church; indeed, they also deserve high praise, when, in circumstances such as the present, they devote themselves to apostolic and charitable works in accordance with the norms which we laid down in the Apostolic Constitution *Sponsa Christi*. [69] They cannot, therefore, be regarded as strangers to human society, seeing that they labour in this twofold way for the spiritual progress of men.

---

[67] St. Ambrose, *De virginitate*, c. 5, 26 (*PL* XVI, 272).
[68] Cf. John 10: 14; 10: 3.
[69] Apostolic Constitution of 21 November 1950 (*AAS* XLIII (1951), p. 20; cf. *supra* 383-387).

17

THIRD PART

PRACTICE OF PERFECT CHASTITY

526   Let us now come, venerable brethren, to the practical application of this teaching of the Church on the excellence of virginity.

Perfect chastity not an essential condition for perfection. To begin with, this must be stated clearly: the fact that virginity is to be regarded as more perfect than marriage does not lead to the conclusion that it is necessary for the attainment of Christian perfection. Holiness of life can, in fact, be attained even without the dedication of one's chastity to God; as proof of this, we have the example of the many men and women who receive public cult in the Church, and who were faithful spouses and exemplary fathers and mothers of families; indeed, it is by no means rare to find married people who are most earnestly striving for Christian perfection.

527   It must also be noted that God does not urge all Christians to virginity as a matter of duty, as the Apostle Paul teaches in the words: *Now concerning virgins, I have no commandment of the Lord, but I give a counsel.*[70] It is only as a counsel, therefore, that we are encouraged to embrace perfect chastity, as a means which can lead those to *whom it is given*[71] more surely and more easily to the evangelical perfection to which they aspire, and to the attainment of the kingdom of heaven. Hence, as St. Ambrose rightly observes: " It is not imposed, but proposed."[72]

528   **A gift of God which invites a free response from men.** From this it follows that perfect chastity demands, on the one hand, that Christians make a free choice before totally dedicating and offering themselves to God, and, on the other, that God himself gives the heavenly gift and grace from on high.[73] The divine Redeemer

---

[70] I Corinthians 7: 25.   [71] Matthew 19: 11.
[72] St. Ambrose, *De viduis*, c. 12, 72 (PL XVI, 256). Cf. St. Cyprian, *De habitu virginum*, c. 23 (PL IV, 463).
[73] Cf. I Corinthians 7: 7.

himself has already taught us this lesson in the words: *All men take not this word, but they to whom it is given . . . He that can accept it, let him accept.* [74] St. Jerome, having pondered deeply on this saying of Jesus Christ, addressed to all the exhortation that " each one should consider his strength, to see whether he is capable of carrying out the precepts of virginity and modesty. For, in itself, chastity is pleasant and attractive to everyone. But we must consider our strength, so that *he that can take, let him take.* The words of the Lord are, as it were, an exhortation to his soldiers, rousing them to win the prize of purity. *He that can take, let him take;* he that can fight, let him fight, let him win and let him triumph." [75]

Perfect chastity is a difficult virtue. For virginity is a difficult virtue. In order   529
to be able to embrace it, it is necessary not only to make a firm and express resolution to refrain completely and always from the lawful pleasures of marriage, but also to master and pacify the rebellious movements of the body and the unruly passions of the heart by constant vigilance and endeavour, to fly from the solicitations of the world and to overcome the temptations of the demon. How true then is the saying of St. John Chrysostom: " The root and fruit of virginity is a crucified life." [76] For as St. Ambrose says, virginity is like a sacrifice, and the virgin herself is " the offering of modesty, the victim of chastity." [77] St. Methodius, Bishop of Olympus, even compares virgins to martyrs, [78] and St. Gregory the Great teaches that perfect chastity is a substitute for martyrdom. " For, though the time of persecution is gone, our peaceful era has its own martyrdom, because even though we do not lay our neck beneath the sword, we slaughter carnal desires in our soul by the spiritual sword." [79] Chastity dedicated

---

[74] Matthew 19: 11, 12.

[75] St. Jerome, *Comm. in Matth.*, 19: 12 (*PL* XXVI, 136).

[76] St. John Chrysostom, *De virginitate*, 80 (*PG* XLVIII, 592).

[77] St. Ambrose, *De virginitate*, L. I, c. 11, 65 (*PL* XVI, 206).

[78] Cf. St. Methodius of Olympus, *Convivium decem virginum*, orat. VII, c. 3 (*PG* XVIII, 128-9).

[79] St. Gregory the Great, *Hom. in Evang.* L. I, hom. 3, 4 (*PL* LXXVI, 1089).

to God calls, therefore, for strong and noble souls, who are ready to fight and win *for the sake of the kingdom of heaven.*[80]

530
Prudent consideration before undertaking this obligation.
Consequently, before entering this narrow path, all those who know by experience that they are too weak for this struggle, should listen with humility to the warning of the Apostle Paul: *But if they do not contain themselves, let them marry. For it is better to marry than to be burnt.*[81] For there are many, in fact, for whom the burden of perpetual continence is undoubtedly too heavy to make it advisable for them to undertake it. Priests, therefore, who have the grave responsibility of assisting with their advice young people who say that they feel a certain inclination for the priesthood or religious life, should exhort them to give careful consideration to the matter, lest they should commit themselves to a course which it cannot be hoped that they will follow firmly and happily to the end. These priests should prudently examine the fitness of candidates in this respect and, wherever it is appropriate, take also the opinion of experts; and then, if prudent doubt still remains, especially on the basis of the previous life of the aspirants, they should use their authority, so that candidates will desist from the intention of embracing the state of perfect chastity, and will not be admitted to sacred Orders or religious profession.

531
Perfect chastity is possible with the aid of grace.
But while chastity consecrated to God is a difficult virtue, it can nevertheless be faithfully and perfectly observed by those who, having carefully weighed the matter, respond to the invitation of Jesus Christ with generosity of spirit and do all in their power to attain it. For by reason of the fact that they have pledged themselves to the state of virginity or celibacy, they will receive from God the gift of grace by the aid of which they will be enabled to carry out their purpose.

[80] Matthew 19: 12.
[81] I Corinthians 7: 9.

Consequently, if there should be some, " who do not feel that
they have the gift of chastity (even though they have vowed it)," [82]
let them not make this the basis of a plea that they are unable
to satisfy their obligations in this matter: " For ' God does not
command the impossible, but by his command admonishes you
to do what you can, and to ask for what you cannot ', [83] and
he gives his assistance that you may be able." [84]

We would recall this comforting truth to those also whose   532
will is weakened by nervous disorders, and whom some doctors,
sometimes even Catholic doctors, are too ready to advise to
seek exemption from their obligation, on the pretext that they
cannot observe chastity without suffering injury to their mental
balance. How much more useful and opportune it would be to
help those who are suffering from this malady to strengthen
their will, and to convince them that chastity is not impossible
even for them, as the Apostle said: *And God is faithful, who will
not suffer you to be tempted above that which you are able, but will
make also with the temptation issue, that you may be able to bear it.* [85]

Means of Safeguarding Chastity

**Vigilance and
mortification
of the senses.**
Now the helps which the divine Redeemer   533
himself recommended as an efficacious means
of safeguarding our virtue are: careful and
unfailing vigilance, whereby we diligently do
all that lies in our power; and constant prayer, whereby we ask
from God that which our own frailty makes it impossible for
us to achieve: *Watch and pray, that ye enter not into temptation.
The spirit indeed is willing, but the flesh is weak.* [86]

This vigilance, at every moment of our lives and in every   534
circumstance, is absolutely essential: *For the flesh lusteth against
the spirit, and the spirit against the flesh.* [87] Anyone who yields,
however little, to the enticements of the flesh, will easily find

[82] Council of Trent, *Sess.* XXIV, can. 9.
[83] St. Augustine, *De natura et gratia*, c. 43, 50 (PL XLIV, 271).
[84] Council of Trent, *Sess.* VI, can. 11.
[85] I Corinthians 10: 13.
[86] Matthew 26: 41.
[87] Galatians 5: 17.

himself falling into the *works of the flesh* [88] enumerated by the Apostle, which are the most shameful and ugliest of human vices.

535   Consequently, we must watch particularly over the movements of our passions and senses, and so control them, by voluntary austerity of life and bodily mortification, that we will bring them into subjection to right reason and the law of God: *They that are Christ's have crucified the flesh, with the vices and concupiscences.* [89] The Apostle of the gentiles says about himself: *But I chastise my body and bring it into subjection, lest perhaps, when I have preached to others, I myself should become a castaway.* [90] All saintly men and women kept a most careful watch over the movements of their senses and passions, and sometimes took very stern measures to curb them, in accordance with the teaching of the divine Master himself: *But I say to you that whosoever shall look on a woman to lust after her hath already committed adultery with her in his heart. And if thy right eye scandalize thee, pluck it out and cast it from thee. For it is expedient for thee that one of thy members should perish, rather than that thy whole body be cast into hell.* [91] It is obvious that what our Redeemer primarily demands of us by this admonition, is that we should never yield to sin, even mentally, and that we should firmly ward off everything that might tarnish even in the slightest degree this beautiful virtue. In this matter, no vigilance, no severity, can be regarded as excessive. And if ill-health or other causes do not permit severe bodily austerities, they never dispense from vigilance and inner self-control.

536   **Flight from occasions of sin.** In this connection it must also be noted, and it is the teaching of the holy Fathers [92] and Doctors [93] of the Church, that it is easier for us to gain the upper hand in the struggle with the blandishments and enticements of sin, if we do not fight directly against them, but rather fly from them, as far as possible.

---

[88] Cf. Galatians 5: 19-21.   [89] Galatians 5: 24.
[90] I Corinthians 9: 27.   [91] Matthew 5: 28-29.
[92] Cf. St. Caesarius of Arles, *Sermo* 41 (Ed. E. Morin, Maredsous, 1937. Vol. I, p. 372).
[93] Cf. St. Thomas, *In Epist. I ad Cor.* VI, lect. 3; St. Francis de Sales, *Introduction à la vie dévote*, part IV, c. 7; St. Alphonsus de Liguori, *La vera sposa di Gesù Cristo*, c. 1 16; c. 15, 10.

According to the teaching of St. Jerome, chastity is better defended by flight than by open combat: " I fly, lest I should be defeated." [94] This flight must be understood to mean, not merely the careful avoidance of the occasions of sin, but especially that in these struggles we should raise our mind and heart to divine things, fixing our thoughts particularly on him to whom we have vowed our virginity. " Gaze on the beauty of your Lover," as St. Augustine [95] advises.

The virtue of young clerics must be protected. Flight and constant vigilance, as the 537 means whereby we are to carefully ward off occasions of sin, have been regarded by saintly men and women of every age as the most effective method of successful combat in this field. But nowadays this opinion does not appear to be held by everyone. There are some who hold that Christians, and particularly sacred ministers, should not be as in former times *segregated from the world*, as they put it, but *present in the world*: consequently, they should *take the risk* and put their chastity to the test, and thus it will be made clear whether or not they have the strength to resist firmly; therefore, they contend, young clerics should see everything in order to become accustomed to view everything calmly and thus to become immune from any and every form of temptation. For this reason they would readily allow young clerics to turn their eyes freely, without any concern for modesty, to whatever is presented to them; to attend motion pictures, even those forbidden by ecclesiastical censors; to read periodicals, even if they are obscene, and to read novels which are on the Index or prohibited by the natural law. The reason which they allege for allowing all this, is that these spectacles and publications nowadays constitute the mental fare of the majority of men, and that those who wish to be of assistance to them must be familiar with their way of thought and feeling. It is not difficult to see how mistaken and harmful is this method of educating the clergy and training them to acquire the sanctity which befits their calling: *He that loveth danger shall*

[94] St. Jerome, *Contra Vigilant.*, 16 (PL XXIII, 352).
[95] St. Augustine, *De sancta virginitate*, c. 54 (PL XL, 428).

perish in it.[96] The admonition of St. Augustine is relevant in this connection: " Do not say that your mind is chaste if your eyes are unchaste, because the eye that is unchaste is the messenger of a heart that is unchaste."[97]

538   This ruinous approach undoubtedly is based on a serious confusion of thought. While Christ said of the Apostles: *I have sent them into the world,*[98] he had previously said of them: *They are not of the world, as I also am not of the world,*[99] and he prayed to his divine Father in the words: *I pray not that thou shouldst take them out of the world, but that thou shouldst keep them from evil.*[100] The Church, which is guided by the same principles, has enacted opportune and wise laws to protect priests from the temptation to evil which can easily assail all those who live in the midst of the world's affairs;[101] by means of these laws the holiness of their lives is sheltered from the cares and pleasures of the lay world.

539   There is even greater reason why the young cleric, since he is to be trained in the spiritual life and in priestly or religious perfection, should be separated from the world's tumult before going forth to engage in combat; he must spend many years in a seminary or scholasticate, where he will receive careful instruction, and gradually and prudently be trained to approach and master the problems which have been brought to the fore in our own time, in accordance with the directives which we gave in our Apostolic Exhortation *Menti Nostrae.*[102] What gardener would expose choice plants, which are still tender, to the inclemency of the weather, in order to test their hardiness, which they have not yet acquired? Seminarians and scholastics must assuredly be treated as young and tender plants, which still need protection and must be prepared gradually to resist and fight.

---

[96] Ecclesiasticus 3: 27.
[97] St. Augustine, *Epist.* 211, 10 (*PL* XXXIII, 961).
[98] John 17: 18.
[99] John 17: 16.
[100] John 17: 15.

538a   [101] Cf. *CIC*, can. 124-142; cf. also, St. Pius X, Exhortation *Haerent Animo* (*ASS* XLI (1908), p. 564-573); Pius XI, Encyclical *Ad Catholici Sacerdotii* (*AAS* XXVIII (1936), p. 23-30; Pius XII, Apostolic Exhortation *Menti Nostrae* (*AAS* XLII (1950), p. 692-4).
[102] *AAS* XLII (1950), p. 690-691.

**Christian
modesty . . .**
Educators of young clerics would be far 540
better and more usefully employed, if they
inculcated upon those youthful minds the
precepts of Christian modesty, which is such a powerful aid for
the preservation of virginity, and is rightly called the prudence
of chastity. Modesty discerns the approaching danger, and warns
against exposing oneself to peril; it also bids us avoid circumstances which the less prudent do not shun. It does not like
impure or unbecoming speech, and shrinks from even the
slightest immodesty; it carefully avoids questionable familiarity
with persons of the opposite sex, for it fills the soul with due
respect for the body, because the body is a member of Christ [103]
and the temple of the Holy Ghost.[104] Anyone who has the adornment of Christian modesty loathes every sin of impurity, and
immediately shrinks from it whenever enticed by its seductions.

Modesty will also suggest and provide parents and educators 541
with the appropriate words in which to instruct the conscience
of the young in regard to chastity: " Therefore," as we said in
a recent Allocution, " this sense of reverence must not be taken
to mean that there should be complete silence on the subject;
and that in giving moral instructions there should be no mention
of it, even with due care and circumspection." [105] Nowadays,
however, there are some teachers and educators who all too
frequently think it their duty to initiate innocent boys and girls
into the mysteries of human generation, in a way which offends
their sense of shame. But in this matter, that just moderation
and restraint should be observed which is required by Christian
modesty.

**. . . based on the fear
of God and humility.**
Now this chaste reserve is nourished 542
by the fear of God, by that filial fear,
founded on the virtue of deep Christian
humility, which inspires us with horror of even the slightest
sin, as our predecessor, St. Clement I, stated in these words:
" The person who is chaste in body should not be boastful, for

[103] Cf. I Corinthians 6: 15.
[104] Cf. I Corinthians 6: 19.
[105] Discourse to the Order of Discalced Carmelites, 23 September 1951 (*AAS* XLIII
(1951), p. 736); cf. *supra*, n. 460.

he knows that it is another who gives him the gift of continence." [106] Nobody perhaps has taught more clearly than Augustine the importance of Christian humility as a protection for virginity: "Because perpetual continence, and especially virginity, is a prized possession among the saints of God, the greatest care must be taken lest it be corrupted by pride . . . The more I see the greatness of this possession, the more I fear lest it should be lost through pride, the thief which would steal it. The only guardian of the possession of virginity is God himself who gave it: *And God is charity*.[107] Charity, therefore, is the guardian of virginity; and the dwelling-place of this guardian is humility." [108]

543 **Recourse to prayer.** There is another point that must be carefully considered: to keep chastity unsullied, neither vigilance nor modesty is sufficient. Recourse must be had also to supernatural helps, namely prayer to God, the sacraments of Penance and the Eucharist, and fervent devotion to the most holy Mother of God.

It must never be forgotten that perfect chastity is a sublime gift from God. On this point St. Jerome concisely remarks: "*It is given* [109] to those who have asked for it, who have wished for it, who have striven for it. For everyone that asks will receive, and he that seeks will find, and to him that knocks, it shall be opened." [110] St. Ambrose adds that the constant fidelity of virgins to their divine Spouse depends upon prayer.[111] And St. Alphonsus de Liguori,[112] with that ardent piety for which he was eminent, teaches that there is no more necessary or sure means of overcoming temptations against the beautiful virtue of chastity, then immediate recourse to God in prayer."

---

[106] St. Clement, *Ad Corinthios*, XXXVIII, 2 (Ed. Funk-Diekamp, *Patres Apostolici*, Vol. I, p. 148).
[107] I John 4: 8.
[108] St. Augustine, *De sancta virginitate*, c. 33, 51 (*PL* XL, 415, 426). Cf. c. 3, 31-32, 38; 412-5; 419.
[109] Cf. Matthew 19: 11.
[110] Cf. Matthew 7: 8; St. Jerome, *Comment. in Matth*. 19: 11 (*PL* XXVI, 135).
[111] Cf. St. Ambrose, *De virginibus*, L III, c. 4, 18-20 (*PL* XVI, 225).
[112] St. Alphonsus de Liguori, *Pratica di amar Gesù Cristo*, c. 17, 7-16.

Confession and frequent Communion. We must, however, supplement prayer by frequent and fervent recourse to the sacrament of Penance, which is a spiritual medicine that purifies and heals. It is also necessary to receive the nourishment of the Eucharist, which is the best "remedy against lust,"[113] as our predecessor of immortal memory, Leo XIII, pointed out. The more pure and the more chaste the soul, the more it hungers for this Bread, from which it draws strength to resist all enticements to sins of impurity, and by means of which it becomes more intimately united with its divine Spouse: *He that eateth my flesh, and drinketh my blood, abideth in me and I in him.*[114]

544

Devotion to the Blessed Virgin. An outstanding means of protecting and nourishing unspotted and perfect chastity, a means which has been proven by experience time and again in the course of centuries, is solid and fervent devotion to the Virgin Mother of God. In a certain sense, all other means are included in this form of devotion; for it is certain that anyone who is sincerely and ardently animated by it, is salutarily inspired to exercise constant vigilance, to pour forth his soul in prayer, and to have recourse to the tribunal of Penance and to approach the Holy Table. Therefore, we paternally exhort all priests, and men and women religious, to place themselves under the special protection of the gracious Mother of God, who is the Virgin of Virgins and the " teacher of virginity," [115] as St. Ambrose declares, and in a particular way, the most powerful Mother of all those who have dedicated and consecrated themselves to the service of God.

545

St. Athanasius [116] observed of old that virginity owes its origin to her, and the same truth is clearly taught by St. Augustine in the words: " The dignity of virginity began with the Mother of God." [117] Following in the footsteps of St. Athanasius,[118]

546

---

[113] Leo XIII, Encyclical Letter *Mirae Caritatis*, 28 May 1902 (*ASS* XXXIV, p. 641).
[114] John 6: 56.
[115] St. Ambrose, *De institutione virginis*, c. 6, 46 (*PL* XVI, 320).
[116] Cf. St. Athanasius, *De virginitate* (Ed. Lefort, *Muséon*, XLII, 1929, p. 247).
[117] St. Augustine, *Sermo* 51, c. 16, 26 (*PL* XXXVIII, 348).
[118] St. Athanasius, *ibid.*, p. 244.

St. Ambrose proposes the life of the Virgin Mary as a model for
virgins: " She it is that you must imitate, my daughters [119] . . .
Let the life of Mary, therefore, be for you the living image of
virginity, a mirror which reflects the beauty of chastity and the
ideal of virtue. From this model you can take a pattern of how
to live, for here you will find clearly expressed the lessons of
uprightness, which show you what you should correct, what
you should copy and what you should preserve . . . She is
the image of virginity. For such was Mary that her life alone is
sufficient to teach everyone [120] . . . Let holy Mary, therefore,
be the guiding principle of your life." [121] " So great was her
grace that she not only preserved for herself the grace of
virginity, but bestowed the badge of integrity upon all those
whom she visited." [122] How true then is the expression of the
same Ambrose: " O the riches of Mary's virginity." [123] Because
of these riches, it is highly profitable for consecrated virgins,
for men religious and priests, even at the present day, to dwell
upon Mary's virginity, in order to observe more faithfully and
perfectly the chastity of their state.

547   But do not be content, beloved sons and daughters, with
meditation on the virtues of the Virgin Mary: fly to her with
the most complete confidence, in obedience to the advice of
St. Bernard: " Let us seek for grace, and let us seek it through
Mary." [124] And particularly during this Marian Year, entrust to
her care your spiritual life and perfection, in imitation of the
example of St. Jerome, who said: " For me, virginity is dedicated
in Mary and Christ." [125]

[119] St. Ambrose, De institutione virginis, c. 14, 87 (PL XVI, 328).
[120] St. Ambrose, De virginibus, L. II, c. 2, 6, 15 (PL XVI, 208, 210).
[121] Ibid., c. 3, 19 (PL XVI, 211).
[122] St. Ambrose, De institutione virginis, c. 7, 50 (PL XVI, 319).
[123] Ibid., c. 13, 81 (PL XVI, 339).
[124] St. Bernard, In nativitate B. Mariae Virginis, Sermo de aquaeductu (PL CLXXXIII, 441-2).
[125] St. Jerome, Epist. 22, 18 (PL XXII, 405).

CONCLUSION

Appeal for priestly and religious vocations. In the midst of the grave difficulties **548** with which the Church must contend at the present day, it is a great consolation, venerable brethren, for us as supreme Pastor, to see that virginity is flourishing throughout the world, and that nowadays, as in the past, it is held in high honour and esteem, even though, as we have said, it is subjected to erroneous criticisms which, we trust, will be short-lived and soon disappear.

We do not deny, however, that our joy is tinged with a certain **549** sadness, since we know that in many countries there is a steady decline in the number of those who adopt the state of virginity in answer to God's call. We have already referred to the chief causes of this development, and there is no need to return to the subject once more. We are confident that those teachers of youth who have fallen into error in this matter will immediately recognize and repudiate their mistakes and earnestly resolve to repair them; we trust also that they will do everything in their power to ensure that the young people entrusted to their care, who may feel the heavenly call to the priesthood or to the religious life, will be assisted by every means to reach that noble goal. God grant that new and even larger companies of priests, men religious and consecrated virgins, equal in number and virtue to the present needs of the Church, will soon go forth to till the vineyard of the Lord.

Exhortation to Christian parents. Moreover, as the sense of our Apostolic **550** duty demands, we exhort fathers and mothers to gladly offer to the service of God those of their children who are called to it. If this involves some sacrifice, or if they feel saddened or annoyed by it, let them give earnest thought to the words with which Ambrose admonished the mothers of Milan: " I have known many young women who wanted to be virgins, but were prevented by their mothers from coming forward . . . If your daughters should wish to love a man, the laws give them permission to select whom they please. Is it the case, then, that those who have the right to choose a man, have no right to choose God?"[126]

Let parents consider what a great honour it is to see their son raised to the dignity of the priesthood, or their daughter consecrating her virginity to the divine Spouse. The same bishop of Milan says with reference to consecrated virgins: "Parents, you have heard . . . that a virgin is a gift to God, an offering of the parents, the priesthood of chastity. The virgin is the victim offered by her mother, by the daily sacrifice of which God is appeased."[127]

551 **Tribute to the priests and men and women religious who suffer persecution.** And now, venerable brethren, before concluding this Encyclical Letter, it is our desire to turn our thoughts and affections in a particular way to those men and women dedicated to the service of God, who, in not a few countries, are suffering bitter and calamitous persecution. Let them take example from those consecrated virgins in the early Church, who submitted to martyrdom with unflinching courage and constancy for the sake of their virginity.[128]

552 May all of them persevere with fortitude, *even unto death*,[129] in their sacred purpose of serving Christ; let them remember that their sufferings, sorrows and prayers, are of great value in the eyes of God for the restoration of his kingdom in their own countries and in the whole Church. And let them be convinced that those who *follow the Lamb whithersoever he goeth*,[130] will sing forever a *new canticle*,[131] which no other can sing.

We ourselves are moved with paternal and compassionate affection for all those, priests, men religious and consecrated virgins, who are valiantly confessing their faith even unto martyrdom; not for them only, but for all those throughout the whole world who are completely dedicated and consecrated to the

---

[126] St. Ambrose, *De virginibus*, L. I, c. 10, 58 (PL XVI, 205).
[127] *Ibid.*, c. 7, 32 (PL XVI, 198).
[128] Cf. St. Ambrose, *De virginibus*, L. II, c. 4, 32 (PL XVI, 215-6).
[129] Philippians 2: 8.
[130] Apocalypse 14: 4.
[131] Apocalypse 14: 3.

service of God, we humbly implore God that he would confirm, strengthen and console them; and we earnestly exhort each and everyone of you, venerable brethren, and your flocks, to join with us in imploring for these souls the divine consolation and the heavenly gifts and graces which they need.

May the Apostolic blessing, which we lovingly impart to you, venerable brethren, to all other sacred ministers and consecrated virgins, especially those *who suffer persecution for justice' sake,*[132] and to all the faithful of your flocks, be a source of heavenly gifts and a testimony of our own special goodwill.

Given in Rome, at St. Peter's, 25th day of the month of March, the feast of the Annunciation of the Blessed Virgin Mary, in the year 1954, the sixteenth of our pontificate.

---

[132] Matthew 5: 10.

LETTER TO CARDINAL VALERIO VALERI ON THE EXALTED MISSION OF RELIGIOUS TEACHERS

31 March 1954

In reply to a message from the French congress of teaching Brothers, the Holy Father, in an official letter to Cardinal Valerio Valeri, prefect of the Sacred Congregation of Religious, was pleased to give expression to the high esteem in which he held the noble mission of Brothers dedicated to the education of youth.[1]

553   The procurators general of eight lay religious Congregations, whose special aim is to instruct and give a Christian education to youth, have addressed to us, after the annual national French congress held last year in Paris, a dutiful letter to inform us of what had been achieved there and their plans for the future. At the same time they have besought us, with all humility and respect, to make known to them our paternal wishes, and to point out what would lead to greater and more fruitful achievements.

This we are glad to do briefly and concisely by means of this Letter.

554   **Responsibility of Christian teachers.** First of all, we are happy in the knowledge that these religious are earnest and untiring in discharge of the mission entrusted to them; it is a mission which can be of the greatest assistance to the Church, the family and to civil society itself. For, indeed, it is a matter of high importance that is in question; youth is the bright hope of the future, and the course of events in the future undoubtedly depends especially on the young people, who are now being trained in literature and every branch of learning, in order to be capable of undertaking the responsibility

[1] *AAS* XLVI (1954), pp. 202-205.

not merely of private business, but also affairs of public concern.[2] If their minds are enlightened by the light of the Gospel, if their souls are informed by Christian principles and their will strengthened by divine grace, then one may hope for the growth of a new generation of youth, which will successfully surmount all the difficulties, dangers and fears by which we are assailed at the present time; and by its learning, virtue and example it will one day succeed in establishing a better and healthier social order.

That is the goal for which lay religious societies also are striving and it is a great consolation to know it, guided as they are by the wise norms which their respective founders left as a sacred heritage.

It is our earnest desire that they should accomplish their task not only with skill, diligence and industry of the highest degree, but also that they should be animated by the heavenly spirit by which human efforts can be made to flourish and yield salutary results. And in particular it is our wish that they should strive to have their students imbued with learning that is not only genuine and free from all error, but also in harmony and fully in touch with the special techniques and methods which have been introduced into the different branches of knowledge in modern times.

Fervent religious life can help the Brothers in this mission. But what is of primary importance is 555 that they should derive from their religious life, which they should live most fervently, the supernatural strength by means of which they will conform to Christian virtue the students entrusted to their care; that is what the mission assigned to them by the Church absolutely demands. For if Christian virtue be neglected or given a subordinate position, neither

[2] The Holy Father repeatedly emphasized the high dignity of the vocation of teaching Brothers, at the same time insisting on their responsibility to the children entrusted to them. In the Apostolic Letter of 15 May 1950, which proclaimed St. John Baptist de la Salle the patron of educators, Pius XII quoted St. Bonaventure: " The only true educator is one who can stamp on his pupil an imprint of beauty, impart to him light and place in his heart manly strength." The Pope went on to draw this conclusion: " This is a thought which should be given careful consideration, especially in our own day, when we find that instruction is not merely divorced from the moral training of children,   554a

literary knowledge nor any other form of human learning avails anything to establish an upright life; indeed it is quite possible, especially at an age when souls are like wax and can be readily turned to evil,[3] that these attainments could become apt instruments of corruption and of unhappiness.[4]

556   Therefore, they shall watch carefully over the souls of their pupils; they shall have a profound understanding of the character of their students, of their hidden inclinations, of their innermost impulses, troubled as they are sometimes by unrest and anxiety, and they shall guide them wisely. As far as possible, they shall take care to banish, without any delay and with all diligence, the deceitful ideas that are a threat to virtue; they shall strive to avert every danger that could tarnish the brightness of the soul, and endeavour so to order the whole setting of their lives that, while the mind is being illuminated by truth, the will also shall be correctly and firmly controlled and moved to embrace all that is good.

The religious of these societies are well aware that the education of youth is the art of arts and the science of sciences;[5] but they know also that for themselves all things are possible by the aid of the divine help which they beseech, as the Apostle of the gentiles said: *I can do all things in him who strengthens me.*[6] They shall, therefore, cultivate piety above all, as befits men who, though not members of a " clerical religious society," are nevertheless legitimately attached to a lay religious society.[7]

but even that it becomes injurious for souls if it be allied with contempt of God and religion. That is why our holy Mother the Church shows vigilant affection to those who have the mission of training adolescents, for it is upon the teachers that the welfare and progress of Christianity largely depends" (*AAS* XXXXII (1950), p. 631).

[3] Horace, *Ars Poetica*, 163.

555a   [4] The Holy Father was gravely concerned for the solidity of the authentic Christian training of young people educated by religious. These are his words to the Fathers of the Congregation of the Holy Cross, 19 July 1956: "Your schools will do more than reflect scholarship. Youth has need not only of a sane and sound culture. It must come to develop a calm and well-balanced judgment, capable of discerning between truth and error, good and evil, justice and injustice. Firmly grounded in convictions planted by faith and reason, they must be strong enough not to be carried away by false illusions or violent passion or a fickle public opinion that measures everything by the rule of immediate, apparent success. Such youth the Church with full reason expects to see passing with sure step from the portals of your schools." (*Discorsi e Radiomessagi*, XVIII, p. 348).

[5] St. Gregory Nazianzen, *Orat.* II (*PG* XXXV, 426).

[6] Philippians 4: 13.

[7] Cf. *CIC*, can. 488, 4°; cf. *supra*, n. 77.

Dignity of vocation of teaching Brothers. Such a lay religious society, though 557 consisting almost exclusively of persons who, by a special vocation of God, renounce the priestly dignity and the consolations which flow from it, is nevertheless held in high honour in the Church; and indeed it provides powerful assistance to the sacred ministers in the Christian training of youth. For as we noted already on an appropriate occasion, " the religious state is by no means reserved exclusively to one or the other of the two groups which exist in the Church by divine ordinance; since both clerics and laics can equally be religious." [8] Now, if the Church has bestowed this dignity on laymen and given this responsibility even to them, that assuredly is the clearest possible indication to everyone that both parts of this sacred army can, with very great benefit, labour for their own salvation and that of others, in accordance with the special canonical regulations and norms by which each of them is governed.

Consequently, no one shall make little of the members of these societies because they do not ascend to the priesthood, and neither shall anyone depreciate the fruitfulness of their apostolate.

Moreover, it is well known to us that these religious so train 558 and educate the youth entrusted to their care, that very many of them, in whom are to be seen signs of the divine calling, are happily led to embrace the priesthood. And among their past pupils, some have been raised to the high dignity of sacred prelates and to membership of the Sacred College. [9]

That is a further reason why these religious societies, while meriting due praise from us and from the whole Church, also have won the grateful recognition of the bishops and of the whole clergy; for they lend powerful assistance to them not only

[8] Allocution *Annus Sacer* to the first International Congress of Religious; cf. *supra*, 557a n. 398.
[9] The Institute of Brothers of the Christian Schools presented to Pius XII, in 1953, a statistical picture of cardinals, bishops, priests and seminarists from 41 countries, former pupils of their schools, who were alive in that year; cardinals 7; bishops 102; priests 15,025; major seminarians 3,313. For France alone, cardinals 2; bishops 29; priests 5,169; major seminarians 786.—Figures taken from *Recrutement Sacerdotal* (April 1954).

in providing proper training for the young but also in encouraging new candidates for Holy Orders, with the aid of divine grace.

Let them continue, therefore, with constantly growing zeal on the path upon which they have set out; let them, together with other religious Orders and societies to whom this same mission has been assigned, devote themselves in concord and with willing souls to the training and education of youth.

MOTU PROPRIO " CUM SUPREMAE " INSTITUTING IN ROME THE PONTIFICAL WORK OF RELIGIOUS VOCATIONS

11 February 1955

On several occasions the Holy Father had manifested his concern at the decline of religious vocations in certain countries. To encourage the growth of vocations, he instituted a special Pontifical Work by the following Motu Proprio.[1]

The Sacred Congregation of Religious, in compliance with 559 our supreme paternal concern, has reported that it is most opportune to establish a primary Work of religious vocations; the purpose of this Work is to arouse in the faithful, by every form of advice, and particularly by the establishment in each region of different Works of this kind, the desire to favour, protect and assist vocations to the state of Christian perfection; also to spread a correct notion of the dignity and utility of the states of perfection and at the same time to summon the faithful from all parts of the world to a communion of prayer and exercises of piety; in view of this report, we, motu proprio and by the fullness of Apostolic authority, will, enact and decree that the Work of religious vocations, to which we give the title Pontifical, be established in the aforesaid Congregation; we add the faculty of admitting to it Works and persons, when that has been requested, and also the faculty of extending, to all who are inscribed as members, indulgences already granted or to be granted in the future and spiritual favours.

This decision shall be firm and permanent, notwithstanding anything whatsoever to the contrary, even things deserving of particular mention.

Given in Rome, at St. Peter's, 11 February 1955, the sixteenth year of our pontificate.

[1] *AAS* XLVII (1955), pp. 266 and 298.

I—STATUTES

560   I—The Pontifical Work for the protection and encouragement of vocations to the states of perfection is the primary Work established by his Holiness Pope Pius XII by the Apostolic Letter *Cum Supremae* issued motu proprio on 11 February 1955.

561   II—This Pontifical Work has its headquarters in the Sacred Congregation of Religious.

562   III—To attain the object for which it was established, the Pontifical Work:

1° Takes care first of all to diffuse a true conception of the nature, utility and excellence of the states of perfection, as this subject is expounded in recent pontifical documents;

2° Promotes works of piety, penance and charity, in order that God may grant many excellent vocations to the states of perfection;

3° Encourages the growth of Works established in each region for religious vocations, and sees that such Works are set up in places where they have not yet been established.

IV—The following can be aggregated to the Pontifical Work:

563   All religious societies and societies which are assimilated to religious societies, Secular Institutes whether of men or of women, monasteries and individual religious houses, the councils of major moderators, both of men and women which now exist in many countries, and all Works constituted specially for the development and assistance of religious vocations.

In addition, the following can be inscribed in the same Work: Ecclesiastical colleges and Catholic associations, and all the faithful, whether clerics or laity, who desire to serve this great Work.

564   V—The Pontifical Work of religious vocations is entrusted to the protection of the holy Family of Nazareth, which " affords a model of the gentle and effective union of the contemplative with the active life " [2] to all the states of perfection.

---

[2] Apostolic Constitution *Sponsa Christi*, 21 November 1950; cf. *supra*, n. 350.

II—NORMS FOR OBSERVANCE OF THE STATUTES

Direction.

His Eminence the Cardinal Prefect of the Congregation of 565 Religious is the president of the Pontifical Work of religious vocations; the vice-president is the Secretary of the same Dicastery.

The Pontifical Work does not in any way take away the autonomy and legitimate liberty of particular Works which are defined and regulated by their own laws.

Inscription.

The petition for aggregation or inscription to the Pontifical 566 Work for the states of perfection, for ecclesiastical colleges and other Catholic institutes or associations, and also for other particular Works of religious vocations, is made by their moderators.

The Pontifical Work, in making the aggregation or inscription, gives a diploma to societies and a special testimonial to individuals.

All inscribed members shall make a modest annual contribution.

Pious exercises.

The following practices are strongly recommended, that 567 God may deign to give excellent vocations to the different states of perfection, together with the assistance required to ensure that the vocations have a successful outcome:

1° Abstinence and fast on the vigils of the Assumption of the Blessed Virgin Mary and of the Nativity of our Lord Jesus Christ, for the special intention of the Work of religious vocations;

2° Prayers said without intermission by each of the states of perfection, each in its turn;

3° The celebration of a *day of religious vocations*, with a pious exercise approved by decree of the Sacred Congregation of Rites and enriched with special indulgences by the Sacred Apostolic Penitentiary;

4° The celebration of a *day of oblation*, in which the sick will offer to the Lord their sufferings and pains for religious vocations in union with the most precious Blood of Christ.

Activity of the Pontifical Work.

568   1° To make provision for the printing and diffusion of writings which will lead to better understanding and higher esteem of the dignity and utility of religious vocations;

2° To persuade priests to avail themselves of every opportunity of treating this theme (e.g., in Lenten sermons, spiritual exercises, novenas, catechetical instructions for adults, etc.);

3° To exhort the faithful to study the documents issued by the Holy See, and also the writings of the holy Fathers and pious authors, concerning the states of evangelical perfection and the religious life;

4° To encourage among the children and adolescents of both sexes, especially those for whom members of the states of perfection are in any way responsible, esteem of the religious life, and to nourish in them the deep desire for Christian perfection;

5° To institute congresses in which this theme will be treated, or at least take steps to see that in other congresses also there will always be something expounded on the subject of religious vocation;

6° To preserve the links and good relations with the religious societies, associations and institutes that are aggregated to it; to give assistance to particular Works and other useful undertakings, to promote and link them together, proposing to them the most suitable assistance to secure the desired object. Reports on all their activities and achievements, set out briefly, completely and accurately, shall be made to the Pontifical Work.

Feast days.   569

The chief feast days of the Pontifical Work will be:

1° The feast of the Holy Family, on the Sunday within the Octave of the Epiphany;

2° The feast of all the holy Founders;

3° The feast of St. Peter and St. Paul, 29 June;

4° The name day of the supreme Pontiff, the supreme moderator of all states of perfection.

LETTER OF THE SECRETARIATE OF STATE FOR THE THIRD CONGRESS OF THE PAROCHIAL TEACHING SISTERS OF FRANCE

10 September 1955

On the occasion of the third congress of parochial teaching sisters of France, in which the theme discussed was: " The woman religious in the community," his Excellency Monsignor Dell' Acqua wrote the following Letter to his Excellency Monsignor Brot, president of the National Commission of women religious; the Letter emphasizes the place of education of the civic sense in the Christian formation of young girls of today.

570   The Holy Father has learned with satisfaction that the Union of Parochial Teaching Sisters, whose happy development he follows with paternal interest, is getting ready to hold its third congress in the near future at Paris, under the presidency of his Eminence Cardinal Feltin; the theme of the congress will be: *The woman religious in the community. Education of the civic sense.*[1]

His Holiness considers that this theme is particularly opportune and topical: for the religious themselves, to begin with, on whom the demands of modern life impose new duties, which they cannot disregard without loss; and then, above all, for the young girls entrusted to their care, who will soon have to exercise, in the Christian spirit, their rights and duties as citizens.

571   At a time when women, having become entitled to exercise the franchise, are called to play their part in the course of public events, it would indeed be incomprehensible that the teachers of young girls should fail to give the necessary training on this matter.

572   Now it has to be recognized that problems of the civic order, which belong in the last analysis to the fourth commandment of God, have not perhaps in the past always fully held their

570a   [1] Some months later, on 11 February 1956, in the Motu Proprio *Nihil Ecclesiae* Pius XII expressed his satisfaction that the congresses of Federations instituted to promote the apostolate of women religious, were developing both their technical competence and skill in the discharge of their responsibility.

rightful place in Christian education. To take only one, but a particularly striking example—how many Catholic women, even nowadays, disregard the electoral obligation, for the reason that care was not taken at the proper time to make them understand the grave consequences which their abstention could involve for the good of society as a whole ! And how desirable it would be that the children of light should seek to give example always, in this department as in others ! They owe it to themselves to yield the first place to no one in their concern for the common good of the country, and to be no less eager for the fulfilment of civic duties than they would when there is question of the domestic or professional virtues. That obviously presupposes a careful formation, begun at an early age, and it is this precisely which shows clearly the importance of the theme selected for the present congress.

And so his Holiness is extremely pleased to felicitate M. l'Abbé Courtois, chaplain general of the Union of Parochial Teaching Sisters and zealous inspirer of this congress, and to invoke on all the participants an abundance of divine light; and as a testimony of his paternal goodwill and a pledge of fruitful labours, he imparts with all his heart the Apostolic benediction.

MOTU PROPRIO "NIHIL ECCLESIAE" APPROVING THE PONTIFICAL INSTITUTE "REGINA MUNDI" FOR HIGHER STUDIES OF WOMEN RELIGIOUS

11 February 1956

The international congress of the states of perfection, held at Rome in 1950, had directed attention to the timeliness of a certain adaptation to the requirements of the present age. The international congress of major superiors, held at Rome in 1952, had accepted the idea of a Roman Institute of the sacred sciences reserved to women religious. This Institute began to function in 1954. In view of the success of the project, the Holy Father, by the Motu Proprio Nihil Ecclesiae, *gave his approval to this Institute and designated it as Pontifical.*[1]

573 Nothing is of greater concern to the Church than that virgins consecrated to God, who profess the evangelical counsels in the states of perfection or other similar institutes, and who devote themselves to the salvation of their neighbours and to manifold good works by the purpose they have undertaken, should make firm progress to the attainment of the sanctity of which they have made profession; and that they should, at the same time, strive to carry out worthily and with unfailing endeavour the apostolic ministries and works of charity, which have been committed to them by the Holy See in the approval of their statutes and institutes.

Since, however, love of God and love of the neighbour are one and the same, the Church rightly demands that the desire for sanctity should become an assiduous striving for constantly fuller and more perfect performance of one's own duties, and for the more thorough preparation of oneself to perform them, sparing oneself no pains.

574 To secure effectively by suitable preparation this highly desirable perfection, at once human and divine, exercised through the performance of various ministries, the Apostolic See has

[1] *AAS* XLVIII (1956), pp. 189-192.

employed all suitable means to encourage and lead, with gentleness and firmness, women religious and other virgins consecrated to God and to the apostolate, to make use of everything that could be useful and fitting for their apostolic mission.

For this reason also all moderators and members of religious 575 societies, loyally obeying the rules and repeated exhortations of the Holy See, have never ceased to urge that individual sisters who, by their vocation and for the sake of the apostolate, have to perform civil or social functions, in addition to other requirements, should be equipped with diplomas, recognised certificates, and other prescribed testimonials for the due and worthy discharge of their responsibilities. For this purpose, special institutes, colleges, academies and schools have been founded or at least promoted and assisted in many ways. Moreover, by means of different courses of lectures and exercises, by the frequent holding of congresses, by the establishment of federations to promote the different apostolates, and by giving assistance of every kind, the Church has earnestly sought that all those who are engaged in active ministries for the love of God and of the neighbour, should have the inseparable accompaniment of technical training and skill in the discharge of their duties, together with religious zeal.[2]

For indeed, according to the mind of the Church, it is inconceivable and inadmissible that all those who by their religious profession and apostolic vocation devote themselves to social duties and professions, could be or should be thought to be

[2] Some years before, His Excellency Monsignor Montini wrote in the same spirit, 575a in a letter to M. l'Abbé Courtois, 1 April 1953, of the importance the Church attaches to Unions of women religious which, by means of their congresses, reviews, meetings, helped the sisters to acquire the necessary competence in the field of their providential activities: "Besides the field of activity which is proper to the two unions of nursing sisters and of teaching sisters, the parish offers a vast field for apostolate to the numerous communities which there exercise their devoted labour; they will find in the Union, which you inspired, possibilities of information and support whose value and worth they appreciate. The notable number of Congregations which work in conjunction with this Union is indeed in itself a proof of its utility and vitality.

"Because she is employed on various tasks, and being in contact particularly with youth, it is important that the parochial teaching sister should keep herself informed of the currents of ideas which, sometimes unconsciously, penetrate the minds of the young, and that she should keep in touch with the progress of proved methods of action or education; it is fitting too that her activity should fit in faithfully with the general lines of the apostolate or of the spiritual formation which the hierarchy encourages."

professionally inferior in the performance and discharge of these duties, to those other women who, for motives that are human, however noble, are employed in the world in the same duties or professions.

576   This applies particularly, and with all the greater reason, to those women religious and virgins consecrated to God who, especially in our own day, are engaged in many different ways in the education, instruction and formation of youth. Their task is an arduous one indeed, not only because of the temperament of the young and the circumstances of the times, but also because of the wider knowledge of science in its manifold forms, of culture and of pedagogy, which has to be acquired in a long course of studies and put to the test of numerous examinations, and because of other similar requirements that are everywhere laid down for teaching.

No one can have any doubt that these women religious who, by vocation, are the teachers and educators of infants, adolescents and young girls—whether they teach in the secondary and higher schools as in most cases, or have charge of girls who are pursuing university studies, even in public extern academies, or are engaged in the important works of their own institutes, directing or training their own religious—should have a higher training, technical and above all religious, which will be at once solid, well assimilated and complete, taking their special position into consideration.

577   In order that members of the states of perfection, and other virgins who are dedicated to perfection and the apostolate, should become first-class educators and teachers, as the times demand, in many places higher schools, academies and institutes, which generally are deserving of high praise, have been opened; in these the sisters are to be competently trained in doctrines and disciplines, especially religious and moral.

578   This fruitful movement of reform and adaptation which, after the solemn congress of the Jubilee year, has never slackened in its efforts to promote so many important initiatives, especially in this field of education and instruction, was the reason why the

³ 26 November to 8 December 1950; cf. *supra*, nn. 394-423.

Sacred Congregation of Religious summoned a meeting of
female superiors general for September 1952;[4] the purpose of
this meeting was to discuss the erection in Rome of a new
institute, which would not only serve as a model for all existing
or future institutes throughout the world, but would in various
respects be their complement and crown.

Consequently the same Sacred Congregation of Religious, by
our command and under our auspices, in order to meet the
wishes of that congress, with the co-operation from every side
of the superiors general, in the course of the Marian Year took
measures for the erection in Rome of the Institute of the Blessed
Virgin Mary, whom we had solemnly proclaimed and crowned
as Queen. This Institute, which has been entitled *Regina Mundi*,
has already given an excellent account of itself in these few years
and it gives us a sure guarantee of those happy results which
we ardently desire; in order, therefore, to strengthen and enrich
it with our pontifical approval, and to make it an outstanding
model and guide for similar institutes intended for virgins
consecrated to God which already exist throughout the world
or will be legitimately founded in the future, motu proprio
and after mature deliberation on our part, we decree and enact
as follows: 579

I—We proclaim as *pontifical*, and grant the honour of this
title to the Institute called " Regina Mundi," which is intended
for the higher training, education and formation in the sciences
and disciplines, especially sacred, of virgins consecrated to God
and to the service of souls.[5] 580

[4] Cf. *supra*, nn. 475-81, the Discourse of the Holy Father to the superiors general
assembled for this congress. 578a

[5] In the periodical *Commentarium pro religiosis et missionaris* (fasc. V-VI, 1954), Rev.
Fr. Goriccho, C.M.F., gave the following particulars on the nature of the new Institute.
" The Institute *Regina Mundi* is, therefore, in a certain way a centre like a university
or a higher school as it is called, which is intended to make it possible both for women
religious and members of Secular Institutes and also for other women consecrated to
perfection and the apostolate, to acquire that solid formation in the sacred sciences
which will give them the appropriate preparation for the internal responsibilities of
direction and formation and for the exterior works of the apostolate . . . Studies last
three years, and at the end of this period pupils, who have successfully stood their
examinations and written and defended their thesis, are granted a diploma which gives
them special rights and, in particular, the right to teach religion everywhere, even in
the higher schools. The subjects prescribed for all pupils are: fundamental theology,
dogmatic theology, moral theology, spiritual theology, sacred Scripture, canon law,

II—This Institute will be governed by the Sacred Congregation of Religious in our name and by our authority, under statutes approved by us. The Sacred Congregation shall be assisted in organizing, ruling and perfecting this our Institute, in accordance with the statutes, by the delegates of the Sacred Congregation of Seminaries and Universities, of the Secretariate of State and of the Vicariate of Rome.

III—To the Institute we grant the right and faculty, in accordance with the statutes, of granting diplomas to the students who have duly performed studies and lawfully passed their examinations; in virtue of these diplomas they will be entitled to teach, in colleges intended for females, whether secular or religious, whatever be their grade, in the measure which will be precisely defined in each diploma. To teach in lay schools intended for males, the prescriptions of law must be accurately observed.

IV—Finally we grant this Institute the faculty, in accordance with the statutes, of aggregating to itself those schools and institutes, and their departments, which are recognized to have an affinity with it. [6]

This we decree and ordain by our authority, anything to the contrary notwithstanding, even things deserving of particular mention.

Given in Rome, at St. Peter's, 11 February 1956, the seventeenth year of our pontificate.

Church history, sacred archeology and art, the liturgy, missiology, catechetics, pedagogy, the social doctrine of the Church, methodology, philosophy (for those who have not already made a sufficient study of it). The free subjects pertain to the sacred sciences or those sciences connected with them, ancient and modern languages (the international character of the Institute makes it an excellent practical school), sacred chant . . . "

580a   [6] A Decree of the Sacred Congregation of Religious, dated 12 March 1957, gives a precise declaration of the norms according to which the Pontifical Institute *Regina Mundi* aggregates or recognizes similar institutes. (*AAS* XLIX (1957), p. 869).

APOSTOLIC CONSTITUTION "SEDES SAPIENTIAE" GENERAL STATUTES FOR THE FORMATION OF RELIGIOUS DESTINED FOR THE PRIESTHOOD

31 May 1956

The Holy Father, in his concern for the human, spiritual and apostolic qualities of religious who have a priestly vocation, brings together here all the principles which should guide their formation. [1]

1. The blessed Virgin Mary, Seat of Wisdom, Mother of the Lord God of knowledge [2] and Queen of Apostles,[3] she to whose veneration we have dedicated a whole year, is rightly regarded as in a special way the Mother and Teacher of all those who embrace the states of striving for perfection and, at the same time, seek to play their part in the apostolic army of Christ the sovereign Priest. In order efficaciously to apply themselves to preparation and training for this sublime religious vocation, which is also sacerdotal and apostolic, they stand gravely in need of the guidance and assistance of her who has been constituted mediatrix of all graces pertaining to sanctification and who is rightly called the Mother and Queen of the Catholic priesthood and apostolate. Therefore we earnestly implore her favour, that as she has been the mediatrix of divine light to us in drawing up these statutes, she may also assist with her patronage those on whom falls the duty of putting these norms into execution.

2. It is by the great goodness of divine providence that, constantly in the course of the centuries, Christ the Redeemer has whispered to souls who are the objects of his predilection, by an inner and quasi-mystic call, that invitation which he had given *viva voce* to the young man who questioned him about eternal

581

582

---

[1] *AAS* XLVIII (1956), pp. 354-365.
[2] Cf. 1 Samuel 2: 3.
[3] Litanies of Loreto.

life: *Come, follow me.*[4] And constantly too, of many who by God's gift have received that call and, like the Apostles, have made the declaration: *Behold we have left all things and followed thee,*[5] our Lord has made *fishers of men,*[6] and has chosen them as workmen to be sent *into his harvest.*[7]

Religious life and priestly life

583   3. This takes place nowadays no less frequently than in former times since the conjunction of the states of striving for perfection with the priestly dignity and the apostolic charge has become ever more frequent and more intimate. For in antiquity monks generally did not possess the priesthood, and only a few of them, being compelled as it were by necessity to receive the priesthood in order to convert the nations to the Christian religion, were practically torn from their own rule; and subsequently, the Mendicants, though imbued with an admirable apostolic spirit, were not all bound by rule to receive the priesthood—even the saint of Assisi himself was not ordained; but the Canons Regular, and especially the Clerics Regular, received and exercised sacred Orders, by divinely received special vocation. Their example has been followed by countless Congregations and clerical societies of the common life. And nowadays, God as always providing for the needs of every age, these are joined by some Secular Institutes which have priest members.

584   4. Besides, at the present time even in the older Orders of the Latin Church which are not formally designated as lay, all the members, with the exception of those called *coadjutores* or *conversi,* are destined for the priesthood; and the priesthood is, moreover, a requirement in those who assume the government of these Orders.

585   5. The Church then, in the present time, has at its disposal a large number of ministers who apply themselves both to the acquiring of perfection by means of the evangelical counsels and also to the performance of apostolic duties. This multitude of

---

[4] Matthew 19: 21.   [5] Matthew 19: 27.
[6] Matthew 4: 19.   [7] Matthew 9: 38.

men constitutes the religious clergy, as it is called, which takes its place beside the diocesan or secular clergy; both of them thrive and flourish in fraternal emulation and with fruitful mutual assistance, under one and the same supreme authority of the Roman Pontiff, without prejudice, of course, to the jurisdiction of bishops.

Need of special rules for the training of religious

6. Now it is realized by everyone that the religious clergy, in order duly and securely to pursue its special twofold aim, has need of rules of great wisdom to guide and promote its training and formation, whether religious or clerical and apostolic. **586**

7. Hitherto this need has been largely met by the statutes or constitutions of the individual societies concerning the training of young religious or the organization of studies. And besides, there is certainly no lack of prescriptions and recommendations of the Holy See on this subject. Nevertheless, for a long time there has been a desire for general regulations, duly co-ordinated and more complete, sanctioned by Apostolic authority and obligatory on all everywhere, so that the success of this great work, which is of such great importance for the welfare of souls, should be ensured and should continue to develop and to be performed with sustained and appropriate endeavour. **587**

8. A work of such importance calls for the constant vigilance of the Apostolic See itself; for, even as diocesan clerical schools, as public institutions in the Church, remain under her active and constant vigilance, exercised through the Sacred Congregation of Seminaries and Universities,[8] similarly and for the same reason the schools belonging to the states of perfection which are recognized and sanctioned by the Church, are public and are subject to the Sacred Congregation of Religious.[9] **588**

9. For these manifold reasons, already in 1944 we decided by our Apostolic authority that, within this same Sacred Congregation, " there should be set up and established a special **589**

---

[8] Cf. *CIC*, can. 256.
[9] Cf. *CIC*, can. 251. Pius XII, Apostolic Constitution *Provida Mater*, art. IV, § 2, February 1947 (*AAS* XXXIX (1947), p. 121; cf. *supra*, n. 242.

committee or commission of competent men to deal with all questions and matters that, in any way whatsoever, pertained to the religious and clerical education, and to the instruction in literary and scientific subjects and training in the ministries, of aspirants, novices and young members of every religious Order and society living in common without vows." [10]

590   10. This Commission, consisting of experts from all religious Orders and all nations, having taken into consideration all the existing documents that were relevant, and having collected information from all quarters in accordance with the circulars addressed to all supreme moderators, [11] had already accomplished an immense work, when the general congress of the states of perfection was announced in 1950. The commission made use of various timely proposals put forward in that congress; it again weighed the various schemata which had already been prepared and revised them, and finally they were submitted for our approval.

591   11. Now, therefore, we enact a number of statutes, which we preface by certain fundamental principles and rules concerning the religious, clerical and apostolic training and formation of pupils, that must always be kept in mind by all.

Vocation

592   12. In the first place, we wish that no one should fail to understand that the foundation of the whole religious life, and of the priestly and apostolic life, which is called divine vocation, consists of two essential elements: the one is divine, the other is ecclesiastical. As regards the first, it must be said that the call of God to enter either the religious or the priestly state is so essential that, if it be absent, then the very foundation of the whole building is wanting.

593   13. The person whom God does not call is not moved or helped by the grace of God. Besides, if it is true in a certain way that a genuine call to any state should be called divine, to

---

[10] Sacred Congr. of Religious, Decree *Quo efficacius*, 24 January 1944 (*AAS* XXXVI (1944), p. 213).
[11] Sacred Congregation of Religious, Circular Letter *Quantum conferat*, 10 June 1944 (*Enchiridion de Statibus perfectionis*, Rome, 1949, n. 382).

the extent that God himself is the principal author of all states and of all dispositions and gifts, natural or supernatural, how much more must not this be said of the religious and priestly vocation? For it is of such sublime dignity, and is enriched by so many great natural and supernatural distinctions that can come only from the *Father of lights, from whom is every good gift and every perfect gift.*[12]

14. And now, to come to the other element of religious and priestly vocation; the *Roman Catechism* [13] teaches that " those are said to be called by God, who are called by the lawful ministers of the Church." 594

15. Now this teaching, far from contradicting what we have said about divine vocation, is on the contrary intimately linked with it. For the divine vocation to the religious and clerical state, inasmuch as it destines one to lead publicly a life of sanctification and to exercise the hierarchical ministry in the Church, which is a visible and hierarchical society, must receive authoritative approval, and be accepted and regulated by the hierarchical superiors to whom the rule of the Church has been divinely committed. 595

16. That is a point that must be attended to by all who are engaged in the recruitment and testing of such vocations. Consequently, they shall never constrain anybody in any way into the priestly or religious state,[14] nor shall they entice or admit anyone who does not genuinely show true signs of divine vocation; likewise they shall not promote to the clerical ministry anyone who shows that he has received from God only a religious vocation; nor shall they force or divert to the secular clergy those who have from God this gift also of a religious vocation; and finally they shall not turn away from the priestly state anyone who is marked clearly as having the divine call to it.[15] 596

17. For it is clear that those who aspire to service in the ranks of the clergy within the state of perfection, and for whom these 597

[12] James 1: 17.
[13] *Roman Catechism* (for the use of parish priests. Edited by Pius V), part II, c. VII.
[14] Cf. *CIC*, can. 971: It is unlawful to force anyone in any way or for any reason into the clerical state, or to turn from it one who is canonically suitable. 596a
[15] Cf. *CIC*, can. 971.

norms are laid down, should have simultaneously all that is required to constitute this manifold vocation—religious, priestly and apostolic; consequently, all the gifts and qualities, which are considered necessary for the fulfilment of these exalted functions, should be found in them.

Need for solid formation imparted by skilful teachers

598   18. Now everyone understands that the germs of divine vocation and the qualities required for it, when they are found to be present, stand in need of education and formation in order to develop and mature. For nothing is perfect at the moment of birth, but gradually goes on to acquire its perfection. In guiding this development, account must be taken of all the conditions—both of the person who has the divine vocation and of the time and place—in order that the purpose intended may be achieved. Hence the education and formation of young religious should be sure, enlightened, solid, complete, wisely and boldly adapted to the interior and exterior requirements of the present day; it should be assiduously developed and vigilantly put to the test in all that concerns the perfection not only of religious life, but of priestly and apostolic life also.

599   19. All this, as we know by experience, can be accomplished only by proved and picked teachers, by men who are distinguished for doctrine, prudence and discernment of spirits, men of wide experience of men and things and eminent for other human qualities; they must also be full of the Holy Spirit and a shining example of holiness and of all the virtues to the young religious; the young, as is well known, are more influenced by right conduct than by words in the whole department of instruction.[16]

600   20. In the fulfilment of this grave responsibility, the first rule for educators shall be that which the Lord enunciated in the Gospel: *I am the good Shepherd: the good Shepherd gives his life for his sheep . . . I am the good Shepherd and I know mine and mine know me.*[17] St. Bernard expressed that teaching in these

599a   [16] Cf. *CIC*, can. 124: Clerics are bound to lead a more saintly interior and exterior life than the laity, and to give them example by excelling in virtue and righteous conduct.
[17] John 10: 11-12, 14.

words: " Learn that you are to be the mothers of your subjects, not their masters; strive to be loved rather than to be feared." [18]

The Council of Trent itself frequently exhorts ecclesiastical superiors: the first admonition which it deems right to give them, is that " they should remember that they are shepherds, not marauders, and that they should so rule over their subjects as not to domineer over them, but to love them as *sons and younger brothers*; they shall endeavour, by exhortation and admonition, to deter them from what is unlawful, lest they be compelled to inflict the due penalties when they do commit crimes. But if they should happen, through human frailty, to commit some sin, then the precept of the Apostle is to be observed, namely that superiors shall *rebuke, entreat, reprove in all goodness and patience*; kindness is more effective than severity with those who have to be corrected, exhortation is more effective than threats, charity is more effective than the exercise of power. But if, because of the gravity of the crime, there is need for the rod, then rigour should be allied with kindness, justice with mercy, and severity should be applied with gentleness; thus, without harshness the discipline that is salutary and necessary for peoples will be preserved, those who have been corrected will amend their ways; or, if they should refuse to repent, others will be deterred from vice by the salutary example of the correction inflicted on them." [19]

Development of the natural virtues

21. All those who in any way have charge of the training of religious shall remember, moreover, that this education and formation is to be imparted in a harmonious progression and with the aid of all opportune resources and methods; and also that it should embrace the man under all the aspects of his vocation, so as truly to fashion him as *a man perfect in Christ Jesus*.[20] In respect of the resources and methods of instruction, it is manifest that those furnished by nature itself and brought to light by human research in modern times, if they are good,

601

---

[18] *In Cantica*, Sermon XXIII (*PL* CLXXXIII, 885B).
[19] Cf. *CIC*, can. 2214 2; Council of Trent, *Sess*. XIII de Ref.; c. 1.
[20] Colossians 1: 28.

are by no means to be despised, but rather to be highly esteemed and wisely admitted; but no error is worse than that which leads a man, in the formation of these chosen pupils, to rely solely or excessively on these natural methods and to relegate to second place or in any way neglect the means and resources of the supernatural order; because, for the attainment of religious and clerical perfection enriched with all apostolic fruits, supernatural resources such as the sacraments, prayer, mortification and other similar things, are not only necessary, but absolutely primary and essential.

602   22. While safeguarding this proper ordering of methods and resources, there should be no neglect of anything that can in any way contribute to the development of body and mind, to the cultivation of all the natural virtues, and to the formation of a manly and complete human personality; on such a solid foundation of natural uprightness and thorough culture,[21] the supernatural training, whether priestly or religious, will thus rest firmly, since the way to Christ will become smoother and more secure for men, the more clearly they see in the person of the priest *the goodness and kindness of our Saviour God*.[22]

Training to sanctity

603   23. However, though great importance is to be attached by all to the human and natural instruction of the religious clergy, the supernatural sanctification of the soul undoubtedly takes first place in the whole curriculum of training. For if the admonition of the Apostle applies to every Christian: *This is the will of God, your sanctification*,[23] how much more does not this obligation fall on one who is not only clothed with the priesthood, but has made public profession of striving for evangelical perfection; one indeed who, by the very fact of his office, is so constituted the instrument of sanctification of others, that the salvation of souls and the growth of the kingdom of God depends in no small degree upon his holiness?

[21] Cf. Philippians 4: 8.
[22] Titus 3: 4.
[23] 1 Thessalonians 4: 3.

24. All members of the states of striving for perfection shall, 604
therefore, remember and frequently reflect before God that it
is not enough for the fulfilment of the duty of their profession,
if they avoid mortal sins, or even venial sins, with God's help;
or if they conform merely materially to the precepts of their
moderators, or even to the vows and obligations which bind in
conscience, or to their own particular constitutions, to which,
as the Church prescribes in the sacred canons, " each and every
religious, superiors as well as subjects, is bound to conform
his life and thus to strive for the perfection of his state." [24]
They are bound to do all these things wholeheartedly and with
ardent love, not merely from necessity but *also for conscience'
sake*;[25] since, in order to be able to climb to the heights of
sanctity and to present themselves to all as living sources of
Christian charity, they should be on fire with burning charity
towards God and their neighbour and carry the adornment of
every virtue.

Intellectual culture

25. When provision has been made for this sanctification of 605
the soul, it will be necessary also to furnish the religious clergy
with a thorough intellectual and pastoral training; in view of
the gravity of this subject and because of our sense of the duty
of our supreme office, we propose to set out and to inculcate
the principles somewhat more fully.

26. The necessity of a solid and in every respect complete 606
intellectual training and formation for these religious, is clearly
evident from the threefold dignity especially which makes them
shining lights in the Church, namely the religious, the priestly
and the apostolic dignity.

27. Religious, whose chief duty it is, by seeking God alone 607
and uniting themselves to him, to contemplate divine things
and to transmit them to others, shall remember that they
cannot at all discharge this saintly duty duly and fruitfully and

---

[24] Cf. *CIC*, can. 593.
[25] Romans 13: 5.
[26] Cf. Pius XI, Apostolic Letter *Unigenitus Dei Filius*, 19 March, 1924 (*AAS* XVI   607a
(1924), p. 137-8); cf. *supra*, nn. 140-1.

be raised up to sublime union with Christ, if they are devoid of that abundance of profound and constantly to be perfected knowledge of God and his mysteries, which is derived from sacred studies.

608   28. The priestly dignity is a shining adornment by reason of which the priest is constituted legate of the *God of knowledge* [27] and is in a special way called the *salt of the earth* and the *light of the world*[28] that is a dignity that demands a full and solid training, especially in ecclesiastical disciplines, a training such as will be capable of nourishing and supporting the spiritual life of the priest himself and will preserve him from error and misleading novelty; and it will also make him a faithful *dispenser of the mysteries of God*[29] and a perfect man of God, instructed for every good work.[30]

609   29. Finally there is the apostolic function, which those who belong to the states of perfection exercise in the Church, each according to his vocation, by preaching to the people, by Christian instruction of children and youth, by the administration especially of the sacrament of Penance, by missions to pagan lands, by the spiritual direction of souls, or finally by their daily contact with the people; this apostolic function will never be capable of producing abundant and abiding fruits, unless they themselves have a full knowledge of sacred doctrine and, by means of sustained study, thoroughly understand it.

610   30. In order to achieve this solid and complete training and formation of the intellect, taking account of the natural development of the young religious and the distribution of studies, religious superiors shall make it their first care and employ every means to ensure that the literary and scientific knowledge of religious students " should at least be no way inferior to that of lay students who follow corresponding courses. If this precaution is observed, the thorough mental formation of the students will be provided for, and it will also be easier to select

---

[27] 1 Samuel 2: 3.
[28] Matthew 5: 13-14.
[29] Cf. 1 Corinthians 4: 1-2.
[30] Cf. II Timothy 3: 17.

candidates when the time comes ";[31] and provision will also be made for the preparation of these students for higher studies and furnishing them with the appropriate equipment.

31. In philosophy and theology, which are to be taught only by competent and carefully selected masters, the prescriptions of the sacred canons, as well as those laid down by our predecessors and by ourselves, shall be strictly observed: especially concerning the reverence for the magisterium of the Church and the absolute fidelity which is to be professed at all times and places and instilled into the minds and hearts of the pupils; the prudence and caution which is at all times to be linked with the diligent and highly commendable examination of new questions which arise with the passage of time; and finally, the strict adherence to the method, teaching and principles of the angelic Doctor, which are to be followed completely in the philosophical and theological instruction of students.[32]

32. With Aquinas as guide and master, theology shall be taught both with the positive and the scholastic method, so that with the guiding light of the authentic magisterium, the sources of divine revelation will be studied with the greatest care and with the appropriate methods, and the treasures of truth derived thence will be clearly expounded and efficaciously defended. For since the deposit of Revelation has been entrusted to the magisterium of the Church alone for authentic interpretation, it is to be explained not by mere human reason and private judgment, but faithfully according to the sense and the mind of the Church herself. Teachers of Christian philosophy and theology shall understand, therefore, that they exercise their function,

611

612

[31] Pius XII, Apostolic Exhortation *Menti Nostrae*, 23 September 1950 (*AAS* XLII (1950), p. 687).

[32] In the Encyclical *Humani Generis*, 12 August 1950, the Holy Father, resuming the terms of his Allocutions to the Jesuits, 17 September 1946 (cf. *supra*, nn. 210-91), and to the Dominicans, 22 September 1946 (*AAS* XXXVIII (1946), pp. 384-5 and 385-9), insisted on the Church's requirements concerning the Thomistic formation of clerics: " . . . the Church demands that future priests should be taught philosophy ' according to the method, teaching and principles of the angelic Doctor ' (can. 1366, § 2); the experience of centuries has made her well aware that the method of Aquinas enjoys singular pre-eminence whether for teaching beginners or for the investigation of profound truths; his doctrine is in harmony with divine revelation, it is a most effective means of establishing securely the foundations of the faith and of gathering safely and putting to good use the fruits of healthy progress " (*AAS* XLII (1950), p. 573).

611a

not in their own right and in their own name, but only in the name and by the authority of the supreme magisterium and hence, subject to the vigilance and direction of that magisterium, from which they have received this quasi-canonical function; consequently, without prejudice to just freedom of opinion on matters still open to discussion, " they shall clearly bear in mind that the faculty of teaching has not been granted to them in order to communicate their own opinions to their pupils, but to impart to them the approved teachings of the Church." [33]

613   33. Moreover, all alike, both masters and pupils, shall always bear in mind that ecclesiastical studies have as their aim not merely the formation of the intellect, but a complete and solid formation, religious as well as priestly and apostolic; studies, therefore, are not to be directed solely to the passing of an examination, but rather to the imparting of a certain lasting stamp to the minds of the pupils, from which they will always derive strength and light for their own needs and those of others, when the occasion arises.[34]

614   34. To secure this, intellectual training must above all be closely linked with love of prayer and with contemplation of divine things; it should moreover be complete, omitting no part of the prescribed disciplines; it should be also coherent and in every respect so arranged and co-ordinated that all the subjects will harmoniously form a single system which is both solid and properly ordered; it shall also be wisely adapted to the refutation of the errors of our time and to answering its needs; while remaining completely in harmony with venerable tradition, it shall be in accordance with recent findings; finally, it shall be effectively directed to the fruitful discharge of pastoral duties of every kind, so that future priests who have received this training will be able readily and accurately to propound and defend sound doctrine for the simple and the learned in sermons and catechetical instructions, to administer properly the sacraments, to promote actively the good of souls and to be helpful to all by word and deed.

613a   [33] Pius X, Motu Proprio *Doctoris Angelici*, 29 June 1914, (*AAS* VI (1914), p. 338).
[34] Pius XII, Discourse to seminarians, 24 June 1939 (*AAS* XXXI (1939), p. 246).

Pastoral training

35. All the requirements for the spiritual and intellectual 615 training of pupils that we have hitherto enunciated, make such an important and vital contribution to the formation of truly apostolic men that, if this due learning and holiness are lacking in a priest, it is proved by experience that he is lacking in every-thing; nevertheless, in order to fulfil our grave responsibility, we must here add that, in addition to holiness and appropriate learning, it is absolutely essential, in order to discharge properly the apostolic ministry, that the priest should have a most thorough and in every respect complete pastoral preparation: a preparation, namely, that will produce and impart genuine skill and dexterity in the proper performance of the manifold functions of the Christian ministry.

36. For if it is customary that everyone, before practising 616 his art, should receive a diligent preparation, a theoretical or technical or practical preparation which is based on a long apprenticeship, who will deny that an equal preparation, or indeed one that is much more careful and profound, should precede the exercise of what is rightly called the " art of arts? "

37. This pastoral formation of pupils should begin with the 617 opening of their course of studies and be gradually completed as they progress; and when the course of theology has been completed, it should be rounded off by a special course of instruction corresponding to the aim of each one's institute; its primary object should be that the future ministers and apostles of Christ will be thoroughly and solidly imbued with and practised in the apostolic spirit and virtues, after the model of Christ himself: namely with ardent and pure zeal for promoting the glory of God, active and burning love for the Church, for the defence of her rights and the preservation and promotion of her doctrine; intense zeal for the salvation of souls, supernatural prudence in word and deed combined with evangelical simplicity; humble self-denial and most docile subjection to superiors, firm trust in God and keen sense of one's duties; manly industry in undertaking and constancy in carrying out projects, assiduous fidelity in performance of duties, great courage in suffering

difficulties and in the performance of arduous tasks, and finally, Christian amiability and Christian refinement that will be attractive to all.

618   38. There is another object to be striven for in the course of pastoral training: namely that the pupils, as their studies progress through various grades, should be instructed in all those disciplines which can help to form in every respect the *good soldier of Christ Jesus* [35] and furnish him with the appropriate apostolic equipment. In addition, therefore, as we have said, to the judicious orientation of philosophical and theological studies towards pastoral action, it is absolutely essential that the future pastors of the Lord's flock should receive, from competent teachers and in accordance with the norms of this Apostolic See, instruction on questions of psychology and pedagogy, didactics and catechetics, social and pastoral and other such problems, which will correspond to modern progress in these sciences and will make them competent and ready to meet the manifold exigencies of the apostolate at the present time.

619   39. To strengthen this apostolic training and formation by practice and experience, it should be accompanied by practical exercises, prudently regulated and following a wise progressive arrangement. It is our wish that this course should be further practised and completed, after ordination, under the guidance of men eminent for their learning, judgment and example, and that it should be continually strengthened without any intermission of sacred studies.

Conclusion

620   40. Having first stated these chief principles by which the work of training, as well as the teachers and their pupils should be informed and guided, we now decree the general norms concerning the individual points of this most important question; having given mature consideration to everything, with certain knowledge and by the fullness of Apostolic authority, we decree that they are to be observed by all whom it concerns. Moreover, by our authority we give to the Sacred Congregation of Religious

[35] II Timothy 2: 3.

the power, by means of ordinances, instructions, declarations, interpretations and other such documents, to give effect to the General Statutes already approved by us, and to do everything that pertains to the faithful observance of the Constitution and the Statutes and Regulations.

Anything whatsoever to the contrary notwithstanding, even things deserving of special mention.

Given in Rome, at St. Peter's, 31 May 1956, feast of the Blessed Virgin Mary, Queen of the world, the eighteenth year of our pontificate.[36]

---

[36] The text of the Apostolic Constitution Sedes Sapientiae is followed by " General Statutes concerning the religious, priestly and apostolic formation of clerics in the States of perfection." These important and detailed Statutes are published by the Sacred Congregation of Religious, which reserves the rights of publication and translation.

DISCOURSE TO NURSING SISTERS

24 April 1957

On the occasion of the first Italian congress of nursing sisters, the Holy Father took the opportunity to deliver to them a discourse which emphasizes the high dignity of their work and their responsibilities.[1]

621   We extend our fatherly welcome to you, beloved daughters, the religious and superioresses of hospitals, clinics and convalescent homes. You have assembled at Rome for your first national congress, in order to study the theme: " Religious life and apostolate, the technique, organization and profession of nursing the sick; " and we have felt that we could not remain absent from this gathering, for indeed it is with supreme joy that we see that the whole world of women religious is astir, proceeding with prudence and daring, actively intent on examining the means and methods which will best serve the renewal of their life and of their apostolic activity.

   This is an indication of your profound conviction that the Church, immutable as she is in her principles and in her essential institutions, is not however immobile, but rather that she lives, grows and adapts herself to the new times and circumstances, in order to be in every age the soul of the world . . .

622   It is unnecessary for us to re-affirm our conviction of the irreplaceable rôle of women religious in many fields of the Catholic apostolate; above all in education and the school, no less than in works of charity. The very missionary activity of the Church has been, now for a long time, almost inconceivable without the participation of the sisters; and even in many regions where the sacred hierarchy is established, the work of the sisters is indispensable for the proper organization of the care of souls. Without their co-operation, the Church might indeed have been compelled to renounce advances on many

---

[1] *AAS* XXXXIX (1957), pp. 291-296.

fronts; and numerous positions that had been secured by laborious endeavour might perhaps have had to be abandoned. By the toil of your motherly hands, beloved daughters, the Church sustains the tottering steps of the old; by the beatings of your heart the Church warms again the souls of little orphans, and through the fervour of your dedicated labour, the Church gives assistance to the sick.

But since you are a body of women consecrated to God, and offered to the Church in the spirit of an abiding holocaust, it is always opportune, indeed sometimes it is necessary, that from time to time the balance-sheet of your activities should be drawn up; on such an occasion there should be an examination of certain ways of life and modes of action, in order to see whether they are still useful and efficacious, as they were in the past.

You are present then at a congress in which assiduous prayer alternates with intense study and lively but calm discussions; you can feel quite assured that this entirely corresponds with our wishes and evokes our confidence. For indeed it seems to us necessary that you should render yourselves an account of what you are bound to be, and of what you are bound to do, so that the extremely delicate problem of assistance to the sick should be completely and wisely examined and resolved. Eminent speakers and lecturers will elucidate, with the clarity derived from their long study and everyday experience, the criteria which should inspire and determine the relations between the life of religious and assistance to the sick. We will confine ourselves therefore to proposing to you a few brief thoughts, in order to make some contribution to the successful outcome of your meeting.

1.—First of all, be true religious.

It is a truth of faith, which we enunciated recently once more 623 in the Encyclical *Sacra Virginitas* [2] of 25 March 1954, that virginity is superior to the married state, because the virgin soul binds ties of absolute and indissoluble love directly with God, indeed with the incarnate God, Jesus Christ. In fact, all that she has received as a gift from God to be a spouse and mother, she offers

[2] Cf. *supra*, nn. 504-505.

20

to him as a holocaust on the altar of a complete and final renunciation. To reach to the heart of God, to love him and to be loved by him, the virgin soul does not pass through other hearts; nor does it stop to dally with other creatures; there is nothing placed between the soul and Jesus, no obstacle, no curtain.

624 Marriage, on the other hand, is indeed a true sacrament, one of the seven sources of grace instituted by Christ himself; it implies the reciprocal offering of one partner to the other; it reaches to a real fusion of their lives and destinies; but in relation to God, there is something which is held back, which is not given at all or is not given completely. It is only virgin souls who make the offering of that which for other loving creatures is an unattainable goal; for them the first step on their ascent is also the last, and the end of their ascent is at once a summit and a profound abyss.[3]

625 You who have been called, by an ineffable design of love, to this state of predilection, should be in fact, whatever may be the sacrifice, that which you are by law.

You should be true brides of the Lord: souls united indissolubly and intimately with him alone; souls without stain, detached from the world of the senses, from the world of money, from the world of vanities. And we willingly acknowledge that countless sisters do correspond fully to the ideal of their vocation or, at least, come very close to that ideal. If

624a [3] On 24 July 1949, in an Allocution to Women's Catholic Action of Italy on Christian Marriage, the Pope already had made a point of stressing the importance of religious vocation: "Do not forget that among the vocations of women there is also the religious vocation, the state of the virgin consecrated to God. Nowadays this observation is all the more opportune, since it is possible that the very proper esteem for apostolic action in the world may have acquired a trace, scarcely perceptible, of naturalism, which would conceal the beauty and rich worth which lie in the total gift to God of the heart and of life." (AAS XLI (1949), pp. 415-21).

624b Similarly, in a Discourse of 19 May 1956 to doctors, on the subject of fertility and sterility, the Holy Father said: "The Catholic Church, depositary of the divine designs, teaches the higher fruitfulness of lives entirely consecrated to God and to the neighbour. Here, the complete renunciation of the family should make possible the completely disinterested spiritual action, which proceeds not from any fear of life and its responsibilities, but from the perception of the true destinies of man, created to the image of God and in search of a universal love, which no fleshly attachment can limit. That is the most sublime fecundity and the most desirable which man can seek, the fecundity which transcends the biological order and reaches into that of the spirit." (AAS XXXXVIII (1956), pp. 467-74).

only there were never amongst them—we do not say betrayals, but not even the slightest indications of infidelity, the least evidences of indifference, coldness or lack of understanding! God alone knows what an increase of flourishing vitality and what a harvest of works the Church would behold. And it is the sick, who are entrusted to your care, who above all would become aware of it and would always truly see Jesus Christ in you.

In order to prevent such a religious life from being endangered or prejudiced by your work of assistance to the sick, you must set yourselves against everything that is opposed to the spirit of absolute and permanent dedication to God.

For example, you must be on your guard against ill-regulated 626 and anxious activity, which leaves no time or calm for Jesus, for listening to him, for asking him what are his wishes, his desires, his preferences, for giving him an account of what you have done, and of how you have accomplished it.

Moreover, you must be on your guard against what would 627 take you away too long or too frequently from the common life; if the common life involves certain renunciations, it is also a strong protection for your interior life and a great exercise of charity.

Be careful of the observance of the spirit of poverty, not only 628 individually, but also collectively. We are well aware of the economic requirements of your clinics, which make it their aim, as indeed they are bound, to be equal to what is demanded for a modern hospital; and we know that it is not always easy in such circumstances to remain wholly faithful to the ideal of poverty. Nevertheless, we believe that we should alert you to the danger of easy temptations, from which women religious who assist the sick are not always exempt: we have in mind certain clinics, where it would appear that in the last analysis the standards are not very different from those of a commercial enterprise.

2.—Devoted assistance of the sick, animated by intensely vivid religious spirit.

629   Ever since man has been liable to sickness, there have always been people concerned to come to his assistance and to care for him, in such fashion as the times and available means permitted. But it was only at a later date that buildings specially and truly established for the purpose of rehabilitating and caring for the sick have arisen, and—it should not be forgotten —that development was entirely the outcome of that universal charity bequeathed to the Church by her divine Founder, as we have had occasion to show on a previous occasion.[4] Nowadays people who had remained for a long time indifferent or out of touch with this problem—and with not a few others—are taking an interest in it. A blessing on their endeavours, and a welcome to all who are willing to offer their help in the great cause of human suffering! But let no one think that the Church can abandon her maternal rôle as the comforter of the sick and the suffering; indeed, there is no one who can take her place completely in her mission to the sick; the sick person has not only a body but also a soul, and it is often more in need of care than the body. And we consider that the first to be aware of that fact are good doctors; they know well how to appreciate the worth of the presence and the work of Catholic nursing sisters.

630   Hence it is our will that there should be no halting on the path upon which you have set out; the goal is the preparation of an increasing body of women religious who will be even better prepared for the tasks which await them beside the sick.

It is for this purpose, beloved daughters, that you have left your family, the family which you had and also the family which you could have had; it is for the same reason that you must not overlook anything that could make you more competent for the direction of nursing establishments and especially for the helping of the sick. For this work, it is not sufficient that you be religious, and even perfect religious; it is necessary too that you should have the indispensable technical knowledge relating to the new methods of treatment, to the new instruments

629a   [4] Cf. *Discorsi e Radiomessagi*, XIV, pp. 155-156 (*AAS* XXXXIV (1952), p. 231).

which have to be employed and to the new medicinal remedies which have to be administered.

Because you are religious, you are bound, like other nurses 631 and even more strictly, to watch over your temperament and to form your character. You need, for example, motherly tenderness in the face of the countless sufferings which call to you for comfort and help; you require gentle firmness when faced with excesses or indiscreet demands on the part of those who are sick; there must be an alert dynamism in your life and, at the same time, a constant calm which enables you to be masters of every situation.

You have need of a readiness, which will never find you unprepared, even in the most unforeseen and unexpected cases; you have need of a patience that is serene and cheerful, and of a capacity for anticipating and making provision, which forgets nothing and overlooks nothing.

We have given the recommendation to admit nothing that could prove injurious to the true religious spirit; likewise we must bring to your notice that sometimes certain horariums and usages could make your work with the sick less efficient and less easy. Superioresses must show themselves prudent and vigilant in this matter also. Your duty is to be religious and at the same time to assist the sick: you must apply your attention to it in order to ensure that both of these requirements are kept in mind and satisfied.

3.—See the Lord Jesus in every sick person.

Whenever a patient, who for some good reason seems 632 deserving of particular consideration, arrives in one of your clinics or hospitals, you know what usually happens: immediately there is a rush of doctors, nurses, everybody offering themselves unsparingly, so that nothing will be wanting to the patient and that he will have no ground for complaint. What would happen then, if one day, unexpectedly, Jesus were to come looking for hospitality? What competition there would be to be near him, what readiness for any sacrifice whatsoever in order to be chosen to keep him company, to comfort him, to care for him! Then any and every show of consideration would appear to you insufficient, any attention would seem too little, any time-table would seem suitable.

Now, it is certain that every sick person is the image of Jesus. The elect one day will ask him: *Lord, when did we see thee sick and visit thee?* And the Lord will reply: *A soften as you did it to one of these my least brethren, you did it to me.* [5]

633   If you had that lively faith: if behind the human countenances —countenances sometimes drawn in intense pain, or grown pale with exhaustion of the organism, countenances inflamed with fever, countenances disturbed by fear of worsening of the malady, countenances calm and resigned—if behind all these countenances, you knew how to discern Jesus in all the wards, lying on all the beds, motionless in that mysterious solemnity of the operating-theatres; then you would no more feel the transition from the chapel to the ward, and there would be no more fear that religious observance would be harmful to assistance of the sick or that assistance of the sick would be prejudicial to religious observance. You would continue to love him equally, everywhere and however he conceals himself. There would be no break of your conversation with him; there would be no distraction, no forgetting of what he is and what are his wishes.

Then it would be easy for you to pass sleepless nights beside the gravely ill, whose vision is growing dim and in whose heart all human hopes are dying; then you will be able to smile in the face of indifference, and even of insults; then you will know how to find fresh new strength, as though the sick person of today were the first to whom you drew nigh; then you will know how to be careful and precise, as though this were the last sick person to whom you are obliged to give your attention before you are called by God.

Beloved daughters; that is what we have deemed it our duty to say to you at the opening of your congress, to which we give our blessing with all the fullness of our heart; we are grateful for all that you have hitherto accomplished and full of confidence for what you will yet accomplish in the future.

The Church, the Pope count upon you; upon your complete dedication, upon your competence and upon your spirit of love.

⁵ Matthew 25: 39, 40.

ALLOCUTION TO THE GENERAL CONGREGATION
OF THE SOCIETY OF JESUS

10 September 1957

In September 1946, the major superiors of the Society of Jesus deemed it necessary to assemble at Rome a general congregation with representatives from all provinces of the Society in order to study the problems created by the post-war situation. A further general congregation of the Society was held in October and November 1957; it led to the creation of new " assistancies " and to a development of the structure of the Society. The Holy Father took advantage of the occasion to declare emphatically a certain number of points, to which he attached particular importance, especially in connection with religious austerity and fidelity to discipline in the service of the Apostolic See.[1]

To all of you, beloved sons, who represent here before us 634
the entire Society of Jesus, assembled together in our city, we
extend a paternal and joyful welcome; and we invoke upon your
labours choicest blessings from him who is the giver of all good
things and from his Spirit of charity.

Your Society, whose " Formula " or resumé of the rule was
submitted for approval by your Father and legislator Ignatius to
our predecessors Paul III and Julius III, was established in order
to campaign " under the standard of the Cross," and to serve
" the one Lord and his spouse the Church, under the Roman
Pontiff, the Vicar of Christ on earth." [2] Moreover, your founder 635
willed that you should be bound by a special vow, in addition
to the three that are customary in religious Orders, namely a
vow of obedience to the supreme Pontiff; and in the celebrated
Regulae ad sentiendum cum Ecclesia which are attached to the book
of the *Spiritual Exercises*, he particularly commends to you: " All
individual judgment being set aside, the mind is to be always
kept ready and prepared to obey the true Spouse of Christ,

---

[1] *AAS* XLIX (1957), pp. 806-812.
[2] *Formula of the Institute of the Society of Jesus*, p. 1, in the Apostolic Letter *Exposcit debitum* of Julius III, 21 July 1550; *Institute of the Society of Jesus*, Florence, 1892, vol. l. p. 23.

and our holy Mother who is the orthodox, catholic and hier-
archical Church "; the ancient version, which your Father
Ignatius himself used, adds the phrase: " which is the Roman
Church." [3]

636   Among the great achievements of those who have gone before
you, deeds in which you take rightful pride and which you strive
to emulate, an outstanding place undoubtedly is held by the fact
that your Society, in its most intimate attachment to the Chair
of Peter, has always striven to keep intact, to teach, to defend
and to promote the doctrine propounded by the Pontiff of that
See with which, " because of its higher authority it is necessary
that every Church, that is, the faithful from all parts, should be
in agreement ";[4] it is also a source of pride that your Society
never tolerated doctrine that was dangerous or savoured of
unapproved novelty. [5]

637   **Obedience.**   It is no less a ground for praise that, in matters
pertaining to ecclesiastical discipline, you strive
to practise that perfect submission of action, will and judgment
towards the Apostolic See, which makes such a valuable contribution " to the more certain guidance by the Holy Spirit." [6]
Let no one rob you of that distinction of correctness of
doctrine and of fidelity in the obedience due to the Vicar of
Christ; and let there be no place among you for that spirit of
" free enquiry," the characteristic of a heterodox mentality
rather than of the Catholic mind, whereby the individual does
not hesitate to challenge at the bar of his own judgment even
statements emanating from the Apostolic See; nor should there
be any toleration of connivance with those who assert that the
norms of conduct and of striving for eternal life are to be determined by what actually takes place rather than what should be
done; nor should unrestricted liberty of thought and action be
allowed to those who regard ecclesiastical discipline as anti-
quated, an empty " formalism " as they call it, from which one

---

[3] *Regulae ad sentiendum cum Ecclesia*, Rule I.
[4] St. Irenaeus, *Adversus haereses*, I, III, c. 3 (*PG* VII, 849A).
[5] *Coll. Decret.*, Decr. 102: *Epit. Instit.*, n. 319.
[6] Apostolic Letter *Exposcit debitum*, l.c., p. 24.

must unhesitatingly set oneself free, in order to serve the truth. If such a mentality, borrowed as it is from unbelieving milieux, were to be allowed without restriction in your ranks, is it not the fact that in a short time there would be found among you unworthy and disloyal sons of your Father Ignatius, men to be cut off without delay from the body of your Society?

Obedience that is completely perfect has been from the 638 beginning the badge of those who fight as soldiers for the Lord in your Society. Your founder went so far as to say: " We will readily allow ourselves to be surpassed in fastings, vigils and other austerities of food and of dress by other Orders, which undertake these things holily each in accordance with its own practice and discipline; but I wish above all that whoever serves God our Lord in this Society should be eminent for true and perfect obedience and abnegation of will and judgment." [7] How pleasing to the Church has not always been this entire and ready obedience shown to religious superiors, the faithful observance of regular discipline, the humble submission even of the judgment to those whom the Vicar of Christ willed to be your rulers, in accordance with your institute which has been so frequently and solemnly given approval by the Vicar of Christ and his predecessors! For, indeed, it is fully in harmony with the Catholic spirit, and sanctioned by the abiding tradition of ancient and venerable religious Orders, with the approval of the Apostolic See, that virtue of which Saint Ignatius has left you his description in the celebrated *Letter on the virtue of Obedience*. And those people are straying far from the truth who consider that the teaching of that *Letter* is to be abandoned, and that in the place of hier-archical and religious obedience there should be substituted a certain " democratic " equality which would permit the subject to discuss with his superior what is to be done, until agreement between them is reached.

In opposition to the spirit of pride and independence, which 639 affects many at the present time, you must preserve undefiled the virtue of true humility, which will make you lovable to God and men;[8] the virtue of complete abnegation, whereby

---

[7] *Letter on the virtue of Obedience*, n. 3.
[8] *Constitution*, p. ix, c. II, n. 2.

you will show yourselves disciples of him who was *made obedient unto death*.[9] Would that man be worthy of Christ, our Head, who flies from the austerity of religious discipline, and seeks to live in a religious society as if he were a man of the world, who pursues at will his own advantage, his own pleasure and comfort? Let those who purport to nullify religious discipline by giving it the empty and now trite title of " formalism " realize that they are acting contrary to the desires and decisions of this Apostolic See; they should understand also that they are deluding themselves, if they invoke the law of charity in justification of a false liberty detached from the vow of obedience; for what sort of charity would that be which neglected the will of God our Lord that is to be fulfilled through the religious life which they have vowed.

The severe discipline, which has been the ornament and the strength of your Order, will keep you equipped and ready for the battles of the Lord and for the so-called " modern " apostolate.

640   **Duties of Superiors.**   A grave obligation concerning this matter falls on all superiors, whether the general, the provincial or the local superior. They must know how to " give commands modestly and circumspectly ";[10] with circumspection and prudence, indeed, as befits pastors of souls, clothing themselves with the gentleness, kindness and charity of Christ the Lord;[11] but they must know how to " command," and, if need be, to do so with firmness, " joining severity, in its own time and place, with gentleness," because they will have to render an account to God of the souls of their subjects and of their progress in acquiring perfection. Although your rules, by a wise prescription of your founder, do not bind under pain of sin, superiors are obliged nevertheless to promote observance of the rules, and they are not free from fault, if they allow regular discipline to be neglected generally. Like a good father the superior will show that trust in his subjects which is customary and fitting in relation to sons; but at the same time, he shall

---

[9] Philippians 2: 8.
[10] Cf. *Rules of Provincial*, 4.
[11] Cf. *Rules of Provincial*, 3.

assiduously watch over them, as a good father is bound to do, and he shall not allow them to gradually depart from the straight path of fidelity.

Your institute has wisely described this duty of superiors, especially local superiors, in relation to the going of subjects outside the cloisters and their dealings with outsiders, the exchange of letters, journeys, expenditure and the handling of money, and even in regard to taking of health cures, in order that all may faithfully fulfil all those exercises of piety, which are as it were the soul of religious observance and of the apostolate. But even the best rules are of no avail, unless those whose duty it is to urge obedience to them fulfil their task firmly and constantly.

Austerity of life. *You are the salt of the earth:*[12] may purity of doctrine and strength of discipline, to which is joined austerity of life, keep you immune from the contagion of the world and make you worthy disciples of him who redeemed us through the Cross.   641

He himself has told you: *He who does not take up his cross and follow me, cannot be my disciple.*[13] That is the reason why your Father Ignatius exhorts you " to accept and desire with all your powers whatever Christ our Lord loved and embraced." [14] And " in order to reach more surely to that degree of perfection, which is so precious in the spiritual life, it shall be the preponderant and most earnest concern of each one to seek in the Lord for greater self-denial and, as far as he is able, continual mortification in all things." [15] In view of the intense interest in new things, which nowadays preoccupies the minds of so many, it is to be feared lest that primary precept of all religious and apostolic life, namely the union of the instrument with God,[16] should be overshadowed, and that " our confidence should be placed " rather " in those natural means . . . which

[12] Matthew 5: 13.
[13] Luke 14: 27.
[14] *General examen*, c. IV, n. 44; *Summary of Constitutions*, n. xi.
[15] *General examen*, c. IV, n. 46; *Summary of Constitutions*, n. 12.
[16] Cf. *Constitution*, p. x, n. 2.

dispose the instrument for the utility of others," [17] contrary to the economy of grace in which we live.

642　　**Poverty.**　To enable one to live that life nailed to the Cross with Christ, faithful observance of poverty, which was so dear to your founder, should make a vital contribution; and we have in mind not merely observance of the poverty which excludes the independent use of temporal things, but rather of that poverty especially towards which this exclusion of independence is ordained; this consists in the very moderate use of temporal things, together with the deprivation of many of those conveniences which men living in the world can quite lawfully take to themselves.

You will, of course, make use for the greater glory of God, with the approval of your superiors, of whatever makes your apostolic work more efficacious; but, at the same time, you will spontaneously deprive yourselves of many things which are not necessary for your purpose, though they are enjoyable and pleasing to nature; you will do this so that the faithful may see in you the disciples of Christ who was poor, and in order that larger sums of money may be reserved for things useful for the salvation of souls instead of being wasted on less austere enjoyments. It is not for religious to take holidays outside the houses of the Order, except for an extraordinary cause, to set out for recreational purposes on journeys that are pleasant but expensive, to have any equipment for personal and private use exclusively, instead of for the common use and benefit, as the nature of the religious state demands. Whatever is superfluous, cut it out with simplicity and courage for the love of poverty and out of zeal for that unceasing mortification in all things, which is a mark of your institute. The use of tobacco,[18] which nowadays is so widespread and a source of pleasure to men in its various forms, must be counted among things that are superfluous. Since you are religious, take steps to have the use of tobacco suppressed among you, in accordance with the spirit of your

---

[17] Cf. *Constitution*, p. x, n. 3.

642a　　[18] Cf. *supra*, nn. 424-30, Circular of the Sacred Congregation of Religious, 10 January 1951, regulating the use of tobacco in the states of perfection.

founder. Religious shall preach, not by words alone but by example, zeal for that penitence without which there is no solid hope of eternal salvation.

Prayer. All these things which we recommend to you, 643 are not " according to man " and indeed appear arduous and exaggerated to nature; they are not only possible, however, but will become easy and pleasant in the Lord, if you are faithful to that life dedicated to prayer, which your Father and legislator expects from you.[19] Your exercises of piety will then be enlivened by the interior fire of charity, if you are faithful to the mental prayer, that prolonged prayer, which the approved rules of your Order daily prescribe. For priests dedicated to apostolic work, the first duty is to vivify their entire activity by that deeper consideration of divine things, and by the burning fire of love of God and our Lord Jesus Christ, which is nourished above all by mental prayer, as we know from the precepts of the saints. Your Order would certainly be turning away from the spirit which your Father and legislator intended, if it were not to remain faithful to the instruction handed down in the *Spiritual Exercises.*

Adaptation and tradition. There is no one amongst you who would 644 criticise or reject innovations, namely those which are conducive to the salvation of your own souls or those of the neighbour, which is the purpose of your Society, merely because they are new. On the contrary, it is completely in harmony with the institute of St. Ignatius, and also the constant tradition among you, to apply yourselves wholeheartedly to any new activities which the good of the Church demands and the Holy See commends, and not to shirk any work of " adaptation," as it is called. But, at the same time, you shall firmly guard and keep intact, against all the attempts of the world and the demon, the traditions which were wisely handed down because they flow from the Gospel itself or are demanded by human nature, namely fallen human nature (that

[19] Cf. *Constitutions*, p. vi, c. 3, n. 1.

is the religious asceticism which your founder learned and took over from the ancient religious Orders).

645

Monarchical authority.

In your institute there are substantial matters of primary importance which cannot be modified even by a general congregation, but only by the Apostolic See, inasmuch as they have been approved in "specific form" since the Apostolic Letter *Regimini militantis Ecclesiae* issued by our predecessor, Paul III, on 27 September 1540. Among these points is the following: "The form of government in the Society is monarchical, and is embodied in the decisions of a single superior."[20] Now this Apostolic See, knowing well that the authority of the general is the very pivot on which rests the strength and health of your Order, does not deem that in this matter any concession should be made to the spirit of this age; quite to the contrary, it is the intention of the Apostolic See that this full monarchical authority, subject only to the superior authority of a general congregation, and of this supreme Holy See, should be preserved intact, though the burden of it may be opportunely lightened, without however in any way infringing the monarchical form of governing.

646

Sanctify yourselves through your Institute.

In a word, "all of you shall make it your constant study to neglect nothing of the perfection which, by divine grace, you can acquire in the complete observance of all the constitutions and in carrying out the particular requirements of your institute."[21] To our predecessor of pious memory, Clement XIII, is attributed a saying, which certainly represents his mind, even though the words may not literally be his; when he was petitioned to allow your Order to withdraw from the institute established by St. Ignatius, he said: "They shall be as they are or they shall not be."[22] That is and continues to be our will also: Jesuits shall be as the *Spiritual Exercises* formed

---

[20] Epitome of the Institute, n. 22, § 3, 4.
[21] *Constitutions*, p. vi, c. I, n. 7; *Summary of Constitutions*, n. 15.
[22] Pastor, *Geschichte der Päpste*, Bd. XVI, I, 1931, p. 651, n. 7.

them, and as their constitutions want them to be. Others in the Church, in praiseworthy fashion under the guidance of the hierarchy, make their way to God by a path that is in some respects different; for you your own institute " is the way to God." [23] This way of life which has so frequently been approved by the Apostolic See, and the works of the apostolate specially entrusted to you by the same Holy See, make these the objects of your striving to excel, in dedicated co-operation with the other workers of the vineyard of the Lord; all of them, under the direction of this Apostolic See and the bishops, are working for the coming of the kingdom of God.

---

[22] *Formula of the Institute*, in Apostolic Letter *Regimini militantis Ecclesiae* of Paul III, 27 September 1540, n. 1; *Institute of the Society of Jesus*, Florence, 1898, vol. I, p. 4.

LETTER OF THE SECRETARIATE OF STATE
FOR THE FOURTH CONGRESS OF
PAROCHIAL TEACHING SISTERS OF FRANCE

12 September 1957

The Union of Parochial Teaching Sisters of France, which in 1955 had taken as subject for its congress the civic formation of young girls of today,[1] selected in 1957 a theme of unquestionable actuality. That point is stressed in the letter which his Excellency Mgr. Dell' Acqua addressed to his Eminence Cardinal Feltin, president of the congress. It is noteworthy that the Holy See has shown increasing interest in unions of both men and women religious which allow them to receive " the additional formation and documentation that are necessary for the proper performance of their activities." [2]

647   The Holy Father has learned that the Union of Parochial Teaching Sisters of France, which came into existence under the auspices of the hierarchy immediately after the last world war, is making preparations to celebrate the tenth anniversary of its foundation by holding a congress, to be presided over by your Eminence, which will be devoted to the subject: " The mission of the woman religious in face of the problems of the workers' world."

648   His Holiness knows and appreciates the services which this institution has rendered in the course of the ten years of its existence. He gladly sends on this occasion his paternal encouragement to those who were the initiators, and especially to the chaplain general of the Union, Abbé Gaston Courtois.

649   Indeed it is particularly opportune at the present moment that sisters who collaborate with the parochial clergy in the various works of education and of the apostolate, should be in a position to receive from a well equipped central organism

---

[1] Cf. *supra*, nn. 570-572, Letter of the Secretariate of State addressed to the Union of Parochial Teaching Sisters on that occasion.

647a   [2] The world congress of the states of perfection, due to be held some weeks later in Rome, 9-14 December 1957, showed that unions of sisters already existed in **twenty-five countries**.

that additional formation and documentation that are necessary for the proper exercise of their activities. The contacts established between these women religious on the occasion of the sessions and congresses organized by the Union, and by means of publications like the review *Educatrices paroissiales*, also make possible a useful comparison of experiences; and they help to combat an isolationism that is frequently prejudicial to the supernatural development of souls and to the effectiveness of their activity. Finally, the conditions of the modern world frequently confront sisters who are dedicated to the active life, with situations or problems which make an admirable and obvious theme for study in common; that is precisely the case for the subject to be studied at the present congress: " The mission of the woman religious in face of the problems of the workers' world." One can say that an exact knowledge of the workers' world, of its psychology, of its sufferings and of its hopes, is indispensable nowadays to anyone, be it priest, man or woman religious, who is endeavouring to permeate that world with the Christian spirit and make it bear fruit there; while, on the other hand, failure to understand these conditions would involve the danger of frustrating, in part at least, the fruits of a zeal and devotion that are highly deserving of praise. The choice of this subject for study is therefore timely, and his Holiness is heartily pleased to invoke on the organizers and speakers of the congress, and on those who will participate in it, the most abundant heavenly blessings. As a pledge of these heavenly favours, and a proof of his own paternal goodwill, the common Father sends to all the Apostolic benediction.

DISCOURSE TO THE MEMBERS OF
THE SECOND GENERAL CONGRESS OF
THE STATES OF PERFECTION

9 December 1957

On the occasion of the priestly jubilee of his Eminence Cardinal Valerio Valeri, prefect of the Sacred Congregation of Religious, the Congregation decided to organize in Rome, in the week 8-14 December 1957, a general congress of the states of perfection, in which the major superiors from many countries would take part. This second general congress (the first had taken place in December 1950)[1] gave an opportunity of reviewing the ground that had been covered in seven years, in seeking an answer to the problem of a better adaptation of Congregations and Secular Institutes. Many important subjects were discussed: the situation of unions of religious, both men and women, in different countries; the practical applications of the Apostolic Constitutions Provida Mater Ecclesia, Sponsa Christi *and* Sedes Sapientiae.[2] *The Holy Father received those participating in the congress on 9 December, when he took the opportunity of giving certain precise directives which clarified the work of the congress.[3]*

650   Under the maternal protection of Mary Immaculate, the most sublime of God's creatures and the model of those who strive for the perfection of the Christian life, you have decided, beloved sons and daughters, to assemble in Rome in order to study the contemporary problems of the states of perfection; at the same time you are celebrating the fiftieth anniversary of the ordination to the priesthood of the most worthy and zealous Cardinal Prefect of the Sacred Congregation of Religious.

In more than twenty-five nations of all the continents, there are in existence today associations of major superiors, both of men and of women religious; these, closely linked with the Holy See and with the ecclesiastical hierarchy of their respective countries, are applying themselves to the task of carrying out

650a   [1] Cf. *supra*, nn. 394-423, the Allocution *Annus Sacer* spoken on that occasion, December 1950, by Pius XII.
    [2] Cf. *supra*, nn. 220-252; 325-387; 581-620.
    [3] *AAS* L (1958), pp. 34-43.

in common the measures of adaptation and organization which are called for by the range and complexity of the apostolate at the present day. We are aware that numerous projects have seen the light in these last years through the enlightened encouragement of your associations; it is sufficient to mention the national or regional congresses of the states of perfection, the sessions of prayer and study, and above all the creation of institutes of higher religious training and culture intended for members of the states of perfection.[4]

Aim of the Congress. The present congress, which is completely in accord with the desire to bring about a constantly more complete engrafting of the states of perfection into the Church, the mystical Body of Christ, proposes to survey the progress made everywhere in the organization of the states of perfection and in their work of adaptation to the requirements of the Church; then to set out clearly the aims to be pursued, the limits to be respected and the principles to be observed in the action of conferences, unions and committees of major superiors; and finally, to elaborate a programme of activities and projects, which will guarantee the effectiveness of the movement of renovation, by tightening the mutual links between the organizations themselves and with the Holy See. 651

The whole programme of lectures and expositions at this congress has the aim of commenting on the three Apostolic Constitutions *Provida Mater*, *Sponsa Christi* and *Sedes Sapientiae*, and also the decree *Salutaris atque* [5] of the Sacred Congregation of Religious, in which are enunciated the norms which must guide the endeavour to adapt and renew. We do not intend to enter here into particular questions which you propose to treat in your sessions; we intend rather to underline certain points of a general character concerning the problem of perfection and that of renewal and adaptation of the means by which individuals and 652

---

[4] Cf. nn. 573-580, Motu Proprio *Nihil Ecclesiae*, which gives approval to the pontifical Institute *Regina Mundi* for the higher studies of women religious. 650b

[5] Cf. *supra*, nn. 220-252; 324-387; 581-620; Decree *Salutaris atque* of the Sacred Congregation of Religious, 26 March 1956 (*AAS* XLVIII (1956), p. 295).

communities strive for perfection. We shall speak first of the perfection of Christian life in general, then of its realization in the groups called " the states of perfection," taking into account first the relations of these states with their members, and then the relations which they have mutually and with the Holy See.

I—THE PERFECTION OF THE CHRISTIAN LIFE

653   It is important first of all to recall that the concept of " perfection " in the strict sense is not identical with that of " state of perfection," and indeed that it is much wider. For in fact one can find heroic Christian perfection, that of the Gospel and of the Cross of Christ, outside any " state of perfection."

We understand therefore the striving for perfection as a habitual disposition of the Christian soul, by which, not content merely to fulfil the duties which bind under pain of sin, the soul gives itself entirely to God to love him, to serve him, and consecrates itself to the service of the neighbour for the same purpose.

654   **Perfection consists in voluntary adherence to God.** The perfection of every free human activity, as that of every reasonable creature, consists in the adherence of the will to God. In one respect, which arises from the very condition of the creature, this perfection is obligatory; one must strive for it under penalty of failing to reach one's last end. There is no need here to go into details about its constituent elements. We mean to speak only of the habitual and permanent tendency which, going beyond all that falls under obligation, takes the whole man to consecrate him without reserve to the service of God. This perfection consists *par excellence* in the union with God, which union is realized by charity; it is in charity, therefore, that it is achieved. It is also called a perpetual and universal holocaust of oneself, which is constantly offered for the love of God and in order to manifest resolutely to him this love.

Ideal of perfection : evangelical counsels and service of the Church. The ideal of Christian perfection is 655 bound up with the teachings of Christ, especially with the evangelical counsels, with his life, his passion and death, those inexhaustible sources whence the heroism of all Christian generations derives its nourishment. It embraces also the work of Christ, that is to say the service of the Church performed for love of the Lord, each one acting in the position and according to the function which falls to him in the totality of the mystical Body.

Secular Institutes and Perfection. Every Christian is invited to strive for 656 this ideal with all his powers, but it is realized in a full and more sure way in the three states of perfection after the manner described by canon law and the Apostolic Constitutions already referred to. In particular, the Constitution *Provida Mater* of 2 February 1947, dealing with " Secular Institutes," grants access to the states of perfection to the greatest possible number of souls, who nowadays aspire ardently for a more perfect life. Undoubtedly this Constitution affirms that associations, which do not satisfy the norms there prescribed, do not constitute " states of perfection "; but it does not at all claim that, outside of these states, there does not exist a true striving for perfection.

We are thinking at this moment of so many men and women 657 of every condition, who take up in the modern world professions and responsibilities of the most varied character and who, for the love of God and to serve him in their neighbour, consecrate to God their person and all their activity. They pledge themselves to the practice of the evangelical counsels by vows that are private and secret, known to God alone; and they accept guidance, in all that concerns the submission of obedience and poverty, from persons whom the Church has judged suitable for this purpose, and to whom she has entrusted the responsibility of guiding others in the exercise of perfection. None of the elements which constitute Christian perfection and an effective striving to acquire it, is lacking in these men and women;

they truly share in it, therefore, even though they are not committed to any juridical or canonical state of perfection.

658 **Christian perfection and adaptation.** It is clear that Christian perfection does not lend itself to any renovation or adaptation in the essential elements of its definition and practical realization. But, since the conditions of modern life are undergoing profound changes, the manner of applying oneself to acquiring perfection will on the other hand call for modifications. These modifications will affect those who live in the states of perfection and those who do not belong to these states; but more especially the latter, particularly if they occupy a high social rank and hold higher responsibilities. For are they not then expected to surround themselves with a certain display of comfort, to take part in official celebrations, to employ costly modes of transport; all of these are things which appear difficult to reconcile with the constant concern for mortification of anyone who desires to follow and to imitate Christ poor and humble? And yet, even in the midst of material goods, they do not in any way deviate from the entire consecration of themselves to God and do not cease to offer to the Lord a holocaust without reserve. That is the achievement of the grace which operates in man according to Christ's word: *That which is impossible with men, is possible with God.*[6]

II—THE STATES OF PERFECTION

659 It is rather the problems of adaptation and renovation within the states of perfection which will engage our attention; and we shall consider first the persons who are members, and then the communities themselves, in their striving for perfection.

I. *The members of the states of perfection*

660 With reference to the individual members, there is only one point that we shall emphasize: what we have said, in the first part of our discourse, on the perfection of the Christian life in general, applies to the members of all the states of perfection

[6] Luke 18: 27.

and constitutes their first and essential obligation, whether they
be superiors or inferiors; they are bound to unite themselves
with God by charity and to offer themselves to him as a holocaust,
to imitate and follow Christ, his teaching, his life and his Cross,
to consecrate themselves to the service of the work of Christ,
the Church, as chosen and active members of the mystical Body.
But once this essential obligation is recognized, they are not
forbidden to give thought to renovation and adaptation of the
means of discharging this obligation, with due respect for
tradition and without contravening prescriptions which the
constitutions regard as inviolable; inferiors shall moreover
observe the religious discipline, which forbids them to arrogate
to themselves what pertains to the competence of the superiors
and to undertake on their own initiative reforms which they
cannot attempt without the authorization of the superiors.

II. The communities themselves

The first point for examination is that of the mutual relations   661
between the community as a whole and the individual members,
superiors or inferiors, who constitute the community. There
are two important elements which call for consideration here:
first, the characteristic spirit, by which the mutual relations of
the communities with their members find expression; second,
the obstacles which are created by certain prejudices against
that religious obedience, upon which the renovation of the spirit
that is proper to the community essentially depends.

An organized society forms a complete   662
Adaptation must whole and possesses a typical character, to
safeguard the spirit the determination of which each of the
of the community. members makes his own contribution.
Every attempt at adaptation, carried out within this particular
grouping, necessarily involves certain modifications of its
characteristic spirit; in other words, one is touching in a certain
way on the innermost fibres of its being. Now every society
has the tendency to keep this spirit intact, as indeed is its right
and duty; it desires to see its members permeated with it and
concerned to make it a vital part of their whole life. The Church

for its part, and the sovereign Pontiffs, when they give approval to a determinate form of life, intend that it should be preserved in all its purity and they carefully watch over this.

663
Role of major Superiors. If it be agreed that major superiors have the right to tell their subjects what is the spirit of their community, a question still remains for all: where is one to find the objective expression of this spirit? Major superiors cannot decide it according to their personal taste or impression, even in all good faith and sincerity. If the major superior is also the founder, and if he has received from the Church the approval of his personal ideas as the norm of a state of perfection, then it is always permissible for him to appeal to his own intentions. But in other cases, the superior must come back to the ideas of the founder as expressed in the constitutions approved by the Church. A subjective conviction, even though supported by one or other passage of the constitutions, is not therefore sufficient. When the superior propounds for the members of his community the true spirit of the founder, he is exercising his rights and the inferiors are in conscience bound to obey him. The rights of superiors and the duties of inferiors are correlative in this respect. The Church and the supreme Pontiffs always intend to defend rights and to urge duties, but within just limits. To avoid exasperation on the one side and the other and to preserve peace, it is sufficient that everyone recognize and put into practice this norm, which for centuries has been the rule of the Church and of the Popes, and which still remains in force.

664
Religious obedience. To come now to the contemporary difficulties of religious obedience, it is notable that the movement of adaptation has provoked a certain tension in this department; not that there is lacking a sincere desire to strive for perfection by means of obedience, but because nowadays there is a certain accentuation of some features of it, which even grave religious of delicate conscience would wish to have disappear. The charge is made in particular that religious obedience imperils the human dignity of the religious,

that it hampers the full development of his personality, and that it warps his orientation to God alone. These objections, it would seem, arise from certain disillusionments suffered personally or seen in others; and appeal is also made to various juridical considerations.

(a) *Not contrary to human dignity;*   665

In order to dissipate a sentiment of sadness, which has its origins in an erroneous interpretation of the principles that govern the religious life or in errors of practical application, let the words of the Lord be first recalled: *Come to me all you who labour and are burdened, and I will refresh you . . . become my disciples, because I am meek and humble of heart and you shall find rest for your souls.* [7] If the Lord uses these words to exhort men to take his yoke upon their shoulders, it is in order to teach them that altogether apart from legal observance, which can easily be burdensome and hard to bear, they have to discover the meaning of true submission and of Christian humility. Far from affronting the dignity of one who submits to them, these give inner freedom; and they make the acceptance of the state of subjection appear not as a constraint imposed from without, but as a committing of oneself into the hands of God, whose will finds expression through the visible authority of those who have the mission of giving commands. The superior for his part shall exercise his powers in the same evangelical spirit: *But he that is the greater among you, let him become as the younger and he that is the leader, as he that serveth.* [8] The firmness therefore which is necessary will always be accompanied in him by profound respect and by the delicacy of a paternal heart.

(b) *does not hinder development of the personality;*   666

Does the religious state constitute an obstacle to the harmonious development of the human personality? Is it true, as some allege, that it compels the human personality to remain in a state of " infantilism "?

[7] Matthew 11: 28-29.
[8] Luke 22: 26.

Why not consider without prejudice the bearing of the men and women who belong to the states of perfection! No one would dare to declare that the majority of them suffer from retarded development in their intellectual and emotional life or in their activity. But, to push the objection further, it cannot be charged either that, at the very least, communities and superiors constrain them in the course of time to adopt modes of thought and action which give colour to this reproach. Those who make the complaint should call to mind that St. Paul, in prescribing for the faithful the goal of a life ordered according to the faith, summons them to advance in the *building of the body of Christ* until they reach *perfect manhood, the mature measure of the fullness of Christ. Thus*, he continues, *we shall no more be children tossed to and fro and carried about* [9] . . . The Apostle, therefore, does not allow the faithful to remain " childish," but demands that they should become " perfect men." Moreover, in the first Epistle to the Corinthians he most explicitly disallows in adult Christians the ways of thought and feeling that are characteristic of childhood: *When I was a child, I spoke as a child, I understood as a child, I thought as a child. But when I became a man, I put away the things of a child.* [10]

667   This passage was already quoted by us in our Allocution of 18 April 1952 on the education of the Christian conscience,[11] as a reminder that the rôle of a sound education is to teach man to make judicious use of his liberty and to be able to do without the educator. Let everyone who belongs to the states of perfection, superior or inferior, apply to himself the words of the Apostle; if they do that, then all danger of " infantilism " will disappear, and that without any calling into question of the respect due to lawful authority or of sincere submission to its decisions.

668   We do not mean to come back here on what we said, in our Allocution of 8 December 1950 to the first congress of the states of perfection,[12] by way of reply to objections put

---

[9] Ephesians 4: 12-14.
[10] I Corinthians 13: 11.
[11] Allocution delivered in French to the members of the congress of the World Federation of Young Catholic Girls.
[12] Cf. *supra*, nn. 394-423.

forward against an alleged lessening of the personal and social worth of the religious; if the rights of the religious are subjected to a certain limitation, the state to which he belongs, and the offering which he makes of himself by obedience, confer on him a dignity which richly recompenses him for the sacrifice freely made.

(c) does not warp the orientation of men to God. 669

Another argument against obedience is drawn from the alleged fact that the dependence of the religious on his superior is contrary to the supreme and direct dominion of God over consciences. To make one man dependent on another even in his personal life and activity, does that not mean that the superior is given prerogatives which belong to God alone?

The Church, in fact, has never defended or approved such a thesis. She regards obedience as a means of leading man to God. Because the motive which inspires obedience is that of union with God, and because it is ultimately directed to the growth of charity, the superior does not at all constitute an obstacle placed between God and the inferior and diverting to his own account the homage addressed to God alone. The superior can issue commands only in the name of the Lord and in virtue of the powers of his office; and the inferior is bound to obey only for the love of Christ, and not for human motives of utility or convenience, and still less because of constraint. Thus, even in the most complete submission, the subject will preserve the joyous eagerness of one who ratifies, by the practical concrete pledge of each day, the total giving of himself to the one and only Master.

Mutual relations of communities. The programme of your second general 670 congress shows that it will treat extensively of the mutual relations of communities, following the line of the movement of renovation and adaptation which you are pursuing. Hence it is not our purpose here to enter into details. Besides, we are certain that the rules laid down by the Sacred Congregation of Religious will be observed faithfully. It will suffice for us to recall that, while preserving the distinctions which exist, and must exist, between communities, it is necessary to strive with sincerity and goodwill towards union and collaboration. There is, in fact, a certain " common good " of communities, which supposes that each one is ready to take account of the others and to adapt itself to the requirements of a co-ordination which necessarily implies some renunciation in view of the general good.

671 The well-known passage of the first Epistle to the Corinthians,[13] in which St. Paul speaks of the mutual relations of the bodily members, applies by analogy to your communities, united as they are by divine grace in the Body of the Church; each one of those who belong to that Body deserves on that ground to have the help and the collaboration of all, with a view to the one single common good, that of the Church. It is easy to deduce from that truth the sentiments of esteem, of goodwill, of kind consideration, of desire to collaborate, saintly rivalry, magnanimous disinterestedness, which will guide the mutual relations of communities. Each member must of course keep to its own nature and to its proper function in the body, but it must also have understanding and respect for the function of the others and know how to reach understanding with them in view of the greater common good.

672 **Relations of states of perfection with the Holy See.** It is scarcely necessary to recall what concerns the relations of the states of perfection with the Vicar of Christ and the Holy See; the prerogatives of the Apostolic See, based on the institution of Christ himself, prerogatives which the Church in the course of the centuries has only clarified and defined, these must remain unshakable and sacred. If every one of the faithful respects them and conforms to them, surely those who are in states of perfection will know how to give an example to all in this matter. It is therefore important to seek after and maintain contact with the Holy See. In the Encyclical *Humani Generis* [14] we have emphasized that the desire to avoid contact and to keep at a distance was an important

[13] I Corinthians 12: 12-27.
[14] 12 August 1950 (*AAS* XLII (1950), pp. 561-578).

cause of the errors and deviations indicated in that document; and that regrettable attitude was in particular to be found in certain members of the states of perfection. This contact with the Holy See, if it is to be effective, must be full of trust, sincerity and docility.

The Apostolic See wishes to receive from you informations 673 and reports which are not merely true, but also frank, and which will enable one to know the true condition of each community in all that has to do with doctrine and life, ascetical formation and observance, religious discipline and temporal administration, and so on. Only thus is it possible to promote the good and to bring timely correction to bear on the evil; for when these favourable dispositions of spirit of which we speak are present, the answers, regulations and instructions of the Holy See bear their fruit.

Answer to the charge of "centralization." There is another subject, namely the 674 alleged desire of the Holy See for "centralization," with which many reproach her, and we do not wish to miss the opportunity of saying a word about it. The word "centralization" can designate a system of government which claims for itself control over everything, deciding and directing everything and reducing subordinates to the rôle of instruments. Centralization of that kind is absolutely foreign to the mind of the Roman Pontiffs and the Apostolic See. But the Holy See cannot renounce its position as the directing centre of the Church. While leaving to the appointed superiors the initiative provided for in the constitutions, it must reserve its own right and exercise its function of vigilance.

What needs to be said on the subject of the renovation and 675 adaptation of the relations of communities with one another and with the Holy See is sufficiently stated, we believe, in your programme. The principles, which we have recalled, will serve as a guide, and we do not doubt that you will know how to study them thoroughly and with profit.

Conclusion. The domain of perfection, in which we have walked briefly in your company, is very extensive and supremely beautiful, but there are still in it unexplored zones. We have directed your attention to perfection in general and to perfection in the state of perfection. Nowadays there are very many clerics and religious, and also lay people, who are interested in these questions; when certain modern notions and principles are brought to bear on these questions, these people see serious and complex problems, the solution to which escapes them, however, despite their keen desire to find it. That is the reason why we have endeavoured to bring them some enlightenment, by recalling the principles which make it possible to give an answer.

By way of conclusion to this Discourse, we shall leave you another thought of St. Paul in the Epistle to the Colossians: *Above all have charity, which is the bond of perfection.*[15] Beyond all problems and discussions, seek above all union with God and you will unceasingly grow nearer to perfection. That is the grace which we desire and implore upon you from the Almighty, while we cordially impart to you our paternal Apostolic benediction.

[15] Colossians 3: 14.

EXHORTATION TO SUPERIORS GENERAL OF RELIGIOUS ORDERS AND INSTITUTES

11 February 1958

The Holy Father received in audience in the Consistorial Hall, on 11 February 1958, the superiors general of religious Orders, Congregations and Institutes which have their general Curia situated in Rome. The following Exhortation was spoken to them in Latin.[1]

It is with great joy, beloved sons, that we salute all you here present, who by the benign design of divine providence are superiors placed in charge of religious striving for evangelical perfection, since you have thus been appointed to share in some way, one that is not unimportant, in our Apostolic office. For, as we recalled some years ago, when addressing the participants in your first congress of the states of perfection, " the reason for the existence of the religious state and the explanation of its value lie in the fact that it is intimately connected with the special purpose of the Church, namely to lead men to the acquisition of holiness." [2] The Church, the Bride of Christ, would not indeed be fully in accord with the desire of Christ the Lord, nor would the eyes of men, bright with hope, look to her as to *a standard unto the nations*,[3] were there not to be found within her fold those who, by the example of their lives even more than by words, shine with added grace from the splendour of the Gospel.

Consequently, for this part of our responsibility, beloved sons, we have taken you as partners in our supreme office; either directly, by delegating to you through the Code of Canon Law some part of our own supreme jurisdiction, or by laying the foundations of that authority of yours which is called " dominative," through our approval of your rules and institutes.

676

---

[1] *AAS* L (1958), pp. 153-161.
[2] Allocution *Annus Sacer*, 8 December 1950; cf. *supra*, n. 397.
[3] Isaiah 11: 12.

It is, therefore, a matter of the greatest concern to us that you should exercise your authority in accordance with our mind and the mind of the Church.

In the aforementioned Exhortation, delivered at the end of the Holy Year of 1950, we expounded at length the things which it particularly behoves your subjects to preserve in this age, and what, on the other hand, it is expedient to renew and adapt. Today it is our intention to define briefly how you, who have to rule those whom we addressed on that occasion, may best collaborate with us for the purpose we have in mind.

677   **Superiors not to be guided by popular opinion or lured by novel ideas.** At that time we gave the admonition that those who belong to the states of perfection should not in any way to the detriment of the eternal truth, yield to the spirit of the philosophy called " existentialism." Now it is the duty of those who are superiors to lead their subjects to the goal of eternal life by the surest possible way, to guide them with enlightened mind by the safe paths of truth, turning neither to the right nor the left, leading them firmly and, if necessary, with a strong hand. As was said by the patriarch of those who in the West strive for evangelical perfection: " The abbot shall not teach or establish or command anything that is outside the precept of the Lord; but rather his teaching or command shall be mingled with the leaven of divine justice in the minds of the disciples." [4] The standards by which superiors of the states of perfection are to guide their subjects shall always be taken, not from what the majority are accustomed to say, nor from what are being spread about as the latest principles of instruction and action, to be given effect now, the older views of the fathers having already been cast aside; nor are these standards to be drawn from what appears most appropriate to men of the world, but from the pure source of revealed truth and from the discipline of the ecclesiastical magisterium. It undoubtedly calls for fortitude to go against the majority view sometimes; but unless the superior is willing at

[4] *Rule of St. Benedict*, c. 2.

times to appear out-of-date to some, how will he keep intact the truth of Christ, that truth which is, of course, always new, but at the same time always ancient? Similarly with reference to the standards which should regulate ascetic teaching and the way of life of the states of perfection (through the Encyclical *Humani Generis* we gave this admonition in an even more serious matter), there are some people nowadays who " in their excessive attachment to innovations . . . are trying to withdraw from the authority of the sacred magisterium and who thus find themselves in the danger of gradually and imperceptibly departing from the divinely revealed truth itself and of leading others into error with them." [5] Certainly it is less serious to go astray in moral discipline than in matters of faith; but error of either kind leads to peril, of its own nature and in its own way, and it undoubtedly retards and impedes us from finding the supreme good as we should.

Superiors shall hold firmly to that doctrine of a well-balanced 678 and solid asceticism, such as has been handed down by the first founders and sanctioned by the long usage of the Church; and they shall not depart from it for any novelties. For we must hold fast to the truth, not because it wins the consent of men, but because it is the truth, either implanted by God in nature or revealed to men by God in his goodness. It may be that there are some who belittle it; but does that make it cease to be the truth and the way to God? A superior, if he is to be prudent, assuredly will be glad to seek and listen to advice from many; he will weigh well and give much thought within himself to the judgment of the wise and learned; he will never so rely on his own judgment as if the danger of error were not always present to everyone on this earth. But after all this, in so far as possible, having first heard those whom the rule has given him as his natural counsellors, with many prayers to the Spirit of Counsel, and after mature consideration of everything, the superior shall take a certain and definite decision; he shall not be afraid to impose it duly on his subjects with paternal and humble firmness, and to regulate their acts and

[5] *AAS* XLII (1950), p. 564.

22

lives in accordance with it. "As it behoves disciples to obey their master, so it is proper for him to order everything with foresight and justice." [6]

A consideration, therefore, which must never be lost sight of by you, however some may cavil at it on the ground that the yoke of religious obedience is too heavy to be imposed on men of the present age: it is the duty of the superior to give firm guidance to his subjects, with all humility, of course, and in the charity of Christ, and also that at the judgment God will demand an account of souls not merely from individuals, but also from those to whose care he committed them. "Whatever be the number of brethren he knows to be entrusted to his care, let him know for certain that on the day of judgment he shall render an account to God of all these souls." [7]

679 **Evangelical perfection demands detachment from the world.**

With the passage of time and as new needs of souls constantly arise, various different forms of leading the life tending to perfection have made their appearance in the Church, under the guidance of the Holy Spirit as one may hope. Each one of them looks for different requirements from its own members; the requirements for monks are not the same as for clerics regular, the demands made on religious are not the same as those made on members of the recently arisen Secular Institutes. But there is one thing which is common to all and will remain such: for anyone who seeks after evangelical perfection, it is necessary that he should withdraw and detach himself from this world, in actual fact to the extent which the individual vocation bestowed by God demands it, and completely as far as attachment is concerned. When we say "this world" we are speaking of the world about which our Lord and Master forewarned his disciples: *You are not of the world*; [8] and the beloved Apostle said: *The whole world is placed in the evil one*; [9] and the Apostle of the gentiles said: *To me the world is crucified and I to the world*. [10]

---

[6] *Rule of St. Benedict*, c. 3.   [7] *Rule of St. Benedict*, c. 2.
[8] John 15: 19.   [9] I John 5: 19.
[10] Galatians 6: 14.

In respect of attachment, whoever intends to live for the Lord and to serve him perfectly, must be a complete stranger to the world; for the Lord is he who is not perfectly served, unless service be given to him alone. And indeed, what created good can be in any way compared with the perfection of God, not to speak of being placed on an equal footing? If anyone has not purged his soul, and does not keep it purged from the pride of the world and its multiform concupiscence, how can he ascend to God on the wings, as it were, of unhampered charity and live united with him? United, that is, not only by that vital coagmentation which we call sanctifying grace, but also by that fervour of charity which is proper to the life of one striving for perfection?

Now what man is there, one who shares in the infirmity which the sin of the first parent involves—unless he belongs to the perfect who are helped beforehand by the grace of God in an exceptional manner—who can remain entirely free from attachment to earthly things, unless he cuts himself off to some extent in actual fact from them, and indeed detaches himself as much as possible and courageously abstains from them? There is no one (apart from the duty of an office committed to one from obedience in the Church) who enjoys all the advantages in which this world abounds, or who has his recreation in the joys and pleasures of the senses which the world offers with ever increasing bounty to its adepts, that does not lose something of the spirit of faith and of charity towards God. Furthermore, anyone who gives way to such laxity over a prolonged period, gradually and imperceptibly will fall away from his purpose of holiness, and will expose himself to the danger that finally the fervour of charity will become so tepid and the light of faith become so dim that he may miserably fall from the exalted state to which he had striven.

Spirit of the Gospel and human wisdom. Your standards of judgment, on doctrines and opinions as well as on courses of action, must be different from the standards of this world; your conduct must be different and so too must be the manner in which you seek to influence other 680 men. Your standards of judging and valuing must be derived from the Gospel of the Lord and from the teaching of his Church; for *it pleased God to save those that believe, by the folly of preaching;*[11] *for the wisdom of this world is foolishness to God;*[12] and indeed what *we preach* is *Christ crucified.*[13] How will one be able to grasp the things that are right,[14] unless, instead of poisoning his mind through constant contact with things of this world, he rather nourishes it diligently by reading and meditating on the things of God, by the study of sound doctrine, by acquaintance with the writings of ancient or modern authors who are eminent for firm faith and solid piety?

681   But similar standards of action must be observed by your subjects. Their longings cannot be for what satisfies them, or for what gives pleasure, or for what is convenient; they must aspire to God alone, whom they will not find save by assiduous restraint of the senses and of the will. Of the will, first of all by humility and the submission of obedience; of the senses, by austerity of life and bodily affliction voluntarily undertaken. For without those supports which are commended in the pages of both Old and New Testament and by the whole tradition of the Church, it is practically futile for the soul to flatter itself that it will make the ascent to love of God and of the neighbour.

682   Even the means by which you will be able to influence men so as to lead them to God their last end, will not they too be different from those which the mind left to itself would judge to be effective? The apostolate of which we are speaking rests absolutely on the necessity of prevenient grace, which will open the hearts and ears of the listeners; and on the need of helping grace, without which nobody performs a good work leading to salvation, and nobody perseveres in good. But the ways of God are not our ways; it is not always *in the persuasive words of human wisdom*[15] that the power lies to move souls to faith and works of salvation, but *in the showing forth of Spirit and power:*[16]

---

[11] I Corinthians 1: 21.
[12] I Corinthians 3: 19.
[13] I Corinthians 1: 23.
[14] Cf. Collect of the Mass of the Holy Ghost.
[15] I Corinthians 2: 4.   [16] I Corinthians 2: 4.

in that mysterious showing forth, which through the sheer sincerity, charity and fortitude of the believer imparts an astonishing capacity to win over souls and to lead them to God. It is not by the new and strange devices, which human ingenuity is constantly inventing, that men are moved to the good, but by the invisible power of grace and the sacraments, especially of Penance and the Eucharist. And again: unless one retires from the world for a time at least, and indeed almost daily takes some free time to give thought to these things with a calm and pious mind in intimate converse alone with the Spirit of Wisdom, will he not become infected with that restless and frequently sterile fever for so-called " action," which is more showy than effective?

Necessity for observance of the Rule. In order that your filial subjects 683 could live in that calm and serenity of spirit which is such an invaluable aid to correct appreciation of divine things, your founders, inspired by the ancient tradition of the Church, coming from the fathers who dwelt in the desert, in accordance with the true wisdom of the Gospel, gave them the protection of what is called discipline or observance. This observance, though it varies in accordance with the different purposes of different institutes, is nevertheless enjoined as obligatory upon all. Its necessity for the goal which you set for yourselves arises from the weakness of human nature itself, wounded as it is by original sin; long experience, both ancient and modern, proves its efficaciousness as a suitable means for attaining the perfection of Christian life; the Church, both by word and deed, has always extolled its holiness.

Human nature is inclined to what is easy, and the observance 684 of discipline, which by the rule is part of the life in states of perfection, is always unpleasant to human nature; to men of our time, since they are more accustomed to a freer life before turning to the state of perfection, it can easily be even more unpleasant. Nevertheless, even in view of this consideration, it is not permissible to depreciate, much less to abandon, the observance, though you rightly have accommodated it and are still accommodating it in non-essentials to the strength of those now coming to you. The words of *Proverbs* are still true, as they were of old: *Hold fast to discipline, do not abandon it; keep it, because it is your life.*[17] What the inspired author says about the discipline which one freely imposes on oneself, cannot the same rightly be affirmed about that discipline which, by making profession of a more perfect life, one takes on oneself and promises to observe? " Those who are impelled by ardent desire of ascending to eternal life, for that reason take the narrow way; . . . not living by their own will or obeying their own desires and pleasures, they walk in accordance with the judgment and command of another; living in communities, they desire to be ruled by an abbot."[18]

685   It is part of your duty to help your subjects with fatherly firmness, by exhortation, advice, reprimands, and even by punishment should it come to that, and to keep them walking in the right path in accordance with the rules of your respective institutes. And no superior has the right, when faced with a negligent or delinquent subject, to throw over on him the responsibility of his office, saying: " He is of age, it is for him to see to it." That is not how the Lord will judge the matter, when he will demand of you an account of the souls entrusted to you: *Behold I will judge the shepherds, I will seek my flock from their hands ;*[19] from the superior who, closing his eyes, has left to themselves sheep however they have strayed or acted foolishly, or who has not kept them with firm staff from erroneous ways, he will demand an account! Fatherly charity, true charity, shows itself not only by blandishments, but also by directing and chastising. This firmness shall never be harsh, never angry or lacking in circumspection; always it shall be righteous and calm; it shall be gentle and merciful, ready to pardon and to help a son who is seeking to arise from an error or fault; and yet there must be no lack of vigilance and it must never grow weary. Your guidance and vigilance must extend not only to what is commonly called the " regular " life, which is led within the walls of the

17 Proverbs 4: 13.
18 *Rule of St. Benedict*, c. 5.
19 Ezechiel 34: 10.

religious house, but to the entire activity exercised by your subjects in the vineyard of the Master. In accordance with the norms prescribed by the ecclesiastical hierarchs to whom this matter pertains, it is your duty to watch over the work of your subjects, so that they will not be guilty of anything harmful to their own souls or contrary to the honour or the well-being of the Church and of souls, but rather will strive for their own good and that of their neighbours.

Union between different Institutes. Your own assembly of superiors 686 general here present, which some time ago met for the first time on its own initiative,[20] continues spontaneously to meet and it has been approved as a permanent institution by the Apostolic See and raised to the dignity of a moral person; from you it calls for the greatest readiness to co-operate in all those tasks for which the Church desires to make use of your labour. You realize thoroughly that all of you form a single army in which, while some are foot soldiers, others horsemen, others archers, all alike are fighting for the same good cause. You have understood how timely, indeed how necessary it is, when the enemy of the name of Christ is daily combining his forces into what he hopes will be one invincible unit, that you and all those who are soldiers for God should join forces for the common victory, each one fighting in his own rank and with his own arms. This unity, which is hindered by the diversity of races, mentalities, customs and other things, will flourish marvellously, if the true charity of Christ, which the Holy Spirit pours forth abundantly, takes deep root in your hearts. This heavenly charity is a gift of God, and if it finds us ready to co-operate,

---

[20] The initiative for the formation of this meeting of superiors general in Rome came from the Very Rev. Fr. Quenard; in 1951, at the end of many years during which he held the office of Superior General of the Assumptionists, he had the idea of bringing together several times at his table some superiors general, notably Very Rev. Fr. Sepinski, Minister General of the Franciscans, and Very Rev. Fr. Janssens, Superior General of the Society of Jesus. Fr. Suarez, the late Master General of the Dominicans and the Superior General of the Redemptorists also appeared there. As a result of the conversations which took place at these friendly gatherings, it was decided to broaden the framework and increase the importance of these reunions, which were immediately encouraged by the authorities of the Sacred Congregation of Religious, though they still retained their character as spontaneous and free meetings.

it will easily solve all the difficult questions which, through human weakness, are wont to arise from narrow preferences for one's own rightly loved Institute. For each one should love his own institute, to which he has been called by divine providence; he should conform his mind and conduct to the norms of his own institute; it is in accordance with the laws of his institute that he shall make choice of and carry out apostolic ministries; but all alike at all times shall act in concord in the service of the same Church, the Bride of the same Lord God and Saviour.

687   **Obedience to the Vicar of Christ.**   From this it follows that the earnest submission, which is shared by all the faithful, to the Chair of Peter and the Vicar of Christ, should be practised in an outstanding manner by you who are striving to reach perfection. This Apostolic See is aware that you will excel others in your obedience to it; it is sure that you are most faithful heralds of the teaching of truth which goes forth from this See; it has the firm hope that you above all will be models and supporters of ecclesiastical discipline. And if at any time, as is the nature of the Kingdom of God on earth in which the good and the evil, the wheat and cockle, are mingled together, there should somewhere be doubt, weakness, error or division, then do you at least, beloved sons, gathered in union with us, defend indomitably the " Kingdom of justice, love and peace." [21] Without the exaggerated self-confidence with which of old Peter, as yet unconfirmed by the Holy Spirit, cried: *Though all . . . not I*,[22] but with no less charity, with humble confidence and relying on the grace of your vocation to the states of perfection, you will be able to proclaim your loyalty. And if others, forgetful of filial affection, should perhaps cause solicitude to this Holy See, we for our part, with God's help, shall faithfully bear in mind the words of the Lord: *Thou art Peter, and upon this rock I will build my Church; do thou . . . confirm thy brethren.*[23]

---

[21] Preface of the Mass of Christ the King.
[22] Mark 14: 29.   [23] Matthew 16: 18; Luke 22: 32.

Strictness in admission of postulants. To ensure that your institutes will 688 always fully meet these wishes of the Vicar of Christ, it will be your duty to admit into the ranks of your institutes only those who are suitable in every way, namely young men selected for their virtue and, as far as is required, for their intelligence and other qualities. Far from your minds be that excessive zeal for gathering an indiscriminate crowd of members, about whom it might be feared that they would prove to be unworthy of your lofty vocation: for such people, far from bringing honour and benefit to the Church, will cause her harm and disgrace. On the other hand, if, in compliance with the norms hitherto laid down by the Church, you recruit only those who are really worthy, God will have a care to raise up such vocations; and by reason of the honour in which it will be held by men, your state will prepare the way for divine grace in the souls of many. Have confidence in God: if you serve him as worthily as possible, he will take care of yourselves and provide for the preservation and prosperity of your institutes.

God grant that an abundance of the light and fervour of the Holy Spirit may descend upon this chosen band of his servants, who among the other soldiers of the same army are most dear to God as they are to us. And while we recall gratefully the sweet miraculous apparitions of the Immaculate Blessed Virgin Mary in the grotto of Lourdes, we ask that the prayer of the same Mother of grace may obtain for you her devoted clients that gift beyond compare. As a pledge of that divine goodness, with overflowing charity to you, beloved sons, to your assistants in the government of your institutes, to all your subjects who are engaged in the struggle throughout the world, and above all to those who are being persecuted by the enemies of God's name, we lovingly impart the Apostolic benediction.

RADIO MESSAGE OF PIUS XII
TO CLOISTERED NUNS OF THE ENTIRE WORLD

19 and 26 July, 3 August 1958

The Holy Father spoke over the Radio to all enclosed women religious, thus granting what he described as an "audience invisible." Nuns of all Orders, in all nations, had been forewarned by the Sacred Congregation of Religious and were listening. The Holy Father's message was broadcast by many countries. In addition, the text of the Exhortation was translated into many languages in the days immediately after the broadcast, and these translations were also broadcast by Vatican Radio. The cloistered women religious of the whole world thus had the joy of hearing the Holy Father speak to them about the contemplative life.[1]

689   Gladly acceding to your request, beloved daughters, we are happy to speak today to all the nuns of the Catholic world, and to talk to them on the subject nearest to their hearts: their vocation to the contemplative life.

Many times, perhaps, you have envied the good fortune of pilgrims, who throng the nave of the basilica of St. Peter or the halls of the Vatican to manifest to us their pride in belonging to the Roman Catholic Church and their joy in receiving the word of the Head of the Church. Now, we have before us the thought of your 3,200 monasteries dispersed throughout the world, and in each of them, your recollected groups, an audience invisible and silent that is however throbbing with the charity that unites you. How could you fail to be close to our mind and heart, you who constitute in the Church a chosen part, one that is called to participate most intimately in the mystery of the Redemption? It is, therefore, with all our fatherly affection that we wish to talk to you about your religious life; that life is identical for you in all its essential elements, but in the different Orders it assumes aspects which vary according to the inspiration of your founders and the historical circumstances which their work has traversed.

[1] *OR* 20 and 27 July, 3 August 1958.

The canonical contemplative life is a path to God, an ascent 690 that is often austere and hard; but it is a way in which the daily round of toil, being sustained by the divine promises, already is lit up by the possession, as yet obscure but quite certain, of him to whom you strive with all your might, God himself. In order the better to correspond to the requirements of your vocation, you expect from us words which will enable you to understand better your vocation, to love it with a purer and more generous love, and to fulfil it more perfectly in the details of your activities.

This ascent to God is not the mere movement of inanimate creatures, nor merely the inclination of creatures endowed with reason who recognize God as their Creator, and adore him as the Infinite Being who immeasurably transcends every thing great, true, beautiful and good.[2] It is more than the ascent of the ordinary Christian life, more even than the striving for perfection in general; it is an ideal of life fixed by the laws of the Church, and for this reason it is called the canonical contemplative life. However, far from being realized in only one rigidly determined type, it takes varied forms according to the character and features that are special to the different contemplative Orders, such as—to mention only Orders of women—Carmelites, Poor Clares, Cistercians, Carthusians, Benedictines, Dominicans, Ursulines. This religious life, diversified according to the different religious families—and even, within each of them, according to those who are subjects—is a path that leads to God; God is its beginning and end, it is he who sustains its aspiring and who fills it wholly.

I.—KNOWING THE CONTEMPLATIVE LIFE

Knowledge of contemplative life as a path leading to God. We wish first to speak to you of 691 knowledge of the contemplative life, as a way which leads to God. If you are to live fully the ideal of the life which you profess, it is important for you to understand what you are and the aim you pursue.

[2] Cf. *Vatican Council, Sess.* III, c. i ; *Denziger,* n. 1782.

The Apostolic Constitution *Sponsa Christi*,[3] of 1 November 1950, includes in its first part an exposition of the state of " virgins consecrated to God " from the beginnings of Christianity down to the recent forms of the institution of nuns. Without repeating what we wrote then, we draw your attention to the interest which a knowledge, summary at least, of the development of religious life for women, and the different forms it has taken in the course of time, would have for you. That knowledge would make you better able to appreciate the dignity of your state, the originality of the particular Order to which you belong, and its links with the entire Catholic tradition.

692

General principles on the nature of the contemplative life. We will dwell here only on the general principles which make it possible to define the nature of the life which you lead, by comparison with other ways of life. For this purpose we can take the sober and sure doctrine of St. Thomas. According to this master of Catholic theology, human activity can be distinguished into the active life and the contemplative life, in the same way as the intelligence, which constitutes the distinguishing quality of man, can be considered under two aspects, active or passive. The intelligence is in fact directed either to the knowledge of truth, a work of the contemplative intellect, or to exterior activity, which belongs to the practical or active intellect.[4] But for St. Thomas, the contemplative life, far from being confined to a soulless intellectualism, also brings the affectivity, the heart, into play. And he sees the ground for this in the very nature of man; for it is the will which brings the other human faculties into action; it is the will, therefore, which will move the intellect to perform its acts. Now the will belongs to the domain of affectivity; thus it is love which moves the intellect in its activity: be it love of knowledge itself, or love of the thing known. Quoting a text of St. Gregory, St. Thomas shows the rôle of the love of God in the contemplative life: " *In quantum scilicet aliquis ex dilectione Dei inardescit ad eius pulchritu-*

---

[3] *AAS* XLIII (1951), pp. 5-10; cf. *supra*, nn. 325-337.
[4] St. Thomas, *Summa Theol.*, II-II, q. 179, a. 1 ad 2; a. 2 in c.

dinem conspiciendam : Inasmuch as, by the love of God, one is set on fire for the vision of his beauty." This love of God which St. Thomas put at the beginning of contemplation, he also places at its term: it reaches its consummation in the joy and the repose which it experiences, when it gains possession of the object loved. [5] Thus the contemplative life is wholly permeated with divine charity, which is the inspiration of its activities and the recompense of its endeavours.

For St. Thomas the object of contemplation is principally the 693 divine truth, the final end of the whole human life; as preparatory dispositions, it calls for the exercise of the moral virtues by the subject; as it progresses, it makes use of other acts of the intelligence; before reaching the goal of its search, it finds support in the visible things of creation, which are a reflection of the invisible realities; [6] but its ultimate perfection, that it finds only in the contemplation of the divine truth, the supreme beatitude of the human soul. [7] How many misunderstandings, how much narrowness of view, how many erroneous judgments would be avoided, if, when speaking of the contemplative life, care were taken to recall the teaching of the angelic Doctor, which we have sketched in its essential features.

" Sponsa Christi " and the nature of contemplative life.
We must now determine in what 694 consists the canonical contemplative life which you practise. Let us take the definition of it in the Apostolic Constitution *Sponsa Christi*, *Art* 2, § 2 of the *General Statutes of Nuns*: " By the canonical contemplative life is understood, not that interior and theological life to which all souls in religious societies and even in the world are called, and which each soul everywhere is capable of leading in itself; it is rather the exterior profession of the religious discipline which, by the enclosure, or by exercises of piety, prayer and mortification, or finally by the works to which nuns dedicate themselves, is so orientated to the interior contemplative life that the entire

[5] *Ibid.*, q. 180, a. 1 in c.
[6] Cf. Romans 1: 20.
[7] St. Thomas, *Summa Theol.*, II-II, q.180, a. 4 in c.

life and activity can easily and should be effectively imbued with
desire for it." [8]

The articles which follow this enumerate a series of other
constituents of the state of nuns: the solemn vows of religion,
the pontifical enclosure, the divine Office, the autonomy of
monasteries of nuns, the federation and confederation of
monasteries, monastic labour and finally the apostolate. Our
intention is not to go into detail on each of these points, but to
give a brief explanation of the definition just quoted.

695

What the contemplative life is not.

Let us first determine what the contemplative life is not. It is not, as the
words themselves say, " that interior and
theological life to which all souls in
religion, and even in the world, are called, and which each
soul everywhere is capable of leading in itself." [9]

696
The Constitution *Sponsa Christi* does not add any further
distinction to this negative aspect of the definition: it gives clearly
to be understood that it will not treat further of this aspect of the
religious life and, therefore, that it is not addressing itself to
those who practise this kind of life and no other. It also points
out that all are called to this kind of life by Christ, even those
who live in the world, whatever therefore may be the state to
which they belong, even the married state. But because that
Constitution does not make mention of it, we should like to
refer to the existence of a form of contemplative life practised
in secret by a small number of people living in the world. In
our Allocution of 9 December 1957, at the second international
congress of the states of perfection,[10] we said that we find
nowadays Christians who " pledge themselves to the practice of
the evangelical counsels by vows that are private and secret,
known to God alone; and they accept guidance, in all that
concerns the submission of obedience and poverty, from persons
whom the Church has judged suitable for this purpose, and
to whom she has entrusted the responsibility of guiding others

---

[8] *AAS* XLIII (1951), pp. 15-16; cf. *supra*, n. 358.
[9] Loc. cit., p. 15; cf. *supra*, n. 358.
[10] *AAS* L (1958), pp. 34-43; cf. *supra*, nn. 650-675.

in the exercise of perfection." These people lead a life of authentic Christian perfection, but outside any canonical form of " the states of perfection." And we used the following words as our conclusion: " None of the elements which constitute Christian perfection and an effective striving to acquire it, is lacking in these men and women; they truly share in it, therefore, even though they are not involved in any juridical or canonical state of perfection." [11] This statement we can now repeat with reference to a way of life, in which one strives for perfection by the three vows and in a private manner, independently of the canonical forms visualized in the Apostolic Constitution *Sponsa Christi*, and yet within the contemplative life. The exterior conditions necessary for this kind of life are undoubtedly more difficult to realize than for the active life, but nevertheless it is possible to find them. These people are not protected by any canonical enclosure, and they practice solitude and recollection in a heroic manner. In the Gospel of St. Luke, we find a fine example: that of the prophetess Anna, a widow from seven years after her marriage, who had retired to the Temple, where she served the Lord night and day, in prayer and fasting.[12] Such a private form of the contemplative life is not unknown to the Church, which grants approval to it in principle.

Primacy of contemplation in the canonical contemplative life.

The positive part of paragraph 2 of the Constitution *Sponsa Christi* defines the canonical contemplative life as " the exterior profession of the religious discipline which . . . is so orientated to interior contemplation that the entire life and activity can easily and should be effectively imbued with the desire for it." Among the prescriptions of religious discipline, the text enumerates enclosure, exercises of piety, prayer and mortification, and finally manual labour with which the nuns must occupy themselves. But these particular matters of detail are referred to only as means to serve the one essential reality: interior contemplation. What is primarily required is that the

697

[11] *Ibid.*, p. 36; cf. *supra*, n. 657.
[12] Cf. Luke 2: 37 f.

nun unite herself to God by prayer, meditation, contemplation, that all her thoughts and actions be permeated by his presence and directed to his service. Should this be lacking, the soul of the contemplative life would be absent, and no prescription of canon law could make up for it.

698   Certainly, the contemplative life includes more than contemplation; it comprises many other elements besides; but contemplation holds the first place in it; we say even that it pervades it completely; not in the sense that it does not allow one to think or do any other thing, but because it is contemplation, in the last analysis, which gives it its signification, its value and its orientation. The preponderant place of meditation and contemplation of God and of the divine truths, over all other means of acquiring perfection, over all practices and over all forms of organisation and federation, that is what we wish to underline and support with all our authority. If your being is not anchored in God, if your spirit does not unceasingly come back to him as to an irresistible point of attraction, then one would have to say of your contemplative life what St. Paul, in his first Epistle to the Corinthians, said of certain Christians, who misunderstood the spiritual gifts and neglected to put charity in the first place: *If I have not charity, I am only a sounding brass and a tinkling cymbal . . . If I have not charity, I am profited nothing.*[13] Undoubtedly, a " contemplative life " without genuine contemplation would also deserve to have said of it: *It profiteth nothing*.

Just as the human body, though equipped with all its organs, but without the soul, is not a human being, similarly all the rules and all the practices of a religious Order do not constitute the contemplative life, when contemplation itself, which is its vital principle, is lacking.

[13] I Corinthians 13: 1, 3.

Formation of female religious to the contemplative life. If theoretical explanations, such as the outline we have just given, can contribute to the enrichment of your knowledge of the contemplative life, the daily practice of your vocation for its part brings a variety and abundance of instruction. For centuries, saintly women—Carmelites, Cistercians, Carthusians, Benedictines, Poor Clares, Dominicans, Ursulines—by faithful observance of their rules and constitutions have attained to a profound understanding of the nature and exigencies of the contemplative life. From the moment of their entry into the cloister, the candidates are instructed in the rules and usages proper to their Order, and this formation of the spirit and the will, begun in the noviciate, is continued throughout the entire religious life. This is the aim of the instructions and spiritual direction, which are given by the superiors of the Order or by the confessors, directors of souls and preachers of retreats. The nuns, who live by a spirituality that is distinctive, generally receive direction and counsel from priests belonging to the male branch of the Order and who have the same spiritual approach. Moreover, for centuries the Church has cultivated particularly mystical theology, which has proved not only useful but necessary for the direction of contemplatives; it gives them sure direction and helps greatly to detect illusions and to discern the authentically supernatural from pathological states.

In this delicate terrain, even women have rendered signal services to theology and directors of souls. It is sufficient to mention here the writings of the great Teresa of Avila who, as you well know, for the solution of the difficult questions of the contemplative life, preferred the advice of an experienced theologian to that of a mystic lacking in clear and dependable theological learning.

To deepen by means of daily practice the sense of the contemplative life, it is important to have a mind receptive to the teaching given, to receive it with attention and with the desire to penetrate its meaning, each one according to the measure of her previous training and her capacities. It would be equally mistaken to set too high or too low an aim, to purport to follow only the one way, identical for all, and to demand of all the same

699

700

23

efforts. The superioresses responsible for the formation of their
subjects will know how to follow the happy mean; they will
not look for too much from simple natures, and they will not
force them beyond the limits of their capacities. In the same way
they will not oblige a nun from Asia or Africa to adopt a religious
attitude in every detail similar to that which a European sister
will adopt quite naturally. A young girl carefully educated and
with extensive culture will not be kept to a form of contemplation that is sufficient for those who have not the same gifts.

701   It happens sometimes that the reproaches of St. Paul against
the wisdom of the world, in his first Epistle to the Corinthians,
are quoted to offset the legitimate desire of nuns to reach a
level of contemplative life that corresponds to their aptitudes.
The words of the Apostle are recalled to them: *We preach a
crucified* [14] *Christ*, and also the passage: *I decided to know nothing
amongst you, but Jesus Christ and him crucified.* [15] But this is a
misunderstanding of the meaning of St. Paul, who is denouncing
the vain pretensions of human learning. The desire to possess
an adequate spiritual formation has nothing in it that is reprehensible and it is no way opposed to the spirit of humility and
renunciation, which is demanded by sincere love of the Cross
of Christ.

Beloved daughters, we here conclude the first part of our
exposition, and we invoke upon you the light of the Holy
Spirit, that he may assist you to realize the splendour of your
vocation and to live it fully. As a pledge of those favours, we
cordially impart to you our paternal Apostolic benediction.

II.—LOVE OF THE CONTEMPLATIVE LIFE

702   If we might have summarized the first part of our Allocution
by saying to you: " Realize what you are! ", we will entitle
this second part: " Love what you are! " This love will lead you,
by the path that is distinctively your own, to God who is issuing
a personal call to you. We will examine in turn the principal
motives which you have for loving the contemplative life, the

---

[14] I Corinthians 1: 23.   [15] *Ibid.*, 2: 2.

attitude which you should take towards it, and the special features which distinguish this attachment to the contemplative life.

Motives and sources of love for the contemplative life. I. Love has no real worth unless the object of love is lovable in the full sense of the word, namely that it is good in itself and capable of communicating this goodness to others. Now is not God the supreme good, both in himself and in the work of his creation, and above all in the work of the Redemption which reveals the love of the Father for mankind? 703

St. John says: *By this hath the charity of God appeared towards us, because God hath sent his only begotten Son into the world, that we may live by him.*[16] How can man respond to such an unheard of proof of the divine love, except by humble and complete acceptance of it? In another passage St. John says: *And we have known and have believed the charity which God hath to us—God is charity: and he that abideth in charity abideth in God, and God in him.*[17] That is the essence of the contemplative life: to abide in God by charity, in order that God may abide in you. And your daily strivings have no other aim but that of putting your mind and heart into constantly more intimate contact with the Lord, who manifests himself and invites you to take part in his work of redemption, in his Cross and in the extension of his Church. While this holds good for every Christian, it is true, first of all, for those who have committed themselves to a state of perfection. And here again the ways of God will vary: your religious profession and the contemplative life which you have chosen dedicate you more exclusively to the pursuit of union with God, in accordance with the particular spirit of your Order and the personal graces which the Lord grants to you. Love therefore the contemplative life in the form it offers itself to you, with its own special demands, and inasmuch as it guides you to the perfection of divine charity and keeps you within its influence. That is your principal motive for loving the contemplative life. 704

There are other motives which, though not of the same

---

[16] I John 4: 9.   [17] *Ibid.* 4: 16.

importance, can contribute nevertheless to vindicate and strengthen your interior conviction. They are to be found in sacred Scripture, in the attitude of the Church towards the contemplative life, and in the fruits which the contemplative life produces. Undoubtedly, the significance of the texts and facts, which we are about to present, takes us beyond the domain of the contemplative life; but they apply to it in a very special way, and they will help to purify and consolidate the love which you bear to your vocation.

705   Scripture contains many texts which speak of the consecration of man to God and to Christ. These passages are so rich in meaning that they will not reveal their hidden content save to those who will take the pains to meditate on them and to deepen their understanding of them in prayer. Through these words the Holy Ghost himself, who inspired them, continues to bring home to every nun the intensity of the call to the contemplative life and the riches which it implies.

Thou shalt love the Lord thy God . . . that is the greatest and the first commandment.[18]

The unmarried woman and the virgin thinketh on the things of the Lord.[19]

They follow the Lamb whithersoever he goeth.[20]

Now this is eternal life; that they may know thee, the one true God and Jesus Christ whom thou hast sent.[21]

Elsewhere, Scripture evokes the riches hidden in Jesus Christ, our God and Lord, the riches of his love for us, from which assiduous contemplation gradually draws back the veil.

The Word was God . . . the Word was made flesh . . . and we have seen his glory.[22]

Thou art the Christ, the Son of the living God.[23]

My Lord and my God.[24]

The contemplative nun knows well the crucified Lord and the significance of the cross which, each day, she takes between her fingers. She will often bring to mind the exclamations of

[18] Matthew 22: 37-8.
[19] I Corinthians 7: 34.
[20] Apocalypse 14: 4.
[21] John 17: 3.
[22] John 1: 1, 14.
[23] Matthew 16: 16.
[24] John 20: 28.

St. Paul: *With Christ I am nailed to the Cross . . . Christ lives in me . . . who loved me and delivered himself for me.*[25] *Who then shall separate us from the love of Christ? . . . For I am sure that neither death nor life . . . nor any other creature, shall be able to separate us from the love of God, which is manifested in Christ Jesus our Lord.*[26]

The works of penitence and mortification, which form part of the contemplative life, put into practice the statement of St. Paul: *I fill up those things which are wanting of the sufferings of Christ, in my flesh, for his body, which is the Church.*[27]

These few passages of Scripture fill with profound joy the soul of the contemplative who meditates on them, and they effect an even closer attachment to God and to Christ. They are an invitation to the contemplative to understand and to follow out lovingly a vocation which leads her, without any turning aside, to the love of God and his incarnate Son.

When the Church declares that the contemplative life is worthy of the highest esteem, when it gives to it the approval of its full authority and confers privileges on it, when it inaugurates it by a solemn liturgy and surrounds it with abundant protective measures to ensure its realization, one can certainly see in all that a proof of the esteem in which the Church holds the contemplative life, and consequently a serious ground for dedication of oneself to it. From among the numerous ecclesiastical documents which speak of it, we shall select three: the Apostolic Constitution *Sponsa Christi*, the benediction and solemn consecration of virgins in the *Roman Pontifical* (whose ancient solemn forms are reserved to nuns by art. III § 3 of the Apostolic Constitution *Sponsa Christi*), and the Encyclical *Sacra Virginitas*[28] of 25 March 1954.

The Apostolic Constitution *Sponsa Christi*, in its historical section, shows the high esteem which the Church professes for the institution of virgins and nuns. It recalls " the esteem and maternal affection that gently inspired her dealings with virgins consecrated to God " from their beginnings. It insists further-

706

more, as we have shown, on the importance of contemplation, to which all other monastic exercises are subordinated.

From the " Consecration of Virgins " we take the words spoken to them by the bishop when he gives the habit and other symbols of their state: " I unite you as spouse to Jesus Christ, Son of the Father Almighty, that he may keep you free from sin. Receive therefore the ring of faith, the seal of the Holy Spirit, that you may be called the spouse of God and, if you serve him faithfully, be crowned for eternity." [29]

The Encyclical *Sacra Virginitas* in its first part treats of the excellence of virginity. It proves this excellence first of all by the texts of the Gospel and the very words of Christ, then by the declaration of the Apostle of the gentiles on virginity chosen for the love of God; it quotes St. Cyprian and St. Augustine, who show forth its powerful effects; it underlines the importance of the vow which gives to virginity the stability of virtue; it shows its superiority to marriage; it sheds light on all the divine blessings which virginity brings down and the admirable fruits which it produces.

707   This last point, which is treated also in the Apostolic Constitution *Sponsa Christi*, deserves particular consideration, because it will arouse in you an even more profound and more convinced adherence to your contemplative life. We could speak at length on the details of the life of the great contemplative saints, St. Teresa of Avila, for example, or St. Teresa of the Child Jesus, both of them Carmelites; but we prefer to appeal to your own personal experience and to that of your community life.

The nun, who devotes herself wholly and sincerely to her task, does not fail to experience in herself the fruits of her efforts and to appreciate them. Her life, exteriorly, follows the course fixed by the daily time-table and the exercises of the rule; interiorly, it matures and is deepened, passing through the phases of consolation and trial, of light and darkness, which leave intact the soul's intimate union with God. Thus, notwithstanding obstacles from within and from without, despite failures

---

[29] *Roman Pontifical*: De benedictione et consecratione virginum.

and weaknesses, the nun progresses, with assurance of God's help, until the moment, sometimes unexpected, when she hears the words: *Behold, the bridegroom cometh; go ye forth to meet him.*[30]

We exhort you, each one of you individually, to apply yourselves with all the strength at your command to the duties of your state as contemplatives; you will thus experience ever more fully the effects of that state and will find in that a new motive for attachment to it. We would wish then to put you on guard against discouragement and faint-heartedness. Undoubtedly, it is your duty to give whole-hearted collaboration with grace, you must struggle with your faults and exercise yourselves in virtue; but leave to God the care of causing you to grow and bear fruit. It is he who, at the opportune moment, *will strengthen, confirm and make you unshakable.*[31] If you possess these dispositions, you will forge ahead, supported by God's power and overflowing with the joy of having been chosen for this life.

This personal experience will be enriched by what you will observe in your community. If, instead of dwelling on the faults and human weaknesses that are inevitable, you attend above all to the sincere efforts of others not to fall short of their religious ideal, you will easily realize the influence of their interior life and their union with God; you will also be moved to admiration, in the smallest details of community life, of the delicacy of a fraternal charity which flows immediately from their love for Christ, who is seen in his members. The splendour of that charity, which is often veiled during life itself, sometimes reveals itself with sudden radiance as soon as death has applied its seal; then you will say with the Psalmist: *Indeed there is reward for the just.*[32]

[30] Matthew 25: 6.
[31] I Peter 5: 10.
[2] Psalm 57: 12.

709   **Attitude to be**   **II.** Having considered the reasons
     adopted towards the   which impel you to love of the con-
     contemplative life.   templative life, we will now speak of
                                the attitude which you should adopt out
of fidelity to this love. Already, in the first part of this discourse,
we underlined the importance of " interior contemplation " and
its superiority to the other elements which are the necessary
means that accompany it: the enclosure, the exercises of piety,
prayer and mortification and work. Here we consider how the
nun acts in face of this combination of obligations.

To begin with, it is obvious that sincere attachment to the
religious life exludes every species of " legalism," in other words
the temptation to stick to the letter of the law, without fully
accepting its spirit: that would be unworthy of nuns, who bear
the name *spouse of Christ* and wish to serve him above all by way
of disinterested love.

Equally unacceptable would be a sort of " eclecticism," a
wholly subjective choosing between certain obligations that one
admits and others that one does not accept. No Order worthy
of the name will accept a candidate who would intend to observe
only a part of the rules and constitutions.

710   The contemplative life is austere; the human sensibility does
not accept it without resistance, but the desire to give oneself
to God willingly embraces the practices of penitence and continual self-denial. The nun who is on fire with fervour for her
vocation can apply to herself the words which the Apostle of
the gentiles spoke of the Christian community: *I have espoused
you to a single spouse, as a pure virgin to be presented to Christ.*[33]
We can add: " To the crucified Christ." The nun who is attached
to her vocation will always take as the rule of her interior life
the words of St. Paul: *I fill up those things which are wanting of the
sufferings of Christ, in my flesh, for his body, which is the Church.*[34]
That is the law of genuine love, to which the words of St.
Augustine are also applicable: " The one who loves feels no pain,
but every pain is hard for one who does not love." [35]

[33] II Corinthians 11: 2.
[34] Colossians 1: 24.
[35] *In Joann. Evang.* Tr. XLVIII, c. x, n. 1 (*PL* XXXV, c. 1741).

Work forms part of the contemplative life. The law of ancient 711
monastic life: "*Ora et labora*, pray and work," has lost nothing
of its wisdom and its necessity. Work, moreover, is a command
of nature itself, which has given the powers of body and soul
to man; it places on him the obligation to provide for his
subsistence and stimulates him to improve his condition of life
and to augment his means of knowledge and action. The Lord,
for thirty years, led a life of toil at Nazareth, and his apostolic
ministry caused him heavy fatigue. St. Paul, in his incisive
manner, writes to the Thessalonians: *If anyone will not work,
neither let him eat. For we have heard that there are some among you
who work not at all . . .*[36] And he himself affirms that he had
laboured with his own hands to earn his bread and not to be
a burden on the Christians.[37] The Apostolic Constitution
Sponsa Christi several times stresses the obligation of nuns to
work in order to earn their daily bread; it follows that anyone
who follows the contemplative life and accepts it without
qualification also fully accepts the law of work.

The positive determinations of ecclesiastical law concerning 712
the canonical contemplative life are many; even if some of them
have not great importance, all nevertheless should be observed.
The Lord has clearly said: *He that shall break one of these least
commandments and shall teach men to do likewise shall be considered
the least in the kingdom of heaven; but he that shall do and teach,
he shall be called great in the kingdom of heaven . . . I am not come
to destroy the law, but to fulfil it.*[38] Anyone who loves the contemplative life will consider this delicacy of conscience and this
fidelity in the smallest details as one of the dearest of duties.

But on the other hand, there must be no narrowness of mind 713
and heart in any way. The liberty of the inner man was willed
and given by God: *You have been called to liberty; only make not
liberty an occasion to the flesh . . . it is in order that we remain
free that Christ has liberated us.*[39] This liberty of Christ, which
the Apostle here describes, consists in the power to accomplish
the works of the Spirit which are opposed to those of the flesh:
charity, joy, peace, longanimity, obligingness, goodness, trust in

---

[36] II Thessalonians 3: 10-11.   [37] Cf. Acts 20: 34; 18: 3.
[38] Matthew 5: 19, 17.   [39] Galatians 5: 13, 1.

others, gentleness, self-mastery: *Against these, there is no law.*[40] Even before St. Paul, Christ had determined in an even more incisive fashion, with reference to the observance of the sabbath, the meaning of Christian liberty: *The sabbath was made for man, and not man for the sabbath.*[41] Since the Lord did not hesitate to express himself in this way, one can affirm as a general statement that the law is for man, and not man for the law. That does not suppress the obligation of observing the law, but it safeguards the liberty and tranquillity of the inner man. The bearing of each law must be exactly understood, according to whether it is a divine or a human law, essential or non-essential. It is an error to place the law above man, as if it were something absolute and not a means for him to attain his end. Jesus had said of the Pharisees: *They bind on men's shoulders heavy and insupportable burdens.*[42] We are satisfied that a nun who is sincerely attached to the contemplative life, will have no difficulty in reconciling delicacy of conscience in the observance of her duties and the prescriptions of the rule, with the peace which flows from the tranquillity and liberty of the inner man. You will be subject to the rules by your observance of them; but, by living in union with the Spirit of God and his love, you will be above them.

714 **Characteristic features of this atitude.** III.—Finally we would wish to say a word about the physiognomy, the characteristic stamp, which should mark your interior attitude.

The first things one expects to find in a nun are simplicity and humility; the love of the contemplative life should exclude all desire for notice, for admiration, for prominence. To be seen by others, that was the desire of the Pharisees which our Lord severely reprimands in the Sermon on the Mount.[43] By remaining unnoticed, you will also avoid certain psychological deviations, which are more frequent in women and belong to woman's temperament.

We have considered the contemplative life as an ascent to God, in order to offer him your mind and heart. This offering,

---

[40] Galatians 5: 23.   [41] Mark 2: 27.
[42] Matthew 23: 4.   [43] Cf. Matthew 6: 1-6, 16-18.

inspired by supernatural motives, is nourished by the theological virtues of faith, hope and charity. The love of contemplation will be authentic, only if it is constantly supported by these virtues. It is that which will give it a typically Christian character, and it will not appear merely as a psychological phenomenon of the religious order, the kind which the comparative history of religions shows to have existed at all times and amongst the most diverse nations.

In order to put to the test the sincerity and the purity of *715* your charity, it will suffice for you to recall the celebrated description of it which St. Paul gives in the thirteenth chapter of his first Epistle to the Corinthians, which you will have already many times made the subject of your meditations. God grant that your everyday behaviour may constantly approach more closely to the ideal depicted in that celebrated passage!

Generous dedication does not go with constant tension, with constraint, with a continual struggle with obligations that are unwillingly borne and that would be rejected if that were possible. It is possible that God permits such a trial for a time in order to purify the soul; but it can also happen that it will lead to breakdown, to catastrophe both interiorly and exteriorly.

We are not considering cases where neurotic or psychotic factors enter in. We are envisaging only the case of normal individuals, nuns who have had such a breakdown or who are heading for it. There can be no question here of studying the diagnosis, therapeutics or prognosis of these cases. But there is a psychic factor, a characteristic quality of the fervent practice of contemplation, which is capable of forestalling such catastrophes. It is the conscientious acceptance, unceasingly repeated and full of joy, by the nun, of the life of each day. This is the indestructible optimism, not of hysteria, but the calm and firm optimism of our Lord who said: *I am not alone, but the Father is with me;* [44] it is the unshakable confidence of the nun in him who has said: *All you that labour and are heavy burdened, come to me and I will refresh you.* [45] These considerations and these sentiments are the factors that determine her interior attitude. She

[44] John 16: 32.
[45] Matthew 11: 28.

knows by experience what she must bear, but she wishes to regulate her life in accordance with the word of the Apostle: *God loves the cheerful giver.*[46] What St. Paul wrote to the Corinthians about the material gifts intended for the poor of Jerusalem, the nun understands it and wishes to apply it to something much more vast: the giving of her whole being and her entire external activity. Joy and constant happiness are the typical marks of the sincere surrender of self. One detects them at the beginning of the first Epistle of St. Peter; he presupposes them and takes note of them in the Christians to whom he is writing, who have already turned to Christ: *Jesus Christ, whom not having seen, you love . . . in whom also now, though you see him not, you believe and believing shall rejoice with joy unspeakable and glorified, receiving the end of your faith, the salvation of your souls.*[47]

716   To each one of you we say: God grant that faith, hope and the love of Christ will give you something of the jubilation which Peter discerned among the Christians to whom he wrote. At the end of his letter he comes back on the same thought; he exhorts the Christians to consider the sorrows of this world as inseparable from their life on earth and as a means to attain to glory: *Cast all your care on him . . . after you have suffered a little, he himself will perfect you, and confirm you and establish you.*[48] It is this same idea which St. Augustine expresses towards the end of his *City of God*: the earthly life with all its sorrows will have an end, and we shall then go to God, and our joy in the possession of him will have no end! " *Ibi vacabimus et videbimus; videbimus et amabimus; amabimus et laudabimus. Ecce quod erit in fine sine fine:* There we shall be at rest and shall see; we shall see and love; we shall love and praise. That will take place at the end without end." [49]

This is the inner conviction that should sustain your life and give you the strength to follow it with courage to the end, without slackness or taking back, and thus to make it a perfect offering to God.

---

[46] II Corinthians 9: 7.
[47] I Peter 1: 8-9.
[48] I Peter 5: 7, 10.
[49] *De civitate Dei*, 1, XXII, c. xxx, n. 5 (*Pl.* XLI, c. 804).

III.—LIVING THE CONTEMPLATIVE LIFE

Practice of the contemplative life in relation to knowledge and love of contemplation.

I.—When dealing with the knowledge and the love of the contemplative life, in the first two parts of this Allocution, we did not omit to stress the practical application of the principles which we were recalling. To make the meaning of our exposition easier to understand, it was important not to confine ourselves to theoretical and abstract aspects of the subject, but also to take into account the practical consequences that a more profound understanding and a purer and more ardent love of the contemplative life would have on the actual practice of contemplation.

It will not be necessary, therefore, to repeat in this third part what we have already explained. Having recalled the need to translate into action that which one has come to know better and to love better, we will envisage the practical realization of the contemplative life, both in its essential element, namely contemplation itself, and in its secondary elements, particularly monastic labour.

As we stressed in the first part of our Allocution, the knowledge of the contemplative life is enriched and deepened by the daily fulfilment of its obligations. The love of the contemplative life necessarily involves certain attitudes, through which this love is manifested and without which it would be only an illusion. In this unceasing interplay, which normally conditions the regular progress of a religious life, the predominant element will always be the interior life, which gives their meaning and value to the exterior actions. It is from man's heart that purposes, good or evil, come: [50] and it is the intention that explains man's actions and gives them a moral value. But this intention by itself is not enough; it is further necessary that it be really put into effect: *He who has my commandments and keeps them, he it is who loves me,* [51] said Jesus. And again: *You are my friends, if you do what I command.* [52] On the other hand, one who neglects to

717

718

---

[50] Cf. Mark 7: 21.   [51] John 14: 21.   [52] John 15: 14.

give practical effect to the divine precepts finds that he is excluded from the kingdom: *Not everyone who says " Lord, Lord," will enter the kingdom of heaven, but he who does the will of my Father.* [53]

719 **Realisation in practice of the essential, namely interior contemplation.** II.—These same principles apply also to the contemplative life; the desire for it, however ardent, is not enough! It is further required that one apply oneself to it in practice, and that one accept all the renunciations that are necessary for the attainment of it. Now contemplation, understood as the adherence of mind and heart to God, is the essential element of the contemplative life. We established that in the first part of our Allocution and we cited the principal texts which prove it. Let us mention two other texts, taken from the Instruction *Inter cetera* of 25 March 1956, which recall, with reference to a practical point, the pre-eminence of contemplation in your life. " Minor enclosure does not permit any and every form of ministry, but only those which are compatible with the contemplative life, whether of the entire community or of the individual nuns." [54] " These ministries . . . are to be undertaken with discernment and moderation, with due respect for the character and spirit of each Order, in such a way that, instead of disturbing or interfering with the authentic contemplative life, they will rather nourish and strengthen it." [55] " Such activities are: the teaching of Christian doctrine, religious instruction, the education of young girls and children, retreats and spiritual exercises for women, preparation for first Communion, works of charity for assisting the sick, the poor, etc." [56] The contemplative life does not consist essentially in the outward profession of a religious discipline; that discipline, in fact, is only the framework for contemplation; the discipline sustains, encourages and preserves the contemplative life, but it does not constitute it. Consequently, to repeat what we have already

---

[53] Matthew 7: 21.
[54] *AAS* XLVIII (1956), p. 520, n. 41a; cf. *supra*, n. 387a.
[55] *Ibid.*, n. 41b.
[56] *Ibid.*, n. 41c.

said, we exhort you insistently to give yourselves with your whole heart to contemplative prayer, which is the essential task for the sake of which you have renounced the world.

There is to be no confusing of this matter of principle with the question of the frequency and the length of exercises of piety. The intensity of an exercise is not necessarily in proportion to its length. The active ministries permitted to nuns do not allow them to devote long hours every day to contemplative prayer; they have however sufficient free time to satisfy this essential obligation.

III.—The Apostolic Constitution *Sponsa*   720
Subsidiary elements *Christi* distinguishes the "proper and
that complete essential constituents which directly
contemplative life. affect the canonical contemplative life of
nuns as their primary and principal aim," from other elements that are not essential to it, but serve to complete and to ensure it, such things as the enclosure, and exercises of piety, prayer and mortification.[57] In articles 6 and 7, the same Constitution treats of the nature and juridical structure of monasteries of nuns, their autonomy and the possibility of forming federations or confederations.[58] On some of these points the Church lays down precise demands which must be satisfied; on others she expresses only an invitation and desires that thought be given to the matter and that the suggestions be weighed with good-will. Let monasteries and Orders of nuns have esteem for their own special character, protect it and remain faithful to it; that is their right, and it would be unjust not to take account of it; but they must not defend it in a narrow, inflexible spirit, and still less with a certain stubborness which is opposed to any form of timely development and would not lend itself to any form of adaptation, even when the common good demands it.

It may happen that a nun is asked to leave her monastery   721
and settle in another, in the interest of some greater good or for a weighty reason. No one, of course, can impose on a religious, contrary to her will, obligations which go beyond

---

[57] Cf. *AAS* XLIII (1951), p. 10; cf. *supra*, n. 340.
[58] *Ibid.*, pp. 17-19; cf. *supra*, nn. 372-382.

what she has undertaken by her vows; but one can raise the precise question as to how far stability constitutes an essential of the rights of nuns. The Holy See has the right to modify the constitutions of an Order and their prescriptions concerning stability; but if these changes touch on essential points of the existing law, the members are not bound, in virtue of their vows, to accept the new constitutions: they must be given the opportunity of separating themselves from Orders which are undergoing changes of this kind. However, a nun can spontaneously renounce her rights and agree to the request which is made to her and which the Holy See approves.[59] We are not unaware of what such a procedure means and how much it may cost a religious; but we exhort her to accept the sacrifice, unless there be even graver reasons to the contrary.

722   When there is question of secondary matters that play only a complementary part in the religious life, monasteries and nuns should be prepared to accept exchanges of ideas and the collaboration which the Holy See proposes to them. In particular, they shall endeavour to establish relations which are as cordial as they are respectful with the Sacred Congregation of Religious, especially as the Congregation has no intention of disregarding acquired rights, but desires to take account of the views of monasteries and Orders of nuns. This collaboration is particularly desirable when there is question of forming a federation of monasteries or Orders, or even a confederation of federations.

The text of *Sponsa Christi* shows that there is no question of doing violence in these matters to the rightful independence of individuals, but rather of protecting and assuring it. Strive therefore to collaborate with the competent ecclesiastical authority, in order to promote the adaptation and healthy development which the Church desires.

---

[59] Cf. *ibid.*, art. 7, 8, n. 3; cf. *supra*, n. 382.

How to realize one particular element, work. IV.—The application of the norms 723 concerning work is a matter of great concern to us, because it affects the interests of contemplative monasteries and of all the Orders of women contemplatives, and also the interests of the whole Church which, in many places, is looking for a combination of all available resources.

As we have already spoken above of the necessity of work in general and of its suitability for contemplative Orders, we will confine our attention now to the application of the dispositions of the Constitution *Sponsa Christi*.

In the first part of that Constitution we said: " We are moved, indeed constrained, to introduce these reasonable adaptations of the institute of nuns by the full information on the matter that we have received from all parts of the world, and by the certain knowledge derived from this information of the grave need in which nuns frequently, not to say always, exist. Indeed there are not a few monasteries which, alas! are practically dying from hunger, distress, privation; . . . in addition, there are monasteries which, though not living in dire need, not infrequently are languishing because they are completely segregated and cut off from any other monasteries. Besides, rules of enclosure which are sometimes too strict can often lead to grave difficulties." [60]

The normal and most immediate way to meet this distress 724 is the work of the nuns themselves. Hence we call upon them to apply themselves to it, so as to be able to secure for themselves the means of subsistence, and not to think first of having recourse to the charity and help of others. This appeal is made even to nuns who are not in grave need, and who are not therefore obliged to gain their daily bread by the labour of their hands. You will be able therefore, in that way, to earn the means required to satisfy the precept of Christian charity towards the poor. We also invite you to train and cultivate your manual skills, as well as to adapt yourselves to contemporary conditions, as is laid down in article VIII, § 3, n. 2 of the Constitution *Sponsa Christi*. [61]

---

[60] *AAS*, loc. cit., pp. 10-11; cf. *supra*, n. 342.
[61] Apostolic Constitution *Sponsa Christi*, *AAS* XLIII (1951), p. 19; cf. *supra*, n. 385.

That same article sums up the norms concerning monastic labour, laying down first of all that " monastic labour, in which nuns of the contemplative life also must engage, should as far as possible be in harmony with the rule, constitutions and traditions of each Order." [62] Certain constitutions make provision for specified works, generally of an apostolic character; others, on the contrary, do not determine anything precise on the matter. This monastic labour " should be so organized that, together with the other sources of income . . . it will ensure for the nuns a secure and appropriate livelihood." [63] Local Ordinaries and superiors are obliged to see to it " that the nuns never want for the work which is necessary, suitable and remunerative." [64] Finally, the article underlines the obligation in conscience which binds nuns not only to earn their bread by the sweat of their brow, but also to make themselves constantly more competent, as the actual circumstances demand, for different kinds of work. [65]

Do not allow our call to labour to go unheeded; make use of all the means at your disposal and of every possibility to train yourselves more fully, for your own benefit first of all, or at least in order to relieve the distress of others, if you have no immediate need of your own. Moreover, a serious occupation, one that is adapted to your strength, is an efficacious means of preserving interior balance, or of restoring it, if it has been impaired. Thus you will avoid the harmful effects which the complete seclusion and the relative monotony of the daily life of the cloister could have on certain temperaments.

CONCLUSIONS

725   We bring our Allocution to an end by renewing the call to the apostolate which also concludes the Constitution *Sponsa Christi*, and which is based on the great commandment of the love of God and of the neighbour and on the will of the Church.

Charity towards the neighbour embraces all mankind, all

---

[62] *Ibid.*, art. 8, § 1; cf. *supra*, n. 383.
[63] *Ibid.*, § 2; cf. *supra*, n. 384.
[64] *Ibid.*, § 3, n. 1; cf. *supra*, n. 385.
[65] *Ibid.*, § 3, n. 2; cf. *supra*, n. 385.

their needs, all their sufferings, and it is specially concerned with securing their eternal salvation. This apostolate, with which the Church charges nuns, is performed by them in three ways: by the example of Christian perfection which draws souls to Christ without words; by public and private prayer; and by their zeal in assuming, in addition to the penitential exercises prescribed by the rule, others prompted by their generous love of the Lord. In the dispositive part of the Constitution *Sponsa Christi*, different forms of the apostolate are distinguished, varying according to the different forms of contemplative life. Certain nuns, in virtue of their constitutions, devote themselves to works of the exterior apostolate; they shall continue that apostolate; others, by their constitutions, are dedicated to the contemplative life alone, but in fact they perform some forms of exterior apostolic work, or did so in former times; these nuns shall continue or resume these activities, adapting them to contemporary circumstances; there are still other nuns who, in law and in fact, live only the contemplative life. They shall abide by that, unless they are compelled by necessity and for a limited period, to accept certain apostolic activities. It is clear that these nuns who are exclusively contemplatives share in the apostolate of the love of the neighbour under the three forms of example, of prayer and of penance.

We wish, however, by way of conclusion to call to mind 726 an apostolate that is even greater and more exalted, that of the Church, the Spouse of Christ, as understood by the Apostle of the gentiles and St. John.[66]

The apostolate of the Church is founded on her mission to the whole world, to the men of all nations and of all ages, to Christians and pagans, to believers and unbelievers. This mission comes from the Father: *God so loved the world as to give his only begotten Son, that all who believe in him may not perish, but may have life everlasting. For God sent not his Son into the world to judge the world, but that the world may be saved by him.*[67] That mission was handed on by Christ: *As the Father hath sent me, I also send you.*[68]

---

[66] Cf. II Corinthians 11: 2; John 20: 21-23; 21: 16-17; Apocalypse 21.
[67] John 3: 16-17.
[68] John 20: 21.

All power is given to me in heaven and on earth. Going therefore, teach ye all nations baptizing them . . . I am with you all days, even to the consummation of the world.[69] The mission is carried out in the Holy Spirit: *You shall receive the power of the Holy Spirit coming upon you, and you shall be witnesses unto me . . . even to the uttermost part of the earth.*[70] This apostolic mission of the Church preceeds primordially, therefore, from the Blessed Trinity, Father, Son and Holy Spirit, and no one can conceive anything more exalted, more holy, more universal in its origin no less than in its object.

For what, in fact, is the purpose of this mission, if not to bring men to the knowledge of the true God, One in the Trinity of Persons, of the design of the Redemption which he has carried out by his Son, and of the Church founded by Christ to continue his work? The Church has received the whole deposit of faith and that of grace, the whole treasury of revealed truth and all the means of salvation bequeathed by the Redeemer: Baptism,[71] the Eucharist and the priesthood: *Do this in commemoration of me,*[72] the imposition of hands of the Apostles,[73] the remission of sins: *Receive ye the Holy Ghost; whose sins you shall forgive, they are forgiven them,*[74] the government of the faithful by the power of jurisdiction, exercised in the name of Christ and with the abiding assistance of the Holy Spirit.[75] There in a few words you have pictured the divine riches with which our Lord has endowed his Church, so that among all the vicissitudes of the earthly life she may be able to accomplish her apostolic tasks and thus pass through the centuries; and the gates of hell can never prevail against her.[76]

Allow the unconquerable power that animates the apostolate of the Church to take possession of your mind and heart! It will fill you with peace and joy ! *Have confidence, I have overcome the world.*[77] As you climb ever higher, and constantly draw nearer to God, you widen your horizons and become proportionately more capable of orientating yourselves on this earth. Far from shutting you up within yourselves behind the monastic walls, your union

---

[69] Matthew 28: 18-20.   [70] Acts 1: 8.   [71] Cf. Matthew 28: 19.
[72] Luke 22: 19.   [73] Cf. Acts 8: 17.   [74] John 20: 23.
[75] Cf. John 21: 16-17.   [76] Cf. Matthew 16: 18.   [77] John 16: 33.

with God widens your mind and heart to the dimensions of the world and of the redemptive work of Christ which is prolonged in the Church; it is that which will serve to guide you, to sustain your endeavours and to make them fruitful in all good.

We pray the Lord to enrich you with his gifts and to bring to completion the work which he has begun in you for his own greater glory; as a pledge of his favours we impart cordially to each of you our paternal Apostolic benediction.

PRAYER OF HIS HOLINESS POPE PIUS XII
FOR RELIGIOUS VOCATIONS

For many years the Holy Father was pre-occupied by the decline in religious vocations in many parts of the Christian world. He alluded to the subject in precise terms in his Allocution to superiors general, 15 September 1952. He decided on his own initiative to found a Pontifical Work of Religious Vocations by the Motu Proprio Cum Supremae *of 11 February 1955; he composed in his own hand a special prayer for religious vocations.*[1]

Lord Jesus Christ, sublime model of all perfection, who not content with calling unceasingly to privileged souls to ascend to that exalted ideal, also dost draw them by the powerful force of thine example and the efficacious action of thy grace to follow thee on the path to the highest peaks; grant to us that many will understand and decide to correspond to thy gentle inspirations, by embracing the religious state, in which they will have the benefit of thy special solicitude and tender predilection.

Grant thus that never will there be wanting at the cradle of the orphan, at the bedside of the sick, at the side of the aged and the infirm, a messenger of thy charity to represent thee night and day; apart from him there is perhaps no one to extend to them a helping hand. Grant that in the little schools as well as in more celebrated chairs of learning, a voice may always resound, the echo of thy own, to teach the way to Heaven and the particular duties of each one. Grant that no country, however inhospitable or far off, may be deprived of the call of the Gospel which invites all peoples to enter into thy kingdom. Grant that those flames, which will set the world on fire and in which the unspotted holiness of the Church shines forth in all its splendour, will spread and mount aloft. Grant that in every region there may flourish those gardens of chosen souls who, in contemplation and penitence, make reparation for the faults of men and implore thy mercy. Grant that in the continuous immolation of those

[1] *AAS* XLIV (1957), p. 100; *Discorsi e Radiomessagi di Sua Santità Pio XII*, vol. XVIII (1956-1957), pp. 775 f.

hearts, in the purity of those souls white as snow, in the perfection of their virtues, there may always live again on earth the perfect example of the Son of God, which thou camest to reveal to us.

Send to those ranks of thy privileged ones numerous good vocations, souls that are resolved and firm in their decision to make themselves worthy of a grace that is so outstanding and of the holy institute to which they aspire, by the exact observance of their obligations as religious, by assiduous prayer, by constant mortification and by the perfect adherence of their will to all that is thy will.

O Lord Jesus, enlighten many generous souls with the burning rays of the Holy Spirit, substantial and eternal love; and by the powerful intercession of thy most amiable Mother Mary, stir up and keep burning in them the fire of thy charity, unto the glory of the Father and the Holy Spirit who, with thee, live and reign world without end. Amen.

INDEX OF TEXTS OF SCRIPTURE

References are to the marginal numbers. Where a citation is textual,
the number is given in roman type; otherwise it is in *italics*.

OLD TESTAMENT

Genesis

2: 9	120a
2: 15	*350*
2: 24	499
3: 19	269, *350*

Exodus

17: 8-13	*169*
22: 16-17	*482*

Leviticus

15: 16-17	*503*
22: 4	*503*

Deuteronomy

22: 23-29	*482*

I Samuel

2: 3	*581*
2: 3	142, *608*
21: 5-7	*503*

II Chronicles

19: 7	*228*

II Machabees

1: 3	*271*
15: 14	*45*

Job

5: 7	*350*

Psalms

22: 1	313
22: 3-4	313
57: 12	708
103: 30	*272*

Proverbs

4: 13	*684*

Canticle

6: 3	*273*

Wisdom

13: 1	*139*

Ecclesiasticus

3: 27	537
33: 29	*145*
42: 9	*482*
44: 13	*137*

Isaias

11: 12	*676*

Ezechiel

34: 10	*685*

Osee

4: 6	*142*

Malachy

2: 7	*142*

NEW TESTAMENT

Matthew

4: 19	*582*
5: 10	*552*
5: 11	43
5: 13	272, *641*
5: 13-14	142, *608*
5: 17	*712*
5: 19	*712*
5: 28-29	535
5: 48	*228*
6: 1-6	*714*
6: 16-18	*714*
6: 33	*137*
7: 8	*543*
7: 21	*718*
9: 38	*582*
11: 28	*715*
11: 28-29	665
11: 29	2
12: 33	*506*
13: 33	272, *314*
13: 46	*511*
13: 55	*350*
16: 16	*705*
16: 18	*687*
16: 24	*221*
19: 5	*499*
19: 10	*488*
19: 10-11	*504*
19: 10-12	*221*
19: 11	527, *543*

359

INDEX OF CANONS OF THE CODE

Reference are to the marginal numbers.

Reference are to the marginal numbers

CHRONOLOGICAL INDEX OF PONTIFICAL DOCUMENTS [1]

(1) In this Index documents are distinguished as follows :
    CAPITALS: principal documents on the states of perfection.
    heavy type :   other documents published in the body of the text ;
    roman :   documents quoted in footnotes or in the text ;
    italics :   documents merely referred to.

LEO XIII

References are to the marginal numbers.

BENEDICT XV

PIUS XI

25

ANALYTICAL INDEX

Abnegation
Cf. SELF-DENIAL, RENUNCIATION, SPIRIT OF SACRIFICE.

Action
Heresy of –, consequence of naturalism, Ia; – of religious in human society, 37; principles for – by missionaries, 431, by major superiors for more efficacious apostolate, 651; field of – of modern apostolate, 418; persecution, obstacle to – of the Church, 40. Cf. APOSTOLATE.

Active (Life)
Distinction and union between – and contemplative life, 173, 177, 336-337, 350, 411-412, 564, 691-724. Cf. CONTEMPLATION, CONTEMPLATIVE LIFE.

Active (Orders)
Distinction between – and contemplative Orders, 337; theological culture required by –, 142-145. Cf. CONTEMPLATIVE.

Active (Virtues)
Distinguished from passive virtues, 1. Cf. PASSIVE, VIRTUE.

Activism
Warning against –, 1-6, 211. Cf. ZEAL.

Actuality
abiding – of religious Orders, 38; of contemplative Orders, 176-177; of Benedictines, 253, 263-270; of Secular Institutes, 228; – of education given by religious, 45, 570; of theological training, 143; of patrimony of the Church, 416; of patristic writings, 155. Cf. ADAPTATION.

Adaptation
of the Church, 622; – of religious to contemporary age, 131, 264, 320-324, 414-420, 475, 478; of nuns, 338-353, 720-724; of teaching religious, 441, 445-447; of Carmelites, 455; of Secular Institutes, 228, 230, 251, 275, 277; of

nursing sisters, 631; of monastic labour, 388-393, 723-724.
– in expounding doctrine, 144; in constitutions, leaving essentiais intact, 55, 210, 658, 660, 662, 720-722; in the training of young religious, 150, 152, 598, 618; in education of youth, 218, 302, 324, 554, 576, 601, 614; in the apostolate, 644, 650.
Prudence in –, 341, 389; – and tradition, 644, 720-722; and obedience, 323, 664; and perfection, 658, 660.

Administration
of goods of a Congregation: rights of the bishop, 20, 30; cf. TEMPORAL GOODS.
– of sacraments requires sound knowledge of theology, 609.

Admission
Conditions of – into religion, 96-105; – and responsibility of superiors, 62-64, 67, 69-70, 114; qualities needed for – into novitiate, 154. Cf. NOVITIATE, PROFESSION.

Alms
Episcopal vigilance over Congregations living by –, 13, 28, 82.

Apostle
Virtues required in –, 52, 212, 214, 422. Cf. APOSTOLATE.

Apostolate
of the Church, 726.
Mary, Queen of the –, 581.
–, essence of the religious life, 224; of religious Orders, 36, 320, 396, 405, 481, 522-524, 573, 583, 646, 682; – of nuns, 336-337, 344, 348, 351-353, 386-387; – of Secular Institutes, 229, 230, 231, 235, 239, 271, 275, 313-319; – of laity, 506, 522-523; of nursing sisters, 621-633; – of contemplatives, 169-177, 261, 342, 355.
Call to the –, 421-423; necessity of –, 524; importance of –, 622; vocation, foundation of –, 592; conditions of –, 415, 459, 463, 506-508, 639, 650-651;

qualities of –: adaptation, 321, 322,
338, 574, 618; culture, 606, 609;
interior life, 409-413, 640, 643, 682.
Training for –, 446; of young religious,
158, 617; of youth, 181; of laity, 179.
Avoidance of "activism" in – 1a, 211.
Cf. ACTION, MINISTRY, ZEAL.

Approval
of a new Congregation, 59, 61; of a
Secular Institute, 286-288, 295; of a
federation of monasteries, 378; of the
pontifical Institute "Regina Mundi,'
573-580.
– by the Holy See of a pontifical Congregation, 8, 9, 78, 132, 247, 249; by
the bishop of a diocesan Congregation,
8, 11-21, 77, 283.

Aptitudes
required as condition of admission to
religious life, 96; natural –, 456-458,
insufficient without supernatural virtues,
66; – necessary in professors of scholasticate, 158; adaptation of teaching to –
of the individual, 152, 302; especially in
the case of lay brothers, 167; need to
take account of capabilities in undertaking obligation of chastity, 530. Cf.
VIRTUE.

Asceticism
Safeguard of chastity of religious, 327,
330; antiquity of practice of –, 170,
221; tradition of – among Jesuits, 644;
importance of balanced doctrine of– ,
677-678. Cf. CHASTITY, PENITENCE,
RENUNCIATION, SACRIFICE.

Aspirants
Conditions for admission of – into
religion, 102, 105, 688; advice for
recruitment and training of – 149-152,
688. Cf. ADMISSION.

Assistance
to the sick: rôle of nursing sisters, 13,
621-633.

Associations
Cf. COMMUNITIES, SECULAR INSTITUTES,
FEDERATION.

Authority
of the Holy See over Congregations
of pontifical law, 23; approval by
legitimate ecclesiastical – for religious

Orders, 77; – of S. Congr. of Religious
over Secular Institutes, 242-243, 280-
285, 580; – of the Church, 42; of
Ordinaries over Congregations of diocesan law, 84.
– of Superiors: foundation in – of
Christ, 73, 255, 665; duty to exercise
–, 66, 683-685; qualities, 74, 255, 459,
600, 640, 665, 678, 683-685.
– of civil law, 41; respect for –, 478a,
634, 646; contempt for – among
modern youth, 439. Cf. LAW, JURIS-
DICTION.

Authorization
by Ordinary for foundation of establishment held by religious, 83; – by S.
Congr. of Religious for foundation of
Congregations, 57-61, Secular Institutes,
245-246; by S. Congr. for Oriental
Affairs for an Oriental who desires to
enter a Latin Institute, 100. Cf.
AUTHORITY, HIERARCHY.

Autonomy
of monasteries of nuns, 372; federations
of monasteries safeguard the – of each,
349, 373-376, 379; pontifical Work of
religious vocations safeguards—of particular Works, 565.

Benedict (Saint)
Cf. BENEDICTINES, RULE.

Benedictines
Letter to –, 253-270.
Praise of Rule of –: wisdom, 253-258,
677; influence, 259-262; actuality,
263-270.

Bishop
Rights of the – over pontifical Congregations, 9, 10, 22-32; over diocesan
Congregations, 8, 11-21, 78, 81, 83,
84; over Secular Institutes, 232,
244-246, 283, 285.
Duties of the – in relation to recruitment
of religious vocations, 467; prayer for
persecuted priests and religious, 552;
facilitate Confession in religious communities, 194.
Religious Orders auxiliaries to –, 33, 37,
45, 121, 173; obedience of regular
and secular clergy to –, 399-400;
entry of – into religion, 100. Cf.
DIOCESE, HIERARCHY, ORDINARY.

Body
Consecration of – to God in virginity, 493; modesty, respect for –, a member of Christ, 540; need for development of – in education, 602; pagan ways of modern world and seeking for pleasures of the –, 176.

Brothers
Definition, formation, functions of lay –, 166-167.
Teaching –, 168, 301-307, 553-558.
– of Christian Schools, 54-56, 324, 558.

Bruno (Saint)
169-177. Cf. CARTHUSIANS.

Call
Cf. VOCATION.

Cardinal Protector
Rights of – of a Congregation, 85; rights of religious to write freely to –, 122.

Carmelites (Discalced)
Allocution to –, 455-466.

Carthusians
Praise, special vocation, actuality of –, 169-177.

Catholic Action
Necessity and importance of –, 178-183; religious and –, 178-183; – in mission territories, 178; laity and –: formation, 179, importance of their rôle, 506; the young and –, 181-183; Secular Institutes and –, 279, 318. Cf. APOSTOLATE, HIERARCHY, LAITY.

Celibacy
Obligatory for priests of Latin rite, 402; source of grace for priest, 521; reason for –, 503; excellence of – and superiority to marriage, 514; renunciation of marriage in –, 530; – and spiritual paternity, 506a; – in Oriental Church, 502; in Secular Institutes, 239. Cf. CHASTITY, PURITY.

Censure
Powers of bishop in relation to –, 26.

Chant
Gregorian – and divine Office, 174.

Chaplain
appointed by bishop in diocesan Congregations, 21.

Chapter
Rights of –: in pontifical Congregations, 22, 80; for admission into a religious society, 101; in the case of dismissal of a novice, 113; – and adaptation within teaching Orders, 447.

Charity
1. Union with God in – 192, 690-698, 704-705; – towards God, foundation of religious obedience, 459, 681; – towards God and – towards the neighbour, 56, 266, 573.
2. –, measure of perfection, 473; custodian of chastity, 542; motive of chastity, 495-498; contemplative life a form of –, 509, 690-698, 725, mere doing good not –, 413.
3. Sanctity and –, 604, 653; faith and –, 413; obedience and –, 214, 669; renunciation and –, 213; apostolate and –, 351, 617, 720-726; virginity and –, 506-508, 510, 525, 623.
4. Universality of –, 267; works of – and interior life, 411; and adaptation, 338, 478.
5. –, goal of religious, 573, 622, 669, 703-705; –, in contemplative life, 692-693, 702-708; the religious, a messenger of Christ's –, 677; manifestations of – of religious, 35, 38, 45, 131, 151, 183, 258, 453, 629; –, a duty of religious, 53, 71, 267, 423, 660; of superiors, 73-75, 479, 640, 678; of masters of novices, 110; of teachers, 600; of women religious, 325, 336-337, 436, 454.
Practice of charity in Secular Institutes, 239; among Benedictines, 253, 254, 257, 261.
Formation of young religious to –, 165; of women religious to – 699-701.
Community life, an exercise of –, 627.

Chastity
1. *Nature of* –: one of the three vows of religion, 76, 133, 134, 486; spiritual marriage, 494; evangelical counsel, not a precept, 527; a gift of God, 528; sacrifice of self, 489, 529; not a necessary condition for perfection, 526.
2. *Teaching on* – : in pagan religious,

460, 482; in Old Testament, 482, 503; in early Church, 483.

3. *Obligation of* –: for religious, 71, 443; undertaken at subdiaconate, 486; for Secular Institutes, 239, 486; for certain lay people, 486; prudence in undertaking the obligation of –, 530; training in –, 155, 460-462.

4. *Motives for*– : for priest, 502-503; for consecrated souls, love and imitation of Christ, 497-498; for combat against concupiscence, 517.

5. *Practice of* –: 526-547.

6 *Safeguarding of*– : 533-547; grace of God, 462, 531-532; prayer, 462, 533, 543; penitence, 462, 535; vigilance, 529, 534; flight from sin, 536-537; modesty, 540-542; charity, 542; Eucharist, 543-544; devotion to Our Lady, 545-547; sacrament of Penance, 543-544; enclosure, 347.

7. *Worth of* –; and balanced personality, 515-518; – does not impoverish human personality, 520; – and self-mastery, 517; – does not isolate from human society, 446, 525; – and spiritual liberty, 518; – and nervous afflictions, 532; fruits of – for the apostolate, 525. Cf. CELIBACY, PURITY, VIRGINITY, VOWS.

Children

Rôle of religious in Christian formation of –, 48, 507; this formation demands sureness of doctrine, 609; widespread practice of frequent Communion among –, 185; Christian parents should favour vocation of their –, 550; assistance of – due to parents: an impediment to entry into religion, 100. Cf. EDUCATION, YOUTH, VOCATION.

Christ

Cf. JESUS CHRIST.

Christian life

Perfection of – 653-658; renewal of –, aim of religious, 320.

Church

1. *Nature of the Church:* the mystical Body of Christ, 651; the city of God, 43; the soul of the world, 264, 622; a visible, hierarchical society, 595; her mission, 35, 51, 725-726.

2. *Church and religious life:* constant esteem of – for religious life, 4, 131-136, 220-222, 325-326; preference of Church for community life, 223-225; religious life, reflection of holiness of the Church, 512-513.

3. *Church and religious:* place and rôle of religious in the –, 33, 35, 53a, 324, 397, 507, 626, 676; religious in the service of the –, 325, 333, 447, 634-635, 655, 660; purpose of religious Orders also goal of the –, 70, 165, 397, 671; holiness of religious, benefit for the –, 51; utility of religious Orders for the –, 5-6; of contemplatives, 172, 177, 525; of Secular Institutes, 227, 231, 313; of nuns: apostolate, 351-353, work, 350; of teaching sisters, 436; education given by religious, 436; – and persecution of religious Orders, 39-53.

4. *Church and clergy;* differences between secular and regular clergy dependent on decisions of the –, 398; call of the –, an essential element of vocation, 594-595; secular and regular clergy at service of the –, 399-400, 585.

5. *Church and virginity:* – gives an official character to vow of virginity, 326-327; perpetual virginity, source of strength for the –, 461, 482; image of holiness of the –, 512-513; proof of vitality of the –, 625; perfect chastity, honour of the –, 510.

6. *Church and sacred science:* Catholic faith, a patrimony to be preserved by the –, 416; importance of Latin in the –, 153; importance of Thomism in the –, 611a; edification of the –, goal of sacred learning, 218.

7 *Church and adaptation:* founders of religious orders met the needs of their epoch, 415; new conditions bring new requirements in the –, 342; the – adapts itself to these needs, 622; religious must adapt themselves to needs of the –, 644; Catholic Action forms auxiliaries for the –, 181. Cf. MYSTICAL BODY, HIERARCHY, HOLY SEE.

Church (building)

Authorization and vigilance of the bishop in relation to erection of churches and public oratories in religious houses, 24, 32, 83; religious poverty and resources required for decoration of –, 463.

Civic (life)
Education of civic sense of modern girls by parochial teaching sisters, 570-572. Cf. FATHERLAND.

Civilisation
Catholic truth transcends all –, 466; religious Orders, a factor of –, 36, 37, 256, 259, 260, 316.

Clergy
Place of secular – and regular – in the Church, 5, 40, 468, 585, 588; distinction between secular and regular –, 398, 399-400, 467-474; union of secular and regular – in the apostolate, 121, 173, 180, 183, 469. Cf. REGULAR, SECULAR, PRIEST.

Clerical
Definition of – religious society, 77; clerical dignity open to religious and laics, 398; – state and obligation of perfection, 401-402; – vocation and the ministry, 595; history of practice of community life and – life in the Church, 583.

Clerics
Distinction between –, religious and laics, 397, 469; – can enter religious state, 398, conditions, 100, 102; – are not bound to evangelical counsels, 402; religious – bound to perfection because of religious profession, 402; submission of – to bishop, 400; regular – and priesthood, 583; regular – of Mother of God, 301-307; – members of Secular Institutes and perfection, 403; Secular Institutes can be associations of –, 235, 274; incardination of religious –, 225; studies of –, 136, 153; Communion of –, 185; Confession of –, 88, 196; formation of young – to chastity, 537-539; to modesty, 540-541; to holiness, 603; to Thomism, 611. Cf. CLERGY.

Colleges
Vigilance of Ordinaries over –, 31; establishing of – for young aspirants to priesthood, 149; Communion in –, 187; Catholic Action in –, 178-183. Cf. EDUCATION, YOUTH.

Commitment
to chastity, 486; special grace attached to this undertaking, 531; freedom to

undertake this –, 528; – to state of perfection, 704; prudence in regard to contacts with world, 539. Cf. CONSECRATION, VOWS.

Common (life)
Essential to religious life, 76, 77, 134; obligatory for religious, 119, 133, 171; but not for members of Secular Institutes, 231, 236, 241; an exercise of charity, 573; protection for the interior life, 627; practice of – in history of the Church, 583.

Communities
Organization of growth of female – in history of Church, 328-333, 483; preference of Church for profession of perfection in approved –, 223; family character of Benedictine –, 255; mutual relations of members of – and between –, 661-675; adaptation: safeguarding the spirit of –, 662; regulations for Confession in female –, 90-94, 193, 194; and for Communion, 187. Cf. CONGREGATIONS, FEMALE, ORDERS, RELIGIOUS.

Communion
Supernatural means for preserving chastity, 543-544; *Instruction* to prevent abuses of frequent –, 184-209; benefits of –, 184-185, 192, 193; conditions of –, 186, 189, 190, 191; dangers of general –, 187-188, 193, 202, 209; precautions to be taken against this danger, 189-202; advice for avoidance of social pressure, 203-209.

Competence
Required by religious in their ministry, 142; need for – in teachers of young religious, 158, 611; need for – in religious engaged in teaching, 449, 480; – required in all female religious, 573-580; obligation of superior to attend to this requirement, 480. Cf. PROFESSION.

Confession
Co-operation of secular and regular clergy for ministry of –, 121, 142; duty of superiors to facilitate – of their subjects, 193-194; especially of female religious, 196-198; of students in

colleges, 195; –, spiritual remedy to preserve chastity, 543-544. Cf. CONFESSOR, SIN.

Confessor
Regulations for nomination and rôle of – in female Congregations, 29, 89, 90, 93, 94, 194, 195, 196, 198; freedom of female religious in choice of –, 89, 91-92, 193, 196, 197, 201; in Orders of men religious, the superior not the habitual – of his subjects, 88; in colleges, a – available before Communion, 202; likewise at Catholic gatherings, 209. Cf. CONFESSION.

Confidence
in God, 56, 617; in the Heart of Jesus, source of strength, 53; – of states of perfection in relation to Holy See, 672, 687; of superiors in relation to their subjects, 640; of heads of families in teaching sisters, 444, 449.

Congregation
– of Bishops and Regulars, 58-60.
– of Religious; headquarters of pontifical Work of Religious Vocations, 561, 565; authority of – over Institute " Regina Mundi," 580; authority over Secular Institutes, 242, 245, 246, 248, 278‘ 280, 283, 284, 286; – and enclosure, 364, – and tobacco, 429.
– de Propaganda Fide and Institutes dedicated to the missions, 242.
– of the Council : jurisdiction over associations of the faithful which have not the character of Secular Institutes, 243.
Oriental –: jurisdiction over Orientals desirous of entering a Latin institute, 100.

Congregations (religious)
Place of – in the Church, 397; definition of religious –, 77; laws concerning religious – of simple vows, 7-32, 57-61; religious belonging to – of simple vows are not nuns, 356; regulations for foundation and suppression of –, 78-87; – of teaching brothers, 168; missionary religious and the interests of their own –, 433-435; fraternal collaboration between teaching –, 453. Cf. COMMUNITIES, ORDERS, RELIGIOUS.

Congress
Letters or Discourses of Pius XII on the occasion of congresses of religious: to the first international – of religious, 320-324, 394-423; to first international – of teaching sisters, 436-454; to – of superiors general of female Congregations, 475-481; to – of teaching men religious, 553-558; to – of parochial teaching sisters of France, 570-572, 647-649; to – of nursing sisters, 621-633; to second general – of states of perfection, 650-675.

Conscience
1. Training of – in relation to Communion, 189-192; to teach proper use of one's liberty, 667; liberty of – of men and women religious in relation to Confession, 95, 200.
2. Young clerics must be conscious of their responsibility, 617.
3. Professional sense of nursing sisters, 633. Cf. DIRECTOR.

Consecration
– to God, motive of Chisitan virginity,– 492, 493, 496, 505, 506; obligation of religious, 660; of missionaries, 431; of nursing sisters, 625; in the spirit of sacrifice, 622; possible in the world (Secular Institutes), 229, 230, 239, 276, 278, 291, 311; 657, 679, 696.
– to Christ of consecrated virgins, 325, 326; more complete in solemn than in other public vows, 345; Church always showed favour to – to Christ, 221.
Union of – to God and the apostolate, 411, 506, 522-524, 725-726; – and Christian perfection, 653-654; religious habit should express – to Christ, 478. Task of consecrated souls: prayer and contemplation, 140, 677, 691-708; work, 711; generosity of consecrated souls, 679. Cf. COMMITMENT, VOW.

Constitutions
Fidelity to –, condition of effective work, 210-214, 426, 663; obedience to – informed by holiness, 604; means of sanctification, 646; work by nuns in accordance with the –, 383, 711; duty of superiors to have – read publicly, 87. Cf. RULE.

Contemplation
Means of perfection, 694-701; task of consecrated souls, 140, 697; means of union with God, 145; essential nature of contemplative life, 169, 689-726.

Contemplative (life)
History, importance and actuality of –, 169-177; definition of canonical –, 344, 690-701; the –: principal aim of monastic life, 358, 697-698; –, special form of religious life of nuns, 330, 336-337, 357, 690-726; different kinds of nuns and unity of –, 355, 690; –, form of charity towards the neighbour, 509; contributes to good of the Church, 525; enclosure and –, 347, 348, 364, 365, 719, 720; Holy Family of Nazareth, model of union between active and –, 564; union between – and apostolate, 336-337, 342, 350, 355, 387, 411-412, 614; – and virginity, 509; and theological culture, 141. Cf. ACTIVE (LIFE).

Contemplative (Orders)
Distinction between – and active Orders, 337; work in the spirit of penitence in –, 350.

Conversi
In religious Orders, – not designated for priesthood, 584; advice for special training of –, 166-168.

Councils
Texts of –, witness to Church's interest in religious life, 220.
Council of Trent and religious discipline, 62; and virtues of religious, 133; and chastity, 531; on virginity and marriage, 514.
Council of Vatican, 690.

Courage
in adaptation to present-day needs, 447; in struggle for justice and truth, 54; in mortification of senses to preserve chastity, 535; in persecution, 51, 53, 551-552; –, a virtue to be inculcated on young clerics, 617; generous –, feature of Benedictine rule, 254.

Crisis
of female religious vocations, 476-478; reasons for – among the young, and remedies, 437-442.

Critical (mentality)
malady of the age, a danger for the apostolate, 214.

Culture
theological – required by contemplatives, 144, 699; in active religious Orders, 142-145; cultivation of spirit of faith in studies, 163; of spirit of charity and piety in studies, 165.
Intellectual formation directed to supernatural virtues, 163; for the glory of God, 218; object of Catholic school, 301, 304; – of young religious, 605-614; classical – and knowledge of Latin, 464-465; artistic – encouraged by superiors, 480.
Training of *natural virtues* in young religious intended for the priesthood, 456-458, 601-602.
Catholic truth transcends civilisations and cultures, 466; adaptation of training in Christian education, 554; Benedictines and civilisation, 259, 260. Cf. FORMATION, INTELLIGENCE, KNOWLEDGE, CIVILISATION.

Dedication
Religious life, life of –, 131, 458, 679; to Christ, 220, to the Church, 333, 352, 687, to the neighbour, 315, 525; –, a virtue required for teachers, 302; for teaching sisters, 436; for nursing sisters, 633; desire for –, motive for entering religion, 405; – in consecrated virginity, 506. Cf. APOSTOLATE, ZEAL.

Defection
of religious and responsibilities of superiors, 62-75.

Detachment
Spirit of – in religious, 48, 679-682. Cf. POVERTY, SACRIFICE (SPIRIT OF), RENUNCIATION.

Dignity
– *of states of perfection*, 559; application to studies as safeguard of religious –, 145, 606-607; *priestly* – and states of perfection, 583; intellectual formation demanded by –, 606, 608; safeguarding – of religious, 323.
– *of the human person*: give sense of – to the young, 307; chastity and balanced personality, 515-518; chastity does not

impoverish human personality, 520; religious obedience not contrary to –, 665; enriches human personality, 668. *Clerical* – accessible to religious and to laics, 398; – of work shown in teaching of St. Benedict, 269.

Diocesan (law)
Definition of a Congregation of –, 77; regulation for Congregations of –; 7-21, 61, 78, 81, 83, 84, 124.

Diocese
Impediment to entry into religion for cleric attached by oath to service of –, 100.

Director (spiritual)
Vigilance of – in discernment of vocations, 408, 530, 596; in relation to Communion, 189; freedom of female religious in their choice of –, 89, 196. Cf. CONFESSOR.

Discipline
Vigilance of Holy See over –, 673; of bishops and superiors, 32, 683-685; example of teachers in relation to –, 305; obedience, basis of religious –, 638, 660, 638-685, 687; priestly dignity and ecclesiastical –, 638; – necessary for the apostolate, 639; – not to be reduced to formalism, 637, 639; –not to be relaxed, 640; freedom of conscience in –, 200; formation to – in novitiates, 112, and in seminaries, 205. Cf. AUTHORITY, OBEDIENCE.

Discretion
of superiors in respect of Confession of female religious, 196-197, 199-202.

Dispensation
Right of Holy See to give –, 23; of the S. Congr. of Religious, 364; of the bishop, 26, 299; responsibility of superiors in regard to dispensation from vows, 62-75. Cf. VOWS.

Distress
Relief of –, special field of action of religious, 418; poverty and charity of religious in face of contemporary –, 423.

Doctor
Rôle of – in discerning physical aptitude for vocation, 530, 532.

Doctors of the Church
Cf. FATHERS OF THE CHURCH.

Doctrine
Catholic – transcends epochs, civilisations, cultures, 466. Vigilance of Holy See over doctrine of religious communities, 673; of the bishop over – of religious Congregations, 32. Learning (sacred and profane) at service of Catholic –, 143-144, 153, 162; religious have duty to spread learning, 157, 158, 260; solid – required in educators, 599; in the apostolate, 609; union between religious life and –, 215; respect for principles of catholic –, 218-219.

Dogma
Cf. DOCTRINE.

Economic
– conditions nowadays and rule of nuns, 342-343, 723-724; federations of monasteries contribute to mutual – assistance 382; – requirements of hospitals and religious poverty, 628.

Education
Religious life and –: priority of religious life over –, 55-56; religious life not an obstacle to –, 443-447.
The Church and – of the young: fundamental rôle of religious, 45, 48, 436, 622; – of youth: an essential work entrusted to religious, 137, 173, 405, 418, 507, 677; Congregations of Brothers dedicated to –, 168, 301, 324, 553-558.
Aims of education at present day, 306-307, 450, 554, 555a, 667; method of –, 601-602; contemporary difficulties of –, 451, 576; families and –, 45, 149, 444.
Importance of education of young candidates for religious life, 150-151; formation of teaching sisters for education, 446, to be facilitated by their superiors, 480.
Formation to Catholic Action, an essential element of –, 181-183; civic education of girls, 570-572.

Educators (men)
Aim of religious –, 139; need for prudent – for young religious intended

or the priesthood, 598; qualities required in –, 302, 554, 554a, 599-600; – and vocations of the young, 549, 557-558; and training to chastity, 460-462, 540-541; responsibility of Christian –, 554; functions of the –, 556; rôle of the –, 667; importance of the mission of the –, 555.

Educators (women)
Letter to parochial teaching sisters of France, 570-572, 647-649; need for suitable training and culture for teaching sisters, 576; formation of religious teachers in specialized institutions, 577; teaching sisters not strangers to the world, 446. Cf. EDUCATION, TEACHING, YOUTH.

Election
of superiors of diocesan Congregations, 19. Cf. SUPERIORS.

Enclosure
Protection for religious life, 330, 347; 364; obligation of – for postulants, 98, need for adaptation of –, 338, 339, 342 – 348, 364, 387a.
Pontifical –; 336, 338, 347-348, 363, 367; major –, 347, 364; minor –, 348, 355, 365, 367; enclosure, necessary condition for solemn vows, 366; federation of monasteries not contrary to law of –, 349.
Episcopal –, 25, 32.
Duties of superiors in relation to –, 640.

Error
Affirmation of Catholic truth against contemporary –, 466; enquiry into the sources of –: method of understanding, 440; sympathy for those in –, but not for – itself, 219.

Eucharist
Cf. COMMUNION, EUCHARISTIC SACRIFICE.

Eucharistic sacrifice
Primary motive of priestly chastity, 503; gives efficacy to prayers of contemplatives, 169. Cf. COMMUNION.

Evangelization
of pagan nations, missionary vocation, 431. Cf. MISSIONS.

Evangelical counsels
Foundation and *raison d'être* of religious Orders, 33, 53a, 221; observance of –, essential to religious state, 76, 130, 134, 220, 229, 407, 421, 474: practice of – in the world: purpose of Secular Institutes, 235, 271, 290, 403, 657; private vows, 696; practice of – as means towards perfection, 4, 43, 407, 653, 655; position of secular and regular clergy in relation to –, 402, 407, 469; perfect chastity and –, 504, 527. Cf. GOSPEL, STATE OF PERFECTION, VOWS.

Examination
by Ordinary of rules of a new institute, 11-12, 60, 287; – of postulants, 63-64, 67, 69-70, 105.

Exempt
Definition of an – religious society, 77; conditions for foundation, 83, and suppression, 84, of an – religious house; – religious and obedience to the Ordinary, 374, 400; confessors of – houses, 196.

Existentialism
Warning against –, 410, 677.

Experience
required for education of young religious, 599; diocesan – of associations seeking to become Secular Institutes, 287. Cf. COMPETENCE, PROFESSION.

Expiation
Cf. PENITENCE.

Faith
Means of union with God, 146; virtue required in apostles, 212, in educators, 554; constituent of vocation, 454; a comfort in face of ingratitude, 53; patrimony of the Church to be preserved, 416; life of – in answer to persecutions, 50; genuine charity proceeds from living –, 413.

Science and –: need for union between – and science, 218; sacred learning is knowledge of mysteries of the –, 141; learning at the service of the faith, 143; profane knowledge not hostile to –, 161; studies and spirit of –, 163; pride in science and loss of –, 164; scholastic method combines reason and –, 160, 161.

Christian education and –, 306, 319, 442, 450, 454, 554; virginity a witness of –, 510; a religious should be competent to defend the –, 158; courage of confessors of the –, 552; nursing sisters and spirit of faith, 633; adaptation and the –, 419; – in contemplative life, 716.

Faithful
Jurisdiction of Pope over all the –, 400, 672; example and assistance given to – by religious, 121, 135a; distinction between associations of the – and Secular Institutes, 274, 279, 284; formation of – for Catholic Action, 179; duties of –: frequent Communion, 185, prayer for persecuted religious, 552. Cf. LAITY.

Family
Holy Family of Nazareth, model for nuns at work, 350; patron of Work of religious vocations, 564.
– life in religious houses, 255, 458, 479; – and religious education, 149, 444, 449, 554; – life and Secular Institutes, 231; – life and priestly ministry, 529; and virginity, 492; and spiritual progress, 499, 624b; and apostolate, 500, 522-524; and vocation, 550; and education of children to purity, 541. Cf. CELIBACY, MARRIAGE, VOCATION.

Fatherland
Devotion of religious to –, 45, 48; missionary religious and –, 138, 431; Christians in service of welfare of –, 572.

Fathers of the Church
Relevance of writings of –, 155; concern of – with religious life, proved by numerous texts, 220-222.
Teaching of –: charity of brides of Christ, 495-496; virginity: in the primitive Church, 325-337, 482-484, 490-498, 501-503, 511, 513-514, 516, 524, 527-529, 531, 536-537, 542-543, 545-547, 550; union of faith and learning, 139, 144-145, 147, 153, 161, 163, 164; education, 554a, 556, 600; fidelity to Holy See, 636; frequent

Confession, 195. Writings of – to be studied by priests, 144; by the faithful, 568.

Fear
of God, foundation of modesty, 542; religious state not a refuge for timorous souls, 404; – of superior and dangers of abuse of Communion, 187.

Federation
Purpose of – of monasteries, 376, 382; autonomy of monasteries and –, 349, 373, 375, 376, 379, 382; Holy See and –, 349, 376, 377, 378, 380, 381.

Female
Pontifical texts addressed to – Congregations: 313-319, 436-454, 475-481, 570-572, 621-633, 647-649, 689-726.
History of female communities, 328-333.
– Congregations, 13, 86. Cf. RELIGIOUS.
Young girls, 438. Cf. EDUCATION.
Women in public life, 451, 570-572.

Fidelity
of *God* in giving grace, 532.
of *religious*: to spirit of founders, 54, 137, 210-219, 303, 322, 422, 663, 678; to constitutions, 71, 183, 210-214, 333, 389, 425-426, 678; to teachings of magisterium, 217-219, 313, 466, 611, 635, 672, 677; to Thomism, 159-162, 216.
of *nuns* to their vocation to apostolate, 386-387.
–, a virtue necessary to religious, 457, 617; bond of – between members of Secular Institutes, 311. Cf. OBEDIENCE, OBSERVANCE.

Formation
General Statutes for – of religious destined for the priesthood, " Sedes Sapientiae," 581-620.
1. *Importance* of –, 155, 554; purpose of novitiate, 126, 128; purpose of ecclesiastical studies, 613; formation of perfect Christians, purpose of education, 450; primacy of religious – in novitiate, 126, 128; –, goal of Catholic school, 301.
2. *Qualities* of –, solid, 598-600; based on culture and natural virtues, 602,

605, 615; intellectual – and culture, 464; – and adaptation, 321, 574; and vocation, 454.

3. *Duty of superiors* to ensure –, 62-63, 65, 67, 70, 480a, 480b, 610; duty of *religious*: to possess –, 142, 454, 480, 630; to impart –, 45, 48, 112, 139, 449, 553-558; special obligation of masters of novices, 112, educators, 139, 553-558, 609, teaching sisters, 499, Secular Institutes, 230, 241.

4. *Effective* – facilitated by the constitutions, 446; federations of monasteries, 382, 648; methods of Jesuits, 211.

5. – *of young religious*, 179-180, 610; of aspirants, 149-152; of novices, 155, 382; of lay brothers, 166-168; of young clerics, 615-619; of youth in general, 139, 181, 307, 449, 451, 454, 553-558, 570-572, 609; of children, 48; of laity, 179, 507; foundation of establishments for – of young religious, 575, 577.

6. – *of soul*, 554, of character, 449, 556, of consciences, 189-192.

7. *Formation to* sanctity, 603-604, 605, 615; apostolate, 181, 574; contemplative life, 699-701; purity, 537, 539; labour, 480; pastoral work, 605, 615-619; discipline, 112; the ministry, 142; fidelity, 451; spirit of sacrifice, 307; Catholic Action, 179-181; good citizenship, 570-572. Cf. EDUCATION.

Foundation
of religious houses, in accordance with canon law, 78-87; rights of Holy See over –, 11a; of bishops over –, 12, 24, 42; – of Congregations of simple vows, 57-61, 220, 252; of Secular Institutes, 238-241, 244, 246, 285, 286; – of the Carthusians, 174; – of federations of monasteries, reserved to Holy See, 349, 377; history of – of religious life, 221, and of Orders of nuns, 335; – of pontifical Work of religious vocations, 559-569; of Institute " Regina Mundi," 578; – of Catholic Action groups in colleges, 178-183.

Founders
Numerous – of religious institutes canonized, 47; religious should follow example of their –, 51, 263, 415;

fidelity of religious to spirit of their –, 54, 137, 210-219, 303, 322, 422, 663, 678; respect for will of –, 80; holiness desired by –, purpose of religious, 75; encouraged sacred study, 147.

Fraternity
Cf. CHARITY.

Fruitfulness
of virginity, 506-509, 510, 624b; virginity, a reflection of the – of the Church, 513; – of witness given by Christian home, 523. Cf. GRACE.

Glory of God
Zeal for –, purpose of religious, 50, 70, 131, 137, 163, 169, 218, 263, 431, 617.

God
God alone is absolute wisdom, 164; faithful in giving necessary graces, 520, 532; kingdom of God, 552, 687, 725-726.
Love of –, confidence in –, knowledge of –, consecration to –, fear of –, glory of –, obedience to –, the priest and –, the superior and –, union with –, virginity, a sacrifice to –, call of –. Cf. *Corresponding words.*

Goodness
Cf. CHARITY.

Gospel
and Christian perfection, 653, and contemplative life, 705-706; – simplicity, virtue of religious, 617; authority of superiors to be exercised in spirit of the –, 665; light of the – in Christian education, 554; evangelical perfection and separation from the world, 679; right coming from the – to lead the religious life, 42. Cf. EVANGELICAL COUNSELS.

Grace
Necessary – never wanting, 532; – and God's call, 593; efficaciousness of –, 679; – obtained by prayer of contemplatives, 177; – in Christian education, 554; in religious life, 679; – and chastity, 462, 517, 531-532; – proper to virginity, 520-521; to marriage, 519, 624; lay brothers have same spiritual favours as other religious, 166.

Habit (religious)

should express consecration to Christ, 478; should express religious simplicity and modesty, 445; should be adapted to contemporary requirements, 478; special – for each Institute, 58, 78, 119, 133; difference in – for postulants and novices, 98; taking of – at beginning of novitiate, 106; members of Secular Institutes have not protection of –, 231.

Hatred

of world for Church and persecution of religious orders, 43, 49.

Hierarchy

Organization of – in the Church, 397, 595; interdiocesan and universal hierarchical organization in Secular Institutes, 277; apostolate of religious in union with –, 650, 676; authority of – and religious Orders, 77; cooperation of Secular Institutes with –, 297; obedience to – not to be replaced by a " democratic " egalitarianism, 638, 687. Cf. CHURCH, BISHOP, MAGISTERIUM, ORDINARY.

History of the Church

History shows constant concern of Church for religious life, 220; – to be taught in scholasticate, 158. Cf. CHURCH.

Holiness

Christ, model of –, 2.
– and charity, 604; – independent of state of life, 472; relation of religious life to –, 224, 225; reflection of holiness of Church, 325.
Religious and –: purpose of religious life, 75, 263, 322, 397, 417, 573, 595; numerous religious canonized, 47, 262, 405; – required in: apostles, 212; contemplatives, 169, 177, 333, 335, 689-690; educators, 158, 599; Jesuits, 646; Benedictines, 253; brothers, 166; members of Secular Institutes, 234.
Formation to –: 70, 603-605, 615.
Evangelical counsels and –, 130; – and virginity, 501, 510, 512-513, 526; and marriage, 519-520.
Theology and –, 147; science and –, 144; persecution and –, 51. Cf. PERFECTION.

Holy See

Supreme direction of religious institutes by – 35, 676; rights of – over foundation and suppression of religious houses, 57-61, 78-87; concern of – for religious Orders, 132, 136; in particular for persecuted religious, 39-53; relations of states of perfection with –, 650, 672-674, 687.

Vigilance of – on application of regulations of " Sedes Sapientiae," 588; duties of – in relation to missionary institutes, 435; authority of – over federations of monasteries, 349, 376, 377, 378, 381. Knowledge by religious of decrees of –, 87; obedience of religious to –, 478a, 687; attachment of Jesuits to –, 634, 636, 646; right of religious to correspond freely with –, 122. Cf. POPE, HIERARCHY, MAGISTERIUM.

Holy Spirit

Light of – for consecrated souls, 679, for educators, 599.

Hospitals

Vigilance of bishop over – managed by religious, 13, 31, 83; –, result of charity of the Church, 629; rôle of sisters in –, 629; economic requirements of – and religious poverty, 628. Cf. NURSING SISTERS.

House

religious –: definition, 77; conditions of foundation of religious –, 81-84; special – for novitiate, 107, 128, 156; confessors in religious –, 88, 196, 201; difference between religious – and family home, 458; community – for members of Secular Institutes, 241, 292, 300; educational establishments: formation to Catholic Action, 181-183; custom of frequent Communion in educational establishments, 185-187.

Humility

A virtue that is never out of date, 2, 658, 678, 714; religious should give the example of –, 71, especially educators, 436; – and religious obedience, 665, 678; necessity of – in studies, 164-165; –, foundation of modesty, 542; special characteristic of Benedictines, 254, of Jesuits, 639;

humble duties of lay brothers, source of graces, 167. Cf. PRIDE.

Ignatius of Loyola (Saint)
Fidelity of Jesuits to spirit of –, 212, 634-636. Cf. JESUITS.

Imitation
of Christ in religious life, 220, 407, 660; supreme motive of perfect chastity, 497-498; imitation of Christ at Nazareth in contemplative life, 172; of the Holy Family in work of nuns, 350; imitation of example of founders, a duty of religious, 137. Cf. JESUS CHRIST, MODEL.

Impediments
Nature of impediments to entry into religion, 96-105. Cf. ADMISSION.

Indigenous (clergy)
Collaboration between – and missionaries, 432.

Infantilism
Practice of religious obedience and –, 666-667.

Infidels
Evangelization of –, purpose of missionary vocation, 138, 431, 507. Cf. MISSIONS, SALVATION.

Institutes
Difference between – and religious Orders, 6; religious – in the service of the Church, 35; fidelity to purpose of –, 54; obedience of religious to rules of –, 137, 678; mutual aid between provinces of the same –, 151; rules for postulancy, 97, and novitiate, 126, 128, in Institutes; missionary – and the Holy See, 435; understanding between different missionary –, 435; missionary does not seek interests of his own –, 431; master of novices of clerical – should be a priest, 110; entry of Orientals into a Latin –, 100; – of men have not authority over Congregations of women, 86; approbation of Institute for higher studies of women religious, 578-580. Cf. ORDERS (RELIGIOUS), SECULAR INSTITUTES.

26

Intelligence
Quality of educator, 554; of novice: necessary, 154, but not sufficient, 64; enlightened by light of the Gospel, 554; formation of intelligence of young religious, 464-465, 610. Cf. CULTURE, STUDIES.

Interior life
Distinction between – common to all and canonical contemplative life, 358, 690-701; –, pedagogical resource for teaching sisters, 313; – nourished by study, 146-148; – protected by community life, 627; apostolate and –, 409-413, 643; formation of novices to –, 155.

Jesuits
Discourses to –, for twenty-ninth general congregation, 210-219, and for thirtieth general congregation, 634-646. Specific characteristics of –: fidelity to doctrine, 215-217, to St. Thomas, 216, 636, to constitutions, 210-214, to the Pope, a special vow, 635; complete obedience, 214, 637-638.
Virtues required in –: 213-214, 639-645; in particular, respect for spirit of St. Ignatius, 212, in order to sanctify themselves by means of their institute, 646; third year of probation, 211.

Jesus Christ
Teacher and model of perfection, 2; call of – to perfection, 33, 130; ideal of perfection traced by –, 35; Christian perfection that of the Cross of –, 653; model of authority for superior, 73, 640; model of chastity, 495-498, 520, 531.
Love of religious for –: leave all things to follow him, 75, 213, 220; – in Benedictine life, 257; teaching sisters, 436, 447, 454; nursing sisters, 625, 626; contemplatives, 704-705, 716; love of – in religious obedience, 669.
Imitation of –: contemplative life, 172; vow of obedience, 407; dignity of labour, 269; duty of religious, 660.
Religious, an image of –, by interior life and sacred studies, 146; missionary, ambassador of –, 431; vows and the liberty of –, 4, 713; see – in every sick person, 632-633.
Consecration to –: favoured by the

Church, 221; of consecrated virgins, 325, 494, 496, 625, 705-708; expressed by religious habit, 478.
Teaching of – *on virginity*, 488-489; love of –, motive of virginity, 494-499, 623; virginity, reflection of holiness of –, 512-513; virginity, spiritual marriage between – and soul, 494, 625; respect for body, member of –, by modesty, 540.

Joy
through religious obedience practised in charity, 669.

Jurisdiction
of the Pope over dioceses and the faithful, 400; delegated to superiors, 676; of cardinal protector of institute over religious, 85; of the Ordinary over Congregations of pontifical law, 9, 10, and exempt Congregations, 77. Cf. LAW, AUTHORITY.

Justice
Virtue necessary in religious, 71, 457; required in educators, 600; the education of youth a duty in –, 151; – in wages of employees, 463; spirit of – in labour, 269; appeal for – in relation to rights of religious schools, 444.

Knowledge
of God, necessary for religious, 141; *of the world*, necessary for the apostolate, 415; *of the contemplative life*, 691-701; – necessary for educational work, 440, 576; – of working-class life, 649; *humane* –: limits, 164; *professional* – required for teaching sisters, 480; for nursing sisters, 630. Cf. DOCTRINE, SCIENCE, STUDIES, TEACHING.

Laity
Definition of a religious society, 77. Distinction between clerics, religious and –, 397-398; Secular Institutes and associations of clerics or of –, 235, 274; perfection to be striven for by –, 471, 657, 696; perfect chastity practised by numerous –, 486; – and Catholic Action, 179; and apostolate, 524; lay apostles in works of education, 436; Christian charity and good works of –, 413. Cf. APOSTOLATE, CATHOLIC ACTION, FAITHFUL.

Latin
Importance of – in the Church, 153, 464-465.

Law
Distinction of *divine* – between clerics and laics, 397; *divine* – and secular and regular clergy, 398-400; cleric not obliged by *divine* – to evangelical counsels, 402.
Civil – and solemn vows, 346. Cf. CANON LAW, DIOCESAN, PONTIFICAL, CONSTITUTIONS, RULE.

Law (Canon)
Extracts from Code of – on spirit and obligations of religious life, 76-125; numerous prescriptions of –, proof of concern of the Church for religious life, 220, 222; need for regulations supplementary to –, reason for "Provida Mater Ecclesia," 226-229; reminder of prescriptions of – concerning Confession of female religious, 196-198. For canons of the Code cited in this work, cf. INDEX OF CANONS OF THE CODE.

Lay Brothers
Definition, training, functions, 166. Instructions for special training of –, 166-168; in religious Orders, – not destined for priesthood, 584. Cf. CONVERSI.

Liberty
and religious vows, 3, 4, 33, 406-407; and virginity, 489, 495, 499-500, 502; – from impediments: condition of admission into religion, 96, 105, 113, 114; – of Confession of women religious, 88, 89, 90-92, 95, 193, 196-198, 199-202; freedom to abstain from Communion, 207, 209; freedom of opinion on controverted questions, 466, 612; distinction between charity and false –, 639; education of conscience and –, 667; freedom of schools, 444.

Love
of God and the neighbour. Cf. CHARITY.

Loyalty
a natural virtue required in religious, 457; – in the relations between the Holy See and states of perfection, 672.

Magisterium

Concern of – for religious life, 221; fidelity to teaching authority, 217, 636; of Jesuits particularly, 217, 636, of Carmelites, 466; teaching given in name of –, 611-612. Cf. CHURCH, HIERARCHY, HOLY SEE, TEACHING.

Major (enclosure)

347, 363-364, 366. Cf. ENCLOSURE, MINOR, MAJOR, SUPERIORS.

Man

Religious should become – of God, 162, a perfect –, 456; purpose of education: to form the entire –, 601-602; – of future will be what youthful training makes him, 554; teach – how to use his liberty, 667; obedience does not warp man's orientation to God, 669. Cf. DIGNITY, PERSONALITY.

Marriage

and entry into religion, 100; and personal perfection, 473, 499, 519, 525; and virginity, 461, 477, 488-489, 491-495, 501, 504-505, 514, 520-521, 623-624; –, a sacrament, 501, 519, 624; place of – in the Church, 522-524; duties of married people, 499. Cf. CELIBACY, CHASTITY, FAMILY.

Martyrdom

fruit of virginity, 510; practice of perfect chastity comparable to –, 529. Cf. COURAGE, PERSECUTION.

Mary

and religious, 581; queen of Catholic priesthood, 581, of the apostolate, 581; –, model of perfection, 650; – and perfect chastity, 543, 545-547; Marian year, 547.

Mass

Approval of priests by bishop or cele bration of –, 29; daily attendance at –, obligatory in principle for religious, 120; conventual – in all monasteries of nuns, 371. Cf. EUCHARISTIC SACRIFICE.

Master

of novices: rights and duties, 111, qualities, 70, 110, 155, functions, 112; teachers of scholasticate, 158-159; religious, teachers of divine and human

sciences, 260, 262; examples of discipline by teachers of Catholic schools, 305; duty of pupils to cooperate with their –, 304-307; formation of –, 575, 577; competence required in teachers, 611-612. Cf. TEACHERS, TEACHING.

Meditation

daily –, obligatory for religious, 120; –, safeguard of vocation, 71; means of perfection, 167, 211; leads to union with God, 146; task of consecrated souls, 140; – on virtues of Mary and chastity, 547. Cf. SPIRITUAL EXERCISES, PRAYER, CONTEMPLATION.

Mendicant (Orders)

can seek alms with the sole permission of superior, 123; – monks not obliged by rule to priesthood, 583. Cf. QUESTING.

Ministry

Vows a preparation for exterior –, 34; religious Orders, auxiliaries in ministry, 35, 45, 121; secular and religious clergy exercise – in dependance on bishop, 399-400; competence and formation required for – of religious, 142, 156; resources necessary for – and religious poverty, 463; – of priest, 503, 595. Cf. APOSTOLATE.

Minor (enclosure)

348, 355, 363, 365-367. Cf. ENCLOSURE, MAJOR.

Misery

Cf. DISTRESS.

Mission

of the Church: salvation of souls, 35, 42, 51; of teaching sisters, 448-454; and working-class life, 647; of teaching brothers, 553-558; of religious clerics, 613; of St. Bruno, 174. Cf. CHURCH, RELIGIOUS.

Missionary

Missionaries, ambassadors of Christ, 431; praise of –, 46; vocation of religious to be –, good of souls, 431; – vocation, motive for entry into religion, 405; directives of Pope to –, 138, 431-435.
Duties of missionaries: collaboration

with local Ordinaries, 432-434; with other religious, 433-435; love of mission as second homeland, 431; sureness of doctrine, 609.
– rôle of Benedictines, 260; discourse to Missionaries of the Kingship of our Lord Jesus Christ, 313-319.

Missions
Encyclical on the –, 431-435; –, a rôle of religious, 137, 142, 507, 622; Catholic Action in mission territories, 178; resources required for – and religious poverty, 463. Cf. EVANGEL-IZATION, INFIDELS, SALVATION.

Model
Christ, – of perfection, 676; of gentleness and charity in giving commands, 640; Mary, – of perfection, 650; of virginity, 546; founders, a – for religious, 51, 137, 263, 303, 415; religious should be a – of all virtues for Christian people, 45, 135a, 157, 162, 169, 172, 305, 313, 327, 423, 425, 599; nuns, 352; teacher of scholasticate, – of holiness, 158.

Modesty
Give example of –, duty of religious, 71, 425, 457, 640; religious habit, an expression of –, 445; immoderate use of tobacco, contrary to exterior –, 425. Cf. HABIT.
Basis of chastity, 540-541; in education to chastity, not to be identified with silence, 460, 541. Cf. CHASTITY.

Monastery
Holiness in monasteries, 333; –, cradles of civilization, 36, 256; foundation of –, by Holy See, 80; enclosure in –, 98, 347-348, 344-366; federations of –, 349, 379, 380; autonomy of –, 372, 376; conventual Mass in –, 371. Cf. MONASTIC, NUNS.

Monastic (life)
Definition of a – Congregation; rights of Holy See over – Congregations, 80; formation to – life, 67; indispensable conditions so that religious life may have –character, 358-359. Cf. CONTEM-PLATIVE (LIFE), RELIGIOUS.

Mortification
Cf. PENITENCE, RENUNCIATION, SAC-RIFICE (SPIRIT OF).

Mystical Body
Church, the – of Christ, 651; religious, as members of –, at the service of the Church, 660; should be mutually in union, 671. Cf. CHURCH.

Naturalism
Warning against –, 1a, 624a; union with God, remedy against –, 641. Cf. ACTIVISM.

Novelty (spirit of)
Danger of – in theology, 218-219, 611; adaptation and –, 414; distrust of –, cause of clash between generations, 439. Cf. PRIDE.

Novice
Conditions for admission of –, 17, 102; dress of –, 58, 98; liberty of – to leave Institute, 113; dismissal of –, 113; work by –, 126-129; qualities of –, 154; importance of formation of–, 150, 155, 539, 688; qualities required in master of –, 110-112; rights of superiors over novices, 22.

Novitiate
Aim of –: formation to religious life, 126, 155; training for vows of religion, 33; – and responsibility of superiors, 62-70; admission to – by superiors, 101; right of Ordinaries over –, 17, 105; conditions, rule and general features of –, according to canon law, 99, 100, 106-113; validity of –, 114; second year of –, 126-129; advice for time of –, 154-155; common – in case of federations, 382.

Nuns
Statutes of–: " Sponsa Christi," 354-387. Definition of –, 77, 354-356; distinctive character of –: solemn vows, 360-362; – in history of Church, 325-337; enclosure of –, 25a, 98, 363-367, 694, 697; adaptation of – to contemporary conditions, 338-353, 720-724; maintenance of essentials of canonical form, 340, the contemplative life, 357, 694-701.
– and public prayer, 352, 368, and

and obedience to –, 400; autonomy of monasteries and obedience to –, 373; relations of Ordinaries with Secular Institutes, 231, 250, 298-299; – and permission to quest by mendicant Orders, 123-124; co-operation of missionaries with local Ordinaries, 432, 434; confessions of women religious and rôle of Ordinaries, 89, 90, 91, 94, 196-197; right of religious freely to correspond with –, 122. Cf. BISHOP.

Ordination
Attestation of – required by cleric seeking to enter religion, 102; obligation of chastity at major Orders, 486. Cf. PRIESTHOOD.

Oriental (Church)
and ecclesiastical celibacy, 502; Orientals joining a Latin institute require authorization of S. Congr. for Oriental Church, 100.

Old Testament
Virginity in the –, 482, 503. Cf. SACRED SCRIPTURE, INDEX OF TEXTS OF SCRIPTURE.

Pagans
Cf. INFIDELS.

Parents
Cf. FAMILY.

Passive (virtues)
No really – virtues, 1; so-called – virtues always relevant, 2; praise of – virtues, 177.

Pastor of souls
The good –, model of charity and zeal, 525; superiors not to forget that they are –, 640; educators are the – of young religious, 600.

Pastoral
– formation of religious clerics, 605, 614, 615-619. Cf. MINISTRY.

Paternity
spiritual – of men and women religious, 507-508.

Patience
Example of –, duty of religious, 71; natural virtue of – required by religious,

457; required by nursing sisters, 631, 633; a requirement in superiors to ensure observance of rule, 74; necessary in educators, 600; union of – and works, 411. Cf. PERSECUTION, SUFFERING.

Peace
Mission of Church, 51; needed by society, 52; religious life not idle –, 404; religious, workers for–, 45, 256, 260; contemplatives, – offering for all, 169; obedience, source of inner –, 254; – and supernatural spirit, 270; St. Francis of Assisi and spirit of –, 319.

Pedagogy
Importance of –, 455; for teaching sisters, 450-452; for teachers in scholasticates, 158; sources of –, 303. Cf. TEACHER, TEACHING.

Penance (sacrament)
Cf. CONFESSION, CONFESSOR.

Penitence (virtue)
Means of perfection, 33; foundation of hope of eternal life, 642; utility of – for Church, 177; life in religious houses, exercise of –, 458, 679-682; obligation of – for contemplative religious, 174, 350, 710; prayer and –, 169; chastity and –, 462; and religious vocation, 562; and use of tobacco, 425, 427. Cf. RENUNCIATION, SACRIFICE (SPIRIT OF).

Perfection
1. *Nature of* –, 471-474, 653-655; charity and apostolate, 351; based on natural virtues, 456; juridical concept of –, 474; –, aim of religious life, 421; canonical state of –, basis of ecclesiastical legislation, 224.
2. *Distinction* between – and state of –, 474, 653, 696; between secular and regular clergy in relation to –, 401-402, 467, 469, 471, 473.
3. *Models* of –: Christ, 2, Mary, 650.
4. *Evangelical counsels* and –, 3, 4, 33, 43, 130, 407, 696.
5. *The Church, magisterium* and –, 221, 222, 223, 224, 467-474.
6. *Obligation* of –: for religious in general, 118, 133, 146, 166, 397-402; striving for –, essential duty of religious,

77, 134, 481, 660, 675, 679; –, purpose of vows, 34, 35, 397.
For novices, formation to –, 155; for Jesuits, institution of tertian year, 211; for contemplatives, solitude a means of –, 170; for nuns, 331, 352, 385; for Secular Institutes, through life in the world, 228, 229, 231, 235, 239, 275, 278, 283, 297, 403, 656, 657; outside canonical forms of life, 696.
Congress of religious, search for –, 395.

7. *Self-denial* and –, 417; virginity and –, 499, 526-527; adaptation and –, 658; theological culture and –, 141, 146, 598; persecution, stimulus to –, 49. Cf. STATE OF PERFECTION, HOLINESS, SANCTITY.

Perpetual
– vows, preceded by simple vows, 115; – profession, preceded by temporary profession, 114. Cf. VOWS.

Persecution
of religious Orders, 39-53; of Brothers of Christian schools, 54-56; value of – for Church, and fidelity of persecuted clergy, 552. Cf. MARTYRDOM, PATIENCE.

Personal
Distinction between – sanctity and state of perfection, 471-474; – sanctity and virginity, 490, 501; – sanctity in marriage, 473, 519.

Personality
Religious obedience not incompatible with respect for human –, 459, 665-668; chastity and balanced –, 515-518; chastity does not impoverish –, 520. Cf. DIGNITY, MAN.

Philosophy
Rules to follow in teaching –, 611-614; teaching of – by Jesuits, 215; according to method of St. Thomas Aquinas, 159-160; in scholasticates, 152, 156; reason and –, 161; particular views permitted in – when they are not dangerous to faith, 466. Cf. STUDIES, SCHOLASTIC, THOMISM.

Piety
Foundation of virtues, 165; to be nourished by rules that are live and adapted to conditions, 322; –, virtue

necessary for masters of novices, 110, for novices, 154; formation of young to –, 70, 150, 165.
Exercises of piety: soul of religious observance and apostolate, 640; a safeguard of public profession of virginity, 327; in Secular Institutes, 239, 290.
Eucharistic piety and Communion of children, 185, 205; devotion to Mary required to safeguard chastity, 543, 545-547. Cf. HOLINESS, SANCTITY, INTERIOR LIFE.

Pontifical
Congregations of – law, 7-10, 22-32, 61, 77, 78, 124, 247, 249; federations of monasteries are of –, 380.
– enclosure, cf. ENCLOSURE.
– Work for religious vocations, 559-569.
– Institute " Regina Mundi " for higher studies of women religious, 573-580. Cf. POPE, HOLY SEE.

Pope
Supreme superior of all religious, 85, 400, 676; jurisdiction of – extends to all dioceses and all the faithful, 400; constant concern of –s for religious life, 220; rules enacted by –s for safeguarding dignity of discipline, 62; papal esteem for Carthusians, 175, Carmelites, 455, teaching brothers, 301-307, teaching sisters, 436, missionaries of Kingship of Christ, 313; encouragement from – for congress of religious on adaptation, 320; – and Secular Institutes, 234; and Catholic Action, 178, 183; Jesuit vow of fidelity to –, 634-635. Cf. PONTIFICAL, HOLY SEE.

Postulants
Conditions for admission of –, 17, 62-64, 67-69, 102; regulations concerning –, 98-99; supernatural motives of –, 96, 150.

Poverty
Vow of –, essential of religious state, 76, 119, 133, 134.
St. Francis of Assisi, model of –, 318-319; religious should give example of –, 423, 425; in use of tobacco, 425-427; – among Jesuits, 642; in Secular Institutes, 239; – of nuns in present-day economic conditions, 342.

Spirit of –, to be safeguarded in hospitals, 628; – and comforts of modern life, 658; religious – and resources required for apostolate, 463; formation of novices to –, 155. Cf. DETACHMENT, VOWS.

Power
of S. Congr. of Religious over religious, 242, 245, 246, 248, and Secular Institutes, 278, 280, 284, 286; – of bishops over Secular Institutes, 244; – of superiors, 77; – of confessors, 93, 94, 196; religious and – of State, 35. Cf. AUTHORITY.

Prayer
a means of perfection, 33; source of strength, 53; supernatural aid in pedagogy, 303, education, 601; means of preserving chastity, 462, 533, 543; means of apostolate, 352.
Duty of men religious, 45, 71, 140, 169, 177, 183, and of women religious, 333, 368, especially of nuns, 352, 689-690.
Union between – and work, 411, 711, 724, and teaching, 614.
Virginity and fruitfulness of –, 509.
– for vocations, 559; – for persecuted priests and religious, 50, 552. Cf. MEDITATION, DIVINE OFFICE, SPIRITUAL EXERCISES, EUCHARISTIC SACRIFICE.

Preaching
Essential part of apostolate of religious, 36, 142, 162, 180, 260; duty of chaplain, 21; – demands sureness of sacred doctrine, 609; – of virtue and example of religious, 36; – on vocation, 568; on Communion, 189; on Catholic Action, 178-180. Cf. TRUTH.

Precept
Christian perfection and observance of –s, 653-654; observance of –, essential in religious life, 76, 130, 134; perfect chastity, not a precept, but an evangelical counsel, 526-527. Cf. EVANGELICAL COUNSELS.

Pride
Danger of – in studies, 164; in non-Christian practice of virginity, 491. Cf. NOVELTY.

Priest
Rights of superiors over Congregations of –s, 32; collaboration of religious with bishops, 37, 45, in dependence on bishop, 399; in clerical institute, master of novices is a –, 110; Secular Institutes complement apostolate of –, 231; lay brothers who are not priests, 166-167.
The –, light of world, salt of the earth, dispenser of mysteries of God, 608; sacred learning necessary for –, 140, 142, 144; the – and the world, 538; – and chastity, 502-503. Cf. CLERGY, PRIESTHOOD.

Priesthood
Mary, queen of –, 581; General Statutes for formation of young religious intended for priesthood, "Sedes Sapientiae," 581-620; vocation, basis of –, 592; motives for entry into religion and entry into –, 405; dignity of –, 323, 583, and intellectual culture, 606, 608; religious life and –, 583-585; union between religious life and –, 583, 584, 597; Catholic Action and –, 181. Cf. CLERGY, PERFECTION, PRIEST, VOCATION.

Primitive Church
Virginity in the –, 220-225, 325-337, 483-485, 493-495; heroism of virgins in the –, 551. Cf. FATHERS OF THE CHURCH.

Private (vows)
Distinction between public and – vows, 326; – vows in Secular Institutes, 657. Cf. VOWS.

Privilege
– granted by Holy See to colleges, etc., 31; danger of –s for religious life, 66; Congregations of pontifical law quest by – of Holy See, 124; perfection not exclusive – of religious, 467. Cf. DISPENSATION.

Probation
Rights of bishop concerning time of – for associations seeking to become Secular Institutes, 288. Cf. ADMISSION.

superior of – 85, 399-400, 676; services rendered by – to bishops, 35-37, 432, 434.

4. *Responsibility of superiors* towards –, 62-75, 677-685.

5. – *in the world*: services to civil society, 35-37, 45, 46, 48, 52, 53a, 135a, 405; example given by – to faithful, 423, 425.

6. *Distinction* between –, clerics and laity, 397, 398, in relation to perfection, 467.

7. *Obligations* of –: 118-122, 133; holiness, 467, 603, 660; charity, 53; fidelity to spirit of founder, 51; interior life, 146-148; penitence, 430.

8. *Studies* of –: 141-145, 146-148, 153, 156, 163.

9. *Formation* –: 456, 581-620.

10. *Activities* of –: apostolate, 142, education, 45, 48, 139, teaching, 553-558, works of charity, 506, missions, 431-432; Catholic Action, 178-183.

11. – and adaptation, 320-334, 720; Confession of –, 88-95, 201; persecuted –, 39-53, 551.

Religious (women)

Pontifical documents concerning –: "Sponsa Christi," 325-387, "Sacra Virginitas," 482-552.

1. *Consecration to Christ*: 490, 495-496, 622, 625, 701, 704-705.

2. *In the service of the Church*: rôle of –, 507; numbers of –, 485; rights of bishop in relation to –, 13; duties of superiors towards –, 19, 479, 480.

3. *In the world*: rôle of –, 525; apostolate of –, 481, 573; works of charity of –, 506; among working-class, 647.

4. *Studies* of –: 573-580.

5. *Vocation* of –, 550.

6. *Different forms* of –: nuns, 332, 354, 689-726; missionaries, 434; teachers, 436-454, 480; nurses, 621-633; parochial educators, 570-572, 647-649.

7. *Confession* of –: 88, 89, 90, 95, 196-201.

8. *Persecution* of –: 551-552.

9. *Unions* of –: 575a, 648.

Religious State

Definitions of –, 76-77, 134, 220, 225, 397-398; legislation concerning the –, 78-87, 224, 226-229; Secular Institutes and the –, 229, 232, 235, 276, 278,

294, 403; priesthood and the –, 467-474, 583, 597; motives for embracing the –, 404-405, 470; the – and holiness, 397, 417, 603; and chastity, 486; and poverty, 424-430; and apostolate, 412; the – not a refuge for timorous souls, 404; relations of the – with Holy See, 672-674. Cf. RELIGIOUS LIFE.

Religious life

is of *divine* origin, 33-34, 140; *nature* of –: leave all to follow Christ, 75; life dedicated to Christ, 220; reflection of holiness of the Church, 512; sign of union with God, 442; *Church* and –, 326, 330; history of – in Church, 221; – has many forms, 131; *essential marks* of –, 421-423; fundamental features and contemporary problems of –, 394-423; *vocation* and –, 404-405, 592; *priestly life* and –, 583-585; *family life* and –, 275, 458; *primacy* of –, 55-56; *holiness, apostolate* and –, 224; *obedience*, basis of discipline of –, 459; *care of sick* and –, 621-633; *formation* to –, purpose of novitiate, 126, 154-155; knowledge and esteem of –, 568, 684-716.

Renunciation

Self-denial, way to perfection, 417; religious life, life of –, to follow Christ, 75, after example of Christ, 43; – of world, duty of religious, 71, 679-685; of Jesuits, 213, 639, 641; of contemplative Orders, 172, 709-716; of consecrated virgins, 325; of members of Secular Institutes, 239, 290; in religious houses, 458; – of family to be compensated by community life with family spirit, 479; – in the practice of chastity, 446, 489, 493, 495, 518, 529, 623, 624b; formation of young religious to spirit of –, 601, 617; the faithful, 319; co-operation between communities involve certain –, 670; – in persecution, 50. Cf. PENITENCE, SPIRIT OF SACRIFICE.

Reserved cases

Powers of bishop in –, 26; powers of confessor in – in religious communities 196.

Respect

Natural quality required in religious, 457; obedience and respect for human dignity, 459, 665; – for tradition in adaptation, 660; – for eternal truth and doctrine, 219; – for Thomism, 611; – in teaching chastity, 460; modesty, – for body, member of Christ, 540; – for rules of novitiate in employment of second year novices, 126; – in practice of frequent Communion, 192; – for prescriptions of Holy See, 672; – for confederations of institutes, 277; – for liberty of subjects by superiors, 90-92, 95, 193, 196, and for their dignity, 665; mutual – between communities, 671, 686. Cf. AUTHORITY, OBEDIENCE.

Responsibility
of superiors, 62-75, for souls of their subjects, 640, 677-688; – for professional training of teaching sisters, 480a, 480b, 575, 610; – of Christian educators, 554, 554a; – of those who depreciate Christian virginity, 477. Cf. AUTHORITY.

Retreat
Cf. SPIRITUAL EXERCISES.

Revelation
Principles of theology based on –, 161, 612; scholastic method combines – and philosophy, 160.

Rights
of the *Church* and attacks on religious, 40, 42; of the *Ordinary* in question of foundation or suppression of religious houses, 78-87; over Secular Institutes, 244, 292-299; in relation to religious recruitment, 467; of *superiors* over postulants and novices, 97, 101, 113, 115, 126; of the master of novices, 111. – of religious in accordance with Code of Canon Law, especially, 86, 92, 112; – of religious as citizens, 35, 48, 53a; – of parents over the education of their children, 444.
Juridical – and monasteries of nuns, 373.

Rule
Observance of –, essential obligation of religious, 71, 77, 118, 120, 133, 137, 683-685; –, safeguard of vocation, 67; means of perfection, 33; dignity of discipline, 62; formation to apostolate, 56; means of apostolate, 352; in spirit of mortification, 352; – must be live

to correspond to spirit of founders, 322. Approval of – by Holy See, 132; vigilance of bishop concerning observance of –, 32; qualities and duties of superiors in relation to keeping of –, 74; knowledge of – required in teachers of young religious, 600.
Carthusian –, means of sanctification, 177; characteristics and wisdom of Benedictine –, 253-270; juridical – of Secular Institutes, 282-300, adaptation, 230; work by nuns in conformity with –, 383, 711, 723-724.
Gradual precision of – of states of perfection in Church history, 222; – of Congregations of diocesan law, 11, 15, 19, 60; – of Congregations of simple vows, 57-61; of Secular Institutes, 220-252.
Necessity of special – for formation of religious, 586-591. Cf. CONSTITUTIONS.

Sacrament
Vigilance of bishop concerning administration and reception of –s in Congregations, 32; duty of chaplain, 21; –, supernatural aids vital to education, 601; marriage, a –, 501, 519, 624; virginity not a sacrament, 519.

Sacred Scripture
Teaching of –, 158, 215.
For texts cited, cf. *Index of Texts of Scripture.*

Sacrifice (spirit of)
Perpetual virginity, a – to God, 461; – in the contemplative life, 525; – in the practice of chastity, 529, 533, 535; the – of obedience and human dignity, 668; – by teaching sisters, 436; formation of young to spirit of –, 48, 145, 307. Cf. PENITENCE, RENUNCIATION.

Salvation (of souls)
Mission of the Church, 51; needs of society, 52; aim of religious life, 34, 70, 131, 169, 174, 417, 421, 506, 617; purpose of missionaries, 138, 431; of the Catholic school, 301; obligation of religious, 71; – and contemplative life, 495, 497, 719, 726; practice of virginity for – of oneself and others, 490, 496-498, 506; forgetfulness of – in modern paganised world, 176. Cf. EVANGELIZATION, MISSIONS.

Sanctity, Sanctification
Cf. HOLINESS.

Scandal
Dispensation of vows, – to faithful, 62 ; avoidance of –, duty of religious, 71.

Scholastic
– method, essential foundation of theological studies of religious, 159-162, 612. Cf. PHILOSOPHY, THEOLOGY, THOMISM.

Scholasticate
Regulations for period of –, 156-165; formation of young clerics in –, 539; vigilance of Holy See over –, 588. Cf. NOVITIATE.

School
Purpose of Catholic –, 301-307, 450; bishop and –: right of visitation, 31, 32; authorization necessary to open a –, 83; apostolate in schools: motive for entering religion, 405, and joining a Secular Institute, 317; preference of heads of families for schools managed by women religious, 444; equality of civil rights for schools directed by female religious and State schools, 444. Cf. PUPILS, TEACHERS, TEACHING, BROTHERS.

Science (Knowledge)
Priest repository of – of God, 608; apostolate and –, 36.

Sacred –: knowledge of God and of mysteries of the faith, 141; in the service of the faith, 143; nourishment of interior life, 146; study recommended by founders, 147; required in priests, 140, 144, in educators, 168; – and holiness, 144; theology a –, 161. *Profane* –: in the service of sacred doctrine, 162; and faith, 161, 218; and glory of God, 218; progress of profane sciences and holiness, 323, 418, 466, 615.

Formation to –, 158, 615; purpose of the Catholic school, 301.

– and adaptation, 323; Benedictines and –, 256, 259, 260; no pride in –, 164. Cf. CULTURE, DOCTRINE, STUDIES, KNOWLEDGE.

Secular (clergy)
Church and – clergy, 40, 585; distinction between – and regular clergy, 398, 467-474; – clergy at disposition of bishop, 399; holiness and – clergy, 401-402, 467, 469, 472-473. Cf. CLERGY, REGULAR, SECULAR INSTITUTES.

Secular Institutes
Definition of –, 229, 235, 272, 403, 656-657; – are public states of perfection, 278, 403; juridical character of –, 232, 283, 403.

Distinction between – and religious, 236, 276, 403; and clerical state, 583; and associations of the faithful, 274, 279, 284, 286-288.

Legislation: " Provida Mater," 220-252; " Primo feliciter," 271-279; " Cum Sanctissimus," 280-300; declaration of S. Congr. of Religious, 308-312. Cf. specially, 230-234, 237, 235-252, 292.

Foundation of –, 238-239, 244, 246, 289-293.

Purpose of –, 229, 234, 235, 271; general characteristics, 313-319; place in the Church, 230, 403; Secular Institutes in service of the Church, 228, 231; of Catholic Action, 182, 279; a light in the world, 272, 275, 314, 315, 319.

Relations of – with Holy See, 242-243, 247-249, 278, 280, 284, 286; with bishops, 244-245, 250, 285, 298, 299; with Institutes of regulars, 296; mutual juridical bonds of members of Secular Institutes, 240, 291.

Interior government, 251, and hierarchical organization, 277, 295.

secular institutes and chastity, 486; and vocations, 279, 563.

Self-control
Natural virtue required in religious, 457; – and chastity, 511, 518, 529, 535; formation of youth to self-control, 307. Cf. CHASTITY, COURAGE, PATIENCE.

Seminaries
Vigilance of Holy See over –, 588; formation of young clerics in –, 539; creation of minor – for young aspirants to religious life, 149; practice of Communion, 185, 187, 205, and of Confession in –, 195; study of Latin in –, 153. Cf. STUDIES, VOCATION.

Service
Religious orders in – of the Church, 35, 45, 46, 48, 52, 53a, 213, 325, 447, 622, 660; and of civil society, 36-37, 259, 314; rule of Jesuits: – of Christ and the Church, 634; – of neighbour in Secular Institutes, 657; enclosure, protection for – of God, 347; the Christian in the – of his country, 572; Christian perfection and – of God and the neighbour, 653-655; sacred science in – of the faith, 143; profane science in – of sacred doctrine, 162; virginity and – of God, 505, and of the neighbour, 496-499; exercise of authority means –, 665. Cf. APOSTOLATE, CHARITY, CHURCH, SOCIETY.

Sick
Religious and –: approval of special Congregations for care of –, 13; care of –, motive for entry into religion, 405; Benedictines and care of –, 258; rôle of consecrated souls in relation to –, 507, 622, 625; combination of religious life and assistance to the –, 621-633; formation of nursing sisters, 480, 630.
Sick person and Jesus Christ, 632-633. Nervous illness and practice of chastity, 532.
Sick female religious and liberty of Confession, 97, 197-198, and of Communion, 208.

Silence
means of perfection, 211; modesty not – in education to chastity, 460, 541.

Simple (vows)
Legislation for Congregations of – vows: " Conditae a Christo," 7-32; – vows must precede perpetual vows, 115; nuns and – vows, 355, 356, 361, 370. Cf. vows.

Simplicity
evangelical –, required in religious, 617; religious habit, an expression of evangelical –, 445; –, characteristic of Benedictine rule, 254.

Sin
Original –, 517; flight from occasions of –, 536, 537, 540; – avoided for love of God, 604; avoidance of –, beginning of Christian perfection, 653;

reparation for –, characteristic of contemplative Orders, 169; confession of grave – before Communion, 191, 193. Cf. CONFESSOR, CONFESSION, PENANCE.

Society (civil)
Principles of religion, foundation of –, 264; benefits of religious Orders for civil –, 2, 5, 35-37, 42, 45-48, 51-53, 121, 135, 162, 183, 256, 263, 268, 350, 405, 583; Secular Institutes and –, 231, 315, 317; Christian education in service of –, 48, 305, 554; work of men and –, 269; renovation of civil – by Catholic Action, 178. Cf. CIVIC, WORLD, FATHERLAND.

Solemn (vows)
more solemn form of public vows, 345-346; nuns are religious of – vows, 354, 360-362; pontifical enclosure and – vows, 347, 348, 366, 367. Cf. vows.

Soul
Sanctification of souls, mission of the Church, 35; and of religious, 36, 71, 183, 431, 617, 725; consecration of the – to God in virginity, 493-494, 499-500, in the contemplative life, 704-705; blossoming of the – in education, 554, 602; religious life not an escape for timorous souls, 404. Cf. SALVATION.

Spectacles (shows)
Renunciation of –, duty of religious, 71; danger for chastity, 537.

Spiritual Exercises
Means of preserving virginity, 327; apostolate of religious towards the clergy, 180; prescribed by constitutions, obligatory for religious, 99, 113, 120.
Exercises of piety: soul of religious obedience and apostolate, 640; – in Secular Institutes, 239, 290, 657.
– of St. Ignatius. Cf. IGNATIUS, JESUITS.

State
Cf. CIVIC, FATHERLAND.

State of Perfection
Distinction between perfection and –, 401-402, 467-474, 653. Cf. RELIGIOUS STATE, PERFECTION.

Statutes

of nuns, "Sponsa Christi," 354-387; for the formation of religious intended for priesthood, 581-620. Cf. CONSTITUTIONS, RULE.

Strictness

with oneself to safeguard chastity, 535; union of – and kindness in superiors, 479, 640; for educators, 600; – in discipline, necessary for modern apostolate, 639, 688; –, mark of Benedictine rule, 254. Cf. AUTHORITY, PRUDENCE, VIGILANCE.

Studies

of religious: purpose of "Unigenitus Dei Filius," 130-168 and of "Sedes Sapientiae," 581-620.

– necessary for all religious, 71; for contemplatives, 141, and active religious, 142-145; purpose of ecclesiastical –, 613; – nourish interior life, 146-148, 303, 607, reciprocal effect on spiritual life, 614; solid secondary – required for young religious, 610, for aspirants, 151-152, for novices, 155, for scholastics, 156; religious study for laymen, 568; need for study of Latin, 150, 153, 464. Foundation of Pontifical Institute for higher – of women religious, 573-580. Cf. FORMATION.

Submission

Cf. OBEDIENCE.

Suffering

for Christ, reason for joy and encouragement, 43-44; – of missionaries, 46; human – and charity of the Church, 629. Cf. PATIENCE, PERSECUTION.

Superiors, Superioresses

1. The *Pope*, supreme superior of all religious, 85, 400, 676, 687; Allocutions to superiors general, 475-481, 676-688.

2. *Authority* of – representative of God's authority, 665-669; does not usurp divine prerogatives, 669; to be exercised in evangelical spirit, 665.

3. *Rights* of –: of diocesan Congregations, 18, 19; of pontifical Congregations, 9, 10, 22; of Congregations of priests, 32; of nuns, 373; in relation

to foundations, 78, 80, 84; administration, 30; admission to profession (postulancy, novitiate), 27, 97, 105, 113, 114, 115, 121, 123, 126; concerning use of tobacco, 428.

4. *Duties* of –: ensure respect for spirit of the Order, 87, 663, 677-688; formation, 62-75, 101, 102, 479-480, 610, 617; studies, 147-148, 154, 156, 158; lay brothers, 166-168; nuns, 385, 391-393; Jesuits, 640.

5. *Obedience* due to –: 604, 660; Jesuits, 214, 638; nuns, 390; in adaptation, 323, 720-721; in Secular Institutes, 231, 241.

6. – and adaptation, 323, 447; and Confession of women religious, 88, 90-92, 193, 196-197, 199-202; and Communion, 187, 203-209; and Catholic Action, 178-183.

Union of – with view to apostolate, 650-651; major –, members of Work of religious vocations, 563. Cf. AUTHORITY, OBEDIENCE, RESPONSIBILITY.

Supernatural

Union with God by contemplation of – truths, 146, 691-701; – spirit, source of peace and eternal happiness, 270; – motives of candidates for religious life, 150, 596; – formation in Catholic schools, 301; distinction between – and natural virtues, 457-458; between – charity and natural beneficence, 413; diminution of – spirit, danger of existentialism, 410.

Teachers

Tribute by Pope to teaching brothers, 301-307; dignity of mission of religious –, 553-558; aim of teaching sisters, 447; activity of teaching sisters, 436; qualities required in teaching sisters, 448-453; special formation of teaching sisters, 454; teaching sisters and young girls, 437-442. Cf. TEACHING, MASTER.

Teaching

Work of charity towards the neighbour, 56, 259; – and apostolate, 36; –, one of chief activities of men religious, 142, 215, and of women religious, 436-454, 622; importance of teaching religion, 151-152; – to be adapted, without

Unity
of Church, amidst variety of religious orders, 334-347.

University
Religious orders and –, 36.

Validity
Conditions for – of novitiate, 100, 107, and profession, 114-117; – of Confession of female religious, 91.

Victim
Contemplative religious consecrated to God in spirit of sacrificial –, 172, 622.

Vigilance
of Holy See and formation of religious, 588, and missionary institutes, 435; of Ordinaries over work by nuns, 392-393, Secular Institutes, 231; of superiors over work by nuns, 392-393, in supervision of religious, 63, 66-67, 71, 74.
– to safeguard chastity, 529, 533-535. Cf. PRUDENCE.

Virginity
Apostolic Constitution " Sponsa Christi," 325-387; Encyclical " Sacra Virginitas," 482-552, Radio Message, 689-726.
1. *Nature* of –: official character given to vow of – by Church, 326-327; public profession of – approved by Church, 326, 330; –, essentially Christian, 482; consecration of soul and body to God, 490-492, 493, 623; a complete giving, 494, 623; sacrifice of self, 461, 529; a gift of God, 528; spiritual marriage, 494; witness of faith and charity, 510; ideal of purity, 511; image of holiness of union between Christ and Church, 512-513; image of fruitfulness of Church, 513; source of strength for Church, 461; not a sacrament, 519; not obligatory for attaining perfection, 526.
2. *Excellence* of –: 488-513; prized in whole world, 548.
3. *Errors* concerning –, 477, 514-525.
4. *Marriage* and –: 461, 489, 492, 495, 499, 504-505, 519, 623-624.
5. *Fruits* of –: personal sanctification, 499, 501, 510, 525; liberation of soul for spiritual progress, 499-500; union

with Christ, 520; acquisition of self-control, 511; spiritual fecundity, 506-509, 624b.
6. *Mary, model* of –, 545. Cf. CHASTITY, PURITY.

Virgins
brides of Christ, 494; pontifical documents concerning consecrated –, 325-387, 482-552, 689-726. Cf. CONSECRATION, VIRGINITY, RELIGIOUS.

Virtue
1. Distinction between active and passive –, 1-2.
2. *Obligation* of –: for founders of Orders, 12; all religious, 38, 133, 263, especially apostles, 52, 212, master of novices, 110, teaching sisters, 436, and nursing sisters, 626, 631, 633, and educators, 302, 554, 599-600.
3. *Means of acquiring* –: religious life, a call to –, 324; vows, a source of –, 33; evangelical counsels, 43; charity and piety, basis of other –, 165; meditation, 167, 547; work, 350, 711; Benedictine rule, 253.
4. *Formation* to –: by education, 45; of novices, 70, 115; of young clerics, 617; of children, 48.
5. *Virginity* and –: 327, 403, 490, 493, 529, 537-539.
6. *Preaching* of –, 36.
7. *Persecution* and –, 49, 50, 51.
8. Christian – of our age, 420.
9. *Natural* –: importance, 455-458; development of – in formation of young religious, 601-602, 688.

Vocation
1. *Nature:* 592-595; call of God, 131, basis of all religious life, 592; distinction between priestly and religious vocation, 596-597.
2. *Fidelity* of priest to – through sacred learning, 140; of nuns to their – to apostolate, 386-387.
3. Holy See and –: 136; responsibility of superiors and –, 62-75; missionary –, 431; teaching –, 454, 557.
4. *Duties* towards –: action in favour of –, 524; of educators, 558; of families, 548-550; of directors of conscience, 408; to found establish-

ments for young people with –, 149,
596; to encourage – in Secular Institutes, 279.
5. – in history of the Church, 582;
virginity and – of women, 624a; crisis
of –, 476-478; foundation of pontifical
Work of religious –, 559-569. Cf.
RECRUITMENT.

Vows

1. *Nature* of –: not a shackle on liberty,
3, 4; –, a source of virtues, 33;
essential to religious state, 76-77,
134, 421; object of –, 34.
2. *Different kinds* of –: perpetual, 97, 115.
Private –: for Secular Institutes, 227,
236, 239, 312, 657; distinction
between – and *public* –, 326, 486.
Public –: 326, 486; distinction between
– and *solemn* vows, 345.
Simple –: 7-32, 57-61, 115, 356.
Solemn –: 345; – and enclosure,
347-348, 366; and nuns, 354, 360-362;
and contemplatives, 367.
3. *Observance* of –: and holiness, 604;
essential duty of religious, 118, 130,
147; by lay brothers, 166; by nuns,
354, 356, 360-362, 704; by teaching
sisters, 454; by Jesuits, 635.
4. *Formation* of novices to observance
of –, 155, 530; retreat before pro-
nouncing –, 113.
5. – of *obedience*: to the Pope by all
religious, 85, 400, 687; special – of
Jesuits, 635; errors on the nature of –,
406-408.
6. – of *chastity*: 486; official character
recognized by Church, 326-327; enclosure, safeguard of –, 347.
7. *Dispensation* of – and responsibility
of superiors, 62-75. Cf. CONSECRATION,
EVANGELICAL COUNSELS, COMMITMENT.

Will

of God: personal holiness and acceptance
of the will of God, 471, 678. – *of
founder* to be respected, 80.
Total abnegation of self-will, characteristic of Jesuits, 637; practice of
obedience and one's own will, 407;
Christian education and formation of –
of young, 554.

Witness (Testimony)

of virginity, 510-511; of Christian
families in the world, 522-524.

Wisdom

God alone is absolute –, 164; –,
required in religious, 71; – necessary
in founders of Congregations, 12; – of
Benedictine rule, 253-258; – in
adaptation to contemporary conditions,
321-323. Cf. PRUDENCE.

Word of God

Cf. PREACHING.

Work (labour, toil)

Dignity of – and teaching of St. Benedict,
269.
Intellectual –: element of vocation and
a help for teaching sisters, 454; formation of teaching sisters to – and
responsibility of superiors, 480, 480a,
480b. Cf. STUDIES.
Manual –: of nuns, 344, 350, 383-385,
388-393; of contemplatives, 385, 391-
393, 711, 713, 723-724.

Works

–, fruit of state of perfection, 412;
– of charity, special function of men
religious, 131, 135a, 137; and of
women religious, 338, 622; – of
education, obligation for religious, 151;
– of apostolate and adaptation, 321;
contemplative life, 355, 719-721; of
Secular Institutes, 239; of nuns,
386-387, 719-721; danger of activism
in –, 211; danger of critical spirit in –,
214; religious poverty and resources
necessary for –, 463; federation of
monasteries helpful to –, 349. Cf.
APOSTOLATE, PONTIFICAL WORK FOR
RELIGIOUS VOCATIONS, 559-569.

World

Church, vital rôle in –, 264, 622;
renunciation of –, duty of religious,
71, 495, 625, 679; enclosure, protection from the –, 347; chastity and
virginity do not make strangers to –,
466, 525; need for knowledge of the –,
538, 539, 649.
Adaptation, does not mean yielding to
spirit of the –, 323; protection of
religious spirit against –, 50, 679-685;
witness of Christian family in –, 532;
hatred of – for Church, cause of
persecution, 43-44, 49, 53; pagan
ways of present day world, 176.

Religious apostolate in world: aim of Secular Institutes. Cf. SECULAR INSTITUTES.

Youth

Hope of better society through Christian education, 554. Education of –, work of men religious, 137, 553-558, of women religious, 436-454; chief concern of religious educators, 139, 301, 304-307, 554; of special Congregation of Brothers, 168, 301, 553-558; adaptation of teaching to capacities of –, 302, 304.

Formation of – demands sureness of doctrine, 609.

Formation of young religious and Holy See, 589-590; first requirement, to make young religious perfect in natural virtues, 456.

Formation of girls, special vocation of teaching sisters, 454; to Christian fidelity, 451; to citizenship, 570-572; difficulties of this work: conflict between generations, 437-439.

– and vocation, 149, 524, 530, 549, 557-558; impart to – esteem of religious life, 568.

– and chastity: prudent formation, 460, 541; training in modesty, 540-541; protection of virtue of young clerics, 537-539.

– and habit of frequent Communion, 185, 187, 202; and Catholic Action, 181-183. Cf. CHILDREN, EDUCATION, FORMATION.

Zeal

Apostolic virtue, aim of religious, 320; outcome of religious obedience practised in charity, 669; – of religious Orders, 38; various works of – and religious Orders, 131.

– required in apostle, 212, 617; in founders, 12; in superiors, 167; in contemplatives, 177; in missionaries, 431; – to be allied with competence, 385; – and spirit of penance.

– for the truth, 162; for education of aspirants, 151; for the formation of children, 48; as reaction to persecution, 50. Cf. APOSTOLATE.

⚓ M. H. GILL AND SON LTD., PRINTERS, DUBLIN.